C000141448

Discussing Disney

Discussing Disney

°o°

Edited by Amy M. Davis

British Library Cataloguing in Publication Data

Discussing Disney

A catalogue entry for this book is available from the British Library

ISBN: 0 86196 719 3 (Paperback))
ISBN: 0 86196 960 9 (ebook-MOBI)
ISBN: 0 86196 961 6 (ebook-EPUB)
ISBN: 0 86196 962 3 (ebook-EPDF)

Published by
John Libbey Publishing Ltd, 205 Crescent Road, New Barnet, Herts EN4 8SB,
United Kingdom e-mail: john.libbey@orange.fr; web site: www.johnlibbey.com

Distributed Worldwide by
Indiana University Press, Herman B Wells Library—350, 1320 E. 10th St.,
Bloomington, IN 47405, USA. www.iupress.indiana.edu

© 2019 Copyright John Libbey Publishing Ltd. All rights reserved.
Unauthorised duplication contravenes applicable laws.

Printed and bound in the United States of America..

Contents

Contributor Biographies

Noel Brown is a lecturer in film at Liverpool Hope University. His research focuses on children's film, family entertainment, and animation. His books include *The Hollywood Family Film: A History, from Shirley Temple to Harry Potter* (I.B. Tauris, 2012), *British Children's Cinema: From The Thief of Bagdad to Wallace and Gromit* (I.B. Tauris, 2016), *The Children's Film: Genre, Nation and Narrative* (Columbia University Press, 2017), *Contemporary Hollywood Animation* (Edinburgh University Press, forthcoming 2019), and, as co-editor, *Family Films in Global Cinema: The World Beyond Disney* (I.B. Tauris, 2015) and *Toy Story: How Pixar Reinvented the Animated Feature* (Bloomsbury, 2018). He is currently in the process of editing an *Oxford Handbook of Children's Film*.

Jemma D. Gilboy is a Senior Lecturer in Animation Studies at Nottingham Trent University, teaching modules on animation/film theory and aesthetics, and animation history. Her research focuses on meme theory and its application to relationships among the fans, authors and producers of The Simpsons and other animated texts, as well as to productive memetic activity by fans. She studied practical animation in her under-graduate work in Canada, and in further undergraduate and postgraduate study narrowed her focus onto the theoretical sides of filmmaking, animation and online participation. She is renowned for having a Simpsons analogy for everything.

Helen Haswell received her PhD in Film from Queen's University Belfast in 2018, where she has taught courses on cinema and postmodernism. Her research focuses on the development of digital animation and its contemporary aesthetic, the studio narrative of Pixar Animation, and Pixar's relationship with the Walt Disney Company following the 2006 Disney-Pixar merger. She has presented several conference papers and written articles on computer-animation, including work on nostalgia and film industry. Most recently, she published a book chapter in *Toy Story: How Pixar Reinvented the Animated Feature* (2018). She is a visiting lecturer at Leeds Trinity University and Ulster University, where she teaches modules on Disney and animation.

Joshua Hollands is a PhD Candidate at UCL Institute of the Americas. He is currently completing a thesis, funded by the Wolfson Foundation, which examines the history of homophobic workplace discrimination in the United States South and Southwest. His academic love of Disney animation and history was encouraged by Amy Davis while he was an undergraduate student in American Studies at the University of Hull.

Christopher Holliday teaches Film Studies and Liberal Arts at King's College London specializing in film genre, international film history, and contemporary digital media. He has published several book chapters and articles on digital technology and computer animation, including work in *Animation Practice, Process & Production* and *animation: an interdisciplinary journal*. He is the author of *The Computer-Animated Film: Industry, Style and Genre* (Edinburgh University Press, 2018), and co-editor of *Fantasy/Animation: Connections Between Media, Mediums and Genres* (Routledge, 2018) for Routledge's AFI Film Readers series that examines the historical, cultural and theoretical points of intersection between fantasy and animation.

Dorene S. Koehler, PhD earned an MA and PhD in Mythological Studies with emphasis in Depth Psychology at Pacifica Graduate Institute. She published her first book, *The Mouse and the Myth: Sacred Art and Secular Ritual*, in 2017. It explores the intersection of spirituality and popular culture at Disneyland. She teaches Humanities and Interdisciplinary Studies at Southern New Hampshire University's College of Online and Continuing Education. She also teaches Classical Myth, Shakespeare, Harry Potter, and Disney Studies to middle school children at Gifted Homeschooler's Online Forum. Dr. Koehler resides in Santa Barbara, California, USA with her husband Bruce and their cocker spaniel dog Lucy.

Catherine Lester is Lecturer in Film and Television at the University of Birmingham. Prior to this, she was a teaching assistant and PhD candidate at the University of Warwick, where she completed her PhD thesis on horror films for children in Hollywood cinema. This work is the basis of her forthcoming monograph, entitled *Horror Films for Children: Fear and Pleasure in American Cinema* (I.B. Tauris).

Oliver Lindman holds a Bachelor's Degree in music from the University of Sussex, where his main area of focus was film music. After returning to his native Sweden, he has continued building on his interest in music as a storytelling tool, gradually finding his way into musical theatre. In 2016, he co-founded the Malmö-based association Samsa Musikteater, through which he is currently co-writing and producing his second musical. He has also recently completed a two-year course in dramatic writing at the Biskops-Arnö Writing School. A long-time fan of music in Disney films, this is his first academic venture into Disney.

Kodi Maier is a PhD candidate at the University of Hull. Their doctoral thesis, *Dream Big, Little Princess: Interrogating the Disney Princess Franchise from 2000 to the Present Day*, investigates the evolution of the Disney Princess franchise and its impact on female gender roles in the United States. Other research interests include fan studies, queer studies, and comics. Their most recent publication, "Camping Outside the Magic Kingdom's Gates: The Power of Femslash in the Disney Fandom", published in *Networking Knowledge: Journal of the MeCCSA Postgraduate Network*, discusses how the Disney femslash fandom manipulates Disney animated texts to create their own queer fairy tales. They are also a regular contributor to the Society for Animation Studies's blog, *Animation Studies 2.0*.

Chris Pallant is a Reader in the School of Media, Art and Design at Canterbury Christ Church University. He is the author of *Demystifying Disney* (2011), *Storyboarding: A Critical History* (2015) and editor of *Animated Landscapes: History, Form and Function* (2015) and *Animation: Collected Published Writings* (2019). He is also the Founding Series Editor of Bloomsbury's *Animation: Key Films/Filmmakers*. Chris has written journal articles and book chapters on a range of topics, including the "cartoonism" of Tarantino's films, performance capture technology, the animated landscape of New York, and the work of Rockstar Games. He currently serves as Vice-President for the Society for Animation Studies and is Festival Director for Canterbury Anifest.

Alexander Sergeant is a Lecturer in Film and Media Theory at Bournemouth University. His research expertise includes the history of Hollywood fantasy cinema, psychoanalytic theories of phantasy, film theory and spectatorship, and critical theories of gender. He has published on these subjects in a variety of academic journals and edited collections. He is the co-editor of *Fantasy/Animation: Connections Between Media, Mediums and Genres* (Routledge, 2018).

Lauren L. Smith graduated from the Film Studies Department at the University of Hull in 2018 – Discussing Disney was her first (and to date only) academic conference. Though she now works in media planning, her passion for film, Disney, and gender representation continues.

Introduction

Amy M. Davis

Disney

It's a family name. The name of a company. A place name (albeit in abbreviated form). It's a studio. To some, it's a genre. For most, it means Mickey and Minnie Mouse. Snow White and seven dwarfs. Princesses and musical adventures. Fantasy, romance, and escapism. Childhood, both actual and remembered. It's a spoonful of sugar to help the medicine go down, and the happiest place on Earth.

But to some, it is "The Rat". A sexist throwback to clichéd and damaging gender roles. Hard-core delusional pabulum for the emotionally immature. An example of the ultimate in corporate greed and excess. As one meme famously declares, it is a people trap built by a mouse.

But love it or loathe it – get it or not – Disney is important. Begun in 1923 by Walt and Roy Disney, The Disney Brothers Studio (as it was known in its first two years) arose from the failure of Walt Disney's first studio, Laugh-O-Grams, and for its first three decades, Walt Disney Productions (the name it was given in 1925) existed as a small but hugely-respected independent studio that, despite its praise and multiple awards, was in a near-constant fight for financial survival on the fringes of Hollywood at a time when the industry – to include access to film distribution networks – was carefully controlled by the eight major Hollywood studios.[1] That it was once an independent production company at the mercy of corporate giants is something that it is very easy to forget now that it is a corporate giant itself. As I write this in July 2018, Disney – already the world's largest entertainment corporation – is in the process of negotiating its $52.4 billion purchase of Twenty-First Century Fox (as it is now known); it was even reported on 3 April by a number of UK news outlets that, according to Mark Sweney in a report for *The Guardian*, 'Disney has "expressed interest" in buying Sky News, a move that would clear media plurality concerns and pave the way for its own $66 billion (£47 billion) takeover of most of Murdoch's 21st Century Fox, including all of Sky'.[2] According to an article on CNBC.com, Disney's CEO since 2005, Robert Iger, saw his fiscal 2017 compensation reach $36.3 million.[3] In contrast to Disney's purchasing power and its CEO's earnings, Disney's theme park employees are struggling just to afford the basics. According to the *Orange County Register*, "… the cost of living is 87 percent higher in Orange County than the US average …"; it goes on to note that, "The county's 2017 Workforce Indicators Report … found that Orange County renters making the mean wage of $19.89 an hour would have to work 70 hours a week to afford a two-bedroom apartment".[4] In another article, the *Orange County Register* notes that "85 percent [of Disneyland employees] now earn less than $15 an hour with more than half earning less than $12…".[5] It is hard for such an enormous – and enormously successful – company to justify such a financial – and moral – disparity in its dealings.

For many years now, Disney has been the largest entertainment corporation in the world. But even more significantly – at least to those of us who study popular culture in its many forms – Disney has been a hugely-significant institution for much of the twentieth and all of the twenty-first centuries, to include during those years when it was an independent studio. Its assets include creations that have become iconic even while they have stood in as symbolic of the company itself. Its most famous and important creation, Mickey Mouse, is so masterful that, despite his various redesigns and uses since his creation in 1928, and despite the many ideas and entities with which he is associated, he can be visually reduced to three circles – °o° – and almost everyone, across a range of ages and nations, will still recognise him, and in doing so, will also think "Disney". There are precious few people left in the world for whom Disney was not a feature of at least some part of their childhood, and for many, Disney is a life-long source of enjoyment. Putting aside the various franchises that Disney now owns that have brought their own loyal fan-bases with them (Star Wars and Marvel being the two that, arguably, stand out the most in this respect), the Disney theme parks, Disney-branded movies, and the Disney-branded television shows (not to mention the thousands and thousands of Disney merchandise lines created since their first, tiny foray into merchandising in 1929) have, as a group, remain hugely popular, even as the popularity of individual films and shows have naturally fluctuated over time. Disney may be a corporation, but for many the name "Disney" carries the warm and fuzzy connotations of fantasy, adventure, romance, and – perhaps most fundamentally – wholesome, high-quality, family-friendly entertainment. This identity for the brand seems to have emerged during the childhood years of the Baby Boom in the 1950s; it was strengthened during the 1960s as other studios and filmmakers began to challenge the strictures of the old Hays Code, a reality that saw a majority of films released in the United States in the early-to-mid 1960s go into cinemas without either a rating certificate – there was no Ratings System in the US until 1968 – and create a situation for audiences whereby they had no external guarantees about a film's content. In this pre-Ratings environment, the Disney name on a film came to mean "safe" – a film anyone in the family could go to see without having to worry about the kinds of depictions of sex and violence increasingly featured in mainstream films of the period – and, in that sense, functioned as a de facto, unofficial "G" rating. By the time the MPAA's Ratings System came into force in November 1968, Disney's association with family entertainment was firmly established.

First and foremost, for most people, Disney means animation. Though by no means the first American studio to produce animated films, Disney nonetheless came to define the form within its first two decades of operation. It was not the first to add sound to its films, but it was the first animation producer, in Mickey Mouse's debut short *Steamboat Willie* (1928), to use fully-synchronised sound that was essential to conveying the film's narrative (and was beat to the post of being the first Hollywood studio to release a '100 percent all-talking film' by just four months when Warner Brothers released *Lights of New York* on 18 July 1928; *Steamboat Willie* debuted theatrically on 18 November 1928). Likewise, Disney led the way in the use of colour cinema: its *Silly Symphony* short *Flowers and Trees* (1932) was the first theatrically-released film to use what was then the new full-colour 'Process 4' (or, as it was/is better known, 'Three-Strip') Technicolor process. Though not (contrary to popular myth) the first to make a feature-length animated film, its *Snow White and the Seven Dwarfs* (1937) was nonetheless a pioneering film in its use not only of animation technologies like the multiplane camera, but also (and amongst other things) in its use of music as a narrative device.[6] Furthermore, although *Snow White* continued to utilise (albeit at a higher level) existing animation technologies, it was nonetheless a game-changer in that its planning and pre-production stages saw a greater awareness of the need for – and an increased uptake of – artistic training (to include fine art instruction) amongst Disney studio artists. Disney was the first animation studio to encourage and support better art education for its staff, and the links established by Disney with the Chouinard Art Institute in Los Angeles led eventually to the establishment of CalArts (California Institute of the Arts), as well as the creation of programs of instruction, training, and education for those aspiring to be professional animators. All of this helped to foster a working environment which not only allowed, but also actively encouraged, artists to experiment – to play – and has seen the medium – and therefore the animation industry as a whole – continue to expand and develop throughout most of its history, up to and including the present day.

But beyond that, Disney has engaged actively with many other forms of popular entertainment. Disney first began to dabble in live-action films – albeit films that combined animation and live-action – in the immediate post-war period, and moved into fully-fledged live-action film making in 1950 with their adaptation of *Treasure Island*, directed by Byron Haskin. An area of the studios that has continued to grow, Disney has made far more live-action films to date even under the Disney label (as opposed to Touchstone, et cetera) than it has animated films (features and shorts combined). Also beginning in 1950, Disney began its first forays into television via a Christmas Day special called *One Hour in Wonderland* that was broadcast by NBC. It launched its first series, *Disneyland*, in October 1954 (on ABC), both as a series in its own right and as a way to exhibit the building of – and generate excitement for – their next major entertainment project, their first theme park, Disneyland, which opened in Anaheim, California in July 1955. Like its film divisions, both Disney's television and theme park divisions have continued to grow exponentially since the 1980s in particular, when Disney began expanding its theme park operations outside of the United States into Japan, France, and most recently into mainland China. Underpinning all of its ventures since the 1920s has been its involvement with merchandising; engaged with only sparingly for Oswald the Lucky Rabbit, Disney became heavily involved in merchandising in the early 1930s, primarily (though not exclusively) with its merchandising of Mickey Mouse. Always a crucial source of revenue for Disney, in the modern era in particular its merchandising, far from simply subsidizing its box office earnings, has the potential to make as much as – if not more than – the actual film. By mid-2015, for example, Disney's 2013 film *Frozen* had grossed $1.3 billion at the box office, and brought in $107.25 billion for its merchandising.[7] *Frozen* merchandise has continued to sell well ever since. And beyond all of these entertainment, commercial, and cultural productions that can unequivocally be designated as "Disney", there are the franchises and businesses that Disney has acquired over the last thirty-plus years that are not so easily "branded" as "Disney". Yet in some cases, particularly for the Star Wars and Marvel franchises, Disney is at least perceived by fans as having had an impact on these universes (whether that is good or bad depends on the opinions of individual fans). Star Wars has been heavily incorporated into the "Disney" brand; Marvel less so. But does that mean that Star Wars is now "Disney"? Or is it simply the case that Disney owns it, distributes it, and merchandises it? The fact that, unusually in the case of such franchises, Disney has increasingly incorporated it into the Disney brand through, amongst other things, crossover merchandise (Mickey dolls dressed as Jedi, for example) and Star Wars "lands" at Disneyland, California, and Walt Disney World, Florida, might suggest something more radical than we usually see with the franchises Disney has purchased; certainly the campaign to make Princess Leia a

Disney Princess would suggest that there is a group of fans who are enthusiastic about this merger of brands.

In September 2014, I hosted an academic conference at the University of Hull. Titled "Discussing Disney" (like this book), the conference's theme was Disney – anything Disney. In my call for papers, I made it clear that I was willing to consider *anything* in the wider world of Disney Studies. That call for papers yielded some amazing stuff, and there were indeed papers on everything from Disney princesses, music, and animation to Disney's live-action films, the theme parks, Disney fandom, and criticisms of Disney. In the end, twenty-two papers (including the keynote) were delivered over the two days of the conference, and in between panels, at lunches and breaks, discussion continued on a variety of topics. A number of themes came up again and again (with discussions of the Disney company's use of the word "Classic" so particularly recurrent that it was eventually dubbed "the C-Word" by the delegates present). But, unsurprisingly, the topic which most held sway at the conference, at least in terms of the general and "extracurricular" discussions, was the very nature of what has become known as "Disney Studies". What do we mean when we say "Disney", after all? These days, "Disney" means more than the things that I began this introduction with. It has grown – and continues to grow – and potentially encompasses multiple brands, franchises, and companies that, on the surface at least, have nothing to do with the traditional idea of the Disney brand. These include television channels (to include ABC and ESPN); character/fantasy worlds such as the Muppets, Marvel Comics, Star Wars and Indiana Jones … even the Simpsons must now be welcomed into the Disney (or perhaps that should be "Diz-nee") family. Whether this niche field of Film/Animation/Cultural/Pop Cultural Studies (take your pick) will come to encompass such diverse properties remains to be seen. Certainly, in their work for my final-year Disney Studies module, my students, whose subject areas are either single- or combined-honours within Film Studies, Media Studies, and American Studies, are already addressing these areas, noting their less-traditional association with "Disney" and asking important questions about what it means for one company – one corporate giant – to have so many properties, brands, fan groups (and fan types) under one umbrella. That Marvel and (in particular) Star Wars are already making their presence known at the Disney theme parks (complete with a Star Wars-themed "land" at Disneyland and Walt Disney World opening in 2019, and even a Star Wars-themed hotel at Disney World) simultaneously have caused excitement and dismay amongst both Disney fans, who want the Disney parks to stay "Disney", and fans of the other brands, who are horrified at what some might see as their beloved brands' "Disneyfication" – its being diluted and polluted by the traits they associate with Disney. How all of this will play out in the longer term remains to be seen, of course; what matters desperately to some fans does not phase others in the slightest; likewise, once the dust has settled completely and these Disney acquisitions have belonged to the company for a few decades, it may cease to matter for the newer generations of fans. Likewise, how these acquisitions will impact both the popular and the scholarly definition(s) of "Disney" remains to be seen. For now, students and academics tend to treat these brands as corporate acquisitions, examining them in terms of economics, corporatization, and fan controversies; they acknowledge the Disney link, but nonetheless tend to see these "satellite" brands as something ultimately separate from the "real" House of Mouse.

So ... how, in this book, is "Disney" to be discussed?

From the original twenty-two papers presented at the conference, I invited fourteen scholars to submit chapters; of those, twelve are included here. They cover four major areas: Disney history, the workings of the Disney studio and Pixar Studios (another formerly-independent brand that Disney has integrated), Gender and how it manifests in a variety of Disney forms, and (last but by no means least) a section that looks at some of the ways that Disney (to include the academic study of the field) has been reinterpreted by others.

The *History* section begins with Dorene S. Koehler's examination of Walt Disney's persona, "A Return to 2719 Hyperion Avenue: Walt Disney as Archetypal Trickster". Looking at Walt both historically and from a Mythos perspective, Koehler links Walt Disney (or perhaps that should be ⱲAⱢⱦ ⅅⲓⲋⲚⲈⱷ) to the many faces of the "Trickster" archetype, and links the use of his persona not only to the ways that the Disney company has presented him, but also to his appearance as a character in several recent biopics and biographical documentaries. She uses Depth Psychology to get closer to not only Walt the Persona, but also to how fans perceive and understand him. As Koehler notes, her analysis "... suggests that this interest in Walt – in his prime, successful, the fearless visionary – reflects a general cultural interest in genesis myths, and that these liminal in-between times are often the realm of the trickster archetype, an archetype that Walt Disney embodies both as a historical figure and as a mythic image. As with all these archetypal images, the images of Walt are greater than the man himself."

The history section continues with Joshua M. Hollands' look at the potential politics of an early Disney short, *Alice's Egg Plant* (1925), in "Animating America's Anticommunism: *Alice's Egg Plant* and Disney's First Red Scare". Hollands examines the short both as an artefact of a moment in American history when the first "Red Scare" was a current event, and also as evidence of Walt Disney's own political leanings as a man in his early twenties ... a man who, as a child, first taught himself how to draw by copying the cartoons in such Socialist periodicals as *Appeal to Reason*, to which Walt's father, Elias Disney – a committed Socialist – was a sub-scriber. By examining the short both within the context of the era in which it was made and as it hints at Walt Disney's own understanding of the Red Scare, Hollands notes that "… both sides of the labour dispute are mocked in *Alice's Egg Plant*, and any narrative indication that we should favour one side over the other is ultimately made tenuous".

The *History* section concludes with Alexander Sergeant's discussion of the making and reception of *The Black Cauldron* (1985), "High Fantasy Disney: Recontextualizing *The Black Cauldron*". In doing so, Sergeant also examines Disney's use of the "Classic" label, as well as how *The Black Cauldron* does not fit easily (if at all) into what, by the 1980s, was understood as the Disney brand, particularly in light of the film's strong connections with "high" Fantasy as a genre. By looking at *The Black Cauldron* not only within the context of the cycle of Hollywood-produced High Fantasy films of the early 1980s, but also as part of how Disney sought to reach an audience whose attitude towards the Disney film brand had changed significantly since the 1950s and '60s, Sergeant notes the longer-term impact of the film's box-office disappointment. As Sergeant argues, the successes of the late 1980s and 1990s at Disney, in many important ways, can be traced back to the experiment of making and releasing *The Black Cauldron*, particularly with the period's heightened emphasis on fairy tale and folklore sources for its animated films. He asserts, ultimately, that "… the importance of understanding some of the artistic traits of *The Black Cauldron* is not simply that it might allow us to reclaim or reconsider a film dismissed by many as a commercial and artistic folly, but that such an analysis provides a way of examining the studio's wider relationship to the fantasy genre outside the domains of dominant narratives emphasised through quantitative labels such as 'Classic' and 'Renaissance'".

The next section of the book, "Inside the Studio", offers readers a look into how Disney's live-action and animation studios have approached film making during the last half century. The section begins with Noel Brown's chapter "'That Corner of the Disney Studio that is Forever England': Disney's Vision of the British Family", which looks at the representations of Britishness and in particular the British family in some of Disney's films of the 1960s and '70s. To do this, Brown focuses on four of Disney's live-action films from this period as case studies: *Greyfriars Bobby* (1961), *Mary Poppins* (1964), *Bedknobs and Broomsticks* (1971), and *Candleshoe* (1977). However, he acknowledges that Disney's "fixation with Britishness" ex-tended to its animated films as well during this period, and argues that, rather than focusing on British stories and characters as a way to link itself to a kind of imagined "prestige" that might be associated (by some) with Britishness, in fact this use of the British family allowed for a kind of "neutrality" for American audiences in a period turbulent enough that, as

Brown notes, it has been described as being akin to a "second American civil war". Yet, Brown argues, this does not mean that these films are either "politically withdrawn or ideologically displaced". Rather, "Each [film] identifies problems in society and in the family in microcosm, that an enlightened or inspirational outsider must resolve; each reasserts the nurturing, protective qualities of the literal or symbolic family; and each places emphasis on young children and mature adults, marginalising or altogether dispensing with older teenagers and young adults".

Next, Helen Haswell analyses the impact that Disney's work with – and later in its acquisition of – Pixar has had on the Disney studio's animated films. Her chapter, "Fix it Felix! Reviving Disney Animation Using the Pixar Formula", particularly focuses on the post-"Renaissance" era of the Disney studio. As its own animated offerings began to decline significantly in popularity while, from its release of *Toy Story* in 1995, Pixar enjoyed hit after hit with both the public and critics; a decade later, Haswell notes that "Disney's own market research confirmed that mothers with children under the age of twelve generally rated Pixar's brand higher than Disney's". Additionally, for the first time in its history, Disney's animated feature films began to experience genuine competition from multiple animation studios, as well as witnessing (and joining in only latterly) a genuine technological revolution in animation production with the rise of digital animation in the feature film market. However, once Disney had purchased Pixar in 2006 and John Lasseter was installed as Chief Creative Officer of Disney, the studio's output began to turn around, particularly with its release of *Tangled* in 2010, which, Haswell notes, "was the [Disney] studio's first number one hit in 16 years". Of course, the subject of Haswell's chapter is an on-going story, even necessitating a last-minute revision of her chapter due to Lasseter's ouster from Disney/Pixar as a result of his problematic treatment of female staff at the company finally becoming public and believed – and therefore punishable – as a result of the #MeToo movement, and his replacement at Pixar by Pete Docter (Jennifer Lee, co-director of *Frozen*, 2013, has taken over the leadership of Disney's animation studio; she is the first woman to hold this position, and the latest to hold a role first occupied by Walt Disney himself). This leadership change – both of personnel and of having separate Chief Creative Officers for each of these animation studios – far from problematizing Haswell's study, in fact makes it more salient, since at the heart of her work is an examination of whether Pixar's acquisition by Disney has benefitted Pixar or Disney more. Her conclusion is that, as of 2017, Disney was the primary beneficiary; only time will tell whether this latest evolution in the studios' lives maintains or changes that trajectory.

The "Inside the Studio" section concludes with Christopher Holliday's essay, "Let It Go? Towards a 'Plasmatic' Perspective on Digital Disney", in which he discusses the notions that surround the idea of the "Disney Formula" – an idea which has a very long history within critical, popular, and scholarly discourse – and looks at it in relation to the impact that turning to digital animation technologies has had upon Disney animation. Noting that "… the phrase 'Disney formula' has become embedded deep within the recesses of America's cultural memory, uttered as part of a global vernacular denoting the perceived uniformity of Disney products and testifying to Magic Kingdom hegemony", Holliday unpacks and interrogates this notion, and looks at how scholars have shown this notion of Disney as "formulaic" to be inherently problematic. He does this by examining how the idea of a Disney formula first emerged in the discourse of film critics about the studio (as well as in the writing of Sergei Eisenstein), and looks not only at how the idea of the formula has evolved, but also at how the idea of the formula struggles for relevance in the face of scholarship that has shown that, in fact, this notion of Disney is ultimately erroneous. By examining the Disney films of the digital era in particular, Holliday shows that "A duel between *formulaic* and *plasmatic* thinking presents an effective means of understanding the period of Digital Disney, painting (and now pixelating) a picture of Disney's computer-animated films that is altogether more nuanced and complex".

The third section of the book includes four chapters that examine Disney in relation to various aspects of Gender Studies, focusing primarily upon how Disney interacts with ideas of femininity and feminism. The section starts with Lauren L. Smith's examination of the use and presence of cosmetics in "Perfect Brides or Beautified Baddies: Characters' Use of Cosmetics in Disney's Feature Animation". Smith distinguishes between what cosmetics can signify about a character's moral stance, but also notes that, when we see a character obviously applying cosmetics, they are used "… to highlight the artifices present in either the characters or the situations being depicted". Smith focuses on five scenes in five films where we see characters actually applying facial cosmetics, and looks at both how these characters apply (or remove) their makeup, noting the ways that appearance is commented on by the films' narratives, particularly when it is one of the three villains we see using beauty products: Madame Medusa of *The Rescuers* (1977), Ursula from *The Little Mermaid* (1989), and Yzma from *The Emperor's New Groove* (2000). This chapter, in its examination of cosmetics, focuses as much on the significance of seeing characters actively using cosmetics as it does on the inherent artifice created by makeup, concluding that the use of cosmetics "… can be seen as a means of highlighting and reflecting the artificial aspects of the particular scenes in which they are used or in the people which they are used by". Given how understudied the areas of costuming, cosmetics, and grooming in general are within the area of animation studies, this chapter is a rare examination of characters' appearances within animation, and considers cosmetics for animated characters in very similar ways to those applied to live actors.

As with cosmetics as a form of costuming within animation, music too is (at the time of this book's publication, at least) an overlooked area of animation studies. Oliver Lindman's examination of gendered music in Disney, "From Operatic Uniformity to Upbeat Eclecticism: The Musical Evolution of the Princess in Disney's Animated Features", seeks to bring attention to how music is used to accompany the princess characters, as well as contextualizing Disney's use of music within the larger area of film music studies. Indeed, Lindman acknowledges that his paper is only part of the beginning of academic exploration of Disney's music, and notes that "Expanding on the topic of audiences and sociocultural meanings of music is necessary for more in-depth studies of the [Disney] films". At the core of his analysis is Lindman's assertion is that "The musical development of the animated Disney princess is a slow but reasonably steady process of gradual liberation from the early Hollywood conventions of scoring stereotypical womanhood". Much of the chapter is an analysis of those changes, to include careful analysis of how Howard Ashman and Alan Menkin's incorporation of Broadway musical styles of the 1980s would impact how we understand the Disney animated musical. Ultimately, Lindman stresses the power that music has for enabling the audience to connect to the character singing, arguing that "... when music is foregrounded, emotional borders between characters and audience are often thinnest". He notes that this is true not only when someone is watching the film, but also later, both when listening to songs from the film (such as when listening to a CD) and when engaging with the film's non-musical merchandise.

From examining the music that links the Disney princesses, we move on to Kodi Maier's dissection of how Disney lets any bride-to-be play Princess for a Day. In "Princess Brides and Dream Weddings: Investigating the Gendered Narrative of Disney's Fairy Tale Weddings", Maier places the Walt Disney World wedding pavilion within the contexts of both the modern wedding industry and ideas about the Princess as an aspirational fantasy figure. These two ideas are brought together by an examination of how both Disney and the wedding industry (to which Disney is a relative late-comer) construct the aspirations of the modern bride; they note that, when those connected to the wedding industry (and even those who are not) ask such questions as "what woman doesn't dream of being a fairy-tale princess on her wedding day", they "... demonstrate that the bride's desires for a lavish 'fairy tale' wedding are merely constructed; they are *naturalised* by language that implicitly reinforces the idea that fantasising about the 'perfect' 'fairy tale' wedding is an inherent component of a woman's femininity". Maier interrogates the assumptions that underlie this bias (since, after all, there are many women who had no desire to play "princess" when they were little girls, and likewise a great many women who never, as children or as adults spent time dreaming about their wedding day). Maier, in looking at these issues, also notes the secondary role of the groom in all of this, thereby reinforcing the gendering of not only weddings, but also the hyper-consumerism that has come to be associated with weddings since the 1950s. They conclude by tying this to how Disney caters to all brides and grooms, in this way (arguably) privileging the betrothed couple's Disney fandom over their fantasies (or lack thereof) of having a Disney princess wedding. After all, Maier notes, "Those who wish to eschew the Cinderella/princess theme can opt for an international theme in Epcot, a Hollywood theme in Disney's Hollywood Studios, or a luau at the Polynesian Resort". If, of course, you have the budget for it!

The Gender section concludes with Catherine Lester's "Frozen Hearts and Fixer Uppers: Villainy, Gender, and Female Companionship in Disney's *Frozen*". In this chapter, Lester looks at the ways that Elsa plays into ideas about the villain, but ultimately subverts these notions through the film's depiction of Elsa's relationship with her sister, Anna. This, Lester argues, "… marks a significant change in the representation of women, girls, and female relationships in Disney's animated fairy tales". Lester contextualizes Anna and Elsa within the larger subject of the Disney princess (and the villains they must face as part of their narratives). Arguing that *Frozen* offers audiences a departure from what might be seen in earlier Disney films, Lester notes that it is likely the differences the film offers that made it so appealing to audiences, particularly when it comes to the relationship between the sisters and the various "red herrings" about the identity of the film's villain: "With its portrayal of Hans … *Frozen* is in the intriguing position of a Disney film criticising Disney's own tropes, and using them against the audience to challenge ingrained assumptions about what villainy does or does not look like".

The final section of the collection, "Outside the Studio", discusses issues regarding how Disney has been depicted and/or perceived by others. It begins with Jemma D. Gilboy's examination of the "Simpsonification" of Disney in "The Violentest Place on Earth: Adventures in Censorship, Nostalgia, and Pastiche (Or, *The Simpsons* Do Disney)". Taking the three most common types of Disney references to be found in *The Simpsons* – the theme parks, a version of the life of Walt Disney, and Disney films as they can be related to *The Itchy and Scratchy Show* (arguably the most prominent of the various shows-within-the-show to be found in *The Simpsons*), and states the core of her examination in this chapter as being an attempt "… to determine what – beyond being Disney outputs – these three elements have in common that makes them particularly tempting to the producers of *The Simpsons* [to target]". Gilboy contextualizes her discussion within an examination of the Post-modern elements of *The Simpsons* and the (arguably related) fashion for Disney defamation, as well as where on the spectrum of loving Disney and loathing Disney one might find the creatives who have contributed to *The Simpsons* since their series debut in 1989.

The section – and the book as a whole – concludes with Chris Pallant's chapter "Disney Pluralism: Beyond Disney Formalism", an essay which has grown out of his keynote speech for the conference though, as he notes, has evolved to take into account not only the goals of this book, but also subsequent popular reactions to groups of scholars gathering together to discuss Disney, in particular the excellent "SymFrozium" held at the University of East Anglia in May 2015 ... that despite its many thoughtful, highly intelligent, and entirely scholarly papers (I was one of the keynote speakers, so I may be somewhat biased), was nonetheless treated with disdain by a popular press – and a public – who by and large were not there to witness the day, but reacted with misguided scorn and disdain that such an event had even occurred. Pallant's focus, however, is the idea of "pluralism" in relation to Disney. As he puts it, "With the unwieldy scale of contemporary 'Disney' in mind, my use of pluralism in this chapter is intended to foreground the fact that what 'Disney' was/is/means is not defined by any one individual – whether that is The Walt Disney Company or an online commentator going by the pseudonym 'V'. As we continue through a period of scholarly upheaval, where the meaningfulness and funding of Arts and Humanities is increasingly defined via metrics con-ceived for – and far better suited to – STEM subject areas, scholars committed to the study of 'Disney' as an object of significant historical and cultural importance need to continually re-evaluate how they frame and communicate this work."

As to why it is important to think about these issues, Pallant concludes by stating that, "At a time when large corporations like Disney are seeking to manage our journey through life, it is critically important that we continue to interrogate the terms on which we interact with them. By adopting a pluralist framework, we might find a more nuanced and flexible means with which to negotiate the 'Disney' world in which many of us now live." This very neatly and effectively sums up my own goals in hosting the *Discussing Disney* conference, in putting together this collection, and – indeed – informs my teaching of popular culture as a whole, to include within my final-year module, *Disney Studies*. Disney is everywhere; as it continues to acquire more media properties, it becomes more pervasive than ever before. As an enormous corporation whose reach is global, it has enormous potential to shape our lives, and therefore has great power – as do all corporations – to shape our lives for good or ill, regardless of whether or not, in the ordinary run of things, an individual does or doesn't consider themselves to be a Disney fan. But The Walt Disney Company has something that the vast majority of corporations do not – it has not just one face, but two: Walt Disney and Mickey Mouse. It has a warm, safe, familiar branding connotation that makes us more susceptible as a society to trust it – even in some cases to love it. We *need* to discuss Disney – how it came about, the key individuals who have shaped it since its founding in 1923 (as well as the experiences of its founder, Walt Disney, prior to 1923), how it evolved as an animation leader, how it began to branch out into other areas of entertainment while keeping its (at times, rather diminished) animation studio as the heart and soul of its brand and its increasingly family-friendly identity, and how it has continued to change since the death not only of Walt Disney, but also the deaths of those whose family ties to the studio could most shape it: Walt's brother Roy O. Disney in 1971, Roy's son, Roy E. Disney, in 2009, and Walt's daughter, Diane Disney Miller, in 2013 (who never worked for the company, but who nonetheless carried great clout as Walt's only surviving child). In discussing Disney, we are discussing not just a film studio, not just a corporation, but a significant aspect of western popular culture. To not discuss it is to ignore one of the greatest forces of the twentieth and twenty-first centuries.

Bibliography

Anonymous. "Disney shareholders vote against CEO Iger's pay package", *CNBC.com*, published 9 March 2018, https://www.cnbc.com/2018/03/09/disney-shareholders-vote-against-ceo-igers-pay-package.html

Robehmed, Natalie. "The 'Frozen' Effect: When Disney's Movie Merchandising is Too Much", from *Forbes* Online, 28 July 2015. https://www.forbes.com/sites/natalierobehmed/2015/07/28/the-frozen-effect-when-disneys-movie-merchandising-is-too-much/#2f01805522ca

Roosevelt, Margot. "Disney unions' ballot drive seeks to raise wages up to $18 an hour for hospitality companies that take Anaheim subsidies", *Orange County Register* online, published 28 February 2018, updated 4 March 2018. https://www.ocregister.com/2018/02/28/disney-unions-ballot-drive-seeks-to-raise-wages-up-to-18-for-hospitality-companies-that-take-anaheim-subsidies/amp/?utm_source=dlvr.it&utm_medium=twitter&__twitter_impression=true

Roosevelt, Margot. "Disneyland Resort workers struggle to pay for food, housing and medical care, union survey finds", from *Orange County Register* online, published 27 February 2018, updated 7 March 2018. https://www.ocregister.com/2018/02/27/disneyland-resort-workers-struggle-to-pay-for-food-housing-and-medical-care-union-survey-finds/

Sweney, Mark. 'Disney Offers to Buy Sky News to Ease Murdoch's £11.7bn Takeover', *The Guardian* online, https://amp.theguardian.com/business/2018/apr/03/disney-offers-to-buy-sky-news-to-ease-murdochs-117bn-takeover

Endnotes

1. These studios, known as the Big Five and the Little Three, were (respectively) Warner Brothers, Twentieth Century Fox, MGM, Universal, and Paramount; RKO, United Artists, and Columbia. Between 1930 and 1953, Disney's films were distributed by Columbia (1930–32), UA (1932–37), and RKO (1937–53). By 1953, the distribution and exhibition networks' ownership had been dismantled sufficiently that Disney was able to form its own distribution company, which it initially named Buena Vista Distribution Company, Inc.

2. Mark Sweney, 'Disney Offers to Buy Sky News to Ease Murdoch's £11.7bn Takeover', *The Guardian* online, https://amp.theguardian.com/business/2018/apr/03/disney-offers-to-buy-sky-news-to-ease-murdochs-117bn-takeover.

3. "Disney shareholders vote against CEO Iger's pay package", *CNBC.com*, published 9 March 2018, https://www.cnbc.com/2018/03/09/disney-shareholders-vote-against-ceo-igers-pay-package.html

4. Margot Roosevelt, "Disney unions' ballot drive seeks to raise wages up to $18 an hour for hospitality companies that take Anaheim subsidies", *Orange County Register* online, published 28 February 2018, updated 4 March 2018. https://www.ocregister.com/2018/02/28/disney-unions-ballot-drive-seeks-to-raise-wages-up-to-18-for-hospitality-companies-that-take-an aheim-subsidies/amp/?utm_source=dlvr.it&utm_medium=twitter&___twitter_impressio n=true

5. Margot Roosevelt, "Disneyland Resort workers struggle to pay for food, housing and medical care, union survey finds", from *Orange County Register* online, published 27 February 2018, updated 7 March 2018. https://www.ocregister.com/2018/02/27/disneyland-resort-work-ers-struggle-to-pay-for-food-housing-and-medical-care-union-survey-finds/

6. Though the first film to be screened cinematically that used Disney's re-designed version of the multiplane camera was its 1937 short *The Old Mill*, *Snow White and the Seven Dwarfs* was the film for which the technology was actively developed. *The Old Mill*, though an Oscar-winning short, nonetheless effectively functioned as a test film for Disney's development of the vertical multiplane camera.

7. Natalie Robehmed, "The 'Frozen' Effect: When Disney's Movie Merchandising is Too Much", from *Forbes* Online, 28 July 2015.https://www.forbes.com/sites/natalierobehmed/ 2015/07/28/the-frozen-effect-when-disneys-movie-merchandising-is-too-much/#2f0180 5522ca

I.
History

Chapter 1

A Return to 2719 Hyperion Avenue: Walt Disney, the Animated Trickster

Dorene S. Koehler

"[Walt] Disney always promised a fantasy in which one could exercise the privileges of childhood ... This will to power also explained why animation was his preferred medium. In animation one took the inanimate and brought it to life, or the illusion of life. In animation, one could exercise the power of a god."[1]

From the Surrealism of the 1920s to the contemporary obsession with the cult of celebrity, few storytelling mediums have been as influential as those of Hollywood. Perhaps none of Hollywood's icons are as largely and globally influential as Walt Disney. The psychological power of moving picture arises from how films make us feel. Both as individuals and as a broader culture, films resonate because they reflect some sort of truth. They crawl inside and move that ineffable mystery that is the human soul. They reflect who we are, who we have been, and who we are becoming and, in doing so, offer an opportunity for psychological insight, bringing with it the chance to challenge and transform.

According to the Oxford English Dictionary, the term *anima* derives from the Latin word meaning soul or life force. Walt Disney's name is synonymous with the medium of animation, a process that uses artistic renderings to imbue inanimate images with life. Walt's animated characters and signature are icons, infused with life and recognizable all over the world. Since the 1920s, Disney's creations – Oswald the Lucky Rabbit, Mickey Mouse, and many others – have captivated audiences. The man himself, however, is often shrouded in ambiguity.

For all the stories that circulate about Walt Disney, it is virtually impossible to completely distill history from myth.[2] As is the case with all historical persons of mythic significance, some are comfortable remembering the mythic incarnation of them, and some search for the certainly of historical facts about them. As one might expect, finding a balance between the myth and history is complicated. The process lends itself to projection, often making mythic personalities both controversial and multifaceted. This is certainly the case with Walt Disney. Love him or hate him, there is no mistaking the power of both his richly detailed creations and the stories that are told about him.

In recent years, the mythic icon that is Walt Disney has emerged stronger and more prevalent than ever in Disney culture. This might suggest that after decades of mourning his death and attempting to inject the company with new energy, those in charge of running The Walt Disney Company recognized the void Walt's absence created in their actual process of storytelling. The following analysis suggests that this interest in Walt – in his prime, successful, the fearless visionary – reflects a general cultural interest in genesis myths, and that these liminal in-between times are often the realm of the trickster archetype, an archetype that Walt Disney embodies both as a historical figure and as a mythic image.[3] As with all these archetypal images, the images of Walt are greater than the man himself.

In 2001, an attraction devoted to the history of Walt's life, *One Man's Dream,* opened at Walt Disney World's Disney-MGM Studios theme park.[4] This seems to be the beginning of a reinvestment by the Walt Disney Company in Walt's image because, after this attraction opened, his image slowly began to reemerge. In 2009, an organization called D23 was launched.[5] In August of that same year, the D23 hosted their first event, the D23 Expo. This three-day event at the Anaheim Convention Center, filled with thousands of Disney fans, included a booth heralding a new museum. Initially an internet resource, The Walt Disney Family Museum became a physical space in October 2009.[6] Around that same time, Walt's image reemerged at the parks in Anaheim. Merchandise arrived with quotes and images of him, much of which regularly sold out.

At the D23 Expo in 2011, Disney Imagineering released plans for a $1 billon expansion at Disneyland Resort which included extensive renovations of Disney California Adventure and The Disneyland Hotel. In demographic studies done at the park, cast members found that patrons felt Disney California Adventure somehow missed the magic Disneyland had. One central aspect of that renovation was a re-theming of Disney California Adventure's Main Street into *Buena Vista Street,* intended to be Disney's experience of Los Angeles when he arrived in 1923.

In 2013, Walt Disney Pictures released *Saving Mr. Banks,* a biopic originally intended to tell the story of the life of PL Travers, author of *Mary Poppins.* To no one's surprise, Walt Disney hijacks the screen. In film, as in life, his presence is infectious. Tom Hanks' performance is layered with emotion and effectively-created illusion.[7] In 2014, two more films arrived: *As Dreamers Do*, an independent project bolstered by crowd funding and telling Walt's story from birth to his move west; and *Walt Before Mickey*, a film version of the book by the same name that tells the story of Walt's early career.

On May 22, 2015, two new offerings from The Walt Disney Company continue to bring Walt's image to the public. Brad Bird's film *Tomorrowland* (2015) is an epic adventure based on Walt Disney's philosophies of utopia and progress. The film relies heavily on the mythically and historically iconic 1964/65 World's Fair at which WED Enterprises offered exhibitions for PepsiCola (*It's a Small World*), General Electric (*Carousel of Progress*), The State of Illinois (*Great Moments With Mr. Lincoln*), and Ford (*Magic Skyway*). It places the welfare of the future directly into the hands of the heirs of Walt Disney's mythic voice. On the same day, Disneyland Resort launched a celebration for the 60th anniversary of the park with several new attractions. One in particular, *World of Color*, evokes Walt's image. The show titled *The Wonderful World of Walt Disney* features moving images projected on water that include footage of Disney's early work, the opening day of Disneyland, an interactive video asking Walt if he would do it all again, and lastly a shimmering white outline of Walt and Mickey walking away hand in hand. Lastly, PBS scheduled a four-hour, two-part film, *Walt Disney* (14 and 15 September 2015, PBS), that focused on his life and achievements.[8] These are just a few of the projects that have arrived in the last decade that focus on Walt Disney, a large percentage of which focus on him as a young man, following his early career from the late 1920s to the beginning of the *Disneyland* television show in 1954.

From the perspective of myth analysis, this interest clearly indicates Walt Disney's archetypal resonance. In contrast to a historical perspective that would seek to find truth in fact about Walt, a mythological perspective allows for truth in the *image* of Walt and in what he represents. It allows, much like animated film itself, for truth to come through a painted image of him as metaphor, archetype, and icon. This kaleidoscopic image, and the ensuing level of cultural projection that follows it, both suggest that Walt Disney's central mythic significance is as a trickster figure.

Like all archetypes, the trickster is difficult to define, in part because the interpretation of archetypal images is as complex as the human experience itself. Depth psychologist C.G. Jung spent his life examining the effects of what he called the *archetypes* and the collective unconscious on mythology. He theorized that the human soul or *psyche* comes to a sense of identity through the images we create, and that the purpose of these images is to grasp at an understanding of the psychic energies that make up our emotions and our psychological experiences. The entirety of mythic expression, he notes, is humanity's way of coming to know itself. He writes, "The collective unconscious appears to consist of mythological motifs or primordial images ... In fact, the whole of mythology could be taken as a sort of projection of the collective unconscious."[9] In other words, the motifs and images that make up our stories are universal – each is a prismatic projection of the collective human psyche.

To Jung, an archetype is an energetic concept, not completely unlike Plato's theory of forms. He theorizes that there is a difference between archetypes (which he saw as universal concepts: father, mother, warrior, trickster), and the archetypal images that we can physically experience: our fathers, our mothers, our soldiers, and the tricksters in our stories. The creation of a hermeneutic for these psychological energies is the basis of Jungian interpretation of mythic archetypal images. Whether in film, television, printed word, spoken word, or any other aspect of story, archetypal images are the characters who bring understanding to our psychological realities.

Conventional Jungian theory identifies the trickster archetype as the psychic energy of the shadow, or that of which we are unconscious. In her book *Shadow and Evil in Fairy Tales*, Jungian theorist Marie Louise von Franz amplifies this concept of shadow, though she warns against any attempt to codify it with definitive answers.[10] Jung himself argues that the trickster is the shadow itself. Although some theorists equate shadow with evil, it simply means the totality of what is unconscious. It is the often ignored, repressed, and unattended to parts of who we are. It represents the unknown, and the unknown, if not made conscious, can often manifest itself in harmful or negative ways. As a representative of the shadow, trickster figures bring the unconscious to consciousness – an experience which can often make us uncomfortable because it often does not care about upholding the status quo. For this reason, the shadow is often misunderstood as a negative construct. On the contrary, an experience with the shadow can bring delight as often as it brings discomfort.

Just like Walt Disney the man, tricksters defy the rules of the gods. They are often impish, desirous of mischief for its own sake or simply for fun. They appear in every mythology, and are often, though not exclusively, presented in the form of a male.[11] In Irish myth, the trickster is the leprechaun; in Native American myth, he is the coyote; in Greek myth, he is Hermes. Trickster figures love to complicate myth by doing exactly what they please. They are storytellers, magicians, and, masters of creating what Ollie Johnston and Frank Thomas called an "illusion of life".[12] The particularities of Walt Disney as a trickster image speak to the power of subversion in the process of mythmaking, and the history of The Walt Disney Company demonstrates clear evidence for the ebb and flow that exist when tension is in play between different archetypal energies. In other words, the most trickster-esque thing about Walt Disney may be the fact that he often does not seem like a trickster at all. This interpretation of Walt Disney welcomes the ambiguities of paradox; as a trickster, he can simultaneously be Mickey Mouse, Uncle Walt, the dreamer, the visionary, the tyrant, the misogynistic, racist anti-Semite, the anti-communist patriot, the genius, the messiah, the family man, the every man, hero, the shrewd moneymaker, and the cult leader.

The God of the Crossroads

Virtually all of the world's mythologies cast the trickster in the role of gatekeeper or god of the crossroads. They rarely stick to their home, preferring instead to open up new opportunities.[13] They are the archetypal travelers, roaming everywhere so that they can subvert systems anywhere. As such, they are generally most interested in thresholds – the places where beginnings and endings intersect. As Walt Disney once said, "We keep moving forward – opening up new doors and doing new things – because we're curious. And curiosity keeps leading us down new paths."[14] Tricksters serve as a witness to the process of threshold crossing. They often offer themselves as a guide to the underworld, ushering humanity into the transformation of death, both literal and metaphorical.

There are many different images of this god of the crossroads, but the Haitian gods or loa known as Papa Ghede[15] and Brave Ghede[16] are perhaps the clearest examples of this. Though they are slightly different in presentation, all images of Ghede are generally characterized as a male figure in a suit with a black top hat and skull face. Those with knowledge of Disney's animated films will recognize this character as evocative of Dr. Facilier in *The Princess and the Frog* (2009).[17] Ghede is a lord of death and the guardian of the graveyard. Dark and frightening though he may seem to those outside the tradition, he is not often feared in the context of Voudou practice. As a metaphor for death itself, he represents more than just the end of physical life. He is the transformation of consciousness – the loa to whom practitioners of Voudou appeal for their opening into the realm of the divine. He stands at the gate of the graveyard, allowing entrance to the spiritual powers of the ancestors. These figures are responsible for holding and controlling the power of transformation, or what ritual scholars refer to as liminality.[18] As travelers, crossroads gods represent all the collective wisdom of humanity, both conscious and unconscious, and they are the ones who grant access to it.

Walt Disney is also presented in this way, though his image takes on a different form and offers a completely different kind of transformation of consciousness. In contrast to an image that recognizes the transformation process as dangerous and frightening, he is presented as a kind and welcoming crossroads guardian. Statues at Disneyland and in Disney California Adventure, as well as at the Magic Kingdom in Walt Disney

World, Florida, both depict Walt as a gatekeeper, presiding over and facilitating entrance into the realm of Disney imagination. In both of the Anaheim parks, these figures of Walt occupy a central space, known specifically at Disneyland and Disney World's Magic Kingdom as "The Hub". Much like a vestibule of a church, Main Street Disneyland/the Magic Kingdom, and Buena Vista Street at Disney California Adventure, both function as a threshold crossing into sacred experience. They orient the visitor into the myths they are about to inhabit, and prepare the guest to enter the Disney experience. Yet the parks does so in subtle, but vastly different ways.

Main Street at Disneyland transports the guest into Walt's imaginal projection of turn of the century Missouri. It places the guest in the era of Walt's birth and childhood as though it were a contemporary era, not over a century ago. It recreates an experience of a very specific time in American history, when cities began to flourish and the railroad made travel much more possible for the average American; when the county fair and the World's Fair still brought a sense of wonder at the mysteries being discovered, but before Americans faced the potential of utter annihilation during two World Wars and The Great Depression.

As a visitor travels down Main Street, one is transported into this earlier era: smells of popcorn and candy are piped through the air, ragtime music plays, cast member costumes evoke the fashions of the time, and the buildings reflect "turn of the (twentieth) century" garb. This is the world that is largely responsible for Walt's beliefs in possibility and progress; after all, Walt Disney was born in the midst of the Progressive Era (1890–1920), which saw numerous changes and improvements in the daily and working lives of ordinary Americans. As one is bathed in a sense of comfort and reassurance about the era and the American mythic experience, one approaches The Hub – a circular center that serves as a kind of compass entrance into the parks. At both parks, The Hub is raised focal point with benches and flowerbeds punctuating the area. At each cardinal direction of the circle, there is a foot entrance, and in the center are circular, raised flowerbeds and a centrally located statue of Walt Disney and Mickey Mouse. Once the guest crosses this threshold presided over by Walt and Mickey, they are free to make their way through to the other ands of the park.

The *Partners* statue in Disneyland/the Magic Kingdom depicts Walt Disney and Mickey Mouse holding hands. They face out toward Main Street, Walt with an arm that can be seen both as outstretched as if waving hello, beaconing the guest to come to him and Mickey, and also as Walt looking out across the horizon, describing to Mickey (who is looking up at Walt) what he sees. This iconic statue presents Walt in his middle age, as he was when Disneyland first opened in 1955. He is recognizable as the host of the *Disneyland* television show, wearing his trademark suit. He stands tall, an icon on high, as his role is also as guardian to watch over the kingdom he has created. He is the archetypal Wise One, imparting his vision to future generations. Walt himself said, "Disneyland would be a world of Americans, past and present, seen through the eyes of my imagination – a place of warmth and nostalgia, of illusion and color and delight".[19] At The Hub, Walt Disney opens a crossroad to the park's "lands", each of which can be interpreted as representing core Disney values: imagination (Fantasyland), mythic history (Frontierland), the wildness of nature (Adventureland), and faith in progress and the limitless potential of the future (Tomorrowland).

The threshold crossing at Disney California Adventure evokes a slightly different type of Disney experience. In contrast to the kind of old-timey mythic image Walt Disney's mid-west constellates, Disney's Los Angeles is brimming with the kind of youthful energy that the early Disney Brothers Studio and Pixar both represent. As guests at this park move down Buena Vista Street, they are treated to the offerings of Hollywood's Golden Age. Rather than the image of mid-western small town America, Buena Vista Street brims with art and the budding motion picture industry. The colorful tiles evoke the Mexican folk art that is central to Los Angeles city culture, and the jazz musicians represent the youthful exuberance of the years between World War I and The Great Depression. The Hub at the end of Buena Vista Street is similar in construction to the one at Disneyland with one notable difference: the placement of the icon of Walt and Mickey. The central focal point of this Hub is the Carthay Circle Fountain. It stands adjacent to the Carthay Circle Theater, a re-creation of the theater where *Snow White and the Seven Dwarfs* first premiered on December 21, 1937.

Blaine Gibson, the artist and imagineer[20] who created the *Partners* statue, was tapped to create the statue in the Hub of Buena Vista Street. This icon, titled *Storytellers*, presents Walt Disney as a fresh-faced mid-western kid just off the train. It depicts young Walt directly on the ground, no taller than you or I. The statue is placed outside the circle of The Hub, a choice that seems to remind us that this young man has just begun to develop his career. Rather than being dressed in the somewhat more formal standard suit he became known for later in life, this Walt Disney is a dressed in his 1920s-style trousers and sweater, jacket slung over his shoulder, evoking the importance of the eye-catching fashion to the era. He stands next to his traveling trunk, upon which Mickey (depicted in his late 1920s/early 1930s design) is perched. Mickey is smaller (in comparison with Walt) in the *Storytellers* statue than he is in the *Partners* statue; no doubt this indicates that, like Walt, Mickey's own status had grown since his early days.

The two are full of energy and enthusiasm. All of this suggests that at Disney California Adventure, Walt Disney and Mickey Mouse are opening the crossroads to a kind of Californian playground – an environment perfect for Disney artists, where magic and industry co-exist to form a state that guests can build together, rather than being surrounded by a magic kingdom that has been created for them. Guests on Buena Vista Street are invited to experience both the time before the creation of Mickey Mouse – the Disney Brothers' world shortly before Mickey's conception. Moving toward *Hollywoodland*, one is able to visit an attraction dedicated to animation where guests can begin to learn the trade themselves. Moving the opposite direction toward what has been called *Grizzly Peak Airfields*, guests can explore the beginnings of Californian aviation, the natural beauty of the Sierra Nevada Mountains and Yosemite Valley, the fertile farmland of the San Joaquin and Salinas valleys, and the early days of Santa Monica Pier. Although Disney characters are present all over the park at Disney California Adventure, Pixar's emphasis on reinvention is the focus, and with that reinvention comes an emphasis on Walt's early career – the halcyon days of the Disney Brothers' Studio, before the complications of the employee strike and the red scare of communism changed his politics and business practices.

The Illusionist

Perhaps the most obvious trickster-esque aspect of Walt Disney appears through his role as magician or illusionist. Conflated with what *Saving Mr. Banks*' PL Travers calls a "… trickster, a fraudster, and a sneak", the term magician has come to have a negative connotation. The term itself, however, has its roots in ancient religion and the tradition of the shaman. In connection with its role as the god of the crossroads, the trickster magician in mythology is the one who has the ability to travel between realms. Hermes, for example, is the only god who can speak to Olympus, the human realm, and the underworld – and he doesn't cross those realms just for the sake of his love of travel. He does so in his role as messenger. Hermes is also the god of liars – not the capricious liar, but the mischievous liar. This ties his role again to the archetype of the trickster. The magician trickster assumes this role in the human world, therefore, becoming a human version of the messenger to the gods. Again, they do this not for their own sake, but for their community.

They are the dreamers and the visionaries, and are often reluctant to perform their duties, aware as they are of the dangers that exist beyond the human world in the realm of the imagination.[21] Likewise, Walt Disney was reluctant, in his early years, to embrace a public persona as a magician. But, as he became aware that he alone had depth of passion and understanding for his own work, he realized that it was up to him to guide the journey. In *Walt Disney: His Life in Pictures*, Diane Disney Miller writes:

Dad was not really a celebrity until his entry into television, when he became the host of his own show on ABC. He took his lead-ins very seriously, but he also had great fun with them. Once more he was, in a sense, standing in front of the class, offering entertainment.[22]

To the public, Walt has the ability to call up magic at his command: he snaps his fingers and Tinkerbell appears. As he conjures up the illusions he imagines, he returns to his youthful days of acting out storyboards for his animators, only this time, what he did then in private for his artists, is shared with the entire television community.

The Animalistic Shape Shifter

Hollywood is often referred to as a *dream factory*, and films are often referred to as *movie magic*. It makes sense, therefore, that filmmakers embody the archetypal energy of the trickster. Walt Disney, however, is an exceptional example of this. As a human being, he was incredibly mercurial. Biographer Bob Thomas said of him, "Walt had many faces, and the face his showed his family was quite different from the face he showed his animators and his artists. There he was a taskmaster, and a very stern one. He could be very tough, and he would never praise."[23] While visiting within the realm of Disney's stories, the audience never quite knows what kind of character will arrive. When a queen becomes an elderly peddler, or an enchantress morphs into a dragon, it makes sense, because we are in Walt Disney's story.

Perhaps this is true because Disney myths are often presented in the form of animation. Disney myths are sketched and painted. They can literally shape shift in front of our eyes, and the authenticity of the illusion is the hallmark of great animation. However authentic the experience of the story feels, our ability to believe it still begins with the mythic environment that is constellated by Walt Disney and his magic paintbrush. Think, for example, of Mickey Mouse in the "Sorcerer's Apprentice" segment of *Fantasia*. Through Mickey Mouse, Walt becomes the shape-shifting sorcerer *Yen-Sid* ("Disney" spelled backwards). As the character of PL Travers notes in *Saving Mr. Banks*: "Where is she when I need her? I open the door for Mary Poppins, and who should be standing there but Walt Disney". One never knows where he will be or who he will become. In that sense, living or passed on, he is always there plussing the show.[24]

The trickster is primal energy. As such, it connects to the animal kingdom – reflecting its close association with the energy of the unconscious. Walt Disney is often linked to many different animals. In fact, animal characters in Disney animation are more common than human ones, but none are as evocatively resonant of Walt's career as Mickey Mouse. The rabbit may have been first, but the mouse became psychologically indispensable to

Walt. He once noted that Mickey Mouse represented freedom and independence to him.[25] Mickey became a symbol of possibility.

Again, in *Saving Mr. Banks*, he notes that "I fought this battle years ago from the other side ... The mouse is family. It would have killed me to give him up." Though Ub Iwerks and many others refined his look ever since he first goofed his way on screen in *Steamboat Willie* and *Plane Crazy*, Mickey Mouse always has and always will be a reflection of Walt Disney. This is so true that when the time came for Mickey to speak, Walt could not settle on someone to voice him. He had to do it himself, which he did from 1929–1946. Mickey Mouse became a kind of alter ego for him. It often seems as though Mickey was a release for Walt from the pressures of the studio, and that Mickey speaks Walt's inner voice. Mickey, like the mouse in many other myths and legends, represents the power of the small, seemingly-insignificant, vulnerable, and perhaps socially unacceptable, character.

Much like Walt himself, this mouse comes from obscurity to cultivate a powerful persona. It is often easier to accept animal characters in trickster behavior than humans. In the early Mickey Mouse shorts, he is full of mischief. In that way, early Mickey safely makes the social commentary. He pokes fun at cultural icons like Clark Gable and Charles Lindbergh. He fights against the established order or drops a piano on it, so to speak, and he safely takes the audience with him.

The Shadow Shaman

Because of this magical ability to cross realms, open crossroads, and shift form and gender, trickster figures are often conflated with the image of the shaman. This classification, however, misses the nuances of the archetype. As an agent of the psyche's shadow aspects, the trickster relishes the subversion of expectations. The distinction between the archetypes of the shaman and trickster can be summed up in one word: irreverence. Shamans exist to be agents of the divine for the benefit of the people to whom they belong. They embrace the structure they represent. When they travel to the gods, they are welcomed with gifts of wisdom. And they belong in each of the realms they inhabit. They are always at home.

Trickster, however, participates in the same structure, but from an opposite attitude. These figures are never at home. When they travel to the realm of the gods, they are not given gifts; they have to steal them. They exist outside of the structure, and they cling to, rather than transcend, the trappings of human life. As William Doty notes, "Trickster is a humanist ... they don't need or want the structure a shaman works through. Trickster, like a human being, is an earth-bound creature and wishes to fly (and to escape the human condition) is shown to be a frivolous fancy."[26] They refuse to hold to traditional conventions of the gods, because if they did, they would be too bound up in the rules and to a sense of responsibility to both the divine and their community to be able to bring forth the energy of subversion necessary to heal a community.

When Dr. Facilier insists that he's "got friends on the other side", for example, he attempts to present himself as a sacred authority giving gifts that the people who visit him presumably need.[27] But when it becomes clear that those gifts are disingenuous, manipulative gifts, he reveals himself as a trickster villain. At that point, it becomes increasingly clear that those friends are not friends at all, and in fact those powers might be all too willing to consume him for his crimes.

Walt Disney embodied this dynamic between both shaman and the trickster archetypes. As a visionary storyteller, he is literally a traveler to the realm of the archetypal. The projects that come out of Disney's studios often seemed to have the touch of Dumbo's magic feather: sound cartoons, full-length animated features, a television series selling a theme park, and the theme park itself all seemed poised to fail but for one central ingredient – namely, Walt's uncanny ability to reach into the collective unconscious of America (and, in turn, much of the world) and send the message his audience most wanted to hear at the moment they most needed to hear it.[28]

Walt Disney understood American myths of nostalgia and progress better perhaps than almost anyone. As imagineer and Disney legend Marty Sklar once said of him, "This was a man who had one foot in the past ... and one foot in the future".[29] He knew exactly what his audience wanted because in his own imagination he had already seen it. That uncanny ability, coupled with his persona as the kindly Uncle Walt, created his public persona as what Jungians call a wise old man or the *Senex* archetype.[30]

It was this public persona that in the later years of Walt Disney's life provided the kind of mythic reassurance people needed in order to deal with the absurdity of daily life in the nuclear age. He presided over American television with an air of a sacred authority, and that persona was authentic. He believed in the sanctity of the American philosophies he embodied and, indeed, acted as a kind of priest, creating a container for the experience of these sacred ideologies. As an icon of the shaman, he upholds the American system, because essentially, that is what a shaman does. The Walt Disney who dedicates Disneyland with religious leaders and his good friend Ronald Reagan[31] by his side convey the message that society's conventions are what they should be. This is particularly true of the presence of and friendship with Ronald Reagan. As early as the late 1940s, Reagan was already serving as a leader in the Hollywood community. By 1947, he was the president of the Screen Actor's Guild. His presence invokes it a sense of order and the moderate conservative values that typify the mid-1950s. But Walt never quite fits into that mold. Despite his staunchly anti-communist stance and his problematic presence at the House Un-American Activities Committee proceedings,[32] Walt continues to cultivate an image that straddles the space between austerity and progressivism. He may read conservative, but he is never conventional. He consistently pushes forward; subverting himself when one considers him as a filmmaker and visionary, continually subverting Hollywood norms.

During the early years of his career, Walt Disney had no interest in upholding the conventions of the motion picture industry. On several occasions, he noted that he wanted to crack the animation industry. He consistently bucked the system and resisted what was presented to him as his career options. Though they were what might have looked like career-killing moves at the time, decisions like leaving Oswald The Lucky Rabbit to Charles Mintz, taking on the creation of a full-length animated feature, or dreaming up the concept of his own theme park, Walt was always convinced that the ideas and dreams he had for himself would work much better than whatever choices the system had laid out in front of him. In this way, he may be seen as what Hyde Lewis refers to as the trickster who breaks the world in order to fashion it in the image they want to see.[33]

Walt was never satisfied with what was; he always reached for what could be, and what could be, as a reflection of his own imagination, was always the best possible choice as far as he was concerned. This attitude obviously contributed to making him a complicated figure in the public's mind. For every person in Hollywood history that calls him a loving Uncle Walt, another may be found who would call him a black-hearted tyrant. This contradiction is yet another example of the fact that the myths about him bring forth the trickster energy of the shadow to those who encounter and engage them. As trickster shadows shaman, these images are bound to bounce back and forth between reversion and subversion.

The Delight Bringer

Walt was once quoted as saying that "Laughter is America's most important export".[34] As a vessel of irreverent energy from the shadow, the role of the trickster is to bring joy and delight through the silly and the absurd. Trickster figures make fun of the soul's shadow, presenting it through art forms that elevate what might otherwise seem corny or pedestrian. From the Greek gods Dionysus and Hermes to the Irish character of the Leprechaun, the archetypal images of the trickster are often represented as children full of mischief and laughter. Dionysus, god of wine, dismemberment, and merriment, for example, is often believed to be the child Hades and Persephone. In that sense, Dionysus is born of the vulnerability between transformation or death and an archetypal image of girlish innocence. In that sense, he represents the deep joy that comes from an authentic journey from innocence to maturity. One might compare Disneyland to Las Vegas in its Dionysian excess of joy. It may be understood as the light side of a childlike Dionysian experience, in contrast to the dark, grittiness of a night out in Las Vegas.

In his biography *Walt Disney: An American Original*, Bob Thomas addresses many examples of what in the disciplines of depth psychology and mytho-logical studies might be called *Hades consciousness* in Walt's early childhood.[35] Life was never easy for the Disney family. From an early age, Walt had to work on whatever ventures his father considered important at the time, whether it was on the farm or delivering papers in the deep snow of winter in Kansas City, Missouri. One particular interaction with Walt's father Elias seems particularly evocative in terms of understanding the development of Walt's relationship to the archetypal Dionysian child. This experience is one of many that set him toward his own psychological need to connect with archetypes of childhood. He recounts a time when Walt and Elias clashed over Elias' unreasonable expectations. When Elias ordered Walt to the basement to receive a beating, his brother Roy admonished him that at fourteen years of age, he was perfectly capable of stopping the beating before it started.

Walt fought back against his father, grabbing the hammer handle away from him as he attempted to swing it at his son. As his eyes filled with tears, which may have indicated both fear of his son and shame over what he was about to do, Elias fled from the basement. He never hit Walt again. This instance seems to be pivotal, if only for the sake of metaphor, in the context of Disney's life. By all accounts, Walt loved children. He adored his niece and relished every moment he could spend with his daughters. But his love of children and childhood also carried a mythic significance for him. As an adult, Walt cultivated a childlike consciousness. The darkness he remem-bered in his childhood and his own loss of innocence can be seen as his catalyst for embracing childlike joy as a part of his persona, as illustrated both by the Peter Pan's Flight attraction at Disneyland the *Disney After Dark* episode of the Disneyland television show.[36]

Like Dionysus, Peter Pan, and frankly so many of us, Walt Disney's journey to the joys of childhood came through the psychological pain of psycho-logical dismemberment and familial abandonment. His experience of being dragged away from his imagination in childhood to the stark, cold world of his father's making was punctuated by the subsequent joy of his continued return to the ecstasy of the art class and theater that he loved so dearly. And because he himself found it so healing, he dedicated his life to offering it to as many people as he could.

The myth of Hermes and Apollo also offers insight into Walt Disney's obsession with the childlike trickster energy. Hermes, the god of circuitous communication, is also presented as a child who is affable, cute, and filled with laughter.[37] He represents the aspect of the trickster archetype that rules the creation of entertainment, though perhaps not entertainment itself. Hermes creates the first musical instrument when, hours after his birth, he escapes from his nurse and fashions a lyre out of a tortoise shell and sheep intestines. Apollo may be the god of musicians–the one who oversees the technical, rational brilliance of a crafted piece of musical art–but the infant Hermes creates the structure for it. He does so simply because he wants the music.

In that sense, he is the catalyst for art. The same is often said about Walt Disney, particularly as regards the creation of Disneyland. He built the park, some say, because he wanted a place to play. Animator Ollie Johnston, one of what is often called Walt's Nine Old Men, noted that "He was the best story man in the studio – the best story man in Hollywood, really".[38] In the early part of his career, the Disney Brothers Studio was his playground. It was the place where Walt could attempt to fashion creations that redeemed his sense of the joys of childhood through the genre of animation.

Conclusion

It is clear that, as a mythic image, Walt Disney embodies the trickster. The next logical question one might ask is, why does that matter? Ultimately, all discussion of archetypal theory has as its aim the movement toward psychological healing. The trickster is generally presented as a villain, and in its role as a villain seems to be the anti-Disney figure. The care with which The Walt Disney Company and the Disney family craft Walt's image might suggest that, consciously, they wish to present him as a hero. Any attempt to present him otherwise always stirs up controversy. For example, when Meryl Streep was interviewed about her work with Disney and referred to Walt as an old misogynistic anti-Semite, many Disney blogs buzzed with first-hand accounts subverting that opinion.[39] Other negative depictions of Disney's problematic, cultural realties continue to circulate in contemporary popular culture from time to time. Filmmaker Spike Lee has argued that Disney's work furthers racist stereotypes.[40] His critiques of films like *Dumbo* and *Song of the South* continue to be relevant today.[41] They have merit, but when they become personal charges against Walt himself, they are challenged by the few Disney cast members and legends that remember Walt personally. Animator Floyd Norman continues to be particularly outspoken on the topic.[42] This conversation will continue, as satirists such as animated series *Family Guy*[43] also takes the occasional swipe at Disney. The prevalence and malleable nature of these images in contemporary culture reinvigorate the presence of trickster energy connected to Walt Disney.

But these historical concerns influence mythological analysis if one only understands the trickster in binary terms of good and evil. As an archetypal image of wholeness, within it lie all humanity's projections – a kind of cultural scapegoat onto which we project fear, insecurity, doubt, pain, trauma, and feelings of inadequacy. Jung quite succinctly writes that as a collective shadow figure, the trickster is a "… summation of all the interior traits of character in individuals".[44] In other words, all the archetypal energies of our psyches are in shadow until made conscious through the alchemical shenanigans of the trickster.

Walt Disney's trickster beacons those participating in his myth to heal the broken parts of their inner child and turn them into joy. His trickster advocates not that we become childish, but that we become childlike, and that we take our adult selves with us for the sake of balancing the two. In life, Walt understood this. He was sentimental, by all accounts much more so than his wife, Lilly, or any other member of his family. It is his sentimentality that breaks in to offer healing and reassurance to those who are desperately in need of it.

Archetypally, he breaks in by insisting that story has to have heart; by insisting that we stop over-analyzing life and that we focus on relationship, community, fun, and play. He breaks in by daring to suggest that it is acceptable to be corny. He also suggests that we remember the importance of overturning the system. The archetypal Walt Disney carries our projections neatly and securely. He does not mind if we see him as a simple country fellow or as a slick media mogul. As a trickster, he hopes you missed the sleight of hand he just pulled. And that young Walt – that Depression-era kid bucking the establishment – he doesn't care what anyone thinks of him. He just smiles, raises an eyebrow, flashes a grin, keeps telling his stories, opens your wallet, grabs Mickey's hand, and keeps moving forward.

Bibliography

Boer, Charles. *The Homeric Hymns*. Chicago: Swallow Press, 1970.

Disney, Walt, and Dave Smith. *The Quotable Walt Disney*. New York: Disney Editions, 2001.

Doty, William and William J. Hynes, William. Eds. *Mythical Trickster Figures Contours, Contexts, and Criticisms*. Tuscaloosa: University of Alabama Press, 1993.

Fuchs, Cynthia, Ed. *Spike Lee Interviews*. Jackson: University of Mississippi Press, 2002.

Gabler, Neal. *Walt Disney: The Triumph of the American Imagination*. New York: Knopf, 2006.

Hyde, Lewis. *Trickster Makes This World: Mischief, Myth, and Art*. New York: Farrar, Straus and Giroux, 1998.

Jung, C. G. The *Structure and Dynamics of the Psyche (1916/58) CW 8*. New York: Taylor and Francis, 1973.

Jung, C. G. *Archetypes and The Collective Unconscious CW 9*. New York: Taylor and Francis, 1973.

McNeely, Deldon Anne. *Mercury Rising: Women, Evil, and the Trickster Gods*. Woodstock, Conn.: Spring, 1996.

Pelton, Robert D. *The Trickster in West Africa: A Study of Mythic Irony and Sacred Delight*. Berkeley: University of California Press, 1980.

Schroeder, Russell K. *Walt Disney: His Life in Pictures*. New York: Disney Press, 1996.

Thomas, Bob. *Walt Disney: An American Original.* New York: Simon and Schuster, 1976.

Thomas, Frank, and Ollie Johnston. *Disney Animation: The Illusion of Life.* New York: Abbeville Press, 1981.

Turner, Victor W. *The Ritual Process: Structure and Anti-structure.* Chicago: Aldine Pub., 1969.

Von Franz, Marie Louise. *Shadow and Evil in Fairy Tales.* Rev. ed. Boston: Shambhala, 1995.

Waddell, Terrie. *Mis/takes: Archetype, Myth and Identity in Screen Fiction.* London: Routledge, 2006.

Endnotes

1. Neal Gabler, *Walt Disney: The Triumph of the American Imagination*: (New York: Knopf, 2006), xvi.

2. Diane Disney once said that she often worried that her father had become a cultural icon like Ronald McDonald. She worried that the historical man behind the company was becoming lost to the mythic image of him. She feared that if this happened, the physical man that was her father would be lost to the ages. This concern was the impetus behind the creation of The Walt Disney Family Museum.

3. This should be no surprise, as we have certainly seen our share of apocalypse stories in the last decade, and the often forgotten twin of apocalypse is revelation/genesis.

4. In 2008, the name of Disney-MGM Studios was changed to Disney's Hollywood Studios.

5. D23 stands for Disney 1923. It refers to the year Walt came to California.

6. The original website was launched in September of 1999. The museum's physical space is located in the Presidio of San Francisco. It may seem like a strange place to have a museum dedicated to a Hollywood man, but the Disney family moved up to the San Francisco Bay area after Walt's death. This beautiful museum houses interactive exhibits, film screenings, classes on Disney history and animation, and rotating special exhibitions, such as one about to open that will explore Disney's relationship with Salvador Dali. Visit their website at http://www.waltdisney.org

7. In December of 2013, I attended an event at the Walt Disney Studios. At that event, I was given a screening of the film. Part of that event was a tour of the historic animation building. While inside we went into Walt Disney's original office, which was filled with pictures meant to evoke the 1960s. One picture stood out. It was a picture of the original Mickey Mouse Club with Tom Hanks photo shopped in as Walt. So complete was the illusion that precious few of the people filing through to partake the experience even noticed the change.

8. http://www.lastgenpodcast.com/disney-magic-hour/2015/6/4/walt-disney-pbs-trailer-looks-incredible

9. C. G. Jung, *C.W. Structure and Dynamics of the Psyche Volume 8*: (*CW 8*. New York: Taylor and Francis, 1973), 152.

10. Marie Louise von Franz. *Shadow and Evil in Fairy Tales*: (Boston: Shambhala, 1995).

11. Deldon Anne McNeely's book, *Mercury Rising: Women, Evil, and the Trickster Gods* subvert the idea that all tricksters must be male. She suggests that simply by virtue of its nature as a shape-shifter, the trickster must be in some senses androgynous. Disney's characters seem to support this idea. All manner of female characters pour out of the magical imagination of Walt Disney as they appear before the eyes of the patron.

12. Frank Thomas and Ollie Johnston, *Disney Animation: The Illusion of Life*: (New York: Abbeville Press, 1981).

13. "Tricksters seem to find exits where there are no exits". William Doty, *Mirrors of the Self: Archetype Images that Shape Your Life*:(Tuscaloosa: University of Alabama Press, 1993), 237.

14. Walt Disney and Dave Smith, *The Quotable Walt Disney*: (New York: Disney Editions, 2001), 85.

15. According to Haitian tradition, Papa Ghede is the corpse of the first man to have died. He is a short dark male figure who likes to smoke cheap cigars and eat apples. He is full of laughter

and irreverence. He stands at the crossroad between life and death, and much like Charon in Greek mythology, bears the responsibility to facilitate the crossing over of souls after death.

16. In contrast to Papa Ghede, Brave Ghede is taller, leaner, and more frightening. He stands at the crossroads of the graveyard and holds the keys to the magical powers of Voudou practice.

17. Some might suggest that Dr. Facilier's character represents a negative portrayal of Voudou in the estimation of Disney animation, but this character as a villain might also be interpreted as one that evokes the dark side of this archetype if left in shadow. The darkness inherent in this archetype carries with it the potential for the kind of cruel self-interest present in Dr. Facilier's character, which is clearly tempered by Mama Odie in the film.

18. Liminality refers to the aspect of the ritual process when the process has begun, but not completed. The liminal occupies the space between worlds, when something is said to be neither one thing, nor the other. Ritual theorist Victor Turner writes extensively about this in his book, *The Ritual Process: Structure and Anti-Structure.*

19. Walt Disney and Dave Smith, *The Quotable Walt Disney*: (New York: Disney Editions, 2001), 46.

20. Imagineer is a term coined by Disney. It is a combination of the terms imagination and engineer.

21. "Film and television seduce us into a world of illusion, excess and permeable boundaries, where we as interactive spectators, are invited to juggle mixed ethical, moral, philosophical and political messages. Keeping all these balls in the air, while being pleasured allows us to come to our own conclusions about the viability of the positions we are watching and how they might apply to our lives beyond the screen thinking through the fragment of analytical psychology, its possible to argue that this intricate activity is presided over by the energy of *trickster*. The archetype can be read as governing the form and function of cinema and television …" Terre Weddell *Mis/Takes: Archetype, Myth and Identity in Screen* Fiction: (London: Routledge, 2006), 27–28.

22. Schroeder, Russell K. *Walt Disney: His Life in Pictures.* (New York: Disney Press), 7.

23. *Walt Disney: The Man Behind the Myth*, Documentary.

24. What Walt called plussing is the continued process of making transforming the parks into something new and more exciting. http://www.waltdisney.org/blog/walts-own-words-plussing-disneyland

25. Walt called Mickey Mouse "a symbol of independence. He was a means to an end. He popped out of my mind onto a drawing pad twenty years ago on a train ride from Manhattan to Hollywood at a time when the business fortunes of my brother Roy and myself were at lowest ebb and disaster seemed right around the corner. Born of necessity, the little fellow literally freed us of immediate worry. He provided the means for expanding our organization to its present dimensions and for extending the medium of cartoon animation toward new entertainment levels. He spelled production liberation for us." Walt Disney and Dave Smith, *The Quotable Walt Disney*: (New York: Disney Editions, 2001), 37.

26. William J. Hynes and William G. Doty, *Mythical Trickster Figures: Contours, Contexts, and Criticisms*: (New York: Farrar, Straus and Giroux, 1998), 95.

27. "… the trickster embodies this (human) striving, opposes the gods and mocks the shamans. In seeking this mastery of the world and the creation of a secular sacredness, the Trickster often fails. In his failures, he becomes a joke, yet laughing at him men are set free" Robert Pelton. *The Trickster in West Africa: A Study of Mythic Irony and Sacred Delight*: (Berkeley: University of California Press, 1980), 10.

28. Dumbo believed that his feather was magic and allowed him to fly, but the reality was that it was the power of his imagination itself that provided him with what he needed to be able to fly.

29. *Walt Disney: The Man Behind the Myth*, Documentary.

30. The word *Senex* derives from the Latin for wise old man. In Jungian psychology, it refers to the image of a wizard or magician. Jungians often interpret the *Senex* as an image of the wholeness of the psyche. He represents the return to wisdom that comes with age.

31. https://www.sagaftra.org/ronald-reagan

32. http://historymatters.gmu.edu/d/6458/

33. Hyde Lewis. *Trickster Makes This World: Mischief, Myth, and Art* (New York: Farrar, Straus and Giroux, 1998), 7.

34. Walt Disney and Dave Smith, *The Quotable Walt Disney*: (New York: Disney Editions, 2001), 175.

35. Depth Psychology and Mythological Studies often use poetic terms to refer to psychological states. The phrase "Hades Consciousness" refers to a conscious focus on deep self-reflection on the darkest aspects of who we are psychologically. This mode of consciousness can be painful, as it uncovers the most unpleasant parts of shadow, but as with all encounters with death, it offers great possibility for healing.

36. https://www.youtube.com/watch?v=X83vEQmo3YE

37. Boer, Charles. *The Homeric Hymns.* (Chicago: Swallow Press), 1970. 33–68.

38. *Walt Disney: The Man Behind the Myth*, Documentary.

39. http://variety.com/2014/biz/awards/meryl-streep-blasts-walt-disney-at-national-board-of-review-dinner-1201035989/

40. Fuchs, Cynthia, Ed. *Spike Lee Interviews.* (University of Mississippi Press), 2002, 203.

41. http://www.nytimes.com/1990/09/05/opinion/l-spike-lee-misreads-the-history-of-film-769890.html

42. https://www.youtube.com/watch?v=sDWYZcHSbCU

43. https://www.youtube.com/watch?v=1EFA5p4WwXQ

44. C.G. Jung, *Archetypes and The Collective Unconscious CW 9*: (New York: Taylor and Francis, 1973), 270.

Chapter 2

Animating America's Anticommunism: *Alice's Egg Plant* (1925) and Disney's First Red Scare

Joshua M. Hollands

Historians who have analyzed Walt Disney's political and social interventions have seldom looked beyond his October 24, 1947 testimony to the House Committee on Un-American Activities (HUAC) or the 1941 animator's strike at the Disney Studio which preceded it.[1] To contemplate Walt Disney's political reputation without considering his earlier work, especially the silent era's *Alice Comedies*, would be a disservice to the historiography of the studio. This chapter analyses one such short, *Alice's Egg Plant* (1925), as a means to understanding more about Disney's political positions and the way in which both Walt Disney himself, as well as the Disney Studio, related to contemporary political events and current affairs.[2] To achieve this aim, this chapter seeks to place *Alice's Egg Plant* within the broad context of post-World War One radicalism and workplace organization. It will question the extent to which it contributed to the "red scare" of the period, and thus assess the extent to which Disney's political and social interventions began earlier than has been previously suggested. In addition, it is necessary to trace the influence of socialism in the Midwest in this period to better understand Disney's early political experiences.

Following the First World War, the United States saw great turmoil in labor relations as communist and anarchist organizations sought to build upon growing antiwar sentiment throughout the country. The Bolshevik Revolution of 1917 in Russia shook the US government and caused fear within the upper classes. Police strikes took place in Boston, a general strike shut down Seattle, and more than half a million steel workers struck in 1919. Added to this was a bombing campaign which targeted key members of President Woodrow Wilson's government and big-business leaders such as J.P. Morgan.[3] To counter these attacks and the fear that communist support was increasing throughout the United States, the government used legislation to outlaw many of the groups. These laws included the "Espionage Act of June 1917, the Trading with the Enemy Act of October 1917, and the Sedition Act of May 1918 [which] all targeted radicals through restrictions on speech and expression".[4] Jeffrey Johnson notes that, "America's socialists immediately felt the sting of these events".[5] Media campaigns saw radical groups like the Industrial Workers of the World (the IWW, aka the "Wobblies") vilified for holding unpatriotic positions. John Haynes notes that the fear of communism often led to miscarriages of justice: "The heated atmosphere of the 'Red Scare', as it was later called, provoked both federal and local agencies to disregard normal legal restraints on official power ... those arrested were in many cases abused and held incommunicado".[6]

Concurrent to the broader context of the Red Scare was the growing success of the Disney Brothers Studio. The *Alice* series of short films helped to create the studio in the early 1920s and gave Disney his first big break into Hollywood. As historian Amy Davis notes, "by and large, the *Alice Comedies* ... were very popular with both the critics and the public".[7] *Alice's Egg Plant* was released half-way through the overall production of the *Alice Comedies* (1923–1927). In some ways, the short can be considered a landmark for the series. It was the first time that the animated cat, Julius, is named on screen.[8] The episode, which features (as is the case for the whole of the series) a live-action girl in a cartoon world, also marks the first *Alice* short not to include Virginia Davis as the title character. Davis' mother refused to take a pay-cut shortly before the second series began filming, and so she was replaced for this episode by Dawn O'Day (the stage name in this period for actress Anne Shirley).[9]

Alice's Egg Plant remains an intriguing yet under-studied short. It sees Alice and Julius managing an egg farm that receives an order for five thousand eggs. However, to fulfill their commitment, they must break a strike that has been instigated by a Bolshevik rooster, Little Red Henski. To do this, Alice and Julius organize a boxing match, charging one egg per entry; by doing so, they manage to trick the hens into breaking their own strike. Merritt and Kaufman argue that this setting is typical for a Disney silent short: "as appealing as the orderly homespun kingdom was to Disney, even more congenial was the notion of a small business of some sort set on a farm or in a village".[10] This short bucks the trend, however, as being one of only a handful of Disney shorts from this era which develops a full narrative arc, as opposed to depending upon a series of comedic gags.[11]

Merritt and Kaufman also suggest that the "idea of social liberation" is present in many of these shorts. They argue, "although there are plenty of Alices and Oswalds in which the hero rescues a damsel in distress, far more characteristic are the silent Disneys where heroes liberate captive hoards of the jailed or simply cooped-up".[12] This short appears, therefore, to be a deviation from this rule, as Alice and Julius, acting as business owners, actually work to keep the hens literally "cooped-up". It is, therefore, of particular interest within the context of the preceding "Red Scare", and as a fictional pre-curser to the later disputes at the Disney Studio.

Some historians argue that the short also signified the beginning of a deteriorating quality of the series. For instance, Merritt and Kaufman note, "the promising and frequently charming interactions between Alice and Julius soon deteriorate into Alice's pro-forma live-action appearances with Alice doing little more than flapping her arms".[13] They go on to suggest that, "for about a year Disney developed the rich possibilities of a comic partnership between a little girl and an animated playmate, but he then appears to have lost interest, turning Julius into a Felix copycat and Alice into a passive observer".[15] Indeed, Michael Barrier notes that, "As the series advanced Alice ... became more and more superfluous, her scenes fewer and fewer, and her filmed actions more and more generic, so that the live action could be combined with animation of almost any kind".[15] While it is possible that Disney wanted to focus on developing an improved quality of animation at the expense of incorporating live action, it is also true to say that the series struggled to match the quality and imagination of its competitors. Barrier goes on to argue that "the *Alice Comedies* offered few witty transmutations like those in the *Felix* and *Inkwell* cartoons. What happened much more often was that a body came apart and reassembled itself with remarkable ease."[16] This is the case with Julius in *Alice's Egg Plant*, as he uses his tail as a whip to intimidate the hens.

The *Alice Comedies* as a series came about during a period of crisis for Walt Disney. It was during production of the first episode/pilot, *Alice's Wonderland* (1923), that Disney's struggling Laugh-o-Grams Studio, which was based in Kansas City, Missouri, finally went bankrupt. The Disney Brothers Studio was quickly created shortly after Walt Disney received a contract from New York-based distributor Margaret J. Winkler, founder of Winkler Productions, who had made Disney an offer to distribute the *Alice Comedies*; production on the series began with a skeleton staff in October 1923.[17] Michael Barrier notes that Walt, "Roy and Kathleen Dollard, whom they hired to ink and paint the animation cels, made up the entire staff".[18] This was alongside Virginia Davis, whom Disney encouraged to move out to Hollywood to continue her acting career. However, "Disney slowly expanded his staff as the *Alice Comedies* established themselves. In February 1924, he hired Rollin Hamilton as the first cartoonist on his California staff; and in July, he lured west Ubbe Iwwerks (or, more frequently, Ub Iwerks)".[19] Iwerks would contribute most of the animation for the rest of the series, including *Alice's Egg Plant*. Bob Thomas, who wrote one of the earliest biographies of Walt Disney (with the family's blessing), notes that Iwerks brought skills that were much needed: "The addition of Ub Iwerks as animator gave the Alice Comedy series an added boost, both in the quality of drawing and the speed with which they were produced".[20] Indeed, Barrier concurs that many of the early shorts were technically lacking and relied heavily on what had gone before. "The animation in the earliest Alice Comedies, by Disney himself, was ... derivative: it recalled the Fables, only it was even more oppressively loaded with shortcuts (so that, for example, a character's body is noticeably rigid while its head or perhaps its eyes move)".[21]

Both through choice and necessity, Walt Disney took on more of a backseat role in the production of the majority of the shorts that would bear his name, as additional staff joined the studio: choice, as he now hired staff who could continue the work, and necessity, as he faced continuing financial difficulties which frequently took his attention away from art. The Disney brothers were financially dependent upon friends and relatives throughout the early days of the studio, requiring loans, such as that from Roy's future wife, Edna, and $200 from an organist at the Isis Theater in Kansas City, whom Walt had worked with previously.[22] The studio was therefore in a constant state of financial distress during its early days. As Thomas notes, "the money flow did not improve, and a note of desperation entered Walt's letters to the distributor".[23] At the end of the first series, in December 1924, however, Disney was able to agree a deal with Charles Mintz (who, by this stage, as Margaret Winkler's husband, was by and large running Winkler Productions) which contracted eighteen more *Alice Comedies* "at $1,800 per picture, plus a share of the profits from rentals to theaters".[24] Thomas notes, "at last the Disney Brothers Studio was on steady footing".[25] Around the time that Disney was producing *Alice's Egg Plant*, he was more financially secure, as Barrier notes, not only did he marry Lillian Bounds in that year and hire new animators, but also, on July 6, 1925, "he and Roy deposited four hundred dollars toward the purchase of a vacant lot on Hyperion Avenue in the Los Feliz district east of Hollywood".[26] It was here that he would create his first purpose-built studio.

A key issue when assessing any of Disney's output is the extent to which Walt Disney himself is responsible for its creation and production. If we are to consider the extent to which *Alice's Egg Plant* is representative of Walt Disney's views or was a political intervention on the part of Disney, it is also necessary to consider Walt Disney's role as its author. This is problematic however, as Disney, by the time of *Alice's Egg Plant*, was already scaling back the extent to which he was involved in the production. Chris

Pallant notes that "Disney constitutes a rather unconventional authorial figure".[27] Disney would later present himself as a "bee", influencing all around him. "I think of myself as a little bee. I go from one area of the Studio to another, and gather pollen and sort of stimulate everybody ... that's the job I do."[28] As such, and as Pallant argues, Disney somewhat reconciles the issue of authorship himself. If, therefore, Disney was happy to accept responsibility for the overall output of the studio and saw himself as influencing every facet, then scholars can accept that he can be held somewhat accountable for the representations in the *Alice Comedies*, even while he was animating less himself. Although he now took a backseat role in the animation, "Disney assumed more control over the animation done by others".[29] Disney focused most of his attention on developing stories; as animator Rudy Ising noted, "he was the one who really sort of put the story together".[30] According to Barrier, this also provided Disney with the time and ability to begin making technological innovations, but still with an eye upon controlling his animators' output. One such example is that of exposure sheets: "In Kansas City, the animators had written on the bottom of their drawings what the cameraman should do ... In Hollywood, Disney began making what came to be called exposure sheets, which amounted to more formal instructions to the camera operator."[31]

The early days of the studio appear to have been marked by a general feeling of harmony amongst the small staff. According to Barrier, "In 1925, there was still a chummy atmosphere very much reminiscent of the Kansas City days. So small was the staff, and so undifferentiated their duties, that Roy Disney washed cels for reuse until a janitor was hired in November 1925."[32] However, this was also a time when Walt Disney was solidifying his position as both producer and employer. The treatment of Virginia Davis, for example, points to Disney settling into an employer's mentality at this early stage of his career. Disney, in his correspondence, had promised Davis' parents that she would receive a monthly salary of $250 per second series episode. Previously, she had received a sliding scale fee of between $100 and $200 for her first series shorts. Now, however, with pressure from Winkler Productions to keep costs down, the Disney brothers effectively tore up Davis' contract.[33] The *Alices*, therefore, can be seen as serving as a bridge between Walt Disney as artist and Walt Disney as employer/entrepreneur, forced to make decisions that directly impacted the creative process based on financial necessity as much as (if not more than) artistic ambitions. For Walt Disney, this was when he began to move away from the role of worker and into the role of manager.

Hens and Wobblies

There are several aspects to *Alice's Egg Plant* which suggest it is simply reiterating reactionary ideas regarding organized labor. First, in using the specific name and initials of the Industrial Workers of the World (IWW), Disney relied upon the audience's own preconceptions of the organization as a dangerous "anti-American" group. In his history of strikes in the United States, Jeremy Brecher summarizes the role of IWW in the following way:

> The "Wobblies" advocated "industrial unionism"–organizing all workers in an industry into one union–in contrast to the "craft unionism" of the AFL. The IWW organized the most depressed and unskilled, such as migrant laborers of the West and the textile mill workers of the East. It proclaimed workers' ownership of industry its objective and saw every strike as a preparation for revolution. It was in many ways more of a social movement than a conventional union; though it was involved in many dramatic strikes, it generally scorned negotiating a continuing relationship with the employers. The Wobblies were brutally repressed by legal and illegal means during World War I; by 1919 they were rarely a significant force.[34]

The IWW were especially strong in the Midwest areas where Disney grew up. While Walt Disney seems never to have spoken of the radicalism that took place around him in Kansas City following the war and during the early 1920s, it would have been hard to miss. Kansas City was a hub of radicalism between 1919 and 1920 as disputes erupted following the end of the First World War, during which inflation raged and employers sought to consolidate their positions.[35] According to Brecher, "Four general strikes developed in different regions of the country ... In Kansas City, Missouri, when laundry workers and drivers struck, a general strike developed in sympathy and lasted a week until the National Guard was called up to break it."[36] Given the fact that Disney and his colleagues were surrounded by class struggle in their formative years in the Midwest, it is of little surprise that they would produce work that incorporates many of the themes of workplace organization and solidarity, regardless of which side (if any) they were on.

One expression of Disney's awareness of this first "Red Scare" is that of linking the IWW with the Bolshevik Revolution in *Alice's Egg Plant*. Brecher recalls, "In the background of everyone's mind was the Russian Revolution and the wave of revolt sweeping the whole world in the wake of the incredible suffering, destruction, and disorganization resulting from the war".[37] Certainly this seems to have entered into consciousness at the Disney Studio. Including a number of markers of "Russian Revolutionary-ness" in Little Red Henski's character design (his beard, his cap, and his satchel, which states his Slavic-style name and its characteristic/stereotypical –ski suffix and which also notes that he comes from "Moscow, Russia"), the character points directly to a postwar fear of the Bolshevik Revolution, and recycled notions that outside agitators were seeking to destroy the United States. That there was an underlying deceptive aspect to his agitation is demonstrated when Little Red Henski removes his beard and hides it, along with his satchel, under the railroad tracks outside the egg plant. Below "Moscow, Russia", the satchel also notes Little Red Henski's affiliation to the IWW, further emphasizing this ideological linkage in popular perceptions of the Wobblies.

In reality, however, the IWW was in fact split in its support for the Russian Revolution, as noted labor historian, Philip Foner remarks: "The IWW saw in the victory of the Bolsheviks the triumph of the very class and principles for which the Wobblies were working".[38] However, the organization became split over the extent to which the new socialist state agreed in their industrial aims. "The Soviet Union did not proceed to base the first Socialist state solely 'on the industrial unionism of the IWW.' As a result, a strong anti-Soviet faction that dominated the IWW General Executive Board was no longer willing to accept 'the state character of the Soviets'."[39] Nevertheless, Foner notes that support in the United States for the revolution was palpable:

> Despite the positions of the leaders of the AFL and IWW, the mass of the membership of both organizations had a single stand: support of the Bolshevik Revolution. Moreover, a strong feeling permeated these two groups of American workers – that it was not enough to extol the Russian revolution – it was also necessary to protect it.[40]

Portrayal of Workers and Activists

William Puette writes of the Little Red Henski character that in "perfecting the stereotype of the foreign communist agitator, Disney loaded this caricature with the sinister images that had emerged since the films of the open-shop drive that had begun twenty years earlier".[41] The "Red Scare" did not target only communist groups; however, *Alice's Egg Plant* should be seen as contributing to a culture which mocked and derided unions and workplace organization. The short was released during the 1920s, one decade before any protections were put in place for workers in private industries, many of whom faced the threat of violence when they attempted union recognition. It is possible to argue that underscoring *Alice's Egg Plant* is a disdain for working-class people. The representation of the hens, who stand in for workers in *Alice's Egg Plant*, are portrayed as blindly following anyone who puts forward an idea. This is evident in their revolt against Alice and Julius at the behest of the Little Red Henski, as well as through their manipulation by their bosses at the boxing match organized by Alice herself.

The comedy value in portraying striking workers as hens and chickens, ready to follow any leadership, was clearly aimed at belittling the IWW and other organized socialists. While the Disney Brothers were able to poke a little fun at the IWW and the notion of strike action, the reality of labor disputes in this era was bloody. For instance, in 1922, strikes in the mining industry saw violence erupt on picket lines. Brecher recalls one particularly bloody episode in the Midwest: "After eight weeks of the strike, the Southern Illinois Coal Company began to reopen its mines in Williamson County with imported strikebreakers under heavily armed guards. When a group of miners tried to talk with the strikebreakers, they were fired on by machine guns and two of them killed."[42] Violence spread throughout the region, and "men began pouring into Williamson from as far as Kansas, Indiana, and Ohio" following the death of another miner.[43] The episode is filled with the violence the wealthy were particularly fearful of, a standoff between armed workers and strikebreakers:

> The protesters were armed with weapons they had seized from hardware stores and American Legion halls. By dusk, 1,000 armed men advanced on the mine in skirmish waves directed by war veterans wearing trench helmets. An airplane, rented at a nearby field, flew overhead dropping dynamite bombs on the strongholds of the strikebreakers. According to a National Guard colonel, "It was a seemingly well-organized, remarkably sober, determined, resolute aggregation of men and boys".[44]

The stand-off ended with the surrender of the mine guards who had become besieged in their own mine. Brecher concludes, "armed miners marched them away, executing the mine superintendent along the way".[45] While this episode is an extraordinary example, it is nonetheless illustrative of class tensions and violence that characterized the period. Notions of class violence are evident in the comedy of *Alice's Egg Plant*. First, the striking hens (workers) lay and throw eggs at Alice and Julius (bosses), thus illustrating how disputes turned violent rapidly at this time. Secondly, later in the boxing match, the bosses capitalize upon a fight between two workers to organize a boxing match. The inference being that while the workers could threaten and enact violence, they were also easy to pit against each other, and their internal disputes used to defeat them. Disney therefore makes clear the class relations at the heart of disputes over industry and production.

The Appeal to Reason – Disney's Socialist Influences

It appears that Disney was joining the chorus of mainstream cultural commentators who attacked Bolshevik, "outside agitators" in the post-WWI period, poking fun at the Little Red Henski, and establishing the audience's alignment with the protagonists, Alice and Julius. To understand why this argument is superficial, one must trace Walt Disney's personal history back to his childhood. Disney grew up in the Midwest and first learnt to draw by copying the cartoons in his father's socialist newspaper. Michael Barrier notes that, "Elias [Disney] was ... a follower of Eugene V. Debs".[46] Debs had been incarcerated in 1894 for leading an infamously bloody strike by workers at the Pullman railroad company. He later went on to become a founding member of the IWW, and faced more jail time for agitating against US involvement in the First World War. Barrier argues, "Elias Disney's socialist beliefs undoubtedly owed something to what he saw of the Pullman strike and its outcome".[47]

Elias Disney, Walt Disney's father, could be described as a serial entrepreneur. Early in life, Elias moved to Florida, where he had ambitions as a citrus grower, planting orange groves with the financial help of his wife's family. Unfortunately, the fruits were devastated by an unseasonal freeze.[48] Later, Elias was working as a carpenter in Chicago when Walt was born in December 1901.[49] When the Disneys moved to Marceline, Missouri, in 1906, Elias continued his attempts at running his own business, buying a farm.[50] "Elias Disney was a highly religious man", notes Michael Barrier, "'a strict, hard guy with a great sense of honesty and decency', in Roy Disney's words. 'He never drank. I rarely ever saw him smoke.'"[51] Elias's mixture of entrepreneurship and socialism led him to attempt to form a union for farmers, the American Society of Equity, "to consolidate farmers' buying power".[52] This contradiction is explored in the Walt Disney biography "written" by his daughter, Diane (ghost written by Pete Martin), in the 1950s: "Politically and economically Grandfather was a mixture. Economically he had been a contractor who built houses and sold them and who had employed workmen. As such he was a capitalist. Yet politically he was an ardent socialist who voted for Eugene Debs every time Debs ran for President."[53] Barrier notes Elias would later mortgage his house to help fund his sons' attempts at building the studio; "apparently, Elias's grudging way with a dollar no longer ruled when his sons were pursuing an entrepreneurial path of the sort he had taken so often himself".[54]

Elias Disney, therefore, was a man full of contradiction – a serial entrepreneur, as well as a committed follower of both Socialism and Christianity, he was nonetheless entirely the type of man who was the *Appeal to Reason*'s constituency. Paul Buhle in his history of *Marxism in the United States* notes the impact of the political movement at the time in which Elias was first seeking out radical ideas. "Amid even the most idealist, indigenous non-class-orientated radicals, Marxist ideas spread widely to and through those who found them useful."[55] One of those for whom this was particularly true was the socialist editor of the *Appeal to Reason*, J.A. Wayland: "for him [Wayland], as for many others, Marxist ideas removed the scales from the eyes, supplied the why and how for the disestablishment of the wicked".[56] Buhle describes this as a specifically American form of socialism: "In the West, among Debs' rural and small town natural constituency, the grass-roots Socialist press forged a mature propaganda apparatus. *The Coming Nation*, later *The Appeal to Reason*, for nearly twenty years one of America's best-selling political weeklies, epitomized the mixture of enraged individualism and idealism in the air."[57] As Buhle makes clear, the type of person who was interested in, and were targeted for, these ideas, were people like the Disneys: "The *Appeal to Reason* readers, as best as one can determine, were predominantly middle-aged Americans from the heartlands: craft workers, farmers and small business-men who would be swiftly marginalized in coming decades of the twentieth century".[58] Steven Watts also notes that Elias' politics had a significant affect upon his son's future career:

> Walt remembered socialism as one of the earliest inspirations for his drawing. As he noted many years later ... "I got so I could draw capital and labor pretty good – the big, fat capitalist with the money, maybe with his foot on the neck of the laboring man with the little cap on his head".[59]

One of those whose drawings young Walt Disney copied was Ryan Walker in the *Appeal to Reason*, "which came to the Disney household every week".[60] Jeffrey Johnson notes the importance of cartoonists like Walker to the cause they advocated: "socialist cartoonists ... used their work with great effectiveness to both enhance and legitimize the socialist message. They mocked financiers and capitalists, celebrated candidates and electoral successes, and chided ignorant and uninformed laborers."[61] Disney would later somewhat deride the work of Walker and others, comparing his versions of their cartoons. "They weren't bad ... I mean they weren't too below the cartoons in *The Appeal to Reason* in quality; but after all, the cartoonist for that paper was no world-beater."[62] Arguably, Disney drew from these formative experiences to produce *Alice's Egg Plant*; it can be argued that, in this instance at least, Disney stood somewhat within the tradition of socialist cartoonists who "mocked capitalists" and "chided ignorant and uninformed laborers" in highlighting how they were manipulated by both the entrepreneurial Alice and the Red Henski. Yet the short goes beyond this, mocking – and ultimately subverting – the efforts of the bosses who attempt such manipulations, showing that they, too, lose out in pitting themselves against their employees. This, it can be argued, is supported by the final gag in *Alice's Egg Plant*: having tricked their workers (the hens) out of the 5,000 eggs that are needed to fulfil an order, Alice and Julius drive off triumphantly, only for the load of eggs they are hauling to fall off the back of the truck and be destroyed. The hens get to enjoy the boxing match, but Alice and Julius remain unable to supply the 5,000 eggs that had been ordered from them. Furthermore, there is no indication that relations with their workers have improved, nor is there any sign that they will be able to find a further 5,000 eggs in time.

In other words, both sides of the labor dispute are mocked in *Alice's Egg Plant*, and any narrative indication that we should favor one side over the other is ultimately made tenuous. Whilst one may assume that the audience's affiliation would remain with the title character of *Alice's Egg Plant*, it was not necessarily the case. This was the first Alice comedy not to feature Virginia Davis, and the actress playing her, Dawn O'Day, has no particular resemblance to Davis, thereby rendering the Alice in *Alice's Egg Plant* something of a stranger to audiences.[63] As such, the loyalty of the audience may have been split between Alice, Julius, and the hens they were exploiting. The last laugh also belongs to the exploited hens as the eggs Alice and Julius tricked from them smash to the ground in the final shot of the short. Thus it is not necessarily fair to suggest that this short is solely anticommunist or anti-working class. Instead, it is a complex narrative of both exploitation and anticommunist imagery used for comedic purposes. The cheeky ending, in which the bosses get their comeuppance, adds further complexity to this assessment, and may even suggest that the short should be viewed as being on the side of the workers after all.

Alice's Egg Plant was released a few years following the height of the Red Scare. As John Haynes notes, "By 1921 the red scare was over. Fears of world revolution faded".[64] Thus any anticommunist sentiment in the short would not have had the same impact as it would have had a few years before. Socialist organizations and their publications had been significantly weakened; Paul Buhle notes the immediate impact of the Red Scare:

> In the "normalcy" of the Harding administration, it would seem difficult to believe that in 1918, Socialism had commanded the attention of so many ordinary Americans. "Not so many years ago", the *Appeal to Reason* mourned in 1921, "hardly a week passed in any community without some Socialist speaker bringing to it the Socialist gospel. Whether it was on a soapbox or whether it was in a public hall, the principles Socialism and our interpretation of current events were delivered amid great enthusiasm ... The number of speakers now on the road you could count with the fingers of one hand. Soapboxers are practically extinct."[65]

John Haynes has written that, "although there remained a broad and deep public dislike of communism, it could be aroused only when events suggested that communism was a real threat".[66] The movement seems to have provided a simple narrative which could be tweaked for comedic value, as *Alice's Egg Plant* effectively demonstrates. William Puette argues that demeaning portrayals of organized labor predated the Red Scare; he notes that some "early silent films were blatant antiunion propaganda. They made heroes out of scabs and depicted union leaders as self-serving, foreign agitators who deserted the workers after a strike and cared nothing for the havoc they caused in the lives of the native populace."[67] While it did contribute and draw upon negative imagery of "foreign agitators", *Alice's Egg Plant* was certainly not the only silent film to do so. Indeed, it must be viewed as part of a wider cannon of anticommunist films that reflect upon the turmoil of the Red Scare during the preceding decade. Puette notes that the image of labor organizers would not change until ten years later, during the Great Depression. "Only after decades of labor strife did the U.S. Congress in 1935 pass the Wagner Act, which finally required private sector employers to recognize and bargain with their workers."[68] Interestingly, it was under these conditions that Disney would later find himself in hot water, with warring workers and the need for the federal government to resolve the labor dispute at his studio.[69]

1941 – Chickens Coming Home to Roost?

To understand the full significance of this short, one must place it within the Studio's later history. About a year after making *Alice's Egg Plant*, the studio was awarded a distribution deal that included its newest character, Oswald the Lucky Rabbit. However, with the increasing workload, tensions began to be felt within the studio. Michael Barrier notes, "The Disney studio in the late twenties was from all appearances not a pleasant place to work. [Hugh] Harman spoke in 1973 of pressure to turn out animation [which was coming from the distributor] and concomitant pressure from Walt Disney to simplify the drawings".[70] A decade and a half of success later, Disney would refuse to negotiate with strikers at his own company, citing outside communist agitators as the cause of the dispute. A full page advertisement in the *Hollywood Reporter* and *Variety* on 2 July 1941 read: "I am positively convinced that Communistic agitation, leadership and activities have brought about this strike, and have persuaded you to reject this fair and equitable settlement".[71] A little over six years later, on 24 October 1947, Disney testified to the infamous House Committee on Un-American Activities (HUAC), citing this strike and pointing out individuals such as union leader Herbert Sorrell as communists.[72] Reading his testimony to HUAC makes clear that, all those eventful years later, the strike still rankled.

Tom Sito has called the 1941 strike, "the civil war of animation".[73] While it was obviously impossible for Disney to foresee the future – and while it is important to remember that the Disney strike was part of a much larger trend toward unionization within the Hollywood Animation industry (nor does it seem to have been the most acrimonious of the Animator strikes; certainly the Fleischer studio strike stands out as one of the more bitter strikes to hit the US animation industry at this time) – it is possible to argue that the conditions that led to the strike were beginning to be put in place at the start of the Disney Brothers Studio. At the time of *Alice's Egg Plant*, Walt contributed less animation, and focused more upon story, yet it was his name solely credited. A key demand for the 1941 strikers would be full credit for their work. In addition, Disney's paternalistic treatment of his workers began in the 1920s. Bob Thomas quotes Walt Disney's bewilderment at his employees' early demands:

> We got all these ragtag pillows all around. Every guy'd have a different one. So one day we got a little money and I talked Roy into letting me buy some new rubber foam cushions. I gave each guy a cushion for his chair. The next thing I knew, all of these fellows were demanding two cushions. I said, "Gosh,

that's the limit. They were happy with no cushions; I give them one cushion and they want two!"[74]

Michael Denning and Holly Allen note that "legend has it that the clowns who sing the song 'We're Gonna Hit the Big Boss for a Raise' in Walt Disney's 1941 feature *Dumbo* were 'malicious caricatures of striking Disney Studio cartoonists' done by the strikebreakers".[75] While it is interesting to contemplate the ways in which the 1941 animators' strike found its way into the animation, it is also of interest to note the way in which *Alice's Egg Plant* somewhat foresaw the tensions in Disney's own workplace. The hens sing "he's a bad papa" about Julius in the 1925 short, yet sixteen years later it was Disney's paternalism that contributed to disastrous labor relations at the studio. Disney began to lose interest in animation at this time, in part due to war costs, difficult distribution and the strike. This was a reversal in his attitude during the *Alice Comedies*, in which live action was used increasingly less.

If it is the case that, as has been argued in this chapter, the *Alice Comedies* were formative for Disney's later animation output as well as his social and political interventions, one must question why more academic focus has not been placed upon Walt Disney's early silent animation. The case is probably that with such limited access to the Disney studio archives, most see it as almost impossible to build upon what has already been written, and certainly there have been very few recent works of scholarship which bother to assess the *Alice Comedies*.[76] Yet this era is viewed by many as the key turning point in Disney's fortunes, the moment in which he first establishes himself as a serious producer. As Merritt and Kaufman argue:

> In that time he graduated from ambitious beginner to experienced producer, with a studio and staff capable of producing animated films that rivaled the best in the business. Speaking of his studio in later years, Disney was fond of saying that "it all started with a mouse" – but in fact the foundation was laid in 1924 by a little girl.[77]

In conclusion, *Alice's Egg Plant* highlights the complexity of Walt Disney's social and political stances during the early part of his career. The short was produced soon after the first American "Red Scare", and used the imagery of that scare; thus, it can be viewed as both drawing from and contributing to anticommunist discourses during the 1920s. Walt's own background of drawing communist-leaning cartoons, his father's contra-dictory beliefs in Socialism, the class tensions that raged in Kansas City, Missouri, and the final shot of *Alice's Egg Plant*, point to a complex history of inspiration for the short.[78] This period of short silent films was a key turning point in Disney's fortunes, who shifted his day-to-day focus from art to business during the 1920s. Though one must of course be cautious about using hindsight to read any kind of intentionality into a single film, nonetheless *Alice's Egg Plant* stands as a fascinating short that gives us some very interesting potential insights into Walt Disney's personal develop-ments in both his politics and in his understanding of his role as the head of his studio.

Bibliography

Barrier, Michael, *Hollywood Cartoons: American Animation in its Golden Age* (Oxford, UK: Oxford University Press, 1999).

Barrier, Michael, *The Animated Man: A Life of Walt Disney* (Berkeley, CA: University of California Press, 2008).

Brecher, Jeremy, *Strike!* Revised and Updated Edition (Cambridge, MA: South End Press, 1997).

Buhle, Paul, *Marxism in the United States: A History of the American Left* (London, UK: Verso, 2013).

Davis, Amy M., *Good Girls and Wicked Witches: Women in Disney's Feature Animation* (Eastleigh, UK: John Libbey Publishing, 2006).

Denning, Michael, *The Cultural Front: The Laboring of American Culture in the Twentieth Century* (London, UK; Verso, 2010).

Disney Miller, Diane, *The Story of Walt Disney (as told to Pete Martin)* (New York, NY; Henry Holt and Company, 1956).

Elza, Cary, "Alice in Cartoonland: Childhood, Gender, and Imaginary Space in Early Disney Animation" in Animation: An Interdisciplinary Journal (2014, vol.9.1), pp.7–26.

Foner, Philip, *History of the Labor Movement in the United States, Volume VIII: Postwar Struggles 1918–1920* (New York, NY; International Publishers, 1988).

Haynes, John E., *Red Scare or Red Menace: American Communism and Anticommunism in the Cold War Era* (Chicago, IL: Ivan R. Dee Inc., 1996).

Johnson, Jeffrey A., "Raising the Red Flag: Culture, Labor, and the Left, 1880–1920" in *Homer Simpson Marches on Washington: Dissent through American Popular Culture* ed. Timothy M. Dale and Joseph J. Foy (Lexington, KY: University Press of Kentucky, 2010), pp.191–201.

Leslie, Esther, *Hollywood Flatlands: Animation, Critical Theory and the Avant-Garde* (London, UK: Verso, 2002).

Merritt, Russell, and Kaufman, J. B., *Walt in Wonderland: The Silent Films of Walt Disney* (Baltimore, MD: The Johns Hopkins University Press, 1993).

Pallant, Chris, *Demystifying Disney: A History of Disney Feature Animation* (New York, NY: Continuum, 2011).

Puette, William, *Through Jaundiced Eyes: How the Media View Organized Labor* (Ithaca, NY: Cornell University Press, 1992).

Susanin, Timothy S., *Walt Before Mickey: Disney's Early Years 1919–1928* (Jackson, MS: University Press of Mississippi, 2011).

Sito, Tom, *Drawing the Line: The Untold Story of Animation Unions from Bosko to Bart Simpson* (Lexington, KY; the University of Kentucky Press, 2006).

Thomas, Bob, *Walt Disney: An American Original* (New York, NY; Simon and Schuster 1976).

Watts, Steven, *The Magic Kingdom: Walt Disney and the American Way of Life* (Columbia, MO: University of Missouri Press, 1997).

Filmography

Alice's Egg Plant (dir. Walt Disney, Disney Brothers Cartoon Studio, 1925)

The Wobblies (dir. Stewart Bird and Deborah Shaffer, 1979)

Endnotes

1. Barrier, Michael, *The Animated Man: A Life of Walt Disney* (Berkeley, CA: University of California Press, 2008), 201.

2. *Alice's Egg Plant* (dir. Walt Disney, Disney Brothers Cartoon Studio, 1925) *Alice's Egg Plant* is available on *Walt Disney Treasures: Disney Rarities: Celebrated Shorts, 1920–1960s* (2005), and online.

3. Haynes, John E., *Red Scare or Red Menace: American Communism and Anticommunism in the Cold War Era* (Chicago, IL: Ivan R. Dee Inc., 1996), 8.

4. Johnson, Jeffrey A., "Raising the Red Flag: Culture, Labor, and the Left, 1880–1920" in *Homer Simpson Marches on Washington: Dissent through American Popular Culture* ed. Timothy M. Dale and Joseph J. Foy (Lexington, KY: University Press of Kentucky, 2010), 199.

5. Johnson, 199.

6. Haynes, 9.

7. Davis, Amy M., *Good Girls and Wicked Witches: Women in Disney's Feature Animation* (Eastleigh, UK: John Libbey Publishing, 2006), 73.

8. Susanin, Timothy S., *Walt Before Mickey: Disney's Early Years 1919–1928* (Jackson, MS: University Press of Mississippi, 2011), 121.

9. Russell Merritt and J.B. Kaufman, *Walt in Wonderland: The Silent Films of Walt Disney* (Baltimore: Johns Hopkins University Press, 1993), 70.

10. Merritt and Kaufman, 20.

11. Merritt and Kaufman, 20.

12. Merritt and Kaufman, 20.

13. Merritt and Kaufman, 14.

14. Merritt and Kaufman, 14.

15. Barrier, *The Animated Man*, 47.

16. Barrier, *The Animated Man*, 48.

17. Barrier, *The Animated Man*, 42.

18. Barrier, *The Animated Man*, 42.

19. Barrier, Michael, *Hollywood Cartoons: American Animation in its Golden Age* (Oxford, UK: Oxford University Press, 1999), 39.

20. Thomas, Bob, *Walt Disney: An American Original* (New York, NY; Simon and Schuster 1976), 75. One must be cautious of Thomas' work, however. There is little citation, and it is an "authorized" biography. Nonetheless, it is cautiously cited by academics working on Disney.

21. Barrier, *Hollywood Cartoons*, 39.

22. Disney Miller, Diane, *The Story of Walt Disney* (as told to Pete Martin) (New York, NY; Henry Holt and Company, 1956) p.92. This account should also be viewed with caution. By all accounts it was not Diane Disney Miller, but an interview with Walt Disney that prompted the book, Miller's name was said to have been used as not to portray Walt in an egotistical way. In Barrier, Michael, *The Animated Man* p.xi – Diane says she felt "uncomfortable with assuming credit for authorship".

23. Thomas, 75.

24. Thomas, 75.

25. Thomas, 76.

26. Barrier, *The Animated Man*, 48.

27. Pallant, Chris, *Demystifying Disney* (London: Bloomsbury, 2013), 4.

28. Pallant, 4.

29. Barrier, *The Animated Man*, 47.

30. Barrier, *The Animated Man*, 47.

31.   Barrier, *TheAnimated Man*, 47.

32.   Barrier, *TheAnimated Man*, 46.

33.   Merritt and Kaufman, 70.

34.   Brecher, Jeremy, *Strike!* Revised and Updated Edition (Cambridge, MA: South End Press, 1997), 116.

35.   Foner, Philip, *History of the Labor Movement in the United States, Volume VIII: Postwar Struggles 1918–1920* (New York, NY; International Publishers, 1988), 111–116.

36.   Brecher, 118.

37.   Brecher, 118.

38.   Foner, 57.

39.   Foner, 58.

40.   Foner, 58–59.

41.   Puette, William, *Through Jaundiced Eyes: How the Media View Organized Labor* (Ithaca, NY: Cornell University Press, 1992), 14.

42.   Brecher, 155.

43.   Brecher, 155.

44.   Brecher, 155.

45.   Brecher, 155.

46.   Barrier, *The Animated Man*, 13.

47.   Barrier, *The Animated Man*, 13.

48.   Miller, 8.

49.   Miller, 4.

50.   Miller, 9.

51.   Barrier, *The Animated Man*, 13.

52.   Barrier, *The Animated Man*, 16–17.

53.   Miller, 9.

54.   Barrier, Michael, *The Animated Man*, 41.

55.   Buhle, Paul, *Marxism in the United States: A History of the American Left* (London, UK: Verso, 2013), 10.

56.   Buhle, 10.

57.   Buhle, 81–82.

58.   Buhle, 96–97.

59.   Watts, Steven, *The Magic Kingdom: Walt Disney and the American Way of Life* (Columbia, MO: University of Missouri Press, 1997), 19.

60.   Barrier, *The Animated Man*, 13.

61.   Johnson, 194.

62.   Miller, 10.

63.   Merritt and Kaufman, 70.

64.   Haynes, 9.

65.   Buhle, 119.

66.   Haynes, 11.

67.   Puette, 13.

68.   Puette, 14.

69.   For detailed discussions of labor relations at the Disney Studios, specifically the 1941 strike and Disney's HUAC testimony, see: Sito, Tom, *Drawing the Line: The Untold Story of Animation Unions from Bosko to Bart Simpson* (Lexington, KY; The University of Kentucky Press, 2006) and

Denning, Michael, *The Cultural Front: The Laboring of American Culture in the Twentieth Century* (London, UK; Verso, 2010).

70. Barrier, *Hollywood Cartoons*,46.

71. Leslie, Esther, *Hollywood Flatlands: Animation, Critical Theory and the Avant-Garde* (London, UK: Verso, 2002), 210.

72. Leslie, 216–218.

73. Sito, Tom, *Drawing the Line: The Untold Story of Animation Unions from Bosko to Bart Simpson* (Lexington, KY; The University of Kentucky Press, 2006), 101.

74. Thomas, 227.

75. Denning, Michael, *The Cultural Front: The Laboring of American Culture in the Twentieth Century* (London, UK; Verso, 2010), 403.

76. For an example of scholarship that has recently focused on the Alice Comedies, see: Elza, Cary, "Alice in Cartoonland: Childhood, Gender, and Imaginary Space in Early Disney Animation" in *Animation: An Interdisciplinary Journal*, Vol. 9, No. 1 (March 2014), 7–26.

77. Merritt and Kaufman, 55.

78. The short was never copyrighted and was subsequently used in an interesting way. *The Wobblies* (dir. Stewart Bird and Deborah Shaffer, 1979), a film documenting the history of the IWW, uses segments of *Alice's Egg Plant* to illustrate their actions.

Chapter 3

High Fantasy Disney: Recontextualising *The Black Cauldron*

Alexander Sergeant

The Black Cauldron (Berman, 1985) is often situated amongst popular accounts of the Disney studio as a low-point in the history of its animated feature production. Produced on an estimated budget of over $25 million and subjected to a decade-long series of production delays, the film opened in the summer of 1985 to apathetic reviews and lacklustre box-office numbers around the globe, out-grossed not only by *The Care Bears Movie* (Selznick, 1985) but by a re-issue of *101 Dalmatians* (Geronimi, Luske & Reitherman, 1961) released that same year.[1] In an interview conducted in August 2011, Jeffrey Katzenberg described the film as "the least successful Disney animation ever made",[2] whilst Michael Eisner, writing in his autobiography *Work in Progress*, similarly described *The Black Cauldron* as the culmination of a decade-long creative "dissatisfaction" amongst the animation staff.[3] In a more generous account of the film, Eleanor Byrne and Martin McQuillan describe *The Black Cauldron* as a "financial, but by no means artistic disaster" whose main contribution to Disney history was nevertheless to nearly bankrupt the company upon its release.[4] Its commercial failure prompted studio's executives to dramatically rethink their approach to their animated film division and, as such, *The Black Cauldron*'s main impact upon Disney history was that it seemed to act as a catalyst for a series of decisions that paved the way for a cycle of commercial and critical successes produced during the late 1980s and 1990s, including *The Little Mermaid* (Clements and Musker, 1989), *Beauty and the Beast* (Trousdale, 1991) and *The Lion King* (Allers and Minkoff, 1994).

Whilst such accounts of *The Black Cauldron* no doubt reflect the commercial reality of the film's box office performance, they are nevertheless ideologically charged and teleological in that they result in a method of analysis that interprets the specific formal and aesthetic features of *The Black Cauldron* against its subsequent commercial failure. As a means of providing a counter-narrative to such discourse, this chapter of *Discussing Disney* offers an alternative account of *The Black Cauldron* that explores some of the circumstances that helped shape Disney's commercial and artistic strategy in the years prior to the film's release. In particular, by situating the film within the wider context of the Hollywood fantasy genre, the chapter considers *The Black Cauldron* as part of a prominent cycle of high fantasy cinema produced by studios during the early 1980s and reflected in films such as *The Beastmaster* (Coscarelli, 1982), *The Sword and the Sorcerer* (Pyun, 1982) and *Ladyhawke* (Donner, 1985). Engaging with this phenomenon of high fantasy, *The Black Cauldron*'s departure from certain narrative and aesthetic conventions associated with Disney allowed the studio film to negotiate its position as one of Hollywood's most historic and prominent producers of fantasy cinema, creating a high fantasy Disney film that would, on the one hand, look to the studio's past whilst simultaneously feel relevant enough for its contemporary audiences. With this wider connection between Disney and the Hollywood fantasy genre in mind, *The Black Cauldron* provides an opportunity to examine the studio's shifting relationship to fantasy storytelling in the decades prior to its release, and to consider what the film's presence (or indeed absence) from the Disney canon reveals about the wider identity of the studio as a whole.

From Fairy-Tale to High Fantasy: The "Classic" Tradition and the Evolution of Fantasy Cinema

The Black Cauldron was commissioned by Disney as a response to a series of volatile market conditions that, by the early 1980s, had threatened to challenge the studio's long-assumed dominance over US popular animation. The preceding decades had initiated within the Disney studio an era of "transition" in which, as Chris Pallant argues, the studio was "seen to stagnate, both creatively and as a corporate entity".[5] Throughout the 1960s and 1970s, Disney was forced to adjust not only to internal issues such as the death of Walt Disney himself in December 1966, but to the wider conditions of post-classical Hollywood. But in this, Disney was not alone; Hollywood's studios collectively suffered throughout this period thanks in part to their inability to recognise shifting audience tastes and first the emergence of, then the changes within, distinct demographics and audience groups. One important demographic group, the teen-market, were largely alienated by the studios' traditional product of classical filmmaking. Hollywood's broader crisis of identity was especially pronounced within the Disney studio, however, given the difficulty it experienced in matching new audience expectations with the public perception of its brand of filmmaking by the 1960s and '70s. To use Sean Griffin's words, "Disney's public image had inadvertently ghettoized its films" by the end of the 1970s.[6] No longer able to produce the kind of commercial successes the studio had enjoyed in the past through a particular kind of animated feature film that exhibited what Wasko terms a "Disney brand of fantasy", the studio's response was to commission a series of projects that attempted to move the company away from what, by this period, was perceived as its traditional position in the marketplace.[7] Producing science-fiction adventures such as *The Black Hole* (Nelson, 1979) and *Tron* (Lisberger, 1982), as well as other darker fantasy efforts such as *Dragonslayer* (Robbins, 1981), *Something Wicked This Way Comes* (Clayton, 1983), and *Return to Oz* (Murch, 1985), Disney's production cycle throughout this era was a somewhat experimental, if generally commercially unsuccessful, attempt to step away from a well-known formula which had come to be more of a hindrance than an assistance to future box office successes.

Produced within this climate, *The Black Cauldron* was noted by many reviewers on its release for its lack of adherence to the oft-cited paradigm of the "classical" Disney formula.[8] As Pallant suggests, the term "Classic Disney" is now often utilised amongst both journalistic and academic commentaries of the studio's output to "periodize animation in a qualitative sense" as well as serving as a critical yardstick with which to measure its individual films against.[9] Drawing its inspiration not from the fairy-tale folklore associated (rightly or wrongly) with Disney's past, but instead from Lloyd Alexander's fantasy series *The Chronicles of Prydain* (1964–68), the narrative of *The Black Cauldron* shared more in common with J.R.R. Tolkien's *The Lord of the Rings* than it did previous examples of Disney filmmaking such as *Snow White and the Seven Dwarfs* (Hand, 1937) or *Cinderella* (Geronimi, 1950), which each exemplify one of the key values associated with the "Classic" Disney model, namely "the use, and co-option, of fairy tale narratives".[10] In a review appearing in *Variety*, the film was criticised for its lack of originality and vision, as well as noted for its stark departure from the type of filmmaking expected from the studio. As the review explained, "beyond an appreciation for Disney's unique animation craft ... elders lacking an innocent influence may never settle with themselves whether 'Cauldron' matches their memory of other Disney classics".[11] Alienated by the "fairly stock sword-and-sorcery", the author questioned the increased violence and sexualised content in comparison with other Disney productions, features of the film that would be discussed elsewhere in other high-profile publications at the time. In his review of *The Black Cauldron* in the *New York Times*, Walter Goodman stated at that: "People old enough to recall their delight at earlier feature animations, no doubt burnished by memory, are not of course the audience at which 'The Black

Cauldron' is aimed. Nor, apparently, is it aimed at youngsters who have a taste for more sophisticated animation of the 'Star Wars' breed of movies".[12] Being neither adventurous enough for new tastes nor traditional enough for audiences who had been raised on the studio's back catalogue, the general critical and popular response to The Black Cauldron viewed the film as either a misguided attempt by the Disney studio to respond to the popularity of the films of George Lucas and Steven Spielberg, or else more simply as an oddity that failed to register with audiences at the time of its release.

The frequent comparisons made between The Black Cauldron and the features of the "Classic" Disney feature suggest a discrepancy between the kind of filmmaking exemplified in The Black Cauldron and the kind of animated feature expected of the Disney stable, an expectation that does not always bear fruit when one considers the sheer diversity of the Disney animated feature beyond the oft-cited paradigm of the typical Disney "formula".[13] Nevertheless, the "Classic" Disney formula does have some relevance to the study of the Disney studio and its broader cultural impact given the fact that the films that such a label claims to represent most closely are often also the films which have provided the studio with its most enduring commercial and successes. "Classic" Disney is also a label given to a period of production during the studio's first twenty years of feature-length filmmaking, an era that showcased a sustained European influence exemplified through the studio's selection of material for adaptation. While Disney was by no means the first Hollywood studio to select European fairy tales as material for adaptation, the success of the studio's first feature, Snow White, did, as Jack Zipes notes, pave the way "for Disney's eventual domination of the children's fairy-tale industry".[14] As Robin Allan argues, the studio's output immediately prior to the release of Snow White reveals the prominent influences of a studio chairman who had grown up in the American Mid-West amongst popular vaudevillian acts based in Germanic culture.[15] Early Silly Symphonies (1929–1939) such as The Skeleton Dance (Disney, 1929) display some of the formal and stylistic characteristics of the nineteenth-century gothic melodrama, while adaptations of the fairy-tales made popular by the Brothers Grimm began to appear in works such as Ye Olden Days (Gillett, 1933) and Three Little Pigs (Gillett, 1933).[16] If a significant characteristic of the Disney brand has been its capacity to produce fantasy on the big screen, then that capacity was influenced as early on as the Laugh-O-Gram period (1921–23) by a distinctly European set of influences that drew closely from the folkloric precursors of the modern fantasy genre.

The "Classic" label, then, was partially forged by the studio's adherence to a certain set of storytelling conventions exemplified in the European fairy-tale. As Marina Warner argues, "Fairy tales are stories which, in the earliest mentions of their existence, include that circle of listeners, the audience".[17] Stemming from oral storytelling, they have remained in existence because of their ability not only to entertain, but also to be remembered by those hearing them, passed on from generation to generation, and inevitably altered and added to in the process. The repetitive and recognisable narratives of fairy-tales, where "complex characters are rare, and the distribution of villainy and virtue is not muddied by ambiguity", are part of the way they are passed between storytellers, allowing one individual to pick up the basic narrative tenets quickly and then use this as the basis for repetition and embellishment.[18] As Zipes argues, "the paradigmatic structure enables teller and listeners to recognize, store, remember, and reproduce the stories and to change them to fit their experiences and desires".[19] The fairy-tale structure is therefore clear and easily identifiable, emphasising clear progression and form over the arguably more complex narrative strategies developed by nineteenth- and twentieth-century novelists.

However, those same literary traditions exemplified in examples of "Classic" Disney were beginning, even by the time of the release of *Snow White*, to be supplanted within US literary culture by a more recognisably-modern form of fantasy writing. The popularity of the fairy-tale collections compiled by those such as the Brothers Grimm and Charles Perrault during the nineteenth century had produced a generation of writers such as E.T.A. Hoffman, George MacDonald, and Charles Kingsley who, informed by the prevailing romantic discourses of the period, set about replicating the tone of such tales in order to provide a similar celebration of irrationality through a more extended literary form.[20] Within the US, the publication of L. Frank Baum's *The Wonderful Wizard of Oz* (1900) witnessed the creation of what Brian Attebery describes as the first "coherent American fantasy world" to rival that of its European predecessors.[21] Described by the author, Baum, as a series of "modernized fairy stories", the *Oz* books managed to popularise a new form of fantasy writing which, although indebted to the storytelling traditions of the fairy-tale, demonstrated some important differences in tone and structure.[22] While the fairy-tale tended to present a world in which magical circumstances appeared with little justification or explanation, Baum imbued Oz with its own geography, history, and anthropology, allowing the kind of magic on display in Baum's novel to be partially justified by placing it in contrast with the more recognisable reality of Kansas.

Influenced by Baum's ability to blend elements of realism and fantasy together, US writers who followed in his wake such as Ron E. Howard and Edgar Rice Burroughs began to develop a format of fantasy writing that built upon the techniques Baum and others had established, channelling them in the service of a far more adult-focused series of short stories and novellas. Appearing in pulp magazines such as *The All-Story* and *Weird Tales* throughout the 1910s, 1920s and 1930s, these stories, as Paul Kincaid argues, served as "Busby Berkeley musicals for the page: big, colourful, often non-sensical spectacles that proved to be the perfect antidote to the stock market crash, the dust bowl and the Depression".[23] Focusing on the sustained presentation of fictional worlds, far-away planets or bygone mythological eras, such pulp efforts offered their readers a release from the tensions of reality and an escape into fantasy, an aesthetic feat that would reach its epochal moment with the far more literary effort of J.R.R. Tolkien's *The Lord of The Rings*, a work that helped to initiate a new era of high fantasy writing given its vast commercial success. As defined by Marshall B. Tymn, Kenneth J. Zahorski, and Robert H. Boyer, high fantasy is a distinct category of fantasy storytelling based on the presentation of a "secondary world".[24] A subgenre of the broader conventions of fantasy storytelling, high fantasy not only became an especially lucrative category for the publishing industry in the subsequent decades following the success of *The Lord of the Rings* but, by the early 1980s, had branched out into a distinctly cross-media phenomenon exemplified by the popularity of role-playing games such as *Dungeons and Dragons* (1974) and emergent video-game platforms such as *Multi-User Dungeon* (1977), *Zork* (1980), and *Ultima* (1981).

During the same time, as the literary fantasy genre went through a process of evolution throughout this era, the Disney studio departed from its own process of evolution that saw it depart from its "Classic" model of fairy-tale adaptation by the end of the 1950s to embrace some of the literary examples that had contributed to this high fantasy heritage. In releasing adaptations of *Alice in Wonderland* (Geronimi, 1951) and *Peter Pan* (Luske, 1953), Disney had turned towards the writings of two individuals – Lewis Carroll and J.M. Barrie – who had both contributed to fantasy's evolution away from its folkloric origins and towards a literary genre bound by a new set of narrative conventions which Disney's adaptations sought in part to emulate. *Alice in Wonderland* in particular was positioned by the studio as Disney's "unreined improvisation upon the fine fantasies of Mr. Carroll", as Bosley Crowther wrote in his *New York Times* review.[25] Described in advertisements placed in trade journals such as *Variety* and *Box Office* as an "all-cartoon musical wonder film", *Alice in Wonderland* was promoted for its eclectic range of well-known characters from the stories of Carroll himself.[26] Disney's adaptations of *Alice in Wonderland* and *Peter Pan* both showcase a desire to place the secondary worlds of Wonderland and Neverland on screen, often to the detriment of their respective narrative structures. Characters meander through more obviously episodic struc-tures in order to display certain iconic passages from the original sources. Coexisting with fairy-tale adaptations such as *Cinderella*, the transition taking place on screen mirrored the changes taking place off screen. As one generation of studio executives was replaced by another within the Disney studio, so too a series of literary influences stemming from European folklore and the fairy-tale was slowly replaced by another stemming from the modern fantasy novel.

Disney's tentative steps towards a kind of animated fantasy that embraced some of the emerging qualities of high fantasy literature continued to emerge in subsequent decades. After returning to the fairy-tale format with *Sleeping Beauty* (Geronimi, 1959), a film that failed to recoup its vast production budget at the time of its release despite its adherence to the fairy-tale formula popularised with *Snow White*, Disney's next fantasy film after *101 Dalmatians* would be an adaptation of popular Arthurian legend *The Sword in the Stone* (Reitherman, 1963). Based on T.H. White's 1938 novel, a book noted by Roger Scholbin for its ability to utilise "contemporary psychological explanations" to bring a modern perspective to the traditional Arthurian legends, *The Sword in the Stone* was a film that, on the one hand, acknowledged Disney's past and, at the same time, incorporated possible visions of a different future.[27] Sequences in which Arthur and Merlin transform themselves into fish to swim through the castle moat, or into squirrels exploring the near-by woods (both sequences which utilised Disney's trademark tendencies towards anthropomorphism) were blended with more action-orientated episodes, including one sequence in which Merlin battles a dragon in the form of the transformed witch Madam Mim. According to *The Hollywood Reporter*, one of "the notable things about *The Sword in the Stone* from a technical point of view is the development of Disney's approach. Much of the sweetness, sometimes saccharine, of the earlier animated features has been dropped ... [and] there is an astringency and rougher strokes in the art work that is not only better art but better drama."[28] The film was praised in the review for the new direction Disney was willing to take, celebrating the studio's departure from a kind of fantasy associated with the fairy-tale and its embrace of some of the conventions of the fantasy genre as exemplified in its literary counterparts. Reporting on its box-office potential, *Variety* was optimistic about the film's commercial possibilities due the "vast circulation" of White's book which "coupled with the public's knowabout concerning high production caliber of any Disney cartoon, doubtless will help the film 'sell'".[29]

With this broader sense of evolution in mind, *The Black Cauldron* need not be seen as an aberration in Disney's catalogue, but instead the culmination of a steady process of evolution from fairy-tale to high fantasy taking place within the Disney animated fantasy feature throughout the mid-twentieth century. Embracing some of the advances made within the literary fantasy genre, Disney adapted and modified the traits of high fantasy to both mould their features in its likeness while also adapting the format to accommodate some of the broader formal and aesthetic traits associated with the studio's back catalogue. Such a negotiation between past and present can be witnessed in *The Black Cauldron*'s opening scene. Beginning with a prologue designed to inform audience members of some of the back-story surrounding the narrative in question, the film opens on an indistinguishable image of black fog and mist, from which an artefact is slowly revealed in the form of the eponymous black cauldron. As the cauldron takes shape, an unseen storyteller (voiced by Jon Huston) proceeds to inform the audience of the significance of this object to Alexander's world of Prydain. In this sense, the beginning of *The Black Cauldron* is reminiscent of certain "Classic" Disney films. *Snow White*, for example, begins with a shot of an ornately decorated book cover that then falls open on its first page revealing the words: "Once upon a time there lived a lovely princess named Snow White". Establishing both the name and characteristics of its central heroine, this moment exemplifies the broader manner in which *Snow White* typifies some of the narrative devices found in eighteenth and nineteenth century folk literature. *Snow White* need not be demonstrated as being "lovely" through her actions on the screen, but is instead made "lovely" incarnate by the formal imposition of the prose, a characteristic that is then enhanced through the stylised nature of her design. Kristian Moen argues this technique "substantially associates fairy-tales with literature and the written word rather than the visual pleasures of theatre or the transformative marvels of cinema", allowing the Disney studio to position itself less as an adaptor than an illustrator of the fairy-tale source; rather than still drawings, however, animation has been used to depict Snow White. Furthermore, the images have reinforced this description of Snow White as "lovely" through her stylised design, relying on conservative ideals of beauty and femininity.[30]

The Black Cauldron's opening sequence, on the other hand, exhibits a different set of aesthetic priorities. Unlike *Snow White*, the prologue does not serve to establish a sense of who the protagonist is, but instead informs the audience of the land of Prydain, in which the story will take place. In this manner, although the sequence bares some similarities to the beginning of *Snow White*, *The Black Cauldron*'s opening prologue in fact has more in common with live-action high fantasy contemporaries such as *Conan the Barbarian* (Milius, 1982), which begins with a very similar voice-over device, as well as Jim Henson's *The Dark Crystal* (1982), a film that uses puppetry to render on screen a complex alternative world indebted to the high fantasy literary heritage. The opening sequence of *The Black Cauldron* culminates in the title card, whose font draws on the ornate designs of Disney's classic storytelling with its quasi-medieval embroidery patterns. Yet, accompanied by a rousing score by Elmer Bernstein, the tone is distinct from the kind of Disney feature such a title card would traditionally accompany. The title card instead serves as an invitation to a grand fantasy world on screen, a world with depth, history and complexity, and a world whose nuances are promised to be revealed in greater detail to the audience as the words of the title travel past the frame and the film itself begins.

Animating High-Fantasy: Sub-Creation Through Hyper-Realism

The aesthetics of high fantasy witnessed in the opening moments of *The Black Cauldron* become a prominent concern of the narrative that follows. Adapted from the first two books of Alexander's *Prydain* series, namely *The Book of Three* (1964) and *The Black Cauldron* (1965), the Disney film takes as its basic plot a familiar-sounding quest narrative based around the trials of a young man named Taran, who lives in the pastoral idyll of Caer Dallben working as an assistant pig-keeper. Unbeknownst to Taran, the pig whom he looks after, Henwen, is no ordinary animal but is instead a creature blessed with the magical ability of foresight, capable of providing visions to those who know how to access her power. Learning of a faraway conspiracy hatched by an evil ruler, The Horned King, who plans to use Henwen's power to locate the mysterious black cauldron, Taran is given the task of journeying out into the wider world of Prydain in order to find a safe home for her. With its cast of supporting characters including Gurgi (a strange woodland creature who is pathetic, comic and sinister in equal measure in a manner similar to Tolkien's most famous character of Gollum), the Princess Eilonwy, and a local bard named Fflewddur Flam, the central dynamic of the film's narrative pits the small, unworldly Taran against the immeasurable forces of The Horned King.

In constructing the narrative around the exploits of Taran, the narrative makes use of a typical device within fantasy literature which Farah Mendlesohn has dubbed "the portal-quest" narrative.[31] The portal-quest narrative functions as a key rhetorical device that allows the author to present information about a secondary world to the reader while the narration itself remains "tied to the protagonist".[32] As Mendlesohn elaborates, "the portal fantasy is about entry, transition and exploration", as characters journey into the alternative world constructed by an author in order that readers might experience it, engaging with pleasure in the elaborate and intricate way the fantasy world functions as a cohesive whole.[33] *The Black Cauldron* – both in Alexander's original and in the Disney adaptation – utilises this narrative not to simply tell a story containing a collection of fabulist characters and circumstances, but to synergise the setting of Prydain and its inhabitants together to project a sense of "arresting strangeness ... a feeling of awe and wonder" that Zahorski and Boyer argue are key to the presentations of alternative worlds in the subgenre of high fantasy.[34]

Beyond the basic tenets of the narrative, Disney's *The Black Cauldron* also attempts to transmit the pleasure of high fantasy to its audiences by harnessing its animated identity to actualise the feelings of awe and wonder that literary fantasy is only able to describe. In his history of popular US animation *From Mice and Magic*, Leonard Maltin describes *The Black Cauldron* as "the company's most ambitious feature-length animated film" produced in recent memory.[35] Whilst criticising certain faults with the storyline and acknowledging its poor commercial performance, Maltin nevertheless praises the film's "striking" use of both animation techniques from Disney's past and for introducing a series of technical innovations that would go on to be utilised in later productions.[36] Directed by Ted Berman, whose experience with the studio extended as far back as his work as a character animator on *Bambi* (Hand, 1942), *The Black Cauldron* was made by a mixture of old studio stalwarts and a new generation of animators who had obtained their first professional experiences either working in Ralph Bakshi's production studios or else at Disney itself whilst working on the pioneering computer effects utilised on the film *Tron*.[37] *The Black Cauldron* blended some of the Disney studio's trademark technologies, bringing back costly techniques such as the multi-plane camera whilst also being the first Disney film to be shot in 70mm widescreen since *Sleeping Beauty*, with new innovations such as Successive Exposure colouring techniques and an early use of computer animation in some of the film's special effects. These techniques were all designed to bring a level of sharpness to the images that had not been possible in the studio's previous reliance on Xerox technology.[38] Despite many of these processes proving to be less than economically viable at the time, the at least partial integration of such technologies attested to the attention to detail of a film made by a team of 68 animators producing approximately 460,800 cells.[39]

This ambitious blend of some of the more complex techniques of Disney's past alongside technological innovations such as computer animation presented within *The Black Cauldron* can also be seen as a response to the rise of a series of competitors who had not only threatened to challenge the studio's long-assumed dominance of the popular animation feature, but also had showcased a new way of utilising animated techniques in the creation of high fantasy. As Disney suffered a string of apathetic box office results throughout the 1970s, Bakshi established himself as an independent director and producer after releasing his adaptation of the adult-orientated animated feature *Fritz the Cat* (1972), a film which, despite a limited release and a production budget of $750,000, took almost the same amount of money at the US box office as Disney's *Robin Hood* (Reitherman, 1973). Labelled by the *New York Times* as the "Iconoclast of Animation", Bakshi's particular style of animation was seen to have "successfully revolted in subject matter and style against the art of animation as practiced by Walt Disney and his disciples".[40] Yet this revolt quickly took Bakshi away from the kind of animated realism exemplified in his earlier works such as *Fritz the Cat* and *Coonskin* (1975) and towards a more commercially-reliable form of high fantasy in films such as *Wizards* (1977), *The Lord of the Rings* (1978), and *Fire and Ice* (1983). Described as "an epic fantasy" in a review appearing in *Boxoffice* magazine, *Wizards* was an animated fantasy film distinct in tone and content from the kind exemplified in the more popular examples of Disney filmmaking.[41] Featuring a multitude of different characters and taking place in a complex alternative world, *Wizards* told an allegorically-infused story of the corrupting forces of technology in which the armies of technology and magic do battle against one another on screen. Bakshi followed up the financial success of *Wizards* by acquiring the rights to J.R.R. Tolkien's novel with the help of producer Saul Zarentz. A commercial success at the time, Bakshi's *The Lord of the Rings* showcased the potential for animation to be used to make a kind of fantasy film that appealed to demographics beyond those traditionally courted by the Disney Studio, and thereby served to acknowledge the evolution that the fantasy genre had undergone throughout the twentieth century.

Alongside Bakshi, ex-Disney animator Don Bluth also emerged as another serious contender to Disney's throne by producing a series of successful productions that, unlike *The Lord of the Rings*, targeted the exact market with which Disney had previously been so successful. Bluth's decision to leave Disney in 1979 was portrayed by some at the time not so much as a rebellion against the Disney product but instead an attempt to renegotiate the Disney product for a new era. In an interview published in *Variety* in May 1982, Bluth expressed his desire to return to the filmmaking that Disney had created during in "Classical" era, termed by Paul Wells as the "hyper-realist" style, and then abandoned in recent years for more cost-effective production methods.[42] The first of these productions, *The Secret of NIMH* (1982), was made by the short-lived Aurora Productions – a company established by former Disney executives Rich Irvine, Jim Stewart, and Jon Lang – and displayed the dual influences of both Disney and the animation that had emerged in recent decades, blending a mixture of hyper-realism with some of the features of popular fantasy storytelling of this era. Described in *Screen International* as "an action fantasy film in the classical style of animation", *The Secret of NIMH* was heralded by critics as both a return to the Disney style and also a sign of contemporary influences, adapting not a fairy-tale, but rather Robert O'Brien's 1971 fantasy novel.[43] The film was simultaneously celebrated by reviewers at the time as a return to the "old standards" of the animation form set by the Disney studio while at same time acknowledging certain narrative innovations that had developed the sophistication of the type of fantasy storytelling on display.[44] Paradoxically, Bluth's early success came from being seen as both more *and* less Disney than Disney; paying greater homage to the studio's legacy without repeating the similar formulas that were associated with that studio at the same time.

Bluth and Bakshi's forays into fantasy filmmaking showcased a variety of techniques in which animation was utilised to replace traditional rhetorical techniques of "sub-creation", a technique first identified by Tolkien in his own work of literary criticism, "On Fairy Stories".[45] For Tolkien, this process of sub-creation was achieved by a writer when he or she had established a series of coherent rules and logical relationships in order to create "a Secondary World which your mind can enter".[46] This process can be witnessed throughout the works of both Bluth and Bakshi, in which the richness of detail in the animation in the works of both individuals respectively is utilised to create a vivid sense of their own secondary worlds on screen. *The Black Cauldron*, in turn, also utilized a variety of techniques in order to establish Prydain as a fully-realised animated realm invested with the detail and richness required for the high fantasy aesthetic.

A key sequence in demonstrating this process of sub-creation through animation can be witnessed early on in Taran's journey. Leaving behind the safety of Caer Dallben for the nearby woods, Taran stops by a nearby pool, at which point he becomes distracted by a series of visions Henwen is able to create in the water of Taran's possible future. Distracted by such visions, Taran inadvertently loses his prized pig in the middle of a thick forest. As Taran looks up, a brief shot showcasing Henwen's absence from his side displays the ornate detail of the location in which he now stands alone. Taran seems dwarfed by the sense of location swarming all around him, as leaves and grasses are seen protruding into the forefront of the cel while, in the background, the fine detail of the grasslands and flowers provide numerous competing focal points, of which Taran's body is but one of many. The moment communicates Taran's own psychological state – projecting the sudden shock he feels at the absence of Henwen through its brief duration and the dominance of setting over character – whilst also placing him within the context of the wider world of Prydain. The forest he stands in is a forest in its own right, given the complexity of detail in its design that allows for a process similar to Tolkien's own literary techniques required for sub-creation.

Taran begins his frantic search for Henwen through the richly designed forest setting, wherein he encounters the creature Gurgi for the first time. As the two characters argue with one another, Gurgi bargains with Taran find help him find Henwen in return for food, or "munchings and crunch-ings"; their exchange is abruptly curtailed by the sound of Henwen's cry. Taran proceeds to chase after the sound, stumbling into an open field to discover that she is being pursued by a dragon. Close-up and point-of-view shots from the dragon's perspective are intercut with fast-moving camera to provide a kinetic energy to the mise-en-scène. Taking place in an open field, the depth of vision gives an enhanced perspective to the speed at which the creature chases the pig; likewise, the surrounding atmosphere highlights the interplay between an occasionally expressionist vision of stylised woods and trees with a realist sense of the clouds behind. As Henwen is eventually carried away by the dragon, Taran stands forlorn on a cliff-top against a backdrop of darkened, crimson clouds. Disney's multi-plane camera is used to add depth to the scenery in a manner that both reflects the vastness of Prydain and the length of Taran's journey to retrieve Henwen. Like the previous shot, Taran is but one of many focal points, the others being the numerous jagged rock contours that are seen in the forefront and background of the shot, as well as the tiny image of Henwen disappearing into the distance which forms the only action point in the shot. The vastness of Taran's journey is reflected in the depth of the frame itself, creating an image in which character and world collate together so that Prydain speaks of Taran's own turmoil just as it inflicts it upon the character.

Similar techniques are used throughout the film to bring depth and richness to the world of Prydain. As Taran journeys further into Prydain, he proceeds to inhabit as series of richly decorated worlds that display an attention to detail in the film's design and setting. Woods are evoked not simply through colour and indistinct patterns, but through an ornate depiction of the colours of the shrubbery and texture of foliage. Wide-angle shots of the group walking in the distance proliferate the narrative, providing a visual bridge from one location to the next as the traditional framing of shots around individual characters and their bodies are replaced by a world of impressive depth, design and scope of vision. On entering the Mordova Marshes, the location is established through a slow, horizontal pan that travels across the various bogs, mosses, and trees that extend beyond the confinements of the image. Initially, the group of companions are heard without being seen as the mise-en-scène prioritises the location over establishing their immediate presence within it. Eventually, the group is introduced into the shot as they appear in the distant background, tiny and wholly subservient to the larger context of their location. In the film's final confrontation, in which the companions are captured by the forces of The Horned King, his castle is again introduced through a similar panning camera, emphasising little details such as the gothic style of architecture and a ground littered by bones, before again establishing character by returning the focus to the companions. There is a sense throughout *The Black Cauldron* that there is more to the land of Prydain than that shown on screen. Like its fantasy contemporaries, the film instead seeks to establish a sense of fully-realised fantasy world indebted to the high fantasy literary tradition.

Conclusion: The Death of "High" Fantasy?

In a fairly typical review of *The Black Cauldron* (this one appearing in the British publication *Monthly Film Bulletin*), Nigel Floyd acknowledged some of the technical innovations on display in the film before insisting that all "the technical resources do not compensate for the absence of the simple, clear storytelling which was once Disney's great strength".[47] As reviewers pined for the Disney of old, the film was seen by many at the time of its release as a misguided attempt to profit on a short-wave cycle of adult-orientated high fantasy filmmaking, a production trend which, by the mid-1980s, already showed signs of being on the wane. With a string of commercial failures, including Ridley Scott's ill-fated fantasy epic *Legend* (1985), along with the financial success of Steven Spielberg's sci-fi adventure *E.T: The Extra-Terrestrial* (1982), studios quickly abandoned their brief foray into the world of "high" fantasy in favour of a more family-friendly brand of production. Yet *The Black Cauldron* was not without some defenders. In its review in *Cinefantastique*, *The Black Cauldron* was celebrated as a "watershed Disney film" that indicated that, "after 52 years of sweetness and light, Mickey Mouse has grown up".[48] In a similarly enthusiastic review appearing in the *Hollywood Reporter*, Dennis Fischer proclaimed that *The Black Cauldron* "carries on the grand tradition of Disney animation" by taking the format into new territories, providing children with "an imaginative tale where characters sometimes have to make difficult choices and where there is action, excitement, adventure and newfound friends".[49] Even a pessimistic report on the film's potential at the box office appearing in *The Film Journal* was not willing to dismiss the film entirely, given its ambition to depart "from fairy-tale subject matter into mythic adventure" in a manner that reflected the change in contemporary taste.[50] The article predicted that the film would provide the studio with "a relatively small loss ... But to the extent that *The Black Cauldron* ensures another generation of feature animation from the studio, even larger losses would represent well-spent R&D costs."[51] The film pointed towards a bright future for Disney as an adaptor of adult-orientated fantasy sagas in the style of its contemporary, and as such represented a promising future for the studio at large.

The events that followed the financial disappointment of *The Black Cauldron* are well documented. Motivated by the film's commercial failure, Disney set out introducing a series of changes to the kind of animated feature production commissioned by the studio that both directly and indirectly led to the so-called "New Disney" or "Disney Renaissance" of the late 1980s and 1990s.[52] This critically- and commercially-successful period of Disney history was made possible thanks to a series of films that, as Allan argues, were all "based on European fairy tales, [and] have an epic dimension that gives them, for the first time since the death of Walt Disney, a classic status that refers us back to the earlier days of *Snow White and the Seven Dwarfs* and *Cinderella*".[53] Epitomised by films such as *The Little Mermaid*, *Beauty and the Beast*, and *Aladdin*, the Disney renaissance was seen as a return to both the standard and to the format of filmmaking most closely associated with the studio. Yet, looking at examples from this renaissance, it is difficult not to see some of the influences of the high fantasy tradition evidenced in the array of underworld characters that populate Neptune's undersea kingdom, the Beast's castle or the Cave of Wonders. The kind of rich world-building on display in such works of the renaissance era indicates the influence of a production team including such individuals as John Musker and Ron Clements, each of whom had worked on *The Black Cauldron* as storyboard artists. As such, the importance of understanding some of the artistic traits of *The Black Cauldron* is not simply that it might allow us to reclaim or reconsider a film dismissed by many as a commercial and artistic folly, but that such an analysis provides a way of examining the studio's wider relationship to the fantasy genre outside the domains of dominant narratives emphasised through quantitative labels such as "Classic" and "Renaissance". By witnessing the evolution of Disney rather than seeking the periodisation of Disney, we might be better placed to understand the specific characteristics of its respective animated feature films.

Bibliography

Adamson, Joe. "What's Cooking in The Black Cauldron", *American Cinematographer* 66:7 (July 1985), 60–68.

Allan, Robin. *Walt Disney and Europe: European Influences on the Animated Feature Films of Walt Disney* (London: John Libbey & Company: 1999).

Anonymous. "1985 Domestic Grosses", BoxOfficeMojo.com, accessed June 7, 2015. http://www.boxofficemojo.com/yearly/chart/?yr=1985.

Anonymous. "Bluth Completes Cartoon Feature", *Variety* (May 19, 1982), 34; Paul Wells, *Understanding Animation* (Abingdon, Oxon: Routledge, 1998), 25.

Anonymous. "Film review: The Secret of NIMH". *Variety* (June 16, 1982), 14.

Anonymous. "Ralph Bakshi will Visit NYC to Plug 'Wizards'", *Boxoffice*, April 11, 1977, E2.

Anonymous. "Stateside: 'NIMH' nearly ready", *Screen International* 328 (January 30, 1982), 6.

Anonymous. "Walt Disney's Alice in Wonderland", Box Office 58.12 (January 20, 1951), a29; "Walt Disney's Alice in Wonderland" Variety (January 3, 1951), 38.

Anonymous. *Hollywood Reporter* (2 October 1963), 3.

Anonymous. *Monthly Film Bulletin* (October 1985), 305–306.

Anonymous. *Variety* (October 2 1963), 6.

Anonymous. *Variety*, July 24, 1985, 16.

Attebery, Brian. *The Fantasy Tradition in American Literature* (Bloomington, IN: Indiana University Press, 1980).

Braund, Simon. "Ask the Boss" *Empire*, August 2011, 112.

Byrne, Eleanor, and Martin McQuillan. *Deconstructing Disney* (London: Pluto Press, 1999).

Crowther, Bosley. "The Screen in Review: Disney's Cartoon Adaptation of 'Alice in Wonderland' Arives at Crierion" *New York Times* (July 30, 1951), 12.

Culhane, John. "Ralph Bakshi – Iconoclast of Animation", *New York Times*, March 22, 1981, D13.

Eisner, Michael with Tony Schwartz, *Work in Progress* (London: Penguin Books, 1998).

Fischer, Dennis. "The Black Cauldron" in *Hollywood Reporter*, July 1985, 3, 18.

Goodman, Walter. "Screen: Disney's Black Cauldron", *New York Times*, July 26, 1985, c5.

Griffin, Sean. *Tinker Belles and Evil Queens: The Walt Disney Company from the Inside Out* (New York: New York University Press, 2000).

Holliday, Christopher. "Let it go? Towards a 'Plasmatic' Perspective on Digital Disney", found in this collection, p. 115.

Kincaid, Paul. "American Fantasy 1820–1950", in Edward James and Farah Mendlesohn (Editors), *The Cambridge Companion to Fantasy Literature* (Cambridge: Cambridge University Press, 2012), 36–49.

Maltin, Leonard. *Of Mice and Magic: A History of American Animated Cartoon* (New York: New American Library, 1987).

Meisel, Myrion. "Buying and Booking Guide" in *The Film Journal* 88.8 (August 1, 1985), 15.

Mendlesohn, Farah. *Rhetorics of Fantasy* (Middletown, CT: Wesleyan University Press).

Moen, Kristian. *Film and Fairy Tales: The Birth of Modern Fantasy* (London: I.B. Tauris, 2013).

Pallant, Chris. "Disney-Formalism: Rethinking 'Classic Disney'" in *Animation: An Interdisciplinary Journal* 5 (3), 341–352.

Pallant, Chris. *Demystifying Disney: A History of Disney Feature Animation* (London: Bloomsbury, 2013).

Rebeaux, Max. "Animation brings the Magic of Sword and Sorcery to Life", *Cinefantastique*, July 1985, 15.

Schlobin, Roger C. *The Literature of Fantasy* (New York: Garland Publishing Inc, 1979), 260.

Tolkien, J.R.R. "On Fairy Stories" in C. S. Lewis (Editor), *Essays Presented to Charles Williams* (Oxford: Oxford University Press, 1947), 38–89.

Tymn, Marshall B., Kenneth J. Zahorski, and Robert H. Boyer. *Fantasy Literature: A Core Collection and Reference Guide* (New York: R.R. Bowker Company, 1979).

Warner, Marina. *From the Beast to the Blonde: On Fairy Tales and their Tellers* (London: Chatto & Windus, 1994).

Wasko, Janet. *Understanding Disney: The Manufacture of Fantasy* (Polity Press: Cambridge, 2001).

Zahorski Kenneth J., and Robert H. Boyer. "The Secondary Worlds of High Fantasy", in Roger C. Schlobin (Editor), *The Aesthetics of Fantasy Literature and Art* (Notre Dame, IN: University of Notre Dame Press, 1982), 56–81.

Zipes, Jack. *The Oxford Companion to Fairy Tales* (Oxford: University Press, 2000).

Endnotes

1. "1985 Domestic Grosses", BoxOfficeMojo.com, accessed June 7, 2015. http://www.boxofficemojo.com/yearly/chart/?yr=1985.

2. Simon Braund, "Ask the Boss" *Empire*, August 2011, 112.

3. Michael Eisner with Tony Schwartz, *Work in Progress* (London: Penguin Books, 1998), 172.

4. Eleanor Byrne and Martin McQuillan, *Deconstructing Disney* (London: Pluto Press, 1999), 27.

5. Chris Pallant, *Demystifying Disney: A History of Disney Feature Animation* (London: Bloomsbury, 2013), 71.

6. Sean Griffin, *Tinker Belles and Evil Queens: The Walt Disney Company from the Inside Out* (New York: New York University Press, 2000), 103.

7. Janet Wasko, *Understanding Disney: The Manufacture of Fantasy* (Polity Press: Cambridge, 2001), 28.

8. Wasko, 112.

9. Chris Pallant, "Disney-Formalism: Rethinking 'Classic Disney'" in *Animation: An Interdisciplinary Journal* 5 (3), 342.

10. Pallant, "Disney-Formalism", 343.

11. *Variety*, July 24, 1985, 16.

12. Walter Goodman, "Screen: Disney's Black Cauldron", *New York Times*, Jul 26, 1985, c5.

13. See Christopher Holliday, "Let it go? Towards a "plasmatic" perspective on Digital Disney" contained in this collection.

14. Jack Zipes, *The Oxford Companion to Fairy Tales* (Oxford: University Press, 2000), 131.

15. Robin Allan, *Walt Disney and Europe: European Influences on the Animated Feature Films of Walt Disney* (London: John Libbey & Company, Ltd: 1999), 16.

16. Allan, 25.

17. Marina Warner, *From the Beast to the Blonde: On Fairy Tales and their Tellers* (London: Chatto & Windus, 1994), 23.

18. Zipes, xviii.

19. Zipes, xvii.

20. For a more extensive account of these developments in the literary fantasy genre, see Maria Nikolajeva, "The Development of Children's Fantasy", in Edward James and Farah Mendlesohn (Editors), *The Cambridge Companion to Fantasy Literature* (Cambridge: Cambridge University Press, 2012), 50–61.

21. Brian Attebery, *The Fantasy Tradition in American Literature* (Bloomington, IN: Indiana University Press, 1980), 84.

22. Cited in Attebery, 94.

23. Paul Kincaid, "American Fantasy 1820–1950", in Edward James and Farah Mendlesohn (Editors), *The Cambridge Companion to Fantasy Literature* (Cambridge: Cambridge University Press, 2012), 46.

24. Marshall B. Tymn, Kenneth J. Zahorski, and Robert H. Boyer, *Fantasy Literature: A Core Collection and Reference Guide* (New York: R.R. Bowker Company, 1979), 5.

25. Bosley Crowther, "The Screen in Review: Disney's Cartoon Adaptation of 'Alice in Wonderland' Arives at Crierion" *New York Times* (July 30, 1951), 12.

26. "Walt Disney's Alice in Wonderland", *Box Office* 58.12 (January 20, 1951), a29; "Walt Disney's Alice in Wonderland" *Variety* (Jan 3, 1951), 38.

27. Roger C. Schlobin, *The Literature of Fantasy* (New York: Garland Publishing Inc, 1979), 260.

28. *Hollywood Reporter* (2 October 1963), 3.

29. *Variety* (October 2 1963), 6.

30. Kristian Moen, *Film and Fairy Tales: The Birth of Modern Fantasy* (London: I.B. Tauris, 2013), 181.

31. Farah Mendlesohn, *Rhetorics of Fantasy* (Middletown, CT: Wesleyan University Press), 1.

32. Mendlesohn, 1.

33. Mendlesohn, 2.

34. Kenneth J. Zahorski and Robert H. Boyer, "The Secondary Worlds of High Fantasy", in Roger C. Schlobin (Editor), *The Aesthetics of Fantasy Literature and Art* (Notre Dame, IN: University of Notre Dame Press, 1982), 57.

35. Leonard Maltin, *Of Mice and Magic: A History of American Animated Cartoon* (New York: New American Library, 1987), 79.

36. Maltin, 80.

37. Joe Adamson, "What's Cooking in The Black Cauldron", *American Cinematographer* 66:7 (July 1985), 60–68.

38. Adamson, 60.

39. Max Rebeaux, "Animation brings the Magic of Sword and Sorcery to Life", *Cinefantastique*, July 1985, 15.

40. John Culhane, "Ralph Bakshi – Iconoclast of Animation", *New York Times*, March 22, 1981, D13.

41. "Ralph Bakshi will Visit NYC to Plug 'Wizards'", *Boxoffice*, April 11, 1977, E2.

42. "Bluth Completes Cartoon Feature", *Variety* (May 19, 1982), 34; Paul Wells, *Understanding Animation* (Abingdon, Oxon: Routledge, 1998), 25.

43. "Stateside: 'NIMH' nearly ready", *Screen International* 328 (January 30, 1982), 6.

44. "Film review: The Secret of NIMH". *Variety* (June 16, 1982), 14.

45. J.R.R. Tolkien, "On Fairy Stories" in *Essays Presented to Charles Williams* (Oxford: Oxford University Press, 1947), 60.

46. Tolkien, 60.

47. *Monthly Film Bulletin* (October 1985), 305–306.

48. Rebeaux, 15.

49. Dennis Fischer, "The Black Cauldron" in *Hollywood Reporter*, July 1985, 3, 18.

50. Myrion Meisel, "Buying and Booking Guide" in *The Film Journal* 88.8 (August 1, 1985), 15.

51. Meisel, 15.

52. Wasko, 32–36; Pallant, *Demystifying Disney*, 89.

53. Allan, 254–255.

II.
Inside the Studio

'That Corner of the Disney Studios that is Forever England': Disney's Vision of the British Family

Noel Brown

Between 1950 and 1979, Disney filmed fifteen of its live-action productions in Britain, initially as a means of reinvesting capital frozen in the UK due to trade restrictions implemented by the post-war Labour government aimed at stimulating local industry. Early films of this type, such as *The Story of Robin Hood and his Merrie Men* (Ken Annakin, 1952) and *Rob Roy, the Highland Rogue* (Harold French, 1953), were comparatively straightforward adventure stories, privileging rugged individualism within a pastoral setting.[1] Disney's British films of the 1960s and 1970s were altogether different, bringing home and family to the forefront of their fictional representations. This chapter focuses specifically on four of Disney's live-action films of the 1960s and 1970s which centre on the British family unit: *Greyfriars Bobby* (Don Chaffey, 1961), *Mary Poppins* (Robert Stevenson, 1964), *Bedknobs and Broomsticks* (Stevenson, 1971), and *Candleshoe* (Norman Tokar, 1977). These films are nostalgic period pieces in which the family is seen to be in jeopardy, before finally and triumphantly being reconstructed in the final act.[2] Each film has at its heart a central dynamic in which a failing and incomplete family is healed and completed by the interventions of an outsider. In *Greyfriars Bobby*, it is the legendary dog, said to have spent 14 years by the Edinburgh graveside of its deceased owner; in *Mary Poppins*, it is Julie Andrews' 'practically perfect' eponymous nanny; in *Bedknobs and Broomsticks*, it is the reformed gentleman shyster Emelius Browne (David Tomlinson); and in *Candleshoe*, it is Jodie Foster's teenage delinquent from Los Angeles, transposed to an archetypal English manor house.

Disney's live-action films have long held a lowly standing, at least when compared with the reception of the studio's animated features, with all their stunning graphic richness and narrative potentialities. Michael Barrier observes that, during the 1950s, 'scorn for Disney's live-action films was a reflex among most critics, and for good reason', and thus Walt Disney 'was not taken seriously as a live-action filmmaker, in Hollywood or elsewhere'.[3] Even more damningly, Richard Schickel later suggested that 'there is really little point in discussing these movies critically'.[4] These sentiments doubtless reflect the films' believed disposability, but are surprising in light of the fact that, between 1953 and 1968, Disney released only five animated features, but more than 50 live-action films. Live-action, in other words, moved to the forefront of Disney's filmic operations. Many of these productions, admittedly, are modest and more overtly child-orientated than Disney's animated films, but they are far from the wholly-superficial exploitation releases they are widely perceived to be. Indeed, as this chapter will argue, Disney's British films reflect deeply-felt contemporary anxieties in the United States concerning social fragmentation and perceived threats to the long-term survival of the family unit. Through their period milieus, they resurrect a lapsed sense of community and family consensus which would have appeared incongruous in films set in present-day America.

In these films, Britain becomes more of a metaphor than a tangible physical location. It embodies an abstract set of 'family values' that were seen by conservative and reactionary factions to be endangered by a multitude of social changes, including spiralling divorce rates, sexual egalitarianism, the civil rights movement, liberalising attitudes towards homosexuals, the rise of counter-cultural 'youth culture' and, more generally, the perceived weakening of the patriarchal hegemony. Britain here represents concepts of civility, gentility and stability, all within a comfortingly familiar social framework which celebrated the sanctity of family and upheld its putative function as a socialising apparatus. Such representations are not to be taken literally, but rather operate on the utopian level; it matters little, within the context in which they were produced and received, that the Victorian and Edwardian families so many of these films resurrect had never existed in the first place. Via their hopeful visions, they posit a means through which contemporary families can withstand the fragmentary forces of late modernity. Central to such representations is Britain's unique relationship with North America, which simultaneously bespeaks distance and familiarity. While acknowledging shared structures, traditions, and belief systems between the two nations, the films also establish a governing dialectic, an informing relationship, between British antiquity and an unseen, but persistently implied, contemporary America. Britain is seen as a progenitive influence, rather than a contemporary equivalent. As such, there is little interest in the socio-cultural or political specificities of modern Britain beyond their nostalgic invocations.

This chapter's title quotation, taken from a 1971 *Monthly Film Bulletin* review of *Bedknobs and Broomsticks*, recognises the centrality of representations of Britain and 'Britishness' in Disney films of the period.[5] While this chapter focuses on Disney's live-action British films, the studio's fixation with Britishness was also strongly apparent in its contemporaneous animated features, especially *Alice in Wonderland* (Clyde Geronimi et al., 1951), *Peter Pan* (Geronimi et al., 1953), *101 Dalmatians* (Geronimi et al., 1961), *The Jungle Book* (Wolfgang Reitherman et al., 1967), and *Robin Hood* (Reitherman et al., 1973). Paul Wells has argued that Disney's fixation with Britain reflected its need to recover its floundering reputation with recourse to the 'literary' (i.e., 'quality') tradition following its postwar fallow period, and underpinned the studio's 'detachment' from its 'own artistic credo and aspiration, and the socio-cultural context in which it was produced'.[6] In other words, Wells regards the prominence of the British milieu partly as an artistic strategy designed to imbue the resulting films with prestige, and partly as a withdrawal from, or even a disconnection with, the period's dominant socio-political concerns. This chapter, however, advances a rather different viewpoint, arguing that the recurrence of Britishness in these films – particularly in relation to the British family – in fact carries powerful ideological resonances.

Victorian and Edwardian British families are a frequent presence in Disney's 1960s and 1970s live-action films. In both Britain and the US, as Neil Smelser has argued, 'the Victorian family persists as a kind of ghostly model' which continues, more than a century since its heyday, to represent 'Victorian stability, solidarity and serenity'.[7] Although, as Smelser observes, 'there were not one but many types of Victorian family' and thus the image is largely illusory, the inherited prototype – what Ann Oakley later termed the 'conventional family' – comprises parents and children residing together in a single-family household.[8] This remained the preferred family type in 1960s and 1970s North America, when the supposed solidarity of the 1950s nuclear family began to give way under the strain of serially rising divorce rates, the rise of the career woman, and a creeping ethos of individualism among the Baby Boom generation, which promoted individual happiness (in whatever form) over that of the collective well-being of the family unit.[9] As Stephanie Coontz has shown, residual associations of the 1950s as a period of stability and family unity is more imagined than real.[10] Nonetheless, it is tangibly felt in this cycle of films, in which the North American nuclear family and the British Victorian family are routinely conflated.

The four films discussed in this chapter, far more being politically withdrawn or ideologically displaced, are intrinsically reflexive. Each identifies problems in society and in the family in microcosm, that an enlightened or inspirational outsider must resolve; each reasserts the nurturing, protective qualities of the literal or symbolic family; and each places emphasis on young children and mature adults, marginalising or altogether dispensing with older teenagers and young adults. In *Greyfriars Bobby*, an animal film adapted from Eleanor Atkinson's supposedly true-life 1912 story of a Skye terrier reputed to have spent fourteen years at the graveside of his deceased owner, the central animal succeeds in galvanising a fractious community in which small decencies and kindnesses have given way to a selfish individualism. Vulnerable members of society, such as Bobby's elderly and penurious owner, Auld Jock (Alex Mackenzie), a homeless and otherwise-unloved man who dies of pneumonia, slip through society's net. In *Mary Poppins*, a similar lack of cohesion is localised in the family unit itself, which is reunified through the interventions of Julie Andrews' titular nanny. Both films identify a problem in the functioning of society (the family and the community being vital mechanisms of socialisation), and over the courses of their narratives undertake to repair it. But as with Dickens's *A Christmas Carol* (1843), change comes not from within, but rather is imposed through magical intervention.

It cannot be coincidence that in both the 1960s films, *Greyfriars Bobby* and *Mary Poppins*, the agent of change is a being of almost transcendent perfection. The legendary animal and the 'practically perfect' nanny are both capable of gaining the trust of children and melting the hearts of adults. Bobby inspires goodness through unwitting example; Mary is a more explicitly didactic figure who provides moral guidance, but the end result is the same: in galvanising a new generation of young citizens, they point the way to an imagined better future. In both films, people need merely to be set back on the right path. Even very sympathetic characters, such as *Greyfriars Bobby*'s kindly restaurateur Mr. Traill (Laurence Naismith), who feeds groups of orphan children in his restaurant, maintains a facade of unfeelingness, as when he sternly rebukes Auld Jock for praising his hospitality after feeding and housing the sick old man. Individuals like the same film's stiff, dour cemetery warden James Brown (Donald Crisp) and *Mary Poppins*' seemingly-tyrannical bank owner Mr. Dawes, Sr. (Dick Van Dyke) are not innately malign or callous, but rather have lost touch with the vital spark of life, deadened by years of grind. The ancient Mr. Dawes, Sr. is so happily reawakened from his decades-long slumber by an amusing joke that he literally laughs himself to death. *Greyfriars Bobby* also ends with uplifting scenes of friendship, reconciliation and inclusiveness, with the formerly taciturn Mr. Brown inviting Mr. Traill into his house for a drink; a chorus of benevolent child and adult voices, intoning 'Goodnight, Bobby', then fade into the music as the dog takes its customary place on the mound above Auld Jock's grave.

Similarly, the children in *Greyfriars Bobby* graduate to a more 'traditional' eschewal of self, instead embracing an idealised sense of community spirit.

As Douglas Brode has argued, there is an idealistic, almost Capraesque populist agenda in the sequences where the poor, orphaned children gather money from the local community to pay for a licence for the stray dog, Bobby.[11] Such selfless acts hopefully posit an alternative manifesto for self-obsessed, individualistic contemporary youth. This was a period in which the 'teenager' was still viewed widely as a potential menace. As Thomas Hine suggests, 'America created the teenager in its own image – brash, unfinished, ebullient, idealistic, crude, energetic, innocent, greedy, changing in all sorts of unsettling ways'.[12] Mistrust of the teenager and of incipient 'youth culture' was partly a holdover from the 1950s US national obsession with juvenile delinquency, which prompted (and was, in turn, exacerbated by) Estes Kefauver's notorious Senate Committee Investigation into juvenile delinquency. Youth culture's most visible manifestations (e.g. teen exploitation films, rock 'n' roll, street gangs, anti-authoritarianism, and substance abuse) were unsettling to what remained a largely conservative society. Disney, no doubt fearful of risking its well-established reputation as a promoter of goodness, order, wholesomeness – in short, the ideological status quo – largely avoided older teenagers, both as a representational figure and as a potential audience base.[13] As a result, children in these films attain greater symbolic force, invested with Romantic child connotations of innocence and goodness, as well as potential for hope and liberation, looking towards an imagined utopian future. The reform of their elders – Scrooge-like adults such as James Brown and Mr. Dawes, Sr. – perhaps constitutes a reminder to adult spectators that the world is still theirs (though it will not be for much longer), and that there is time to change, or rather to regress, to a more 'innocent' and open-hearted acceptance of the world-at-large.

Greyfriars Bobby is by far the most child-orientated of the four films. While noting 'qualities of exact period detail and childlike directness', the *Monthly Film Bulletin* ultimately regarded the film as little more than 'an engaging display of canine charm for children and susceptible adults'.[14] Subsequently, Disney's British films move away from its largely symbolic (if powerfully felt) family relations to a more literal focus on the nuclear family unit, and, related, to a more adult-orientated mode of audience address. As noted above, until *Candleshoe*, which rather belatedly attempts to tap the youth-orientated zeitgeist by casting teenager Jodie Foster in the central role, unwholesome teenagers and young adults are entirely absent. Parents and children viewing together are clearly these films' primary intended audiences, as with other middlebrow Hollywood family musicals of the 1960s, such as *The Sound of Music* (Robert Wise, 1965). Indeed, contemporary responses in the United States highlighted *Mary Poppins*' ability to transcend the largely juvenile appeal of Disney's earlier live-action releases. US trade paper *Boxoffice* praised its 'appeal to audiences of all ages', and this view was shared by members of the National Screen Council – a loose conglomerations of critics, exhibitors, and civic representations assembled by the publication – who variously proclaimed it as 'wonderful fun for the whole family', 'a wonderful classic handled with perfect care' and 'a delicious treat'.[15]

Tellingly, though, another respondent (obviously an exhibitor) noted its strong 'adult' appeal: 'I get the most favourable comments on "Mary Poppins" from fathers! That should make Mr. Disney happy – he's made a man's picture![16] The *New York Times'* registered a similarly powerful attraction to nostalgic adults in *Candleshoe*:

> The chords it sounds, with its evocation of a world of stately homes, formal gardens, family heirlooms, titled women, eccentric ancestors, perfect servants, tea parties, steam engines and classic motorcars can resonate with an older generation in a way they never can among children whose cultural touchstones are more likely to run the gamut from Big Bird to The Hulk to John Travolta and the Bee Gees [...] Kids, take grandma.[17]

But these genteel archaic trappings, pleasantly evocative though they are, are little more than semantic texture. Far more central to their adult appeal are their representations of family and community.

Mary Poppins is such a landmark film that it would seem like dogged literal-mindedness to omit it from consideration on the basis that it was made entirely in the United States. Prior to Warner Bros.' *Harry Potter* film series (2001–11), it was comfortably the most popular 'British' children's film ever in terms of overall attendances, drawing around 14 million UK admissions, placing it at 25th in the BFI's 2004 list of the 100 top films at the British box office. But while it is directed by a British man, adapted from a British novel, mostly populated by British actors, and set in London, it is a peculiarly American fantasy. As a British journalist observed at the time of release, P. L. Travers's five Mary Poppins novels had been 'greeted with rapture by the Americans', but 'the British seem scarcely aware that she exists'.[18] Nor was the film especially well received in Britain upon initial release. *The Times* was not unrepresentative in its verdict that it possessed 'just about everything you could ask for to make up a splendid Christmas entertainment' 'except charm', and in its criticism of the film's uncomfortable line 'between realism and stylisation'.[19] Certainly, the film's reputation in Britain has risen enormously in the intervening years, and its iconic status in the US is beyond doubt. *Mary Poppins* was the sixth highest-grossing film of the decade in North America; it won five Oscars; it was selected for preservation by the National Film Registry in 2013; and it has generated a Disney live-action blockbuster, *Saving Mr. Banks* (John Lee Hancock, 2013), based on the making of the film, and a sequel, *Mary Poppins Returns* (2018).[20]

The film centres on the efforts of a magical nanny, the eponymous Mary Poppins, to repair a malfunctioning Edwardian British family in which the father, Mr. Banks (David Tomlinson), is preoccupied with work, Mrs.

Banks (Glynis Johns) is equally focused on her efforts as a 'suffragette', and the children, Jane (Karen Dotrice) and Michael (Matthew Garber), are lonely and misbehaving. Revealingly, the central family unit is structurally nuclear (the 'typical' family household in 1960s North America) rather than extended (as was more usual in Britain until around 1950).[21] *Mary Poppins* says less about the socio-historical conditions of early twentieth-century Britain than about the dominant national concerns of 1960s North America – principally, the perceived decline of the family, the transition from a middle-class, adult-orientated culture to a seemingly more liberal, youth-dominated one, the middlebrow establishment's response to the counter-cultural movement, and the inexorable rise of symbolic 'others': working women, racial minorities, blue-collar workers, and out (as opposed to closeted) homosexuals.[22] In the midst of what Maurice Isserman and Michael Kazin have described as a second American civil war, the 1960s were marked by a number of political and cultural oppositions, in which 'many Americans came to regard groups of fellow countrymen as enemies with whom they were engaged in a struggle for the nation's very soul'.[23] *Mary Poppins*, interestingly, reasserts the primacy of the white, middle-class, God-fearing nuclear family. In the process, it eradicates all traces of liberalising change, either through non-representation, or, as in proto-feminist Mrs. Banks's case, deconstructive lampooning. Even the filmic form itself, which revives the 1940s Hollywood family musical (see particularly Vincente Minnelli's *Meet Me in St. Louis*, 1944), harks back to older, increasingly old-fashioned, narrative and stylistic patterns.

The linkages between Edwardian Britain and the United States of the 1960s are strengthened by the curious figure of Mary's friend, the chimney sweep Bert (Dick Van Dyke). Early in the film, Bert, in musical portent of Mary's arrival to heal the Banks family, sings:

> Wind's in the east, mist's coming in,
> Like something is brewin', about to begin –
> Can't put my finger on what lies in store,
> But I feel what's to happen [He smiles] all happened before.

The verse adopts a fairy tale-like narrative framing mechanism, akin to 'once upon a time'. Do these words imply that the nature of family transcends changing historical circumstances and cultural norms? This is the first of several instances where Bert is privy to knowledge and insight denied to the film's other characters. Later, he impresses upon Mr. Banks the evanescence of childhood, his sombre tone (and North American cadences, despite the actor's floundering attempts at a Cockney accent) suggesting sentiments relayed back from an age of relative enlightenment. Bert, then – paradoxically – operates as a representative of the film's contemporary (mid-1960s) audience, while retaining an ability to pass in the Edwardian society the film looks to with hopeful nostalgia.

In many ways, the stern, business-like Mr. Banks is heir to domineering, but ultimately sympathetic, classical-era Hollywood family comedy *patres familias* such as *Meet Me in St. Louis*'s Mr. Smith (Leon Ames) and Clarence Day (William Powell) from *Life with Father* (Michael Curtiz, 1947). But whereas those fathers only *appear* tyrannical and consumed by bureaucracy, Mr. Banks really is. His newspaper advert for a nanny demands 'a general [...] who can give commands', and he reproves the children for their own version of the notice, which requests a nanny with 'a cheery disposition', never 'cross or cruel', who will 'love us as a son and daughter'. While the classical-era Hollywood patriarchs were moderated by the presence of level-headed matriarchs who appeared to defer to their husband's authority as putative head of the family, but actually ruled the roost, Mrs. Banks is the polar opposite: seemingly independent and ambitious, but in reality weak-willed, becoming tearful when chastised by her husband, and displaying scant emotional affinity with her children or aptitude in the daily practicalities of mothering. 'Suffragette' Mrs. Banks sings with certitude that 'our daughters' daughters will adore us' for her reformist efforts, yet she is almost as bad as her husband in neglecting the needs of her family by pursuing her own pet cause. The 1940s/50s films had presented audiences with nostalgic images of 'how we used to be', or, more aptly, 'how we *wish we were*'. *Mary Poppins* has a more active agenda: not just showing images of the past for pleasure, but demonstrating how its true and authentic virtues – discipline, education, reciprocity, community spirit – remain relevant.

Throughout, Mary is a locus of precision and order, though of a different kind to the joyless regimen Mr. Banks embodies. She disapproves of the undisciplined, contagious laughter and play of Bert's Uncle Albert (Ed Wynn), who spends his days in ceaseless levity literally floating helplessly in his house, consumed by bouts of convulsive hysterics. Although she reluctantly indulges Uncle Albert, she cautions Jane and Michael against such self-indulgence, which unproductively takes play to the nth degree. But Mary does recognise the importance of play, within certain parameters, as when she treats the children, and Bert, to a tour around a magical animated landscape (the trippiest and most colourful segment in the film). Later the same evening, however, when the children excitedly recall the adventure, she denies all knowledge of it; such play must carefully be regulated, lest it get out of control to the exclusion of all else, as it does with Uncle Albert – the antithesis of the stern, humourless, Mr. Banks. A more desirable state resides somewhere between these two extremes, maintaining Mr. Banks' professionalism while borrowing something of Albert's carefree levity. In juxtaposing Mr. Banks' climactic celebration of childish play with news of his instatement as an executive board member at the bank, the film's ending makes clear that the balance has correctly been struck, ensuring that his newfound ability to access such a condition does not overwhelm his ability to earn a wage and govern his family. Nor, by implication, does it overtake the necessary sobriety of society-at-large (as Plato and Aristotle cautioned against while condemning the unrestrained laughter of the buffoon).

The role of the gently-manipulative matriarch is assumed by Mary herself. Disturbed at frivolous talk of day-trips and subversive lingual tongue-twisters like 'Supercalifragilisticexpialidocious' – Mary's word for when you 'can't think what to say' – Mr. Banks attempts to dismiss her with common-sensical appeals to efficiency and sobriety. However, Mary outmanoeuvres him by voicing her intention to take the children to his bank the following day, so that they may appreciate the value of stocks and shares and learn the philosophy of acquisitiveness. Far too literal-minded to realise that his arguments have been turned against him, Mr. Banks agrees to what he assumes was his idea in the first place. Mary transforms the family through good example, with qualities Bruce Babington sees as embodied more generally by Andrews' filmic persona: 'teacherly, gentle, solicitous, candid, occasionally commanding'.[24] To these may be added her virtues of neatness and order, precision in action, gesture and enunciation, calmness, gentility and etiquette. What elevates Mary from mere pomposity and didacticism is her magical abilities. While her own persona never deviates from the immutable characteristics listed above, she nonetheless allows immersion into a magical 'other world' of manifold possibilities beyond the hermetic one inhabited by Mr. Banks. Intrinsically, Mary represents conservative values of order and stability, but through her magical abilities, she assumes the broader associations of freedom and imagination her pristine, conservative facade apparently repudiates.

One might cynically suggest that *Bedknobs and Broomsticks* is little more than a thinly-veiled imitation of *Mary Poppins*. Roy Disney had intimated as much shortly after Walt's death in 1966, when he voiced his intention to release 'at least one *Mary Poppins* every year'.[25] Though that policy quickly stalled, the two films share their writer-producer (Bill Walsh), director (Robert Stevenson), composer (Irwin Kostal), songwriters (the Sherman Brothers), some of the cast (David Tomlinson, Reginald Owen) and many of the same technicians; Julie Andrews was offered, but rejected, the central role. In fact, Disney had purchased the film rights to Mary Norton's *The Magic Bed-Knob* (1943) shortly after publication, as far back as 1945, and the film was due to enter production in 1966, less than two years after the release of *Mary Poppins*.[26] However, Walt Disney was wary of the films' possible over-similarity, and suspended the project. When production eventually recommenced in 1970, Hollywood's cycle of nostalgic family musicals had passed its box office sell-by-date. The direct resemblances to *Mary Poppins*, which Walt had resisted, were positively embraced under Roy's auspices – an early sign of the excessive parodic sensibilities that bedevilled the final films in Disney's British cycle. Although it was moderately popular in Britain, *Bedknobs and Broomsticks* failed in the US, where it was described in *Time* as 'ersatz Poppins', and by the *New York Times* as probably 'something of a long, uninterrupted sit for the very children for whom it's intended, and an even longer one for those parents and guardians (both adults and teenage) who will probably accompany them'.[27]

Questions of relative artistic worth aside, the differences between *Mary Poppins* and *Bedknobs and Broomsticks* are largely cosmetic. The earlier film's evocation of Edwardian London is advanced to England's south coast at the onset of the Second World War. As with *Mary Poppins*, the central thematic is the (re)construction of a happy, functioning nuclear family. In *Mary Poppins*, this family is already complete, but in *Bedknobs and Broomsticks* an entirely new, surrogate family is composed from three separate sources: the eccentric spinster and white witch, Eglantine (Angela Lansbury); the individualistic conman, Emelius; and orphaned children Charlie (Ian Weighill), Carrie (Cindy O'Callahan) and Paul (Roy Snart), evacuated from war-torn London. The joining together of these disparate factions appears unlikely, given Eglantine's stated aversion to children, Emelius's inability to live by established norms of conduct, and the children's clearly work-ing-class origins. Ultimately, it is war, and the threat of the home invaded and possibly destroyed by a seemingly overwhelming enemy, that forces the family together, just as Mary Poppins provides the impetus in the earlier film. Although Eglantine comes to regard the children as her adopted offspring, the family is shown to be complete only after Emelius returns to the fold in fulfilment of his masculine/paternal responsibilities, having previously refused the children's request to stay and 'be our dad'.

All four films in this study seem determined to prove that warmth, happiness and optimism still have a place in modern society, in spite of the tiresome refrain – much alluded to in journalistic accounts of contemporary society – that we live in an age of harsh cynicism and moral ambiguity. *Bedknobs and Broomsticks*'s musical number, 'The Age of Not Believing', sung by Lansbury, ostensibly addresses the modern, maturing child's inability to dream and imagine:

> When your rush around in hopeless circles,
> Searching everywhere for something true,
> You're at the age of not believing
> When all the 'make believe' is through.

> When you set aside your childhood heroes
> And your dreams are lost up on a shelf
> You're at the age of not believing,
> And worst of all, you doubt yourself.

> You're a castaway where no-one hears you, on a barren isle in a lonely sea –
> Where did all the happy endings go? Where can all the good times be!

You must face the age of not believing,
Doubting everything you ever knew,
Until at last you start believing
There's something wonderful in you!

The film can be seen to extend these sentiments to contemporary society and culture as a whole. Lionel Jeffries's adaptation of E. Nesbit's *The Railway Children*, released a year earlier, articulates many of the same concerns, but aims for documentary-style realism. *Bedknobs and Broomsticks*, by contrast, cannot resist self-reflexively drawing attention to its ideological agenda, making obvious the allegorical function previously only implicit. Furthermore, in the final line's idealistic reassertion of the 'child within the adult' – the adult's ability to access, at will, childlike associations of innocence, imagination and optimism – the film disavows the possibility that the complex and often traumatic processes of 'growing up' might lead to a permanent repudiation of 'childish things'.

Candleshoe, rather than occluding the contemporary realities of growing up, attempts to engage with them and, in the process, negotiate their rough terrain and render them safe. An opening, ten-minute prologue filmed on the streets of Los Angeles introduces us to the streetwise, cynical, self-confessed 'delinquent' Casey (Jodie Foster). With her gang of street urchin friends, she steals food, deliberately provokes a rival gang by pilfering their basketball, evades police patrols and generally causes minor mayhem for her own amusement. Foster's persona is only slightly softened from the teenage New York prostitute she had recently inhabited in *Taxi Driver* (Martin Scorsese, 1976). In both films, she possesses an innate affinity with the depraved city streets and paralysing inability to understand the wider world beyond its confines. She is also an orphan; her foster parents, for whom she steals in order to pay her way, sell her to the mercenary Bundage (Leo McKern), who recruits her in his scheme to swindle a wealthy dowager, Lady St. Edmund (Helen Hayes), owner of the British manor house, Candleshoe, out of her presumed fortune. Casey, it transpires, bears a striking resemblance to Lady St. Edmund's missing granddaughter (and heiress), and she willingly agrees to inveigle her way into the household in return for a share of the proceeds. Foster displays the same appealing juxtaposition of knowingness and vulnerability as in the far more adult-orientated *Taxi Driver*. This combination allows her to perceive, and comment upon, the disparity between the bewildering and uncompromising world of the modern metropolis and the gentility and kinship and family ties characterising the timeless Englishness of Candleshoe.

In Casey, then, the film presents powerful symbols of modernity and modern youth in their least desirable forms. The following exchange between her and Lady St. Edmund is revealing:

Lady St. Edmund: I don't suppose your experience of family life has been a happy one.

Casey: What family life? I'll tell you, the only thing I remember about family life is nothing. Zero. From one foster dump to another. I mean, who really cares about a kid you take in for the welfare money and food stamps? I mean, who really cares? It's a racket, just like everything else. The whole world's a racket. First thing I ever learned. Get up out of bed in the morning with your dukes up, you know? Got 'em up, first punch is yours.

Lady St. Edmund: I see ...

Casey: Yeah, well ... Maybe you do, and maybe you don't.

Lady St. Edmund: But you can't go through life alone.

Casey: I ain't alone. I got me. Listen, if you don't hand it out, you don't have to worry about not getting it back.

Prior to her inevitable transformation at the end of the film, Casey embodies individualism, aggression, cynicism, selfishness, and disregard for friendship, family, and law and order. These undesirable aspects are incongruous because her outward appearance is one of childlike innocence, allowing the film to present the familiar image of youth corrupted by modern vices. Where *Candleshoe* obviously breaks from the cynical, often nihilistic representations of childhood depicted in the likes of *Paper Moon* (Peter Bogdanovich, 1973) and *Taxi Driver* is that Casey is given an opportunity for redemption.

In shifting from Los Angeles to rural England, Casey crosses time zones in more ways than one. Although ostensibly the film is set in the present-day, Candleshoe and its estate appear devoid of the accessories of modern living. The vintage car is just about the only concession to industrialisation, and televisions and modern everyday appliances that may disrupt the antiquarian veneer are missing altogether. In the film's final scene, after Casey's duplicity has been exposed but her allegiance confirmed when she helps her adopted family repel Bundage, Lady St. Edmund elects to accept her as her missing granddaughter after all. Like the borderline criminal Emelius in *Bedknobs and Broomsticks*, Casey brings certain skills that the rather staid, conventional British family lacks, as in the scene where her streetwise hustling allows the family butler, Priory (David Niven), and Lady St. Edmund's adopted orphaned children, to sell far more food at the local street market.

The film's other major concession to modernity is the acknowledgement that 'family' need not be supported by rigid class distinctions or lineage. For all his servitude, Priory is clearly the *paterfamilias*, and the local children Lady St. Edmund takes into the household are her surrogate grandchildren

– and, by the end of the film, Casey's adopted siblings. The film acknowledges that the old certainties of family and community have been disrupted by changing priorities and belief-systems, specifically the role played by divorce, loosening kinship ties (evident in Casey's and the British children's statuses as orphans) and the surging 1970s ethos of individualism.[28] But family may endure in different forms, with the mutual love and support offered by Candleshoe's residents superseding old definitions based on blood ties or class and racial distinctions. The working-class Priory, the oriental British adoptee Anna (Sarah Tamakuni), and the rough-edged American street urchin Casey are all happily and successfully integrated in a new kind of family structure. The film, in its rather artless and idealistic way, seems to assert modern Western society's need to adopt new family structures if the institution is to survive the uncertainties and divisiveness of the new age. Indeed, as Robert and Rhona Rapoport argued in 1982, with sentiments equally applicable to contemporary North America, 'families in Britain today are in a transition from coping in a society in which there was a single overriding norm of what family life should be like to a society in which a plurality of norms are recognised as legitimate and, indeed, desirable'.[29] This new, multiply-sourced family may not offer the same symmetry in form, continuity between the generations or nostalgia for old behavioural patterns, but it does involve much of the same stability.

Youth-dominated mass audiences were not much interested in representations of family, British or otherwise. *Candleshoe* was only the 15th most profitable film of 1978 at the British box office.[30] Ironically, in fixating on the British family unit, Disney had alienated the commercial 'family' market. Spielberg's *Close Encounters of the Third Kind* (1977) ends with its protagonist leaving his family behind in the name of personal fulfilment, while *Star Wars* and *Superman* (Richard Donner, 1978) – the other dominant family blockbusters of the period – deal with family only tangentially. One might argue that such films, through their undeniable affirmations of friendship and fidelity, involve an even broader definition of family than the one advanced in *Candleshoe*. Besides, as *Close Encounters* reveals, by this point there was a growing acceptance that family could be equally stultifying and inhibiting to personal growth and expression (or even function as a locus of madness, as R. D. Laing posited).[31] Disney's ethos could never permit such a disruptive viewpoint to take hold in its own productions, but the decade's most popular family-life films were cynical and adult-orientated, and avowedly true to life, as witness the likes of *Paper Moon* and *The Godfather* (Francis Ford Coppola, 1972). The vulnerable elderliness of Helen Hayes and David Niven in *Candleshoe* might tacitly acknowledge that the older generation, who had provided a solid bedrock, and for whom the family was sacrosanct, has almost had its time. By the time of Spielberg's *E.T. The Extra-Terrestrial* (1982), Oakley's 'conventional family' is broken, struggling on against the odds, bound together by mutual dependency but shattered by the absence of the adulterous father and by the still-present mother evidently on the verge of psychological breakdown. There is no happy reconciliation or lasting magical intervention. E.T. departs, and although Elliot promises to keep him in his heart, the same cannot be seen as definite for the other members of this beleaguered family.

While Disney's preoccupation with representations of Britishness reveals a complex interplay of commerce and ideology, ultimately these films always carried a strong economic underpinning. The relative underperformance of Disney's 1970s British productions – which also included *Diamonds on Wheels* (Jerome Courtland, 1973), *One of Our Dinosaurs is Missing* (Stevenson, 1975), *Escape From the Dark* (Charles Jarrott, 1976) and *Unidentified Flying Oddball* (Russ Mayberry, 1979) – signalled the end of the British cycle. As Wells argues, ultimately the English milieu 'worked as a distanciation from the cultural destabilisation that escalated in the United States'.[32] Such films had entered into too great a conflict with lived experience, and with the new Hollywood family entertainment paradigm. The *Monthly Film Bulletin*'s review of *Escape from the Dark* reveals impatience with its ideological conservatism, criticising the film's 'circumscribed world' in which 'the values of the hierarchical family where father knows best' is persistently 'defended'.[33] Such films, particularly for leftist observers, were altogether harder to stomach in an era of progressive sexual egalitarianism. For other critics, and presumably audiences as well, the objection was more to the films' entertainment value. Ian Christie's witheringly dismissive review of *Candleshoe* in British tabloid the *Daily Express* asserted that Disney films 'featuring human beings [i.e. live-action productions] are the cinematic equivalent of the processed food industry, bland, hygienically wrapped and predictable', caustically adding that 'I'm sure children will love it – as they would a plate of deep-frozen chips'.[34] As these less-than-complimentary responses indicate, the time for such nostalgic, adult-inflected constructions of Britishness had – apparently – passed.

Bibliography

Babington, Bruce. 'Song, Narrative and the Mother's Voice: A Deepish Reading of Julie Andrews' in Bruce Babington, ed., *British Stars and Stardom: From Alma Taylor to Sean Connery* (Manchester: Manchester University Press, 2001): 192–204.

Barrier, Michael. *The Animated Man: A Life of Walt Disney* (Berkeley and Los Angeles: University of California Press, 2007).

Brode, Douglas. *From Walt to Woodstock: How Disney Created the Counterculture* (Austin: University of Texas Press, 2004).

Brown, Noel. *The Hollywood Family Film: A History, from Shirley Temple to Harry Potter* (London and New York: I.B. Tauris, 2012).

Brown, Noel. *British Children's Cinema: from The Thief of Bagdad to Wallace and Gromit* (London and New York: I.B. Tauris, 2016).

Canby, Vincent. 'Angela Lansbury in "Bedknobs and Broomsticks"', *The New York Times*, 12 November 1971; http://www.nytimes.com/movie/review?res=9503E2DB1038EF34BC4A52DFB767838A669EDE.

Christie, Ian. 'The Kind Con', *The Daily Express*, 11 February 1978, 8.

Combs, Richard. 'Bedknobs and Broomsticks', *Monthly Film Bulletin*, November 1971: 216.

Coontz, Stephanie. *The Way We Never Were: American Families and the Nostalgia Trap* (New York: Basic Books, 1992).

Finler, Joel W. *The Hollywood Story* (London: Octopus Books, 1988).

Hart, Denis. 'P is for Poppins', *The Guardian*, 3 June 1963: 5.

Hine, Thomas. *The Rise and Fall of the American Teenager* (New York: Avon Books, 1997).

Jones, Landon Y. *Great Expectations: America and the Baby Boom Generation* (New York: Coward, McCann & Geoghagan, 1980).

Nissel, Muriel. 'Families and Social Chance Since the Second World War' in Robert N. Rapoport et al., *Families in Britain*: 95–119 (p. 118).

Isserman, Maurice, and Michael Kazin, *America Divided: The Civil War of the 1960s* (Oxford and New York: Oxford University Press, 2000).

Oakley, Ann. 'Conventional Families' in Robert N. Rapoport et al (Eds.), *Families in Britain* (London: Routledge and Kegan Paul, 1982): 123–137.

Pym, John. 'Escape from the Dark', *Monthly Film Bulletin*, June 1976: 123.

Rapoport, Robert and Rhona. 'British Families in Transition' in Robert N. Rapoport et al, *Families in Britain* (London: Routledge and Kegan Paul, 1982): 475–499.

Schickel, Richard. *The Disney Version* (Chicago: Elephant Paperback, 1997 [1968]).

Smelser, Neil. 'The Victorian Family' in Robert N. Rapoport et al (Eds.), *Families in Britain* (London: Routledge and Kegan Paul, 1982): 59–74.

Smith, Justin. 'Cinema Statistics, Box Office and Related Data' in Sue Harper and Justin Smith, eds., *British Film Culture in the 1970s: The Boundaries of Pleasure* (Edinburgh: Edinburgh University Press, 2012): 261–274.

Sykes, Velma West. 'Walt Disney's "Mary Poppins" Wins Nov. Blue Ribbon Award', *Boxoffice*, 14 December 1964: 13.

Van Gelder, Lawrence. 'Disney for the Older Set: Dickensian Disney', *The New York Times*, 4 August 1978; http://www.nytimes.com/movie/review?res=9D0DE5DC1F3EE432A25757C0A96E9C946990D6CF.

Wells, Paul. *Animation and America* (Edinburgh: Edinburgh University Press, 2002).

Filmography

Greyfriars Bobby (Don Chaffey, Director), 1961.

Mary Poppins (Robert Stevenson, Director), 1964.

Bedknobs and Broomsticks (Robert Stevenson, Director), 1971.

Candleshoe (Norman Tokar, Director), 1977.

Endnotes

1. For more on Disney's early British films, see Noel Brown, 'Disney in Britain' in *British Children's Cinema: From The Thief of Bagdad to Wallace and Gromit* (London and New York: I.B. Tauris, 2016).

2. Though *Candleshoe* is not a period piece as such, the English setting and characters it depicts lack a degree of modernity in comparison with Casey (played by Jodie Foster) and her 'American-ness'. This will be discussed later in the chapter.

3. Michael Barrier, *The Animated Man: A Life of Walt Disney* (Berkeley and Los Angeles: University of California Press, 2007): 282.

4. Richard Schickel, *The Disney Version* (Chicago: Elephant Paperback, 1997 [1968]): 299.

5. Richard Combs, 'Bedknobs and Broomsticks', *Monthly Film Bulletin*, November 1971: 216.

6. Paul Wells, *Animation and America* (Edinburgh: Edinburgh University Press, 2002): 128.

7. Neil Smelser, 'The Victorian Family' in Robert N. Rapoport et al (Eds.), *Families in Britain* (London: Routledge and Kegan Paul, 1982): 59–74 (p. 59).

8. Smelser, 60; Ann Oakley, 'Conventional Families' in Robert N. Rapoport et al, *Families in Britain*: 123–137.

9. Landon Y. Jones, *Great Expectations: America and the Baby Boom Generation* (New York: Coward, McCann & Geoghagan, 1980): 212.

10. Stephanie Coontz, *The Way We Never Were: American Families and the Nostalgia Trap* (New York: Basic Books, 1992).

11. Douglas Brode, *From Walt to Woodstock: How Disney Created the Counterculture* (Austin: University of Texas Press, 2004): 195–196.

12. Thomas Hine, *The Rise and Fall of the American Teenager* (New York: Avon Books, 1997): 10.

13. Occasional exceptions, such as Fritz (Tommy Kirk) and Ernst (James MacArthur) from *Swiss Family Robinson*, are conventionally rendered as largely angst-free growing children, rather than as potentially disruptive teenagers negotiating an often fraught passage from childhood to adulthood. The protagonist's 'rebellion' in *Johnny Tremain* (Robert Stevenson, 1957) is a distant and ideologically legitimate historical event (i.e. the American Revolution) which upholds American values of heroism and individualism, in contrast to the threatening associations of contemporary youth during the 1950s and 1960s as conveyed in *Rebel Without a Cause* (Nicholas Ray, 1955) and similar films.

14. 'Entertainment Films', *Monthly Film Bulletin*, July 1961: 98.

15. Velma West Sykes, 'Walt Disney's "Mary Poppins" Wins Nov. Blue Ribbon Award', *Boxoffice*, 14 December 1964: 13.

16. Sykes: 13.

17. Lawrence Van Gelder, 'Disney for the Older Set: Dickensian Disney', *The New York Times*, 4 August 1978;http://www.nytimes.com/movie/review?res=9D0DE5DC1F3EE432A25757C0 A96E9C946990D6CF.

18. Denis Hart, 'P is for Poppins', *The Guardian*, 3 June 1963: 5.

19. 'Wonder-Working Nanny Transformed', *The Times*, 17 December 1964: 14.

20. Joel W. Finler, *The Hollywood Story* (London: Octopus Books, 1988): 277.

21. Muriel Nissel, 'Families and Social Chance Since the Second World War' in Robert N. Rapoport et al., *Families in Britain*: 95–119 (p. 118).

22. See Noel Brown, *The Hollywood Family Film: A History, from Shirley Temple to Harry Potter* (London and New York: I.B. Tauris, 2012): 117–124.

23. Maurice Isserman and Michael Kazin, *America Divided: The Civil War of the 1960s* (Oxford and New York: Oxford University Press, 2000): 3–4.

24. Bruce Babington, 'Song, Narrative and the Mother's Voice: A Deepish Reading of Julie Andrews' in Bruce Babington, ed., *British Stars and Stardom: From Alma Taylor to Sean Connery* (Manchester: Manchester University Press, 2001): 192–204.

25.   Schickel: 304.

26.   *Variety*, 9 August 1945: 13.

27.   Vincent Canby, 'Angela Lansbury in "Bedknobs and Broomsticks"', *The New York Times*, 12 November 1971; http://www.nytimes.com/movie/review?res=9503E2DB1038EF34BC4A52 DFB767838A669EDE.

28.   See Tom Wolfe, 'The "Me Decade" and the Third Great Awakening', *New York*, 23 August 1976: unpaginated.

29.   Robert and Rhona Rapoport, 'British Families in Transition' in Robert N. Rapoport et al, *Families in Britain*: 475–499 (p. 476).

30.   Justin Smith, 'Cinema Statistics, Box Office and Related Data' in Sue Harper and Justin Smith, eds., *British Film Culture in the 1970s: The Boundaries of Pleasure* (Edinburgh: Edinburgh University Press, 2012): 261–274. While, at first glance, this is a more-than-respectable result, it was unusually low for Disney films of the period. Furthermore, like other late-1970s live-action Disney films, *Candleshoe* was comprehensively out-performed at the box office by *Star Wars*, *Close Encounters of the Third Kind* and *Superman*, and also grossed less than the low-budget British fantasy film, *Warlords of Atlantis* (Kevin Connor, 1978).

31.   R. D. Laing, *Sanity, Madness and the Family* (London: Tavistock, 1964).

32.   Wells: 128.

33.   John Pym, 'Escape from the Dark', *Monthly Film Bulletin*, June 1976: 123.

34.   Ian Christie, 'The Kind Con', *The Daily Express*, 11 February 1978, 8.

Chapter 5

Fix it Felix! Reviving Walt Disney Animation Using the Pixar Formula

Helen Haswell

Since the 1980s, a number of global media corporations have assimilated all of the key Hollywood studios: Warner Bros., Paramount, 20th Century Fox, Columbia and Universal are among the studios now owned by conglomerates.[1] In fact, The Walt Disney Studios is the 'only major studio to avoid acquisition by a conglomerate', a feat it seems to have managed by becoming one itself.[2] The Walt Disney Company, henceforth shortened to Disney, operates within four business segments: Media Networks, Parks and Resorts, Studio Entertainment, and Consumer Products and Interactive Media.[3] By the end of the 2016 financial year, Disney reported a revenue figure of $55.632 billion with the following break-down: Media Networks $23.689 billion (43%); Parks and Resorts $16.974 billion (30%); Studio Entertainment $9.441 billion (17%); and Consumer Products and Interactive Media $5.528 billion (10%).[4] The company operates television networks ABC, ESPN and Disney Channels Worldwide; owns several theme parks and additional holiday resorts globally; publishes books; and designs, makes, and sells a wide range of consumer products every year. Within the company's Studio Entertainment, or The Walt Disney Studios division, Disney manages seven film production companies for live-action, animation, and nature documentaries; a film distribution company; three record labels; and three theatre production companies. The most recent additions to this division are Marvel Studios, acquired in 2009 for $4 billion, and Lucasfilm, purchased for $4.05 billion in 2012. Disney has reportedly spent over $18 billion on acquisitions since 2005, which have '... delivered north of $12 billion in shareholder value to date'.[5] The purchase of Marvel in particular has proven highly lucrative for Disney: *Guardians of the Galaxy* (2014) made over $774 million worldwide, and, *Avengers: Age of Ultron* (2015) grossed over $1.4 billion worldwide.[6] These franchises, coupled with the wildly-successful *Star Wars: The Force Awakens* (2015), as well as its subsequent spin-off and sequel films, and merchandizing, have cemented Disney as one of the most recognisable media conglomerates in the world.

But what of Disney's own brand? Established in 1923 as the Disney Brothers Studio, the company has its origins in animated film and is arguably most associated with animation (and, arguably, theme parks). Disney Animation is said by some to have reached its peak in the early 1990s during a period that is commonly referred to as Disney's Renaissance, a period that reflects the 'aesthetic and industrial growth at the Studio'.[7] However, from the early 2000s onwards, Disney Animation suffered significant losses from films that underperformed at the box office and furthermore, films that received generally negative critical reviews. Meanwhile, in 1995, Pixar Animation Studios released *Toy Story* (1995), the world's first fully computer-animated feature film. The film was a phenomenal success both critically and commercially, a trend that has continued with subsequent feature films produced by the studio. Pixar soon became the number one trusted brand for family entertainment, a title once held by Disney. In 2005, Disney's own market research confirmed that mothers with children under the age of 12 generally rated Pixar's brand higher than Disney's.[8] In 2006, Disney purchased Pixar for $7.4 billion, a deal which proved invaluable to the rejuvenation of Disney's floundering animation department. Under the guidance of Pixar's John Lasseter and Ed Catmull, Disney Animation has found a new lease of life, evidenced by the commercial and critical success of the studio's subsequent feature films, *The Princess and the Frog* (2009), *Tangled* (2010), *Wreck-it Ralph* (2012), *Frozen* (2013), *Big Hero 6* (2014), *Zootopia* (2016), and *Moana* (2016). It can be argued, in light of this, that Walt Disney Animation Studios has entered a new era, termed here as "the Post-Pixar Period".

Disney and Pixar

The relationship between Disney and Pixar pre-dates the 2006 acquisition by more than fifteen years and has been well-documented by Karen Paik in *To Infinity and Beyond!: The Story of Pixar Animation Studios* (2007), David Price's *The Pixar Touch: The Making of a Company* (2009), and Ed Catmull's *Creativity Inc.: Overcoming the Unseen Forces That Stand in the Way of True Inspiration* (2014). These key texts offer an insight into the history and development of Pixar and the studio's long-standing relationship with Disney. Therefore, the following is a brief overview of the relationship between the two studios in order to contextualise the significance and impact upon Disney Animation by the acquisition of Pixar.

In the late 1970s, Ed Catmull and Alvy Ray Smith were hired by George Lucas to run the Computer Division of Lucasfilm. Here, they developed the Pixar Image Computer for the purpose of designing graphics. In 1982, the small group worked with Lucas' visual effects company, Industrial Light & Magic, to create special effects for *Star Trek II: The Wrath of Khan* (1982) and *Young Sherlock Holmes* (1985). In 1986, Steve Jobs purchased the rights to this technology from Lucas for $5 million and invested another $5 million into the now independent computer graphics company, renamed Pixar. Initially a hardware company, Pixar developed the Pixar Image Computer (PIC), which was purchased by Walt Disney Animation in the late 1980s to convert the studio's ink and paint process from 2D to digital. The technique was first applied to the final scene of *The Little Mermaid* (1989) and was used fully for the first time on *The Rescuers Down Under* (1990). Moreover, the Pixar-produced Computer Animation Production System software (CAPS) enabled Disney animators to combine hand-drawn characters on a CGI background, affording artists the ability to effortlessly manipulate the 3D space, altering depth, colour and shading. The ballroom scene from *Beauty and the Beast* (1991) is one of the better-known examples of the application of this technique. The short sequence demonstrates the freedom of the sweeping 'camera', which parallels the choreography of Belle and the Beast's waltz. The film went on to make $425 million in worldwide box office figures and received numerous awards, including the Golden Globe for Best Motion Picture.[9] In 1992, it became the first animated feature to be nominated for the Academy Award for Best Picture.

Although supplying software for Disney's award-winning films was generating income, Pixar's long-term objective was to create a feature-length computer animated film. In July 1991, following months of negotiations, Disney and Pixar finally signed an agreement that stated Disney would finance the development, production, and distribution of Pixar's first feature film. As David Price explains, 'the terms of the thirteen-page contract were lopsided enough that unless the film were a hit on the level of *The Little Mermaid*, Pixar's earnings from it would be insignificant'.[10] *Toy Story* premiered at the El Capitan Theatre in Los Angeles on 19 November 1995. Following its general release on 22 November, the film was met with an enthusiastic reception. *Variety* called it a 'clever mix of simplicity and sophistication that cuts across all age barriers with essential themes',[11] and *The New York Times* described the film as a 'parent-tickling delight [a] work of incredible cleverness'.[12] *Toy Story* went on to gross $362 million worldwide and was nominated for three Academy Awards, two Golden Globes, and one BAFTA.[13] John Lasseter was honoured with the Special Achievement Academy Award in 1996 for his contribution to creating the first feature-length computer-animated film. However, due to the prominent Disney branding, many reviewers 'credited the film to Disney ... with no reference to Pixar.'[14] In 1997, following *Toy Story*'s phenomenal and unprecedented success, Pixar renegotiated the terms of their contract, agreeing that Disney would support five more original films from the studio over a ten-year period. The new contract dictated that the two companies would 'equally share the costs, profits and logo credit'.[15] Furthermore, the profit-sharing arrangement exceeded box-office revenue to include the sale of related consumer products.

By 2004, Pixar had completed and successfully released three of the five original feature films stipulated in the studio's contract with Disney. The second theatrical release by the studio, *A Bug's Life* (1998), marginally exceeded *Toy Story*'s takings, grossing $363 million worldwide.[16] Yet, *Variety* stated the film surpassed its predecessor in 'both scope and complexity of movement',[17] while *The New York Times* commended the film for its '... jaunty, imaginative use of both extraordinary technology and bold story-telling possibilities within the insect world'.[18] During negotiations for the 1997 contract between Disney and Pixar, the former was explicit that Pixar produce five original features, not sequels, 'thus assuring five sets of new characters for its theme parks and merchandise'.[19] Therefore, *Toy Story 2* (1999) was initially produced as a direct-to-video release. However, fears that the subpar narrative and less than favourable reception towards Disney's previous direct-to-video releases would damage Pixar's budding reputation, the studio re-wrote and re-pitched the film for theatrical release. *Toy Story 2* debuted on 13 November 1999 and was met with an enthusiastic reception, with many fans and reviewers gushing that the sequel was even better than the original. *Variety* said the film was a 'richer, more satisfying film in every respect',[20] and *The Guardian* proclaimed '*Toy Story 2* is not a sequel. It is an upgrade. It is a manufacturer's improvement of staggering ingenuity.'[21] The film grossed $497 million globally.[22] By the time Pixar released its fourth feature film, *Monsters, Inc.* (2001), develop-ments in animation technology pioneered by the studio had not gone unnoticed. Many reviewers noted the realism of Sulley's fur in *Monsters, Inc.*, though *Sight and Sound* stated 'it is the film's careful attention to narrative and characterisation that pulls us in, not the beautifully rendered visuals'.[23] Another box office hit, *Monsters, Inc.* earned $577 million world-wide.[24] Finally, *Finding Nemo* (2003), the third original feature film released as part of the 1997 agreement with Disney, was described as a '... buoyant adventure that entertainingly continues the Disney/Pixar winning streak'.[25] After five enormously-successful films, the studio was once again met with critical praise. Roger Ebert stated:

> *Finding Nemo* has all of the usual pleasures of the Pixar animation style – the comedy and wackiness of *Toy Story* or *Monsters, Inc.* or *A Bug's Life*. And it adds unexpected beauty, a use of color and form that makes it one of those rare movies where I wanted to sit in the front row and let the images wash out to the edges of my field of vision.[26]

The film earned an impressive $940 million globally, becoming one of the highest-grossing animated films of all time.[27] Pixar had clearly proven its worth and attempted to renegotiate their contract terms to be more favourable to the growing studio. During this same period, however, Disney had released a number of animated features that suffered a generally negative reception both critically and commercially. The Neo-Disney Period, as termed by Chris Pallant, describes a '... phase of feature animation [that] diverged both artistically and narratologically, from the style traditionally associated with the Studio'.[28] This period, which runs from 1999–2004, includes Disney films *Fantasia 2000* (1999), *The Emperor's New Groove* (2000), *Atlantis: The Lost Empire* (2001), *Lilo and Stitch* (2002), *Treasure Planet* (2002), *Brother Bear* (2003), and *Home on the Range* (2004). These seven films grossed a combined box office total of $1.1 billion globally, just $160 million more than *Finding Nemo* earned on its own.[29] That is to say, excluding *The Emperor's New Groove*, which made $169 million worldwide, the combined box office takings of the remaining six films during this period was less than Pixar's *Finding Nemo*.[30] Furthermore, the general critical response to these films did not reach the lofty heights of Disney's Renaissance Era. *Atlantis: The Lost Empire, Treasure Planet, Brother Bear* and *Home on the Range* obtained approval ratings of 25% to 56% from top critics on review aggregator Rotten Tomatoes.[31] *Home on the Range* in particular suffered by comparison. *Screen Daily* stated, 'the comedy is fun and the music has its moments, but by Disney standards *Home on the Range* is a lightweight animated offering, with little emotional pull exerted by the studio's best work'.[32] In his review of the film, Roger Ebert said:

> A movie like this is fun for kids: bright, quick-paced, with broad, outrageous characters. But *Home on the Range* doesn't have the crossover quality of the great Disney films like *Beauty and the Beast* and *The Lion King* ... Its real future, I suspect, lies in home video.[33]

The growing success of Pixar's computer-generated feature films during this period arguably displaced hand-drawn traditions within mainstream American animation.[34] In 2004, DreamWorks Animation disbanded its hand-drawn animation department to focus on CG animation, producing a number of successful films including *Shrek* (2001), *Madagascar* (2005), *Kung Fu Panda* (2008), and *How to Train Your Dragon* (2010). Subsequent animation studios such as Blue Sky Studios, which made *Ice Age* (2002) and its sequels, were set up and geared specifically towards CG animation. Following the lacklustre response to the Neo-Disney Period films, Disney too retooled its hand-drawn animation department to focus entirely on digital animation. *Chicken Little* (2005), Disney's first fully computer-animated film, and *Meet the Robinsons* (2007), were once again met with unfavourable reviews, reflected by approval scores of 29% and 50% by top critics on Rotten Tomatoes.[35] *The Guardian* described *Chicken Little* as 'underpowered and dull, even for kids',[36] and *The New York Times* called it a '... hectic, uninspired pastiche of catch phrases and clichés'.[37] Two years later, *The New York Times* reviewed *Meet the Robinsons* as '... one of the worst theatrically released animated features issued under the Disney label in quite some time',[38] while *Time Out* said '... the plot fractures, the pace goes into overdrive and the jokes wear thin'.[39] Nevertheless, *Chicken Little* grossed $314 million worldwide, a significant improvement on the previous year's release, *Home on the Range*, which took just $104 million globally.[40] *Meet the Robinsons* however, received $169 million worldwide.[41]

In 2004, after a very public falling out, Pixar CEO Steve Jobs halted contract discussions with Disney's then chairman and CEO Michael Eisner and announced that Pixar would not be renewing its contract with Disney. The same year, Eisner suffered '... the highest no-confidence vote ever against a chief executive of a major company'.[42] In 2005, Eisner was removed as CEO and replaced with Robert Iger, who immediately approached Steve Jobs with the possibility of a Disney-Pixar merge. On 24 January 2006, Disney announced that it had '... agreed to acquire Pixar for 287.5 million shares of Disney stock, then worth roughly $7.4 billion'.[43] As chief executive of Pixar, Jobs became a member of the board of directors of The Walt Disney Company, while Catmull and Lasseter became President and Chief Creative Officer of both Pixar and Disney Animation Studios respectively.

Disney Animation and the Post-Pixar Period

When Robert Iger took over as CEO, he outlined three clear priorities for The Walt Disney Company: international expansion, technological innovation and a renewed focus on animation. In his 2006 letter to shareholders, Iger reiterated the importance of the acquisition of Pixar and the future of Disney Animation:

> Synonymous with the Disney name is creative strength, and this year we made a tremendous move to build upon that great tradition with the acquisition of another globally recognised powerhouse of creativity and technology, Pixar Animation Studios. Pixar's unprecedented string of hits ... can be attributed to its incredible artistic talent and spirit of innovation. [So] with this important acquisition, we further our commitment to outstanding animation, embracing our heritage and securing our legacy for the future.[44]

However, following the acquisition of Pixar there was speculation that Disney Animation would be shut down, or that Disney would focus solely on hand-drawn animation while Pixar continued to deliver ground breaking CG animation. Key to the acquisition and to the success of both studios was the decision to keep Disney and Pixar completely separate. Therefore, when Catmull and Lasseter assumed their new positions at Disney Animation, their goal was to '... remould Disney into a filmmakers' studio, with an emphasis on perfection', just as Pixar had been predicated.[45] In his 2014 book *Creativity Inc.*, Catmull outlines the changes he and Lasseter made at Disney Animation following the acquisition. Firstly, they shut down Circle 7 Animation, a subdivision of Disney Animation that had been set up in 2005 with the sole purpose of making sequels to Pixar's films, without Pixar's input. Another course of action was to rehire recently dismissed Disney staff, including long-time directors John Musker and Ron Clements. They retooled Disney's hand-drawn animation department in order to '… revive the art form the studio was built on', which had been dissolved following the release of *Home on the Range* in 2004.[46] Although production on *Bolt* (2008) was already underway by the time Catmull and Lasseter took over at Disney, their input notably changed the direction of the narrative. The film, which centres on the eponymous character, a dog who believes his fictional life as a superhero in a television show is real, at one stage included a '… radioactive, cookie-selling Girl Scout zombie serial killer'.[47] During the months following the acquisition, Catmull and Lasseter established the Disney Story Trust. Based on the model of Pixar's Braintrust, the meetings allow the opportunity to discuss, troubleshoot, and screen sequences from current projects. Over a course of a number of these meetings the film, originally known as *American Dog*, was discarded and rewritten as *Bolt*, without the zombie serial killer.[48] The film received a largely positive response, grossing $310 million worldwide, signalling the start of Disney Animation's regeneration.[49] Critical responses to the film, too, were better than any animated film released by the studio in years. *Time Out* said of Disney's first animated film under the guidance of Lasseter, *Bolt* '… is a likeable, dynamic and seductively characterised family entertainment'.[50] *The Washington Post* commented that although the film '… falls short of Pixar's lofty heights … *Bolt* is the most entertaining and well-crafted Disney Animation movie in years'.[51]

Since the acquisition, Disney Animation has also experienced success with its short film programme, introduced by Lasseter to '… rejuvenate the studio's pigeonholed animators, [bringing] a level of creativity back to a studio which, until recently, had been driven by profit margins'.[52] A Pixar tradition since the theatrical release of *Geri's Game* (1997), which played before *A Bug's Life*, the studio prides itself on its short films, primarily established for the purposes of research and development.[53] The initiative encouraged Disney Animation to develop its own technology, resulting in the development of a 2D/CG hybrid, demonstrated in the studio's short films *Paperman* (2012), *Get a Horse!* (2013), and *Feast* (2014). These films express the new identity of the filmmaker-led studio established by Catmull and Lasseter. In fact, the short films are a way of articulating the personality of each studio without the pressure to create something for commercial profit. They are likewise a platform for experimenting with ideas and techniques, and developing in-house talent. This last use of short subjects had been something Disney animation had embraced throughout the 1930s in its *Silly Symphonies* series (1929–1939), but over time the use of shorts at Disney for training and experimentation had been lost for decades. The long history of short films created by Pixar since *The Adventures of André and Wally B.* (1984) tracks the development and progression of computer-generated animation, establishing Pixar as the pioneers of this technology, which is intrinsic to the identity of the studio. The latest shorts produced by Disney Animation re-establishes the studio as forerunners in the development of cutting edge technology, once a priority for Walt Disney himself.[54] *Paperman*, released theatrically with *Wreck-it Ralph*, uses the Disney-developed programme Meander, a '… hybrid vector/raster-based drawing and animation system that gives artists an interactive way to craft the film' that combines hand-drawn animation with computer-generated images.[55] The approach differentiates Disney from Pixar by paralleling the traditions of the studio and suggesting a future for Disney Animation. Similarly, *Get a Horse!*, which screened before *Frozen*, intentionally draws attention to the differences and contrasts between the two styles by recreating the look of first a black and white early 1930s Mickey Mouse cartoon, then a mid- to late-1930s colour Mickey Mouse cartoon, which is cleverly and comically juxtaposed with 3D renderings of the main characters. The studio's most recent short, *Feast*, which accompanied *Big Hero 6* in cinemas, introduces a more painterly approach unlike anything previously accomplished by CG. The film '… explores aggressive stylization, minimizing the exterior line and steeping itself in the possibilities of color, shape, and form … this film is concept art come to life'.[56] *Get a Horse!* was nominated for the Academy Award for Best Animated Short in 2014, and *Paperman* and *Feast* won the award in 2013 and 2015 respectively.

The Princess and the Frog is significant as the first film released by Disney that was completed from start to finish under the studio's new leadership. The film therefore signals the beginning of Disney Animation's Post-Pixar Period, which continues with *Tangled, Wreck-it Ralph*, *Frozen*, *Big Hero 6*, *Zootopia*, and *Moana*. *The Princess and the Frog* reintroduces hand-drawn animation and features Disney's first African-American princess as the protagonist. The film received a generally positive critical response which mainly focussed on the return to traditional animation methods and the portrayal of princess Tiana. Writing for *The Guardian*, Catherine Shoard notes the ways in which the film really pushes boundaries:

> Disney [has] done something much more interesting than making Tiana black, or hand-drawn, or even a career woman. They've created a heroine who's an actual character; a woman whose three dimensions you don't need to don daft specs to see.[57]

Given past criticisms of Disney's promotion of submissive and romantically-driven female characters, this comment is a clear triumph for the studio. It is noteworthy that this observation follows the first Disney animated film released under the guidance of Catmull and Lasseter. Although commended as a progressive, ground-breaking studio, Pixar has not escaped criticisms concerning its lack of female protagonists: out of the eighteen feature films released by the studio at the time of publication of this chapter, only two – *Brave* (2013) and *Inside Out* (2015) centre upon female characters.[58] While the studio generally writes strong and varied females, they generally appear as secondary to male characters as either the carers or love interests of the featured male characters; in Dory's depiction in the eponymous *Finding Dory*, one could argue that we even get the female character positioned as a relatively traditional Damsel in Distress (albeit a forgetful fish damsel) who must be saved by the film's true main character, Marlin.[59] *Brave* was commended for its presentation of the feisty princess Merida and for subverting traditional fairy tale norms, as she neither ends up married nor in love. However, criticisms surrounding her royal background seemed to suggest and support the notion that female-centred stories can only exist in fairy tales. Nevertheless, the positive critical response to *The Princess and the Frog* continued with *Empire* stating the film was "exactly as good as Musker and Clements' earlier efforts [and] a return to the form of Disney's early 1990s classics".[60] *The Times* claimed that *The Princess and the Frog* is "the closest yet that Disney's traditional 2D animation has come to threatening the supremacy of the computer-generated Pixar-style tales".[61] Here, we begin to see a clear shift in the way critics are talking about the two animation studios. During the height of Pixar's success, the studio was commonly referred to as "the New Disney", replacing Disney as the leading animation studio. Now, as the renewed Disney Animation begins gaining traction, the studio starts to be referred to as "the New Pixar". This is not only reflected by the success of Disney's animated features, but also the recognised fallibility of Pixar, suggested through criticisms of the studio's apparent "gender problem" and other issues surrounding the impact of Disney's acquisition of it upon Pixar, which will be discussed later. Regardless, the comment that Disney Animation is "threatening the supremacy" of Pixar seems somewhat ironic given that Lasseter is credited as executive producer on *The Princess and the Frog*. What these critical responses to the film clearly highlight is that, after years of uncertainty, Disney Animation has experienced a sudden moment of rebirth paralleling that of the studio's Renaissance Period. This positive response to Disney's revival continues with the subsequent features released by the studio.

During the years immediately following its acquisition of Pixar, Disney released a further two titles that concern princess or fairy tale narratives. Although the aforementioned *The Princess and the Frog* was received well by critics, the film grossed a somewhat lacklustre $267 million globally, slightly less than *Bolt's* $310 million box office takings, but an improvement on the reception to the studio's pre-acquisition films.[62] This slight dip in box office figures has been attributed to the marketing decisions made at the time. As Catmull explains:

> Leading up to the release of *The Princess and the Frog*, we'd had many conversations about what to call it. For a while we considered the title "The Frog Princess", but Disney's marketing folks warned us: Having the word *princess* in the title would lead movie-goers to think that the film was for girls only. We pushed back, believing that the quality of the film would trump that association and lure viewers of all ages, male and female.[63]

With the word "princess" in the title and predominant princess and fairy tale imagery in the posters and trailers for the film, *The Princess and the Frog* does seem to have suffered somewhat from apparent misdirected marketing. The trailer states, "after 75 years of magic Walt Disney Studios brings a classic tale to life ... in the tradition of Disney's most beloved classics", drawing direct parallels with *Aladdin* (1992), *Beauty and the Beast*, *The Little Mermaid* and *The Lion King* (1994). The trailer situates this film with some of Disney's most successful and highly-rated animated features, making assumptions about the film's impending reception. It also makes specific reference to the fact that this is Disney's first 2 D animated feature in five years. Clearly, the title was problematic in the marketing of this film and also misleading. Although the film is loosely-based on the fairy tale *The Frog King* published by the Brothers Grimm, the narrative plays with fairy tale conventions by making Tiana career driven and uninterested in a romantic conclusion. Furthermore, she becomes a princess only at the end of the film when she marries her frog prince, Naveen. As stipulated by the spell, Naveen must kiss a princess to break the curse that turned them both into frogs. After they are married (while they are still frogs) Tiana becomes a princess, and the spell is broken when they share their first kiss. The film concludes with their transformation back into humans, and Tiana fulfils her dreams by opening a restaurant. The marketing choices for this film determined the decisions made for Disney, and Pixar's, subsequent princess films.

In order to move away from the "princess curse", Disney and Pixar instead opted for more gender-neutral adjectives for the titles of the fairy tale films that followed: *Tangled*, *Brave*, and *Frozen*. Disney Animation's 50th feature film, *Tangled*, is a retelling of the story of Rapunzel. Although the film centres on the coming-of-age of Rapunzel, a trailer for the film focuses almost predominantly on the film's male character, Flynn Rider, implying that he is the film's protagonist. The trailer downplays the role of Rapunzel; in fact, the clip is almost over before she appears. A title in the trailer states, "it takes two to get tangled", indicating that the film concerns two main protagonists, yet Rapunzel hardly features in the trailer. Arguably, down-playing the princess and fairy tale narrative improved *Tangled*'s chances of reaching a wider audience. Once again, Disney's latest animated feature received a positive critical and commercial response, becoming the studio's first number one hit in 16 years. The film received $591 million in worldwide box office revenue and received a nomination for Best Original Song at the 2011 Academy Awards.[64] Moreover, *Screen Daily* stated the film was "an appropriately commingled sense of classic sentimentality and contemporary, gender-equal romance and adventure" and that the film "underscores the still existent pleasures of traditional storytelling".[65]

Released in 2012, *Wreck-it Ralph* is the third film made by Disney Animation during this post-acquisition period. The film centres on the eponymous character in an 8-bit arcade game called *Fix-it Felix Jr.* Having played the "bad guy" for thirty years (and being treated as such by the film's other characters during their "off" hours when the arcade is closed for the night), Ralph decides to abandon his game in search of a medal, believing this will make him a hero. The promotional materials for the film give a sense of nostalgia for the analogue, while demonstrating the most advanced digital technology that was used to create the film. This is something that features in many Pixar films, particularly recent short films *La Luna* (2011) and *Day & Night* (2010), where they demonstrate combined techniques or use CGI to emulate hand-drawn art.[66] *Wreck-It Ralph* performed well at the box office, grossing $471 million worldwide and receiving a generally positive critical response.[67] As mentioned previously, there is a clear shift in the way Pixar and Disney are referred to in critical responses to the two studios' outputs following the acquisition. In particular, the influences of Pixar on Disney's films are commonly referenced up to and including responses to *Wreck-it Ralph*, Disney's first post-acquisition venture into non-fairy tale territory. For example, *The List* states, "this cleverly targeted family romp marks a step up both commercially and artistically for the non-Pixar side of Disney's animation offering",[68] while reviews in *Empire* and *The New York Times* make several references to *Toy Story*.[69] The film was nominated for an Academy Award for Best Animated Film, but lost out to Pixar's *Brave*. The sudden resurgence of Disney Animation has clearly not gone unnoticed, yet the general response up to this point was that the studio's success is the result of the company's purchase of Pixar. While the films have improved substantially, both critically and commercially on Disney's pre-acquisition releases, they still do not quite match up to Pixar's "supremacy". However, Disney's next theatrical release would prove to be a game changer.

Disney premiered *Frozen* on 19 November 2013 at the El Capitan Theatre in Hollywood. Although the film received initial lukewarm responses from critics, the film went on to become an unprecedented success following its general release in the United States on 27 November 2013. To date, the film has grossed over $1.2 billion worldwide, replacing *Toy Story 3* (2010) as the most successful animated film of all time.[70] The film has won numerous awards, including the 2014 Academy Award for Best Animated Film and Best Original Song. It has produced a multi-platinum soundtrack album, sold millions of DVDs, and is an online phenomenon, generating billions of YouTube hits and thousands of fan tributes. Set in the fictional Scandinavian kingdom of Arendelle, *Frozen* is a retelling of Hans Christian Andersen's fairy tale *The Snow Queen*, familiar territory for the studio that has been reimagining traditional stories since *Snow White and the Seven Dwarfs* (1937). The film centres on princesses Elsa and Anna and is a coming-of-age story about the relationship between two sisters. Having learned valuable lessons in marketing on *The Princess and the Frog* and *Tangled*, the teaser trailer, trailer, and posters for the film downplays the female-centred narrative by featuring the film's male counterparts, Kristoff and Hans, as well as its sidekicks, the reindeer, Sven, and Olaf the talking snowman. The trailer is especially misleading over the position of the two female characters, suggesting that there are a number of potential heroes: titles throughout the trailer state, "who will save the day: the ice guy; the nice guy; the snow man; or, no man?" However, the fact that *Frozen* has continued to be a phenomenal worldwide success long after the film has ended its run in cinemas is testament to the film as a whole, rather than the marketing strategies prior to the film's release. The experience and lessons learned on *The Princess and the Frog*, *Tangled* and *Wreck-it Ralph*, as well as the decisions made throughout by Disney's leadership team and directors, culminates with the success of *Frozen*. This includes the progressive narrative, the redefinition of fairy tale tropes, and unconventional characters that were experimented with for the previous two Disney princess films. As *The New York Times* reiterates:

> They are significant departures from tradition in a film that shakes up the hyper-romantic "princess" formula that has stood Disney in good stead for decades and that has grown stale. Treacly, kissy-kissy endings are not enough anymore. Nowadays, a princess has to show her mettle and earn her happily-ever-after stripes.[71]

The film has been seminal to the successful revival of Disney Animation and symbolises the positive impact of the Disney-Pixar merge for Disney. The unprecedented success of *Frozen* establishes it as the pinnacle of Disney's Post-Pixar Acquisition Period, and is the catalyst for the shift towards Disney as the front-runner in mainstream American animation, and the consequent displacement of Pixar. In a 2015 interview with *Screen Daily*, Lasseter noted that there had been many changes to Walt Disney Animation Studios in the 10 years since he and Catmull had taken over:

> We set out to make it a filmmaker-driven culture like it is at Pixar. We changed the model from being executive-driven to filmmaker-driven ... It was quite broken when we came in; the morale was really low. We wanted to let them

make a movie that would be a really big hit. After *Frozen* and *Big Hero 6*, this studio is so confident now, they're on fire.[72]

Another success for the animation studio, *Big Hero 6* grossed $652 million globally and won the 2015 Academy Award for Best Animated Feature.[73] The triumph of Disney's fifth film since acquiring Pixar proves that the filmmaker-led culture set up by Catmull and Lasseter has revived Disney's once floundering animation department.

According to Thomas Staggs, Disney's former Chief Operating Officer, the acquisition of Pixar was beneficial not only to the animation arm of the company, but to The Walt Disney Company as a whole. In the company's 2006 annual report, Staggs indicates the commercial prospects of expanding the merchandise of Pixar's characters:

> The acquisition of Pixar was an important and valuable step for our Company ... We believe that this company-wide impact improves our long-term earnings potential. The success of the integration to date and the wonderful characters and stories that we expect to leverage across the Company for years to come underscore our confidence in the value-creating potential of this acquisition.[74]

Robert Iger claims that his desire to purchase Pixar was strengthened during a parade at the opening of Disneyland in Hong Kong. He noticed that all of the "classic" Disney characters that had been produced within the last 10 years were all from Pixar films.[75] Since the original 1991 contract between the two companies, Disney has owned the rights to Pixar's characters, which have been sold on an array of consumer products. The Disney Store website features an extensive webpage dedicated to products of Disney-Pixar characters.[76] In 2012, the Licensing Letter issued a list of the top 20 best-selling licensed entertainment character merchandise, based on 2011 retail sales in North America. The survey includes physical consumer goods such as t-shirts, stationery, toys and electronics. Disney owns licenses to four of the top five franchises: Disney Princess ($1.6 billion), Star Wars ($1.5 billion), Winnie the Pooh ($1.09 billion) and Cars ($1.05 billion), and a further three Disney-owned properties feature in the top 20: Mickey and Friends ($750 million), Toy Story ($685 million), Disney Fairies ($435 million) and Spider-Man ($325 million).[77] As it was only released in August 2013, Disney Interactive Studios' Disney Infinity does not feature on this list. The official description of the game as "an action-adventure sandbox video game ... that uses collectible figurines that synchronises with the game to allow characters from Disney, Pixar and now Marvel, to interact and go on adventures" features on promotional materials.[78] In January 2014, Disney Interactive Studios announced that three million starter packs had been sold, excluding all the extras that are available to purchase, making it Disney Interactive's most popular and profitable product to date.[79] One of the main draws of Disney Infinity is that the characters can interact and converge narratively, i.e. *Toy Story's* Buzz Lightyear can be in a game with Lightning McQueen from *Cars* (2006), and so on. This is an interesting concept for Disney to take on board for two reasons: first, it is in direct contrast with the "rules" of Disney's most popular character merchandise collection, The Disney Princess Franchise. The characters who feature on these products come from Disney's princess films, namely Snow White, Aurora, Cinderella, Ariel, Belle, Jasmine, Pocahontas, Mulan, Tiana, Rapunzel and Merida. Because these characters are from different narratives, Disney Consumer Division specified that when the characters are featured together on a product, they should not make eye contact in order to preserve their individual mythologies. Secondly, character interaction, or at least references to other characters, has been a brand distinction of Pixar since *Toy Story*. The idea is that every film features an "Easter egg" or a reference to previous films made by the studio.

Since the acquisition of Pixar in 2006, Disney's struggling animation studio has gone from strength to strength. During the first ten years of the Disney-Pixar partnership, Ed Catmull and John Lasseter have honed the methods and practices that made Pixar so successful and have applied these to Disney Animation. The results indicate a renewed trust in the Disney brand, evident from the celebrated commercial success and critical acclaim of the studio's Post-Pixar Period output. Early indications suggest that following years of uncertainty, Walt Disney Animation Studios is once again a leading studio in mainstream American animation. In his book, Catmull poses the question, "could Pixar and Disney Animation flourish independent of one another, separate but equal?"[80] Although Disney is thriving after the acquisition, the result of the merger on Pixar is still yet to be determined. The rising success and increasing box office figures outlined earlier in the chapter peaked with *Toy Story 3*. Since then, Pixar has received criticisms over an apparent gender problem, stemming from the overwhelming male-centred storylines present throughout the studio's back catalogue, a point that has been magnified by the removal of Lasseter as chief creative officer in June 2018, following allegations of misconduct.[81] Further criticisms surround Pixar's string of sequels. As a studio widely commended for its originality, since the acquisition Pixar has released five sequels, *Toy Story 3*, *Cars 2* (2011), *Monsters University* (2013), *Finding Dory* and *Cars 3* (2017); from 2010 to 2017, Pixar has released five franchise films and three original films, which seems fairly unusual for a studio that from 1995 to 2009 released nine original films and just one sequel, *Toy Story 2*. Evidently, the commonplace notion that sequels generally compromise on quality, and that they are made to generate guaranteed box office revenue, has not escaped the once infallible animation studio. Having pushed back the release dates of two original features, *Inside Out* and *The Good Dinosaur* (2015), which resulted in no Pixar film for 2014, the first year without a Pixar film release since 2005, and the announcement of further sequels over the coming years, additional research into the impact of Disney's purchase of Pixar should be undertaken. Nonetheless, it is obvious that, at least in the initial decade after the merger, Disney's acquisition of Pixar has been far more beneficial for Disney Animation than for Pixar. Yet, as both studios enter its second decade following the 2006 merger, and a new phase post-Lasseter, an emphasis on diversity and equality will be expected under the new guidance of Pete Docter and Jennifer Lee.

Bibliography

"*A Bug's Life* (1998)". Box Office Mojo. Last modified August 24, 2017. http://www.boxof-ficemojo.com/movies/?id=bugslife.htm

Adams, Derek. "*Meet the Robinsons.*" *Time Out*, March 20, 2007. Accessed May 18, 2015. http://www.timeout.com/london/film/meet-the-robinsons

Amidi, Amid. "Short Film Review: Disney's *Feast*". *Cartoon Brew*, June 11, 2014. Accessed May 18, 2015. http://www.cartoonbrew.com/disney/short-film-review-disneys-feast-100333.html

Andersen, Hans Christian. "*The Snow Queen.*" In *The Complete Fairy Tales by Hans Christian Andersen*, by Hans Christian Andersen, 270–302. Hertfordshire: Wordsworth Editions Limited, 2006.

"*Atlantis: The Lost Empire*". Rotten Tomatoes. Last modified January 25, 2011. http://www.rottentomatoes.com/m/atlantis_the_lost_empire/

"*Avengers: Age of Ultron* (2015)". Box Office Mojo. Last modified August 24, 2017. http://www.boxofficemojo.com/movies/?id=avengers2.htm

"*Beauty and the Beast* (1991)". Box Office Mojo. Last modified August 24, 2017. http://www.boxofficemojo.com/movies/?id=beautyandthebeast.htm

"*Big Hero 6* (2014)". Box Office Mojo. Last modified August 24, 2017. http://www.boxof-ficemojo.com/movies/?id=disney2014.htm

"*Bolt* (2008)". Box Office Mojo. Last modified August 24, 2017. http://www.boxof-ficemojo.com/movies/?id=bolt.htm

Bradshaw, Peter. "*Chicken Little.*" *The Guardian*, February 10, 2006. Accessed May 18, 2015. http://www.theguardian.com/culture/2006/feb/10/3

Bradshaw, Peter. "*Toy Story 2*". *The Guardian*, February 4, 2000. Accessed May 18, 2015. http://www.theguardian.com/film/2000/feb/04/6

"*Brother Bear*". Rotten Tomatoes. Last modified November 16, 2009. http://www.rottento-matoes.com/m/brother_bear/

Catmull, Ed. *Creativity, Inc.: Overcoming the Unseen Forces That Stand in the Way of True Inspiration.* London: Bantam Press, 2014.

"*Chicken Little* (2005)". Box Office Mojo. Last modified August 24, 2017. http://www.boxof-ficemojo.com/movies/?id=chickenlittle.htm

"*Chicken Little*". Rotten Tomatoes. Last modified November 16, 2009. http://www.rottento-matoes.com/m/chicken_little/

Crook, Simon. "*Wreck-it Ralph*: Game Changer". *Empire*, February 8, 2013. Accessed May 30, 2015. http://www.empireonline.com/reviews/reviewcomplete.asp?FID=137278

Decker, Jonathan. "The Portrayal of Gender in the Feature-Length Films of Pixar Animation Studios: A Content Analysis". Master of Science Thesis, Auburn University, Alabama, 2010.

"Disney Infinity". Disney Infinity. Last modified June 7, 2015. https://infinity.disney.com/en-gb

"Disney Pixar". The Disney Store. Last modified June 7, 2015. http://www.disney-store.co.uk/disney-pixar/mn/1001073/

Ebert, Roger. *"Home on the Range"*. *Roger Ebert*, April 2, 2004. Accessed May 18, 2015. http://www.rogerebert.com/reviews/home-on-the-range-2004

Ebert, Roger. *"Finding Nemo."* *Roger Ebert*, May 30, 2003. Accessed May 18, 2015. http://www.rogerebert.com/reviews/finding-nemo-2003

"Finding Nemo (2003)". Box Office Mojo. Last modified August 24, 2017. http://www.boxofficemojo.com/movies/?id=findingnemo.htm

Failes, Ian. "The Inside Story Behind Disney's *Paperman*". *FX Guide*, January 31, 2013. Accessed May 18, 2015. http://www.fxguide.com/featured/the-inside-story-behind-disneys-paperman/

"Frozen (2013)". Box Office Mojo. Last modified August 24, 2017. http://www.boxofficemojo.com/movies/?id=frozen2013.htm

Grimm, Wilhelm and Jacob Grimm. *"The Frog King, or The Iron Henry"*. In *The Complete First Edition: The Original Folk & Fairy Tales of the Brothers Grimm*, edited by Jack Zipes, 13–15. Oxfordshire: Princeton University Press, 2014.

"Guardians of the Galaxy (2014)". Box Office Mojo. Last modified August 24, 2017. http://www.boxofficemojo.com/movies/?id=marvel2014a.htm

Hammond, Wally. *"Bolt"*. *Time Out*, February 3, 2009. Accessed May 18, 2015. http://www.timeout.com/london/film/bolt-2008

Handrahan, Matthew. "Disney Infinity Sells 3 Million Starter Packs". *Games Industry*, January 20, 2014. Accessed June 7, 2015. http://www.gamesindustry.biz/articles/2014-01-20-disney-infinity-sells-3-million-starter-packs

Haswell, Helen. "To Infinity and Back Again: Hand-drawn Aesthetic and Affection for the Past in Pixar's Pioneering Animation". *Alphaville: Journal of Film and Screen Media* 8 (2014).

Hazelton, John. *"Home on the Range."* *Screen Daily*, April 14, 2004. Accessed May 18, 2015. http://www.screendaily.com/home-on-the-range/4018167.article

Holden, Stephen. "From the Heat of Royal Passion, Poof! It's Permafrost: Disney's *Frozen*, a Makeover of *The Snow Queen*". *The New York Times*, November 26, 2013. Accessed May 12, 2015. http://www.nytimes.com/2013/11/27/movies/disneys-frozen-a-makeover-of-the-snow-queen.html?_r=0

Holt, Jennifer and Alisa Perren, eds. *Media Industries: History, Theory and Method*. New Jersey: Wiley-Blackwell, 2009.

"Home on the Range (2004)". Box Office Mojo. Last modified August 24, 2017. http://www.boxofficemojo.com/movies/?id=homeontherange.htm

"Home on the Range". Rotten Tomatoes. Last modified November 16, 2009. http://www.rottentomatoes.com/m/home_on_the_range/

Kemper, Tom. *Toy Story: A Critical Reading*. London: BFI Palgrave, 2015.

Kit, Borys. "Pete Docter, Jennifer Lee to Lead Pixar, Disney Animation". *The Hollywood Reporter*, June 19, 2018. Accessed July 10, 2018. https://www.hollywoodreporter.com/heat-vision/pete-docter-jennifer-lee-lead-pixar-disney-animation-1121432

Klady, Leonard. "Review: *Toy Story*". *Variety*, November 19, 1995. Accessed May 18, 2015. http://variety.com/1995/film/reviews/toy-story-2-1200443736/

Kois, Dan. "Disney's Eager-to-Please *Bolt* Lives Up to its Studio Pedigree". *The Washington Post*, November 21, 2008. Accessed May 15, 2015. http://www.washingtonpost.com/wp-dyn/content/article/2008/11/20/AR2008112003758.html

Leyland, Matthew. "Reviews: *Monsters, Inc.*" *Sight and Sound* 12, no. 2 (2002): 54–55.

Lohr, Steve. "Disney in 10-Year, 5-Film Deal with Pixar". *The New York Times*, February 25, 1997. Accessed May 18, 2015. http://www.nytimes.com/1997/02/25/business/disney-in-10-year-5-film-deal-with-pixar.html

Maher, Kevin. "*The Princess and the Frog*". *The Times*, January 30, 2010. Accessed May 10, 2015. http://www.thetimes.co.uk/tto/arts/film/reviews/article1864973.ece

Maslin, Janet. "*A Bug's Life* Review: Out-of-Step Ant Sails Out to Save the Hill". *The New York Times*, November 25, 1998. Accessed May 18, 2015. http://www.nytimes.com/movie/review?res=9C02E7DA1639F936A15752C1A96E958260

Maslin, Janet. "*Toy Story* Review: There's a New Toy in the House. Uh-Oh". *The New York Times*, November 22, 1995. Accessed May 18, 2015. http://www.nytimes.com/movie/review?res=9905EEDA1339F931A15752C1A963958260

Masters, Kim. "John Lasseter Taking Leave of Absence From Pixar Amid "Missteps". *The Hollywood Reporter*, November 21, 2017. Accessed July 10, 2018. https://www.hollywoodreporter.com/news/john-lasseter-taking-leave-absence-pixar-missteps-1057113

McCarthy, Todd. "Review: *A Bug's Life*". *Variety*, November 29, 1998. Accessed May 18, 2015. http://variety.com/1998/film/reviews/a-bug-s-life-1200455803/

McCarthy, Todd. "Review: *Finding Nemo*". *Variety*, May 26, 2003. Accessed May 18, 2015. http://variety.com/2003/film/awards/finding-nemo-4-1200541411/

McCarthy, Todd. " Review: *Toy Story 2*". *Variety*, November 17, 1999. Accessed May 18, 2015. http://variety.com/1999/film/reviews/toy-story-2-2-1117759786/

McGill, Hannah. "*Wreck-it Ralph*: Witty and Cleverly-Targeted Family Romp from Disney with Video Game Theme". *The List*, January 18, 2013. Accessed May 30, 2015. https://film.list.co.uk/article/48290-wreck-it-ralph/

"*Meet the Robinsons* (2007)". Box Office Mojo. Last modified August 24, 2017. http://www.boxofficemojo.com/movies/?id=meettherobinsons.htm

"*Meet the Robinsons*". Rotten Tomatoes. Last modified May 5, 2014. http://www.rottentomatoes.com/m/meet_the_robinsons/

Mitchell, Wendy. "Lasseter Wows Cannes with Pixar, Disney Footage". *Screen Daily*, May 20, 2015. Accessed May 22, 2015. http://www.screendaily.com/5088530.article?utm_source=newsletter&utm_medium=email&utm_campaign=Newsletter79

"*Monsters, Inc.* (2001)". Box Office Mojo. Last modified August 24, 2017. http://www.boxofficemojo.com/movies/?id=monstersinc.htm

Montgomery, Colleen. "Woody's Roundup and Wall-E's Wunderkammer: Technophilia and Nostalgia in Pixar Animation". *Animation Studies Online Journal*, September 2, 2011. Accessed November 27, 2013. http://journal.animationstudies.org/colleen-montgomery-woodys-roundup-and-walles-wunderkammer/

O'Hara, Helen. "*The Princess and the Frog*: One Day My Anura Amphibia Will Come ..." *Empire*, February 2, 2010. Accessed May 10, 2015. http://www.empireonline.com/reviews/reviewcomplete.asp?FID=135544

Paik, Karen. *To Infinity and Beyond!: The Story of Pixar Animation Studios*. London: Virgin Books Ltd., 2007.

Pallant, Chris. *Demystifying Disney: A History of Disney Feature Animation*. New York/London: The Continuum International Publishing Group, 2011.

Price, David A. *The Pixar Touch: The Making of a Company*. New York: Vintage Books, 2009.

Rainey, James. "Disney Merges its Consumer Products and Interactive Divisions". *Variety*, June 29, 2015. Accessed June 30, 2015. http://variety.com/2015/biz/news/disney-merges-consumer-products-interactive-1201530606/

Schatz, Thomas. "Film Industry Studies and Hollywood History". In *Media Industries: History, Theory and Method*, edited by Jennifer Holt and Alisa Perren, 45–56. New Jersey: Wiley-Blackwell, 2009.

Scott, A.O. "A Chick Flick with Aliens Falling From the Sky". *The New York Times*, November 4, 2005. Accessed May 18, 2015. http://www.nytimes.com/2005/11/04/movies/a-chick-flick-with-aliens-falling-from-the-sky.html

Scott, A.O. "A Nerdy Orphan Plows Ahead With a Lot of Familiar Novelties". *The New York Times*, March 30, 2007. Accessed May 18, 2015. http://www.nytimes.com/2007/03/30/movies/30robi.html?_r=0

Scott, A.O. "Bad-Guy Avatar Seeks Midlife Career Change". *The New York Times*, November 1, 2012. Accessed May 30, 2015. http://www.nytimes.com/2012/11/02/movies/wreck-it-ralph-with-john-c-reilly-and-sarah-silverman.html?_r=0

Shoard, Catherine. "How *The Princess and the Frog* Really Breaks the Mould". *The Guardian*, February 5, 2010. Accessed May 15, 2015. http://www.theguardian.com/film/film-blog/2010/feb/05/princess-and-the-frog

Simon, Brent. "*Tangled.*" *Screen Daily*, November 8, 2010. Accessed May 10, 2015. http://www.screendaily.com/reviews/latest-reviews/tangled/5020316.article

Spangler, Todd. "Is Disney's Big-Game Hunting Paying Off?" *Variety*, April 2, 2014. Accessed May 10, 2015. http://variety.com/2014/biz/news/is-disneys-big-game-hunting-paying-off-1201151101/

"*Tangled* (2010)". Box Office Mojo. Last modified August 24, 2017. http://www.boxofficemojo.com/movies/?id=rapunzel.htm

Telotte, J.P. *The Mouse Machine: Disney and Technology.* Chicago: University of Illinois Press, 2008.

"*The Emperor's New Groove* (2000)". Box Office Mojo. Last modified August 24, 2017. http://www.boxofficemojo.com/movies/?id=emperorsnewgroove.htm

"The Licensing Letter". The Licensing Letter. Last modified June 7, 2015. http://74.200.231.27/public/department33.cfm

"*The Princess and the Frog* (2009)". Box Office Mojo. Last modified August 24, 2017. http://www.boxofficemojo.com/movies/?id=princessandthefrog.htm

The Walt Disney Company. *Financial Review* by Thomas O. Staggs. Senior Executive Vice President and Chief Financial Officer. The Walt Disney Company Annual Report. 2006.

The Walt Disney Company. *Fiscal Year 2016 Annual Report.* The Walt Disney Company Annual Report. 2016.

The Walt Disney Company. *Letter to Shareholders* by Robert A. Iger. President and Chief Executive Officer. The Walt Disney Company 2006 Annual Report. December 12, 2006.

"*Toy Story* (1995)". Box Office Mojo. Last modified August 24, 2017. http://www.boxofficemojo.com/movies/?id=toystory.htm

"*Toy Story 2* (1999)". Box Office Mojo. Last modified August 24, 2017. http://www.boxofficemojo.com/movies/?id=toystory2.htm

"*Treasure Planet*". Rotten Tomatoes. Last modified September 9, 2008. http://www.rottentomatoes.com/m/treasure_planet/

Wooden, Shannon and Ken Gillam. *Pixar's Boy Stories: Masculinity in a Postmodern Age.* Plymouth: Rowman & Littlefield, 2014.

"*Wreck-it Ralph* (2012)". Box Office Mojo. Last modified August 24, 2017. http://www.boxofficemojo.com/movies/?id=rebootralph.htm

Filmography

A Bug's Life. Directed by John Lasseter. 1998. Pixar Animation Studios/Walt Disney Pictures.

Aladdin. Directed by Ron Clements and John Musker. 1992. Walt Disney Animation Studios.

Alice Through the Looking Glass. Directed by James Bobin. 2016. Walt Disney Pictures.

Atlantis: The Lost Empire. Directed by Gary Trousdale and Kirk Wise. 2001. Walt Disney Animation Studios.

Avengers: Age of Ultron. Directed by Joss Whedon. 2015. Marvel Studios/Walt Disney Studios Motion Pictures.

Beauty and the Beast. Directed by Gary Trousdale and Kirk Wise. 1991. Walt Disney Animation Studios.

Big Hero 6. Directed by Don Hall and Chris Williams. 2014. Walt Disney Animation Studios.

Bolt. Directed by Chris Williams and Byron Howard. 2008. Walt Disney Animation Studios.

Brave. Directed by Mark Andrews and Brenda Chapman. 2013. Pixar Animation Studios/Walt Disney Pictures.

Brother Bear. Directed by Aaron Blaise and Robert Walker. 2003. Walt Disney Animation Studios.

Cars. Directed by Joe Ranft and John Lasseter. 2006. Pixar Animation Studios/Walt Disney Pictures.

Cars 2. Directed by John Lasseter and Brad Lewis. 2011. Pixar Animation Studios/Walt Disney Pictures.

Cars 3. Directed by Brian Fee. 2017. Pixar Animation Studios/Walt Disney Pictures.

Chicken Little. Directed by Mark Dindal. 2005. Walt Disney Animation Studios.

Day & Night. Directed by Teddy Newton. 2010. Pixar Animation Studios/Walt Disney Pictures.

Fantasia 2000. Directed by James Algar, Gaëtan Brizzi, Paul Brizzi, Hendel Butoy, Francis Glebas, Eric Goldberg, Don Hahn and Pixote Hunt. 1999. Walt Disney Animation Studios.

Feast. Directed by Patrick Osborne. 2014. Walt Disney Animation Studios.

Finding Nemo. Directed by Andrew Stanton and Lee Unkrich. 2003. Pixar Animation Studios/Walt Disney Pictures.

Finding Dory. Directed by Andrew Stanton and Angus MacLane. 2016. Pixar Animation Studios/Walt Disney Pictures.

Frozen. Directed by Chris Buck and Jennifer Lee. 2013. Walt Disney Animation Studios.

Geri's Game. Directed by Jan Pinkava. 1997. Pixar Animation Studios.

Get a Horse! Directed by Lauren MacMullan. 2013. Walt Disney Animation Studios.

Guardians of the Galaxy. Directed by James Gunn. 2014. Marvel Studios/Walt Disney Studios Motion Pictures.

Home on the Range. Directed by Will Finn and John Sanford. 2004. Walt Disney Animation Studios.

How to Train Your Dragon. Directed by Dean DeBlois and Chris Sanders. 2010. DreamWorks Animation.

Ice Age. Directed by Carlos Saldanha and Chris Wedge. 2002. Blue Sky Studios/Twentieth Century Fox Animation.

Inside Out. Directed by Pete Docter. 2015. Pixar Animation Studios/Walt Disney Pictures.

Kung Fu Panda. Directed by Mark Osborne and John Stevenson. 2008. DreamWorks Animation.

La Luna. Directed by Enrico Casarosa. 2011. Pixar Animation Studios/Walt Disney Pictures.

Lilo & Stitch. Directed by Dean DeBlois and Chris Sanders. 2002. Walt Disney Animation Studios.

Madagascar. Directed by Tom McGrath and Eric Darnell. 2005. DreamWorks Animation.

Meet the Robinsons. Directed by Stephen Anderson. 2007. Walt Disney Animation Studios.

Moana. Directed by Ron Clements and John Musker. 2016. Walt Disney Animation Studios.

Monsters, Inc. Directed by Pete Docter, Lee Unkrich and David Silverman. 2001. Pixar Animation Studios/Walt Disney Pictures.

Monsters University. Directed by Dan Scanlon. 2013. Pixar Animation Studios/Walt Disney Pictures.

Paperman. Directed by John Kahrs. 2012. Walt Disney Animation Studios.

Shrek. Directed by Andrew Adamson and Vicky Jenson. 2001. DreamWorks Animation.

Silly Symphonies. 1929–1939. Walt Disney Productions.

Snow White. Directed by David Hand. 1937. Walt Disney Productions.

Star Trek II: The Wrath of Khan. Directed by Nicholas Meyer. 1982. Paramount Pictures.

Star Wars: The Force Awakens. Directed by J.J. Abrams. 2015. Lucasfilm/Walt Disney Studios Motion Pictures.

Steamboat Willie. Directed by Walt Disney and Ub Iwerks. 1928. Walt Disney Studios.

Tangled. Directed by Nathan Greno and Byron Howard. 2010. Walt Disney Animation Studios.

The Adventures of André and Wally B. Directed by John Lasseter. 1984. Pixar Animation Studios.

The Emperor's New Groove. Directed by Mark Dindal. 2000. Walt Disney Animation Studios.

The Good Dinosaur. Directed by Bob Peterson and Peter Sohn. 2015. Pixar Animation Studios/Walt Disney Pictures.

The Lion King. Directed by Rob Minkoff and Roger Allers. 1994. Walt Disney Animation Studios.

The Little Mermaid. Directed by Ron Clements and John Musker. 1989. Walt Disney Animation Studios.

The Princess and the Frog. Directed by Ron Clements and John Musker. 2009. Walt Disney Animation Studios.

The Rescuers Down Under. Directed by Hendel Butoy and Mike Gabriel. 1990. Walt Disney Animation Studios.

Toy Story. Directed by John Lasseter. 1995. Pixar Animation Studios/Walt Disney Pictures.

Toy Story 2. Directed by John Lasseter, Ash Brannon and Lee Unkrich. 1999. Pixar Animation Studios/Walt Disney Pictures.

Toy Story 3. Directed by Lee Unkrich. 2010. Pixar Animation Studios/Walt Disney Pictures.

Treasure Planet. Directed by Ron Clements and John Musker. 2002. Walt Disney Animation Studios.

Wreck-it Ralph. Directed by Rich Moore. 2012. Walt Disney Animation Studios.

Young Sherlock Holmes. Directed by Barry Levinson. 1985. Amblin Entertainment/ Industrial Light & Magic/Paramount Pictures.

Zootopia. Directed by Byron Howard and Rich Moore. 2016. Walt Disney Animation Studios.

Endnotes

1. Thomas Schatz, 'Film Industry Studies and Hollywood History', in *Media Industries: History, Theory and Method*, ed. Jennifer Holt and Alisa Perren. (New Jersey: Wiley-Blackwell, 2009), 45.

2. Schatz, 45.

3. Disney's Consumer Products and Interactive divisions were operating separately until the end of 2015. On 29 June 2015, Disney announced that it would combine these divisions starting with the 2016 financial year. See James Rainey, 'Disney Merges its Consumer Products and Interactive Divisions.' *Variety*, June 29, 2015, accessed June 30, 2015, http://variety.com/2015/biz/news/disney-merges-consumer-products-interactive-1201530606/

4. The Walt Disney Company. *Fiscal Year 2016 Annual Report.* The Walt Disney Company Annual Report, 2016. 31.

5. Todd Spangler, 'Is Disney's Big-Game Hunting Paying Off?' *Variety*, April 2, 2014, accessed May 10, 2015, http://variety.com/2014/biz/news/is-disneys-big-game-hunting-paying-off-1201151101/

6. For box office figures, see boxofficemojo.com's entry for *Guardians of the Galaxy* (2014): http://www.boxofficemojo.com/movies/?id=marvel2014a.htm and *Avengers: Age of Ultron* (2015): http://www.boxofficemojo.com/movies/?id=avengers2.htm

7.   Chris Pallant, *Demystifying Disney: A History of Disney Feature Animation* (New York/London: The Continuum International Publishing Group, 2011), 89.

8.   David A. Price, *The Pixar Touch: The Making of a Company* (New York: Vintage Books, 2009), 252.

9.   For box office figures, see boxofficemojo.com's entry for *Beauty and the Beast* (1991): http://www.boxofficemojo.com/movies/?id=beautyandthebeast.htm

10.   Price, 123.

11.   Leonard Klady, 'Review: *Toy Story*.' *Variety*, November 19, 1995, accessed May 18, 2015, http://variety.com/1995/film/reviews/toy-story-2-1200443736/

12.   Janet Maslin, '*Toy Story* Review: There's a New Toy in the House. Uh-Oh.' *The New York Times*, November 22, 1995, accessed May 18, 2015, http://www.nytimes.com/movie/review?res=9905EEDA1339F931A15752C1A963958260

13.   For box office figures, see boxofficemojo.com's entry for *Toy Story* (1995): http://www.boxofficemojo.com/movies/?id=toystory.htm

14.   Tom Kemper, *Toy Story: A Critical Reading* (London: BFI Palgrave, 2015), 98.

15.   Steve Lohr, 'Disney in 10-Year, 5-Film Deal with Pixar'. *The New York Times*, February 25, 1997, accessed May 18, 2015, http://www.nytimes.com/1997/02/25/business/disney-in-10-year-5-film-deal-with-pixar.html

16.   For box office figures, see boxofficemojo.com's entry for *A Bug's Life* (1998): http://www.boxofficemojo.com/movies/?id=bugslife.htm

17.   Todd McCarthy, 'Review: *A Bug's Life*'. *Variety*, November 29, 1998, accessed May 18, 2015, http://variety.com/1998/film/reviews/a-bug-s-life-1200455803/

18.   Janet Maslin, '*A Bug's Life* Review: Out-of-Step Ant Sails Out to Save the Hill.' *The New York Times*, November 25, 1998, accessed May 18, 2015, http://www.nytimes.com/movie/review?res=9C02E7DA1639F936A15752C1A96E958260

19.   Price, 179.

20.   Todd McCarthy, 'Review: *Toy Story 2*.' *Variety*, November 17, 1999, accessed May 18, 2015, http://variety.com/1999/film/reviews/toy-story-2-2-1117759786/

21.   Peter Bradshaw, '*Toy Story 2*.' *The Guardian*, February 4, 2000, accessed May 18, 2015, http://www.theguardian.com/film/2000/feb/04/6

22.   For box office figures, see boxofficemojo.com's entry for *Toy Story 2* (1999): http://www.boxofficemojo.com/movies/?id=toystory2.htm

23.   Matthew Leyland, 'Reviews: *Monsters, Inc.*', *Sight and Sound* 12, no. 2 (2002): 54.

24.   For box office figures, see boxofficemojo.com's entry for *Monsters, Inc.* (2001): http://www.boxofficemojo.com/movies/?id=monstersinc.htm

25.   Todd McCarthy, 'Review: *Finding Nemo*.' *Variety*, May 26, 2003, accessed May 18, 2015, http://variety.com/2003/film/awards/finding-nemo-4-1200541411/

26.   Roger Ebert, '*Finding Nemo*.' *Roger Ebert*, May 30, 2003, accessed May 18, 2015, http://www.rogerebert.com/reviews/finding-nemo-2003

27.   At the time of writing, the film ranks at number nine, though at its peak, it was the highest-grossing animated film of all time. For box office figures, see boxofficemojo.com's entry for *Finding Nemo* (2003): http://www.boxofficemojo.com/movies/?id=findingnemo.htm

28.   Pallant, 111.

29.   See http://www.boxofficemojo.com/

30.   For box office figures, see boxofficemojo.com's entry for *The Emperor's New Groove* (2000): http://www.boxofficemojo.com/movies/?id=emperorsnewgroove.htm

31.   At the time of writing these films have the following rating from top critics: *Atlantis: The Lost Empire* (44%); *Treasure Planet* (56%); *Brother Bear* (25%); *Home on the Range* (36%). See http://www.rottentomatoes.com/

32. John Hazelton, '*Home on the Range*.' *Screen Daily*, April 14, 2004, accessed May 18, 2015, http://www.screendaily.com/home-on-the-range/4018167.article

33. Roger Ebert, '*Home on the Range*.' *Roger Ebert*, April 2, 2004, accessed May 18, 2015, http://www.rogerebert.com/reviews/home-on-the-range-2004

34. Colleen Montgomery, 'Woody's Roundup and Wall-E's Wunderkammer: Technophilia and Nostalgia in Pixar Animation.' *Animation Studies Online Journal*, September 2, 2011, accessed November 27, 2013http://journal.animationstudies.org/colleen-montgomery-woodys-roundup-and-walles-wunderkammer/

35. '*Chicken Little*', Rotten Tomatoes, Last modified November 16, 2009, http://www.rottentomatoes.com/m/chicken_little/ and '*Meet the Robinsons*', Rotten Tomatoes, Last modified May 5, 2014, http://www.rottentomatoes.com/m/meet_the_robinsons/

36. Peter Bradshaw, '*Chicken Little*.' *The Guardian*, February 10, 2006, accessed May 18, 2015, http://www.theguardian.com/culture/2006/feb/10/3

37. A.O. Scott, 'A Chick Flick with Aliens Falling From the Sky.' *The New York Times*, November 4, 2005, accessed May 18, 2015, http://www.nytimes.com/2005/11/04/movies/a-chick-flick-with-aliens-falling-from-the-sky.html

38. A.O. Scott, 'A Nerdy Orphan Plows Ahead With a Lot of Familiar Novelties.' *The New York Times*, March 30, 2007, accessed May 18, 2015, http://www.nytimes.com/2007/03/30/movies/30robi.html?_r=0

39. Derek Adams, '*Meet the Robinsons*.' *Time Out*, March 20, 2007, accessed May 18, 2015, http://www.timeout.com/london/film/meet-the-robinsons

40. For box office figures, see boxofficemojo.com's entry for *Chicken Little* (2005): http://www.boxofficemojo.com/movies/?id=chickenlittle.htm and *Home on the Range* (2004): http://www.boxofficemojo.com/movies/?id=homeontherange.htm

41. For box office figures, see boxofficemojo.com's entry for *Meet the Robinsons* (2007): http://www.boxofficemojo.com/movies/?id=meettherobinsons.htm

42. Price, 240.

43. Price, 253.

44. The Walt Disney Company. *Letter to Shareholders* by Robert A. Iger. President and Chief Executive Officer. The Walt Disney Company Annual Report. December 12, 2006, 2.

45. Pallant, 131.

46. Catmull, 268.

47. Catmull, 258.

48. Catmull, 262.

49. For box office figures, see boxofficemojo.com's entry for *Bolt* (2008): http://www.boxofficemojo.com/movies/?id=bolt.htm

50. Wally Hammond, '*Bolt*.' *Time Out*,February 3, 2009, accessed May 18, 2015, http://www.timeout.com/london/film/bolt-2008

51. Dan Kois, 'Disney's Eager-to-Please *Bolt* Lives Up to its Studio Pedigree.' *The Washington Post*,November 21, 2008, accessed May 15 2015, http://www.washingtonpost.com/wp-dyn/content/article/2008/11/20/AR2008112003758.html

52. Pallant, 131.

53. Although Pixar decided to make short films regularly alongside its features starting with *A Bug's Life* and *Geri's Game*, the studio has been making shorts since 1984.

54. Walt Disney's short *Steamboat Willie* (1928) is commonly referred to as the first fully-synchronised sound cartoon; the studio's early adoption of the Pixar Image Computer and CAPS software demonstrates its interest in the development of technology. For more in-depth research see J.P Telotte, *The Mouse Machine: Disney and Technology* (Chicago: University of Illinois Press, 2008).

55. Ian Failes, 'The Inside Story Behind Disney's *Paperman*.' *FX Guide*, January 31, 2013, accessed May 18, 2015, http://www.fxguide.com/featured/the-inside-story-behind-disneys-paperman/

56. Amid Amidi, 'Short Film Review: Disney's *Feast*.' *Cartoon Brew*, June 11, 2014, accessed May 18, 2015, http://www.cartoonbrew.com/disney/short-film-review-disneys-feast-100333.html

57. Catherine Shoard, "How *The Princess and the Frog* Really Breaks the Mould". *The Guardian*, February 5, 2010, accessed May 15, 2015, http://www.theguardian.com/film/filmblog/2010/feb/05/princess-and-the-frog

58. While one could of course argue that *Finding Dory* (2016) centres around a female character, the fact is that much of the film focuses on Marlin's search for Dory and the self-discovery he has along the way, rather than being primarily about Dory herself.

59. For a full study of the representation of gender in Pixar films see Jonathan Decker, "The Portrayal of Gender in the Feature-Length Films of Pixar Animation Studios: A Content Analysis" (MSc thesis, Auburn University, Alabama, 2010); and Shannon Wooden and Ken Gillam, *Pixar's Boy Stories: Masculinity in a Postmodern Age*. (Plymouth: Rowman & Littlefield, 2014).

60. Helen O'Hara, "*The Princess and the Frog*: One Day My Anura Amphibia Will Come ..." *Empire*, February 2, 2010, accessed May 10, 2015, http://www.empireonline.com/reviews/reviewcomplete.asp?FID=135544

61. Kevin Maher, "*The Princess and the Frog*". *The Times*, January 30, 2010, accessed May 10, 2015, http://www.thetimes.co.uk/tto/arts/film/reviews/article1864973.ece

62. For box office figures, see boxofficemojo.com's entry for *The Princess and the Frog* (2009): http://www.boxofficemojo.com/movies/?id=princessandthefrog.htm

63. Catmull, 269.

64. For box office figures, see boxofficemojo.com's entry for *Tangled* (2010): http://www.boxofficemojo.com/movies/?id=rapunzel.htm

65. Brent Simon, "*Tangled.*" *Screen Daily*, November 8, 2010, accessed May 10, 2015, http://www.screendaily.com/reviews/latest-reviews/tangled/5020316.article

66. See Helen Haswell, "To Infinity and Back Again: Hand-drawn Aesthetic and Affection for the Past in Pixar's Pioneering Animation", *Alphaville: Journal of Film and Screen Media* 8 (2014).

67. For box office figures, see boxofficemojo.com's entry for *Wreck-it Ralph* (2012): http://www.boxofficemojo.com/movies/?id=rebootralph.htm

68. Hannah McGill, "*Wreck-it Ralph*: Witty and Cleverly-Targeted Family Romp from Disney with Video Game Theme". *The List*, January 18, 2013, accessed May 30, 2015, https://film.list.co.uk/article/48290-wreck-it-ralph/

69. Simon Crook, "*Wreck-it Ralph*: Game Changer". *Empire*, February 8, 2013, accessed May 30, 2015, http://www.empireonline.com/reviews/reviewcomplete.asp?FID=137278 and A.O. Scott, "Bad-Guy Avatar Seeks Midlife Career Change". *The New York Times*, November 1, 2012, accessed May 30, 2015, http://www.nytimes.com/2012/11/02/movies/wreck-it-ralph-with-john-c-reilly-and-sarah-silverman.html?_r=0

70. For box office figures, see boxofficemojo.com's entry for *Frozen* (2013): http://www.boxofficemojo.com/movies/?id=frozen2013.htm

71. Stephen Holden, "From the Heat of Royal Passion, Poof! It's Permafrost: Disney's *Frozen*, a Makeover of *The Snow Queen*". *The New York Times*, November 26, 2013, accessed May 12, 2015, http://www.nytimes.com/2013/11/27/movies/disneys-frozen-a-makeover-of-the-snow-queen.html?_r=0

72. Wendy Mitchell, "Lasseter Wows Cannes with Pixar, Disney Footage". *Screen Daily*, May 20, 2015, accessed May 22, 2015, http://www.screendaily.com/5088530.article?utm_source=newsletter&utm_medium=email&utm_campaign=Newsletter79

73. For box office figures, see boxofficemojo.com's entry for *Big Hero 6* (2014): http://www.boxofficemojo.com/movies/?id=disney2014.htm

74. The Walt Disney Company. *Financial Review* by Thomas O. Staggs. Senior Executive Vice President and Chief Financial Officer. The Walt Disney Company Annual Report, 2006, 17.

75. Price, 252.

76. "Disney Pixar". The Disney Store, Last modified June 7, 2015, http://www.disney-store.co.uk/disney-pixar/mn/1001073/

77. "The Licensing Letter". The Licensing Letter, Last modified June 7, 2015, http://74.200.231.27/public/department33.cfm

78. "Disney Infinity". Disney Infinity, Last modified June 7, 2015, https://infinity.disney.com/en-gb

79. Matthew Handrahan, "Disney Infinity Sells 3 Million Starter Packs". *Games Industry*, January 20, 2014, accessed June 7, 2015, http://www.gamesindustry.biz/articles/2014-01-20-disney-infinity-sells-3-million-starter-packs While it has proven to be successful for Disney Interactive, on 10 May 2016, Disney announced it was discontinuing production on the Disney Infinity range. The final playsets to be released were *Alice Through the Looking Glass* (2016) and *Finding Dory*. The Disney Infinity range is still available for purchase.

80. Catmull, 247.

81. In November 2017, *The Hollywood Reporter* stated that Lasseter would be taking a six-month leave of absence from Disney and Pixar following allegations of misconduct. These allegations, which arose amid a wave of sexual misconduct allegations implicating a number of powerful men in Hollywood, led Disney to announce in June 2018, that Pete Docter and Jennifer Lee would be replacing Lasseter as chief creative officers at Pixar and Disney Animation, respectively. See Kim Masters, "John Lasseter Taking Leave of Absence From Pixar Amid "Missteps". *The Hollywood Reporter*, November 21, 2017, accessed July 10, 2018, https://www.hollywoodreporter.com/news/john-lasseter-taking-leave-absence-pixar-missteps-1057113 and, Borys Kit, "Pete Docter, Jennifer Lee to Lead Pixar, Disney Animation". *The Hollywood Reporter*, June 19, 2018, accessed July 10, 2018, https://www.hollywoodreporter.com/heat-vision/pete-docter-jennifer-lee-lead-pixar-disney-animation-1121432

Chapter 6

Let it go? Towards a "Plasmatic" Perspective on Digital Disney

Christopher Holliday

"Is this a motif in Disney's works, or chance? Let's look at other films."
– Sergei Eisenstein, *Eisenstein on Disney*, p.10.

The received narrative commonly shared among – and fostered by – critical and popular accounts of Walt Disney's feature-length animated canon frequently returns to a particularly durable "tale as old as time" seemingly hard-wired into the historical legacy of the studio. Whether Marxist polemic or pragmatic social critique, and wedged between both populist accounts celebrating Disney as children's entertainment and politically-radical criticism that partakes in "the fashionable sport of Disney bashing", the ongoing theoretical engagement with the Disney universe has afforded sustained prominence to the Disney formula.[1] In its role as a structuring principle that carefully controls Disney animation's formal and ideological terrain, the notion of a "formula" pertains to the manner in which, as Janet Wasko puts it, the studio has emphatically crafted "a self-contained universe which presents consistently recognisable virtues through recurring characters and familiar, repetitive themes".[2] For Disney scholars, the formula dually operates as a barometer of quality and moderator of content, arbitrating each film into the Disney canon and ultimately bearing out Disney's animated films as *aggregate art*. Never just single events, Disney's animated films reap the benefits of accrued meanings: speaking a "promise of a particular experience" that reflects their position within a distinct corpus of North American animated cinema.[3] But as the Disney studio has increasingly embraced digital technologies at the expense of cel-animation techniques, the repeated dusting off of the formula as a critical framework appears less viable and valuable to the rigorous study of "Digital Disney". Cued by Sergei Eisenstein's writing on Disney cel-animation from the 1940s, this chapter argues that a more fluid, *plasmatic* framework (rather than *formulaic* approach) is now required to meet the demands of the studio's computer-animated films produced in the post-2005 period. The textual richness of *Chicken Little* (2005), *Meet the Robinsons* (2007), *Bolt* (2008), *Tangled* (2010), *Wreck-It Ralph* (2012), *Frozen* (2013), *Big Hero 6* (2014), *Zootopia* (2016), and *Moana* (2016), and *Ralph Breaks the Internet* (2018) all pose a theoretical challenge to the "once-and-forever given" and "allotted form" of the formulaic tendency, which has otherwise presided over the development of Disney discourse.[4] These are films heavily informed by their *other* identities as computer-animated feature films, rather than being merely overcome by their determining Disney status. By reframing contemporary Disney animation within the emergent codes and conventions of recent computer-animated cinema, this chapter identifies how the new formal currency of Digital Disney can be progressively unlocked, whilst unpacking the Disney formula according to its own plasmatic charge and polymorphous vigour.

Historicizing the formula

While definitions of the Disney formula often settle around its orientation as a "selling point" or "powerful marketing tool" rather than emerging as a precise function of its animated application, for scholars of Disney the term has undoubtedly helped to explain the precise organisation of the studio's animated narratives.[5] Indeed, the first Disney commentators were highly responsive to the mechanics of the studio's repeating pleasures and openly testified to the perceived homogeny of Walt's feature-length cartoons. As early as 1941, renowned American film journalist Bosley Crowther commented in his *New York Times* review of the studio's fourth film, *Dumbo* (1941), that "… this time Mr. Disney and his genii have kept themselves within familiar bounds".[6] A 1941 issue of *Variety* echoed these sentiments, heralding *Dumbo* as a return for Walt "to the formula that accounted for his original success – simple animal characterization".[7] Both reviews position the familiar pleasures of *Dumbo* as a necessary riposte to the more radical *Fantasia* (1940), Disney's ambitious third feature that Crowther had previously praised as an "imaginative excursion" on account of how it "dumps conventional formulas overboard".[8] Such assumptions were seemingly predicated on a presumed (if contestable) formulaic continuity between Disney's feature-length films and earlier *Silly Symphonies* (1929–1939), one that was temporarily ruptured by *Fantasia* as an experimental concert feature.[9] Yet despite the enhanced musicality, abstract psychedelic colour and "highbrow" operatic intentions of *Fantasia* having been supposedly rehabilitated by the more formulaic *Dumbo*, some critics suggested that the former did not fully evade a prescribed constitution. Two years later, in 1942, Horace B. English asserted in an article on *Fantasia* that "the drawings have all the strength and all the now familiar weaknesses of the Disney formula".[10]

Such formulaic language underwriting popular reviews and trade accounts of Disney animation during the early 1940s reflected the critical consensus that the studio enacted cycles of repetition within its narratives, from the character continuity of the *Alice Comedies* (1923–1927) and *Oswald the Lucky Rabbit* (1927–1943[11]) series to the broader ritualism afforded across both the *Silly Symphonies* and their later animated features. Industrial conceptions of the Disney Corporation have since made the formula commensurate with Walt Disney's own pursuit of commercial stability during this period, and central to his conviction that a "scientific approach to the art of animation" could be achieved.[12] As a blueprint patterning industry production, the formula was supported by the studio's industrial growth that was entirely conducive to a system of reproducibility.[13] Disney animated artefacts were mass produced with Fordian economy, whose assembly line of images, all veined with a perceptible "Disneyness", collapsed the distinction between Disney as "art studio" and "factory".[14] This evolution of a creative, "formulaic" coherency within a broader industrial paradigm impressed structural consistency onto the animated form at the same time as animation itself was emerging (thanks to Disney) as a viable commercial industry. Animation historian Leonard Maltin argues that Disney himself "did not invent the medium, but one could say he *defined* it", pointing to the sizeable contribution made by Disney (the man) and Disney (the studio) to the development of the American animated cartoon tradition.[15]

Disney's expansion as a global corporation throughout the 1950s and into the 1960s placed the formulaic consistency of their animated features at new points of intersection with alternate multimedia enterprises (television series, live-action film, merchandising, consumer products and, beginning with Disneyland in 1955, theme parks). The synergistic projection of Disney's image, in turn, situated the formula within the wider signifying system of mass media culture, as the "semiotic significance" and "semantic meaning" of Disney texts became exploited in the business of entertainment.[16] The acceleration of specialist "Disney studies" during the 1990s, however, awarded increased critical definition to the formula as an intellectual category, not least from "textualist" approaches that have continued to give greater intelligibility to Disney's animated feature films by explicating the styles, themes and motifs packaged within the formula. Measured taxonomies elucidate the key consistencies of what Wasko terms the "Classic Disney" formula, drawn primarily from the studio's animated features produced during the Golden Age period in the 1940s and 1950s.[17] Despite multiple versions and several iterations, formal and thematic content is fairly typical across competing schema, identifying Disney as the standard bearer of specific narrative systems of organisations, stock (normally animal) characters, certain treatments of music and comedy, and as a purveyor of what is usually characterised as a "conservative" ideology trading in core values (individualism, optimism, innocence, romance and happiness). Fully ingrained into the hagiographic register of the worldwide Disney brand, this "Classic" formula has since evolved into a catchall term verified by the studio as part of its mission statement for success, becoming carefully co-ordinated capital within the studio's manufacture of fantasy. Ultimately, the phrase "Disney formula" has become embedded deep within the recesses of America's cultural memory, uttered as part of a global vernacular denoting the perceived uniformity of Disney products and testifying to Magic Kingdom hegemony. Nowhere is this more evident than in the contemporary era, where the formula has lost none of its traction in describing the period of Digital Disney.[18] The most commercially successful feature of this era, *Frozen*, has garnered particular attention for its formal resemblances to earlier Disney animation that has precipitated a clear recourse to formulaic language. *Variety*'s Scott Foundas described the film as Disney's "accomplished but formulaic 53rd animated feature", while Sherilyn Connelly, writing in *The Village Voice*, added "It's no secret that Disney princess films are formulaic".[19] Indeed, Connelly's summation that *Frozen* "just confirms that the formula works" reveals the extent to which the formula is so often cast as the primary condition of reading and evaluating Disney's animated texts.

The energy and durability of the "formula" provides a readily discernible label that culturally signifies Disney and permits shorthand identification with the multifarious Disney universe (including its autocratic leader). This is in spite of retrospective criticisms since levelled at the "Classic Disney" formula by scholars who have spotlighted Disney's "hyperrealist" reduction of the animated medium as a graphic art (against the chaotic ingenuity of Warner Brothers' animation unit), or who argue that the studio popularised a formula fashioned to the live-action Classical Hollywood model of narration.[20] Most potent among the formula's ongoing critical application and interrogation, however, is the widely-held perspective that surfaces its innate formulaic constitution or *set form*. Disney animation is here denoted through a predictability of content, fixed narrational norms, regulatory conventions, and repeating regimes of representation encoded into the text *by* Disney and readily accessible *to* a mass (usually characterised as "family") audience. Discussing the formula back in 1995 as a tribute to a commodity-fuelled capitalist imperative, Jack Zipes critiques the studio on the grounds that once Walt realised he had struck upon a recipe:

> He never abandoned it, and in fact, if one regards the two most recent Disney Studio productions of *Beauty and the Beast* (1991) and *Aladdin* (1992), Disney's

contemporary animators have continued in his footsteps. There is nothing but the "eternal return of the same" in *Beauty and the Beast* and *Aladdin* that makes for enjoyable viewing and delight in techniques of these films as commodities, but nothing new in the exploration of narration, animation, and signification.[21]

According to Zipes, then, the "Disney formula" has remained "eternally" untroubled, free since the 1940s to produce a specific orthodoxy of expectations based on a typology of consistent textual features from which the studio has seldom deviated. Any changes in the formula are conceptualised as being of degree rather than kind, refinements to central components rather than seismic shifts that fail to disrupt the homogeneity of Disney's animated output. They are, simply, *copies of copies*. Wasko also argues that the conservative themes and consistent characters of the Classic era have "changed little over the years".[22] However, just as early Disney critics discerned the derivative qualities of *Fantasia* as a "frank experiment" within a supposedly standardised Classical period, contemporary Disney scholars have progressively destabilised such charges of sameness, and acknowledged the studio's canon as greatly expressive of formulaic upheaval.

The "Neo-Disney" phase, a term employed by Chris Pallant to describe the period of the studio's history between 1999 and 2004, has been categorised as a particularly drastic reworking of convention that actively shifted "the Disney aesthetic in a new direction".[23] This stylistically progressive and heterogeneous period of Disney animation, including *The Emperor's New Groove* (2000), *Lilo and Stitch* (2002), and *Treasure Planet* (2002), offered a freedom of composition and an unprecedented "cartoonality", loosening the studio's established hyper-realist vocabulary at the expense of a more "un-Disney like" register. However, the "Neo-Disney" era only intensifies how Disney's animated features have always been impressed with frequent peaks of formulaic disorder. For example, Maltin asserts how *The Fox and the Hound* (1981) "relies far too much on formula cuteness, formula comic relief, even formula characterizations".[24] But Disney's next film (also directed by Ted Berman), *The Black Cauldron* (1985), was a dark fantasy based on Lloyd Alexander's *Chronicles of Prydain* book series that, in James Kendrick's words, "jettisoned the company's increasingly stale musical formula and emphasized action and spectacle, the hallmarks of 1980s blockbuster filmmaking".[25] The mutable shape of Disney animation, and its capability for change, ultimately bears out the studio's formula as always *historically contingent* rather than an *ahistorical* critical concept. Eleanor Byrne and Martin McQuillan argue that "on every occasion the Disney signature does not signify the same thing", and this important distinction holds given the shifting topography of Disney's animated narratives and its impact on the fixity of the formula.[26] Whether Disney's kinship with musical theatre and creative synergy with a Broadway-style during its post-1989 "Second Golden Age", or the representational radicalism of later "Neo-Disney", departures from formulaic convention graph distinct phases of Disney's animated output, helping scholars evaluate films on the basis of derivation and adherence, *reproduction of* and *resistance to* "Classic Disney" principles. But given how the Classic Disney formula has been worked through and reconfigured, discontinued and progressed, by Disney's animated films at regular intervals and on numerous occasions, its predominance as the spine of (or continuum within) analysis remains troubling.

Frequent recourse to the rigid dictations of the "Disney formula" as a longstanding critical framework – derived from a particularly lauded period in the studio's history – has yielded other achievements. Perhaps ironically, scholars applying the formula to Disney animation have disclosed the canon's true constitution as more *chaotic* (and ultimately *less formulaic*) constellations of meaning, comprised of transforming, continually shifting sets of ideological and formal values consistent only in how they change over time. This very changeability, in turn, surfaces how the application of the formula has tended to mistake its historical specificity for longevity, when the Classic template was initially fleeting (lasting until the 1960s), and then quickly rendered obsolete by the films that followed. For Disney scholars, then, the "formula" is often present solely in its absence, a spectre that haunts Disney scholarship and is typically invoked to explain away divergence rather than identify strict adherence. These assumptions fuel the primary contention of this chapter, namely that in the recent period of Digital Disney, the Disney-centric formula is not a necessary condition or prerequisite of these films' critical analysis, but in fact is simply a readymade, expedient one taken from a canonical or "quality" period and subsequently grafted onto the study of its future. The lively instability of Disney animation necessitates a looser, more flexible approach towards its ideological components and textual properties, one that can ably accommodate its jagged animated landscape but also be more receptive to alternate animated (and non-Disney) contexts that circulate around the studio's animated features.

Digital Disney and *Chicken Little*

Given that during the 1940s and 1950s animated production "formulas dictated technique as well as stories", the recent shift within Disney Feature Animation since 2005 from cel-animated processes to computer graphics has introduced a technological dimension to the formula hitherto absent (or certainly presumed to be relatively invisible) among conventional typologies.[27] Disney had, of course, already recognised the potential in the 1980s for digital imagery to be synthesised within its traditional animation workflow, just as the studio has "like no other American cultural institution, always been invested in the technological".[28] Disney's contribution to the arrival of sound cartoons in the 1920s, their designing of the vertical multiplane camera and adoption of the three-strip Technicolor process in the 1930s, their espousal of cost-effective Xerox copying equipment in the 1960s, and the advent of digital "CAPS" technology in the 1980s all represent Disney's successful ventures into the possibilities afforded by modern technology. Yet the contemporary period of Digital Disney represents the fullest realisation of the studio's pencil to pixel conversion. A phase of animated film production marking the tectonic collision between digital animation processes and Disney's aesthetic, the ten computer-animated features produced by the Walt Disney Feature Animation unit between 2005 and 2018 stand as entirely digital entries within the Disney cartoon canon.

Inaugurated by the release of *Toy Story* (1995), the rapid ascendency of the computer-animated film within mainstream Hollywood animation provides a particularly robust and resilient industrial context that envelops Digital Disney. Superseding traditional cel-animation methods as the animated film's principal language, the computer-animated film has been recognised critically for its positive contribution to the U.S. animation industry.[29] The exponential growth in the number of American animation studios making the transition from digital visual effects companies to feature-filmmaking, coupled with their economic viability and renewed critical appeal, has situated computer-animated films as the locus for debates on animation's current commercial strength and quality of production. The Disney studio is firmly implicated within this animated resurgence of the post-millennial period. The critical and commercial achievements of the Digital Disney period – culminating in the global box-office success and cultural ubiquity of *Frozen* – has led to calls among popular reviewers and more "unofficial" fansites and discussion forums that Disney has now entered a "Neo-Renaissance" or "Third Golden Age".[30] However, the films of the Digital Disney era certainly pose a challenge to the authority of the formula as the centrepiece of critical analysis, complicating its place as the default barometer against which the studio's animated features are gauged. Alongside his comparison of Disney's *Bolt* and Pixar's *Wall-E* (2008), for example, Pallant admits that "Disney's CG features reveal the influence of outside forces – namely the features produced by DreamWorks Animation and Blue Sky Studios".[31] Such recognition of alternate, non-Disney contexts to account for formal features and ideological values dislodges studio authorship as the root cause of shared commonalities. These are texts visibly informed, shaped and moulded by their contact with computer-animated films that circulate beyond the Disney canon.

Chicken Little offers a rich case study in this respect. An unofficial remake of Disney's own 1943 short based on "The Sky is Falling" fable, *Chicken*

Little immediately plunders and explodes the constituent parts of the Disney formula. The film begins with a volley of visual allusions intended to itemise with economic efficiency the film's Disney identity, whilst being no less explicit in attacking the formulaic constitution of Magic Kingdom convention. Fading from the Disney studio logo into swirling "pixie" dust – popularised by Tinkerbell from *Peter Pan* (1953) and central to the studio's reproducible "magical" iconography – *Chicken Little* immediately stakes its claim as a "Once Upon a Time" narrative. The falling dust is illuminated onscreen by golden rays of light that bisect the darkened screen at an angle, complemented by "the rising string music that had begun to swell".[32] Buck Cluck's abrasive narration, however, immediately cuts short this enchanting image, and the delivery of his line "How many times have you heard that to begin a story?" verbalises his disregard for the workings of the Disney formula. Similar treatment is afforded later to the ornate fairy tale book that opens to reveal the printed story inside, recognisable from *Snow White and the Seven Dwarfs* (1937), *Cinderella* (1950), and *Sleeping Beauty* (1959), though this time presented through computer graphics. Just as the leather-bound book's pages begin to turn, Buck's voiceover becomes increasingly agitated at the recourse to fairy tale sameness ("Oh no, no – not the book. How many have seen 'opening the book' before? Close the book, we're not doing that!"). Situated between these focused assaults on the particular fairy tale legacy of the studio is another allusion to more contemporary Disney narratology. Initiated by the rhythmical chants of a Zulu refrain, the rousing musical number "Circle of Life" from *The Lion King* (1994) is cued on the soundtrack to Buck's excited proclamation that "here is how to open a movie". But as the shimmering orange sun begins to rise over the Saharan plains, synchronised with the opening bars of Elton John and Tim Rice's song (original cel-animated footage from *The Lion King* is reused here), Buck again concedes that the tone of this opening feels perhaps too second generation ("No I don't think so, it sounds familiar; doesn't it to you?"). It is only when the film ceases in its recollection of Disney's animated history that Buck is able to settle on a degree of originality to these opening images, and he signals that the narrative can properly commence ("here's what we're gonna do"). The eponymous Chicken Little then appears in pristine digital imagery atop a bell tower, his frantic cry of "Run for your lives" directed to the townsfolk of Oakley Oaks accompanied by a swooping virtual camera that rotates dizzyingly around the character's equally "animated" feathered body in ways that register the spectacle of the film's computerized presence.

Within these opening stages of *Chicken Little*, then, the emphasis is clearly on formal regeneration that is delivered through the sequence's self-reflexive structure of transformation. Buck is firmly embroiled in a perpetual renewal of beginnings as (from his detached, yet involved, extra-diegetic position) he pauses, rewinds, replays and ultimately replaces the animated action of *Chicken Little* in the pursuit of the most suitable "Disney" opening. This is a film inevitably part of an established Disney feature film canon stretching back to the late 1930s, yet it strives at every turn to distance itself from such an identity. As Pallant puts it, "The iconographic evocation of traditional Disney introductions and subsequent admission of their staleness serves to position *Chicken Little* as a film which, through an awareness of past Disney convention, could potentially offer something new and different".[33] Despite repeated gestures in its visual register to Disney's classical past and Buck's complementary (rather than complimentary) narration, *Chicken Little* can be implicated into other non-Disney frames of reference to craft a more nuanced understanding of its content. Despite its status as the studio's first all-digital feature, the film can be productively *prised* away from its Disney lineage and instead *prized* according to its coexistent identity as a computer-animated film.[34] Indeed, it is *Chicken Little*'s very desire to distance itself from received notions of Disney that unveils something of this ulterior identity.

An immediate reference point to the self-conscious, deconstructive opening of *Chicken Little* is DreamWorks' computer-animated film franchise *Shrek* (2001–2010). These films actively court comparisons with Disney through a radical anti-Disney sentiment and relentless mocking of "Mouse House" tradition (widely attributed to the acrimonious departure from Disney by DreamWorks CEO Jeffrey Katzenberg in 1994). Based on William Steig's picture book series, the first *Shrek* film opens with the eponymous ogre explicating the standard fairy tale narrative as he turns the pages of the storybook ("Once upon a time there was a lovely princess"). Whereas Steig's original tale begins by describing Shrek's "ugly" mother and father, this computer-animated film adaptation has the ogre unexpectedly curse the romanticism of true love's first kiss ("Like that's ever gonna happen!"), before ripping the printed pages from their binding to use as toilet paper in an outside latrine. The first scenes of *Shrek Forever After* (2010) reprise the destructive tone of the original. A vengeful Rumpelstiltskin is similarly shown destroying the sanctity of the fairy tale book in furious (and unsentimental) rage, actions that mark another physical assault on the narrative traditions of *Snow White* and *Cinderella*. As Jessica Tiffin explains, "Post-*Shrek* contemporary fairy-tale films share a certain ironic distance from their fairy-tale roots, [and] they also have in common their awareness of narrative, or, more accurately, an insecurity about it".[35] In its parody of "Disney" sentimental fantasy and heroic morality, it is clear that *Chicken Little* is ostensibly "doing" *Shrek*, borrowing its deconstructive patter to similarly unpack Disney iconography. But the self-referential opening of *Chicken Little* not only finds a corollary in the *Shrek* franchise that mocks and manipulates Disney's fairy tale archetypes, but shares multiple points of contact with other computer-animated films. *Hoodwinked!* (2006) and its sequel *Hoodwinked Too! Hood vs. Evil* (2011) add another dimension to the familiar image of the fairy tale book. Both films begin with a mobile virtual camera swooping down into the three-dimensional book to have the subsequent action literally unfold within its pages. Evoking more explicitly Buck's narration that begins *Chicken Little*, the opening sequence of *Happily N'Ever After* (2006) similarly obliterates the sealed narrative space and context to acknowledge the spectators' act of watching, and to playfully reveal the premises of its own unique construction. The forward momentum of narrative progression is unexpectedly halted by the intrusive presence of the omniscient narrator, Rick, who pauses the film (so that the sprocket holes of the "celluloid" are visible) and proceeds to outline the film's key characters. Rick's reflexive verbal commentary *upon* the fictional world opens up the film's diegesis to abrupt, unmotivated change, while his demand to take control of the film and "go back a little" recalls the similar demands made on linear progression by the restless Buck Cluck.

Classed on the one hand as a Disney film, *Chicken Little* reveals the residual traces of the irreverent humour and formal exuberance of the preceding "Neo-Disney" phase. The film even bears the stamp of Wasko's "Classic Disney" model, echoing core Disney virtues of individualism and innocence in ways that maintain the formula as viable connective tissue between *Chicken Little* and Disney's prior animated films. However, finding common ground and forging meaningful associations between *Chicken Little* and the emergent conventions of computer-animated cinema activates a new genealogy for Digital Disney predicated on an alternate formal logic. *Chicken Little* can be understood through the ironic distancing of the "post-*Shrek*" fairy tale with its mindfulness of narrative mechanisms played for comedy. Furthermore, the Disney film is itself congruent with the wider "self-referentiality and surface play" that J.P. Telotte argues has been a "consistent pattern" connecting numerous computer-animated films, beginning with the parody of the Western genre that opens Pixar's *Toy Story* and continuing across its "digital brethren" such as *Monsters, Inc.* (2001), *The Incredibles* (2004) and *Cars* (2006).[36] Indeed, *Chicken Little*'s many reminders of its diegetic construction are scored to a series of highly self-reflexive notes played by several computer-animated films. With their intention to manipulate playfully the illusory achievements of digital imagery (as audiovisual façade), the opening sequences to *Antz* (1998), *Toy Story 2* (1999) and *Shark Tale* (2004) all raise to a higher pitch of emphasis the game of digital illusion in which *Chicken Little* openly takes part. Later films even suggest digital illusionism is the product of theatrical effects (*Shrek the Third* [2007]) complete with rolling backdrop and foley artists, or even recourse to a rising stage curtain (*Gnomeo and Juliet* [2011]), to literally "stage" a humorous "surface play" with the geography of virtual space. Released six months after *Chicken Little*, *The Wild* in particular reprises the deconstructive humour of Buck's impulsive narration. The Walt Disney

Pictures logo that opens the film is paused, rewound and then re-started to accommodate the impetuousness of a young lion, Ryan, who interrupts his father Samson's voiceover with claims of storytelling staleness. Rather than falling back on any determining Disney status, *Chicken Little* starts to look like a film whose textual features and narrative pleasures can be extrapolated in excess of the Disney formula, and instead be understood to circulate *among* and *between* multiple computer-animated films.

A plasmatic approach?

Disney's own critical history provides a vocabulary for understanding the logic of this entanglement between both Disney and non-Disney computer-animated films, and with it more readily unpack the syntax of recent Digital Disney. "Plasmaticness" is a term highly animated in its origins, drawn from Sergei Eisenstein's formal appreciation of the *Silly Symphonies* series. It is thus specific to a period of Disney animation prior to the solidification of their "formula for success" with *Snow White and the Seven Dwarfs*.[37] The "plasmatic" attributes of pre-feature length Disney animation are rooted in its formal ecstasy and harmony of technique, generating an intoxication felt in the Russian filmmaker towards the animated figure's "changeability, fluidity, [and] suddenness of formations".[38] Disney animation of the 1920s and 1930s resisted the enslavement and "once-and-for-ever given" of the modern world and its monstrosity, contravening the "mercilessly standardized and mechanically measured existence" of American social order to revel instead in the ecstatic freedoms of the animated line. Early Disney animation, and in particular the shorts *Hawaiian Holiday* (1937) and *Merbabies* (1938), offered for Eisenstein a "liberation of forms from the laws of logic and forever established stability", mocking zoology as they re-conjured a divine omnipotence within the animated image.[39] The "hyperrealism" of *Snow White*, however, would ultimately subjugate the plasmatic potential of the shorts, conquering their freedom with an illusionist reality at the expense of a lost elasticity.

Taken for its historical specificity (if not its poetic resonance), Eisenstein's notion of a formal plasmaticness embedded deep in Disney's cel-animated images provides a way of challenging dominant formulaic thinking. Repeated recourse to the Disney formula as a core principle in understanding and engaging with Disney's animated features awards them a "measured existence", which counters their supremacy as lively animated texts. The formula makes discriminations based on the internal connections along a continuum between a single Disney animated film and those that flank it. A *plasmatic* approach towards Disney's computer-animated films, however, is more reactionary against formalised and formulated logic. It rejects this "once-and-forever allotted form[ula]" to provide Digital Disney with greater "freedom from ossification".[40] Disney's computer-animated films are themselves highly plasmatic, as despite their seemingly-definite form and straightforward appearance as Disney texts, they simultaneously behave like a "primal protoplasm, not yet possessing a 'stable' form but capable of assuming any form".[41] *Chicken Little* is a Disney film *and* a computer-animated film, both at once. These two identities operate in a constant dialogue, speaking to one another to divulge the changeability that suffices as a property of its plasmatic form. The computer-animated films of the Digital Disney period thus hold an "all-possible diversity of form", accruing a variety of textual features and pleasures constrained and rendered dormant by the rigid dictations of the Disney formula, but highlighted anew by an alternate order of analysis that looks outwards to a computer-animated film context. A plasmatic approach to Digital Disney animation, therefore, shifts the frames of reference to invite new readings of Disney animation rooted in the identification of an alternate set of connecting criteria.

The plasmatic potential of Digital Disney – as films residing between poles of continuity and heterogeneity – speaks to a conspicuously spirited strand of Disney studies, namely the wealth of critical perspectives that square the "impoverishment" of American culture by the Disney conglomerate machine to its influential formula. The Disney studio's broader tendency towards adaptation has repeatedly situated notions of a formula in the throes of cultural and historical appropriation, placed on a collision course with pre-existing story material to yield supposedly sanitized versions of popular myths. The Disney studio's fine-tuning of canonical source material (initially European fairy tales) for its animated features unfolds the formula as a key component of "Disneyfication", a process in which there is a creative bargain struck with the authoritative original for commercial imperatives, negotiated through processes of cartoonal corruption, dilution, inflection, and violation that undermine the integrity of the adapted material. Gene Walz claims that "Disneyfication" at the level of production "denotes the company's bowdlerization of literature, myth, and/or history in a simplified, sentimentalized, programmatic way", and in doing so marks the reduction of "complex character and grand narratives to pre-digested formulas".[42] The "Disneyfied" product is thus assigned an imaginary identity at a distance from "authentic" or "credible" representation.[43] It is a pejorative moniker charged with condemning Disney's deformation of culture within its animated features, unveiling how a pre-existing product has been embellished and re-conjured to fit the constraining mould of the studio's formulaic tendencies.[44]

From colonial discovery (*Pocahontas* [1995]) and medieval tragedy (*The Hunchback of Notre Dame* [1996]) to Greek mythology (*Hercules* [1997]) and Chinese legend (*Mulan* [1998]), plentiful evidence paints a picture of how the Disney formula supposedly alleviates "official" historical account. At its most political, then, Disneyfication (a term coined in the 1990s) is grounded in the consumerism of a capitalist culture. It collapses any recognition of the formula into what is perceived to be the studio's pursuit of economic enchantment, deployed to help maintain its *raison d'être* as purveyor of wholesome family entertainment at the "expense" of "histori-cal accuracy". Alan Bryman suggests that as a mode of editing, "to Disneyfy means to translate or transform an object", casting Disneyfication (and his affiliate term "Disneyization") on the side of the studio's calculated assault on American society.[45] Kent Jones adds that "it's not that we [Americans] lack a past, but that we use it so thoughtlessly, forever mining it and melting it down to a malleable substance – the process known as 'Disneyfication'".[46] Echoing Eisenstein's "flexible" terminology, then, both Bryman and Jones argue that Disneyfication reduces history to something resembling an unstable, highly plasmatic construct readily plundered for trivial consump-tion. Responding to such charges of inaccurate, improper anti-historicism, however, Disneyfication simply follows the muddied purity of all written histories that are produced through practices of "condensation, displace-ment, symbolization, and qualification".[47] The ongoing tension between poetics and empiricism that marks the truth of history (historical facts are, of course, non-narrative) – but whose connection Disney has been widely critiqued for gamely exploiting – is even reflected in the more "fictional" histories of fairy tale and folklore no less spiked with issue of disarticulation, appropriation, and translation stemming from their oral storytelling roots. Disney's particular cartoon "historiophoty" (to borrow Hayden White's term) and the adequacy of its own imagistic (graphic) discourse constitutes part of the way we think about – and represent dimensions of our ideas of – history.[48] But Disneyfication in particular alerts us to how the shaping of historical presentation (into *re*presentation) in Disney animation discloses the necessary instability of the formula, one that is conversely cited by scholars as the most durable, fixed weapon working for Disney against historical veracity. Indeed, as the *working through* of stories, cultures, legends and myths so that they might better fit the Disney template, practices of Disneyfication need another corresponding action: that is, a plasmatic, elastic vitality to the formula, which must also stretch in a host of disparate directions within a series of nuanced translations and transformations. As an interstitial process that occurs (and recurs) in the space *between* the principles of the formula and the sanctity of the target text, Disneyfication demands (and requires) a plasmatic pliancy to the formula so that it can more easily shape its values to multiple contexts. An altogether more complex push/pull relationship is therefore at work across critical assump-tions of "Disneyfied" narratives. Within widespread processes of Disney-fication (and as a response to criticisms of its trivialization of local and global histories), the Disney formula must be viewed as a set of principles that are never fixed, but which *always* flex and strain under the weight of its adapted subject matter. Disneyfication can be conceptualised as simply the measure of this strain, a recognition of the Disney formula as plasma. It is not an inventory of Disney's "one-way" cultural imperialism, but a sliding scale that registers any cross-fertilization with, and spread of, Disney's formulaic principles. This includes any concessions made by the studio across its formal and ideological currency. As a process predicated on intersection, Disneyfication is as much to do with the power wielded *by* Disney as it is concerned with the reciprocating transformation and negotiation *of* Disney.

Given the coalition between Digital Disney and the wider computer-animated film context, we might say, then, that *Chicken Little* operates as a Disneyfied retelling of computer-animated films (as new source material). Its narrative openly jettisons what is culturally recognisable as "Disney" within its opening sequence, stretching the formula to foreground anti-Disney ridicule: to be a computer-animated film, it must repeatedly cease to be a "Disney" one. As a more sustained recourse to conceptions of "Classic Disney", however, *Tangled* provides a counterpoint to *Chicken Little* in not pulling away so forcefully from its Disney status, but seeking more readily to embrace formulaic markers for a modern audience. Justin Chang argues that *Tangled* is a hybrid text, "pitched somewhere between Disney classicism and the self-conscious storybook quality of DreamWorks' 'Shrek' movies".[49] Writing in the *New York Times*, A.O. Scott likewise adds that the film marks the "perfect marriage of Pixarian technical bravura and Disneyesque expressive cartooning".[50] Returning the Disney studio to the Princess narrative for the first time within an all-digital context, *Tangled* occupies a place of negotiation, affixing Classic Disney to the same kind of deconstructive, ironic and self-conscious comedy found in the *Shrek* and *Hoodwinked* films. However, the "post-*Shrek*" irony of narrative awareness (embodied principally in the male protagonist, Flynn Rider) is somewhat leavened by a more affectionate treatment of its fairy tale subject matter. Both *Chicken Little* and *Tangled* thus reveal how the films of Digital Disney are rich sites for identifying the various push/pull factors that surface the Disney formula as a more chaotic, plasmatic set of values.

Despite discourses of historical and cultural homogeneity prevailing among received accounts of the Disney formula, there is a protean charge highly operative within its prestige as a taxonomy of values. Such impulses permit the formula to actively move across, contract and modify itself like a "primal protoplasm" as it is (re)shaped to fit the contours of that which is being Disneyfied (a term that no longer needs to be derided, but championed, as one alive to the innate fluidity of the formula). Just as Disney's *Silly Symphonies* for Eisenstein provided audio-visual respite from modernity's shackled lives "graphed by the cent and the dollar", a plasmatic conception of Disney animation is more responsive to the formula's numerous acts of transition and change, openly bypassing the "regulated moments" and structural fixity ordained by prior formulaic analyses.[51] There is certainly a need to reject a rigid understanding of the Disney formula, and think through what is at stake when applying it as an evaluative term. Not only has the formula displayed a frenzied trajectory across Disney's animated features since the Classic era that gave it definition but, as part of the default language of Disneyfication, it must be malleable enough to accommodate Hugo and Hercules in the same breath. Collapsing the structures of the Disney formula, and imbuing its reconstruction with greater critical elasticity and a stronger plasmatic vigour, does therefore not weaken its structure. Rather, its flexibility supports a critical analysis of Disney animation, and affords greater specificity when discriminating between individual films within Disney's animated canon.

Conclusion: a misunderstood mouse

The increasing scope of Disney scholarship continues to colour Disney's animated films with new tones and shades, their drawn (and now digitized) outlines inked in with persuasive ideological critique and formal appreciation. Within ongoing critical discussions of Disney Feature Animation, however, there has persisted a degree of perceived inevitability to the Disney formula that often predicts something of its critical fate. It is one of the many "old coats of critical paint" applied to the Disney Corporation that, while a valuable heuristic, has nonetheless constrained the clarity of those ingredients that make up Disney's complex cartoon concoction.[52] The persistence of the formula as a default point of authority ultimately reproduces what Seán Harrington calls the fetishized imaginary Disney "thing", part of the "frozen image of Disney's classic era" that, despite its fleetingness as a historical period, has subsequently prevailed as a common narrative.[53] The period known critically as Digital Disney – and the computer-animated films that currently comprise this era – peak the anomaly that the Disney formula presides as a stable, "frozen" set of values made available for reproduction or rejection. Disney's computer-animated films are sites of negotiation, and recourse to the Disney formula does not resolve or fully explain the identity of Digital Disney on its own. The formula must therefore assume its place alongside a myriad of alternate frames of reference in the creation of meaning. A duel between *formulaic* and *plasmatic* thinking presents an effective means of understanding the period of Digital Disney, painting (and now pixelating) a picture of Disney's computer-animated films that is altogether more nuanced and complex.

The decentring of the formula as Disney discourse's main critical narrative, and the alignment of the studio's computer-animated films in this inclusive way, bears out the possibility for wider generic thinking. As I have argued elsewhere, it is generative to the study of Digital Disney to perceive this distinct phase as belonging to a wider computer-animated film genre, which allows its narrative, characters, and other formal attributes to be seen in more complex ways.[54] Genre, on occasion, has been cited to explain Disney's animated corpus, with Harrington discussing the "substance of Disney as a genre" as a way of demarcating the scope and expectation of Disney's animated narratives.[55] Given its polyvalence across the poles of production, distribution and reception, the Disney formula does operate in a manner highly reminiscent of how film genre has been increasingly theorised. Yet the recognition of computer-animated films as a genre in their own right provides the opportunity to think through the viability and applicability of the Disney formula as a defining credential. This is because genre criticism complements the analysis of studio brand identity, even accommodating the growing unsteadiness of Disney's formulaic markers. It is, for example, increasingly challenging to identify computer-animated films solely via the signature styles of individual studios. Henry Giroux and Grace Pollock argue that *A Bug's Life* (1998) "is one Pixar film that seems to stick closely to the Disney formula", while Elizabeth Leane and Stephanie Pfennigwerth actually revisit Wasko's Classic Disney template to examine the moralism of Australian computer-animated musical *Happy Feet* (2006) produced by visual effects studio Animal Logic.[56] These evaluations openly sustain the Disney formula as a prevailing yardstick for the analysis of a range of non-Disney animated texts, whilst simultaneously complicating Disney's possession of its own formula. The subsequent acquisition of Pixar by Disney in early 2006 (and the migration of Pixar co-founder John Lasseter between facilities) made the rhetorical boundary between the two studios further porous, precipitating a highly-problematic exchange of narrative and thematic content. Such corporate fluency has added further intrigue to the notion that "audiences are sometimes unsure what is and is not a Disney film", whilst speaking to how definable pleasures and particular kinds of spectator expectations are often attributed by critics and audiences to specific studios.[57] Whether or not this corporate fluency will change following Lasseter's departure, now that Disney Animation and Pixar each has its own head (Jennifer Lee and Pete Docter, respectively), remains to be seen.

Wider generic concerns can work in conjunction with such proprietary textual features (however slippery), yet without the prevailing assumption that a studio-based formula remains the underlying source for the presence of common ground. The orderly grouping of Digital Disney together in a wider *computer-animated film genre* embraces cross-pollination whilst preserving studio specificities, in the same way that it does not violate or void the singularity of individual films. Rather, genre provides a critical framework for better understanding the content, themes and style that underpin the pleasures contained in the computer-animated film narratives. Within a Disney context, the criteria linking *Chicken Little* to *Meet the Robinsons*, but also to *Bolt*, *Tangled*, *Wreck-It Ralph*, *Frozen*, *Big Hero 6*, *Zootopia*, *Moana*, *Ralph Breaks the Internet*, and *Frozen 2* (2019) may therefore emerge from the ulterior features germane to a computer-animated film genre, rather than predicated on (and patterned by) any determining Disney status. Genre also interrogates the two (anomalous) "cel"-animated features produced during the Digital Disney period – *The Princess and the Frog* (2009) and *Winnie the Pooh* (2011) – and asks whether their formal currency is informed by other computer-animated films (beyond obvious technological considerations), or whether their allegiance lies elsewhere. Armed with the possibilities of a more plasmatic, generic analysis, then, a whole host of connections between computer-animated films (both *made* and *not made* by Disney) can be uncovered that dually complement and overwrite the pleasures of the Disney formula, offering an alternate "generic" agreement for identification that manoeuvres outside any prior recognisability of what a Disney text might be. Submitting Digital Disney to further scrutiny can help elaborate the unique visual currencies and formal attributes of other computer-animated films, which then can be organised productively as a viable generic framework that supports their study as a genre of contemporary cinema.

Bibliography

Anon. "Review: 'Dumbo.'" *Variety* (October 1, 1941): 9.

Bryman, Alan. *The Disneyization of Society*. London: SAGE Publications, 2004.

Byrne, Eleanor, and Martin McQuillan. *Deconstructing Disney*. London: Pluto Press, 1999.

Chang, Justin. "Review: Tangled". *Variety* (November 15-November 21, 2010): 28.

Connelly, Sherlyn. "The Disney Princess Formula Works Again in Frozen". *The Village Voice* (November 27, 2013). Accessed June 13, 2015. http://www.villagevoice.com/film/the-disney-princess-formula-works-again-in-frozen-6440221

Crowther, Bosley. "Walt Disney's 'Fantasia', an Exciting New Departure in Film Entertainment, Opened Last Night at the Broadway". *The New York Times* (November 14, 1940): 28.

Crowther, Bosley. "Walt Disney's Cartoon, 'Dumbo', a Fanciful Delight, Opens at the Broadway". *The New York Times* (October 24, 1941): 27.

Davis, Amy M. *Good Girls & Wicked Witches: Women in Disney's Feature Animation*. Bloomington and Indianapolis: John Libbey & Company/University of Indiana Press, 2006.

Eisenstein, Sergei. *Eisenstein on Disney*. Translated by Jay Leyda. London: Methuen, 1986.

English, Horace B. ""Fantasia" and the Psychology of Music". *The Journal of Aesthetics and Art Criticism* 2, no.7 (Winter 1942–1943): 27–31.

Foundas, Scott. "Film Review: Frozen". *Variety* (November 3, 2013). Accessed June 13, 2015. http://variety.com/2013/film/reviews/frozen-review-1200782020/

Giroux, Henry A. "Animating Youth: The Disneyfication of Children's Culture". *Socialist Review* 24, no.3 (1994): 23–55.

Giroux, Henry A., and Grace Pollock. *The Mouse that Roared: Disney and the End of Innocence*. Maryland: The Rowman and Littlefield Publishing Group, Inc., 2010.

Griffin, Sean. *Tinker Belles and Evil Queens: The Walt Disney Company from the Inside Out*. New York: New York University Press, 2000.

Harrington, Seán. *The Disney Fetish*. Bloomington and Indianapolis: John Libbey & Company / University of Indiana Press, 2015.

Holliday, Christopher. *The Computer-Animated Film: Industry, Style and Genre*. Edinburgh: Edinburgh University Press, 2018.

Jones, Kent. *Physical Evidence: Selected Film Criticism*. Middletown, CT: Wesleyan University Press, 2007.

Kendrick, James. *Hollywood Bloodshed: Violence in 1980s American Cinema*. Carbondale, IL: Southern Illinois University Press, 2009.

Leane, Elizabeth, and Stephanie Pfennigwerth. "Marching on Thin Ice: The Politics of Penguin Films". In *Considering Animals: Contemporary Studies in Human-Animal Relations*, edited by Elizabeth Leane, Yvette Watt and Carol Freeman, 29–40. Burlington: Ashgate, 2011.

Maltin, Leonard. *Of Mice and Magic: A History of American Animated Cartoons*. New York and Scarborough, Plume Books, 1987.

Maltin, Leonard. *The Disney Films Fourth Edition*. New York: Disney Editions, 2000.

Merritt, Russell. "Lost on Pleasure Islands: Storytelling in Disney's Silly Symphonies". *Film Quarterly* 59, no. 1 (Fall 2005): 4–17.

Pallant, Chris. *Demystifying Disney: A History of Disney Feature Animation*. London: Continuum, 2011.

Real, Michael. *Mass-Mediated Culture*. New Jersey: Prentice-Hall, 1977.

Roper, Caitlin. "*Big Hero 6* Proves It: Pixar's Gurus Have Brought the Magic Back to Disney Animation". *WIRED* (October 21, 2014). Accessed June 13, 2015. http://www.wired.com/2014/10/big-hero-6/

Scott, A. O. "Back to the Castle, Where It's All About the Hair". *The New York Times* (November 23, 2010): C1.

Stewart, James B. *DisneyWar*. New York: Simon & Schuster, 2005.

Telotte, J.P. *The Mouse Machine*. Chicago: University of Illinois Press, 2008.

Thomas, Bob. *Walt Disney: A Biography*. London: W.H. Allen & Co. Ltd, 1976.

Tiffin, Jessica. *Marvelous Geometry: Narrative and Metafiction in Modern Fairytale*. Detroit: Wayne State University Press, 2009.

Vardalos, Marianne. "Kantian Cosmopolitanism and the Dreamworkification of the Next Generation". In *Investigating Shrek: Power, Identity, and Ideology*, edited by Tim Nieguth, Aurélie Lacassagne and François Dépelteau, 80–102. New York: Palgrave Macmillan, 2011.

Walz, Gene. "Charlie Thorson and the Temporary Disneyfication of Warner Bros. Cartoons". In *Reading the Rabbit: Explorations in Warner Bros. Animation*, edited by Kevin S. Sandler, 49–66. New Jersey: Rutgers University Press, 1998.

Wasko, Janet. *Understanding Disney: The Manufacture of Fantasy*. Cambridge: Polity, 2001.

Watts, Steve. *The Magic Kingdom: Walt Disney and the American Way of Life*. Boston: Houghton Mifflin, 1997.

White, Hayden. "Historiography and Historiophoty". *The American Historical Review* 93, no.5 (December 1988): 1193–1199.

Zipes, Jack. "Breaking the Disney Spell". In *From Mouse to Mermaid: The Politics of Film, Gender and Culture*, edited by Elizabeth Bell, Lynda Haas and Laura Sells, 21–42. Bloomington and Indianapolis: Indiana University Press, 1995.

Filmography

Aladdin. Dir. Ron Clements, John Musker. USA, Walt Disney Productions, 1992.

Antz. Dir. Eric Darnell, Tim Johnson. USA, DreamWorks Animation, 1998.

Beauty and the Beast. Dir. Gary Trousdale, Kirk Wise. USA, Walt Disney Animation Studios, 1991.

Big Hero 6. Dir. Don Hall, Chris Williams. USA, Walt Disney Animation Studios, 2014.

The Black Cauldron. Dir. Ted Berman, Richard Rich. USA, Walt Disney Animation Studios, 1985.

Bolt. Dir. Chris Williams, Byron Howard. USA, Walt Disney Animation Studios, 2008.

A Bug's Life. Dir. John Lasseter. USA, Pixar Animation Studios, 1998.

Cars. Dir. John Lasseter. USA, Pixar Animation Studios, 2006.

Chicken Little. Dir. Mark Dindal. USA, Walt Disney Animation Studios, 2005.

Cinderella. Dir. Clyde Geronimi, Hamilton Luske, Wilfred Jackson. USA, Walt Disney Animation Studios, 1950.

Dumbo. Dir. Ben Sharpsteen, Norman Ferguson, Wilfred Jackson, William Roberts, Jack Kinney, Samuel Armstrong. USA, Walt Disney Animation Studios, 1941.

The Emperor's New Groove. Dir. Mark Dindal. USA, Walt Disney Animation Studios, 2000.

Fantasia. Dir. James Algar, John Hubley, Wilfred Jackson. USA, Walt Disney Animation Studios, 1940.

The Fox and the Hound. Dir. Ted Berman, Richard Rich, Art Stevens. USA, Walt Disney Animation Studios, 1981.

Frozen. Dir. Chris Buck, Jennifer Lee. USA, Walt Disney Animation Studios, 2013.

Gnomeo & Juliet. Dir. Kelly Asbury. UK/USA, Arc Productions, 2011.

Happily N'Ever After. Dir. Yvett Kaplan, Paul J. Bolger. Germany/USA, Vanguard Animation, 2007.

Happy Feet. Dir. George Miller. USA, Animal Logic Films, 2006.

Hawaiian Holiday. Dir. Ben Sharpsteen. USA, Walt Disney Animation Studios, 1937.

Hercules. Dir. Ron Clements, John Musker. USA, Walt Disney Animation Studios, 1997

Hoodwinked! Dir. Cory Edwards, Todd Edwards, Tony Leech. USA, Kanbar Animation, 2006.

Hoodwinked Too! Hood vs. Evil. Dir. Mike Disa. USA, Kanbar Animation, 2011.

The Hunchback of Notre Dame. Dir. Gary Trousdale, Kirk Wise. USA, Walt Disney Animation Studios, 1996.

The Incredibles. Dir. Brad Bird. USA, Pixar Animation Studios, 2004.

Lilo and Stitch. Dir. Dean DeBlois, Chris Sanders

The Lion King. Dir. Roger Allers, Rob Minkoff. USA, Walt Disney Animation Studios, 1994

The Little Mermaid. Dir. Ron Clements, John Musker. USA, Walt Disney Animation Studios, 1989

Meet the Robinsons. Dir. Steve Anderson. USA, Walt Disney Animation Studios, 2007.

Merbabies. Dir. Rudolf Ising, Vernon Stallings. USA, Walt Disney Animation Studios, 1938.

Monsters, Inc. Dir. Pete Docter. USA, Pixar Animation Studios, 2001.

Mulan. Dir. Tony Bancroft, Barry Cook. USA, Walt Disney Productions, 1998.

Peter Pan. Dir. Clyde Geronimi, Hamilton Luske, Wilfred Jackson. USA, Walt Disney Animation Studios, 1953.

Pocahontas. Dir. Mike Gabriel, Eric Goldberg. USA, Walt Disney Productions, 1995.

The Princess and the Frog. Dir. Ron Clements, John Musker. USA, Walt Disney Animation Studios, 2009.

Ralph Breaks the Internet. Dir. Rich Moore, Phil Johnston. USA, Walt Disney Animation Studios, 2018.

Shark Tale. Dir. Vicky Jenson, Bibo Bergeron, Rob Letterman. USA, DreamWorks Animation, 2004.

Shrek. Dir. Vicky Jenson, Andrew Adamson. USA, DreamWorks Animation, 2001.

Shrek 2. Dir. Andrew Adamson, Kelly Asbury, Conrad Vernon. USA, DreamWorks Animation, 2004.

Shrek the Third. Dir. Chris Miller, Raman Hui. USA, DreamWorks Animation, 2007.

Shrek Forever After. Dir. Mike Mitchell. USA, DreamWorks Animation, 2010.

Sleeping Beauty. Dir. Clyde Geronimi, Les Clark, Eric Larson, Wolfgang Reitherman. USA, Walt Disney Animation Studios, 1959.

Snow White and the Seven Dwarfs. Dir. David Hand. USA, Walt Disney Animation Studios, 1937.

Tangled. Dir. Nathan Greno, Byron Howard. USA, Walt Disney Animation Studios, 2010.

Treasure Planet. Dir. Ron Clements, John Musker. USA, Walt Disney Animation Studios, 2002

Toy Story. Dir. John Lasseter. USA, Pixar Animation Studios, 1995.

Toy Story 2. Dir. John Lasseter. USA, Pixar Animation Studios, 1999.

Valiant. Dir. Gary Chapman. UK/USA, Vanguard Animation, 2005.

Wall-E. Dir. Andrew Stanton. USA, Pixar Animation Studios, 2008.

The Wild. Dir. Steve Williams. USA, C.O.R.E. Feature Animation, 2006.

Winnie the Pooh. Dir. Stephen J. Anderson, Don Hall. USA, Walt Disney Animation Studios, 2011.

Wreck-It Ralph. Dir. Rich Moore. USA, Walt Disney Animation Studios, 2012.

Endnotes

1. Janet Wasko, *Understanding Disney: The Manufacture of Fantasy* (Cambridge: Polity, 2001), 4.
2. Wasko, 2–3.
3. Jessica Tiffin, *Marvelous Geometry: Narrative and Metafiction in Modern Fairy Tale* (Detroit: Wayne State University Press, 2009), 211.
4. Sergei Eisenstein, *Eisenstein on Disney*, trans. Jay Leyda (London: Methuen, 1986), 21.
5. Tiffin, *Marvelous Geometry*, 211.
6. Bosley Crowther, "Walt Disney's Cartoon, 'Dumbo', a Fanciful Delight, Opens at the Broadway", *The New York Times* (October 24, 1941): 27.
7. Anon., "Review: 'Dumbo'," *Variety* (October 1, 1941): 9.
8. Bosley Crowther, "Walt Disney's *'Fantasia'* an Exciting New Departure in Film Entertainment, Opened Last Night at the Broadway", *The New York Times* (November 14, 1940): 28.
9. See Russell Merritt, "Lost on Pleasure Islands: Storytelling in Disney's *Silly Symphonies*", *Film Quarterly* 59, no. 1 (Fall 2005): 4–17. As Merritt suggests, "*Pinocchio* [1940], the most amazing structural contraption Disney ever designed, simply builds on the *Symphony* formula" (9).
10. Horace B. English, "*Fantasia* and the Psychology of Music", *The Journal of Aesthetics and Art Criticism* 2, no.7 (Winter 1942–1943): 27.
11. Though technically the *Oswald the Lucky Rabbit* series ran until 1943, it was animated at Disney – its original studio – only until 1928.
12. Bob Thomas, *Walt Disney: A Biography* (London: W.H. Allen & Co. Ltd, 1976), 120.
13. Whereas a more shifting industrial context is framed as the catalyst for sudden formulaic change. For Amy M. Davis, the "Middle Years" (1967–1987) that followed the Classic era is an interstitial phase cued by Walt's waning influence and subsequent death in 1966. Amy M. Davis, *Good Girls & Wicked Witches: Women in Disney's Feature Animation* (Bloomington and Indianapolis: John Libbey & Company/University of Indiana Press, 2006), 137.
14. Steven Watts, *The Magic Kingdom: Walt Disney and the American Way of Life* (Columbia, Missouri: University of Missouri Press, 2001), 166.
15. Leonard Maltin, *Of Mice and Magic: A History of American Animated Cartoons* (New York and Scarborough, Plume Books, 1987), 29.
16. Michael Real, *Mass-Mediated Culture* (New Jersey: Prentice-Hall, 1977), 241.

17. Wasko, 110.

18. "Digital Disney" conventionally means those ten films made in-house at the company's Burbank studios in California as part of its official animated canon. It does not pertain to supplementary short films or television spin-offs, the work of the DisneyToon Studios (a division of Disney specialising in direct-to-video features), the features produced alongside Pixar Animation Studios (whom the Disney Corporation subsequently acquired for $7.4 billion in 2006), or films such as *Valiant* (2005) and *The Wild* (2006), made by Vanguard Animation and C.O.R.E. Feature Animation respectively but distributed by Walt Disney Pictures.

19. Scott Foundas, "Film Review: *Frozen*", *Variety* (November 3, 2013). Accessed June 13, 2015. http://variety.com/2013/film/reviews/frozen-review-1200782020/. Sherliyn Connelly, "The Disney Princess Formula Works Again in *Frozen*", *The Village Voice* (November 27, 2013). Accessed June 13, 2015. http://www.villagevoice.com/film/the-disney-princess-formula-works-again-in-frozen-6440221.

20. Wasko, 114–115.

21. Jack Zipes, "Breaking the Disney Spell", in *From Mouse to Mermaid: The Politics of Film, Gender and Culture*, eds. Elizabeth Bell, Lynda Haas and Laura Sells (Bloomington and Indianapolis: Indiana University Press, 1995), 40.

22. Wasko, 110.

23. Chris Pallant, *Demystifying Disney: A History of Disney Feature Animation* (London: Continuum, 2011), 113.

24. Leonard Maltin, *The Disney Films Fourth Edition* (New York: Disney Editions, 2000), 275.

25. James Kendrick, *Hollywood Bloodshed: Violence in 1980s American Cinema* (Carbondale, IL: Southern Illinois University, 2009), 183.

26. Eleanor Byrne and Martin McQuillan, *Deconstructing Disney* (London: Pluto Press, 1999), 6.

27. Maltin, *Of Mice and Magic*, 211.

28. J.P. Telotte, *The Mouse Machine: Disney and Technology* (Chicago: University of Illinois Press, 2008),7.

29. See Christopher Holliday, *The Computer-Animated Film: Industry, Style and Genre* (Edinburgh: Edinburgh University Press, 2018).

30. Caitlin Roper, "*Big Hero 6* Proves It: Pixar's Gurus Have Brought the Magic Back to Disney Animation", *WIRED* (October 21, 2014). Accessed June 13, 2015. http://www.wired.com/2014/10/big-hero-6/.

31. Pallant, 144.

32. Pallant, 137.

33. Pallant, 138.

34. Produced by Disney's short-lived internal computer graphics division The Secret Lab (previously the Disney-acquired Dream Quest Images), the earlier *Dinosaur* (2000) had already mined the possibilities of digital imagery ahead of *Chicken Little* in its convincing rendering of prehistoric Iguanodons, Brachiosaurus, Carnotaurs and other ornithopod dinosaurs. Yet despite James B. Stewart's claim that *Dinosaur* was Disney's "first computer-generated animated feature", it is in fact a live-action/CGI hybrid (its lush Mesazoic-era landscapes were actually composited footage of Venezuela's Canaima National Park). Nonetheless *Dinosaur's* heavy use of computer graphics progressed the digital aesthetic for the Disney studio's feature films, even though the film itself remained absent from Walt Disney's Animated Classics canon until 2008 (when it was included by the studio as number thirty-nine, pushing *The Emperor's New Groove* up to number forty). In the UK, however, *Dinosaur* is often omitted from the official series, replaced by C.O.R.E.'s *The Wild*, which otherwise assumes the number forty-six position in the Classics range at the expense of *Chicken Little*. For more on the production background of *Dinosaur* and *The Emperor's New Groove* see James B. Stewart, *DisneyWar* (New York: Simon & Schuster, 2005), 356.

35. Tiffin, 230.

36. Telotte, 163–168.

37. Sean Griffin, *Tinker Belles and Evil Queens: The Walt Disney Company from the Inside Out* (New York: New York University Press, 2000), 29.

38. Eisenstein, 21.

39. Eisenstein, 22.

40. Eisenstein, 21.

41. Eisenstein, 21.

42. Gene Walz, "Charlie Thorson and the Temporary Disneyfication of Warner Bros. Cartoons", in *Reading the Rabbit: Explorations in Warner Bros. Animation*, ed. Kevin S. Sandler (New Jersey: Rutgers University Press, 1998), 51.

43. For a more in-depth discussion of Disneyfication see Henry A. Giroux, "Animating Youth: The Disneyfication of Children's Culture", *Socialist Review* 24, no.3 (1994): 23–55.

44. As a counterpoint to Disneyfication, the recent coining of "Dreamworkification" suggests a comparable negotiation between the "culture industry" and "popular imaginary", in this case pertaining to how a radically subversive and "damaging" worldview ("supportive of neoliberalism") is calculatingly encoded by the DreamWorks studio into its computer-animated film narratives. Marianne Vardalos, "Kantian Cosmopolitanism and the Dreamworkification of the Next Generation", in *Investigating Shrek: Power, Identity, and Ideology*, eds. Tim Nieguth, Aurélie Lacassagne and François Dépelteau (New York: Palgrave Macmillan, 2011), 80–102.

45. Alan Bryman, *The Disneyization of Society* (London: SAGE Publications, 2004), 5.

46. Kent Jones, *Physical Evidence: Selected Film Criticism* (Middletown, CT: Wesleyan University Press, 2007), 85.

47. Hayden White, "Historiography and Historiophoty", *The American Historical Review* 93, no.5 (December 1988): 1193.

48. White, 1194.

49. Justin Chang, "Review: Tangled", *Variety* (November 15–21, 2010): 28.

50. A. O. Scott, "Back to the Castle, Where It's All About the Hair", *The New York Times* (November 23, 2010): C1.

51. Eisenstein, 3.

52. Byrne and McQuillan, 14.

53. Seán Harrington, *The Disney Fetish* (Bloomington and Indianapolis: John Libbey & Company/University of Indiana Press, 2015), 1.

54. Holliday, *The Computer-Animated Film*.

55. Harrington, 70.

56. Henry Giroux and Grace Pollock, *The Mouse that Roared: Disney and the End of Innocence* (Maryland: The Rowman and Littlefield Publishing Group, Inc., 2010), 114; Elizabeth Leane and Stephanie Pfennigwerth, "Marching on Thin Ice: The Politics of Penguin Films", in *Considering Animals: Contemporary Studies in Human-Animal Relations*, Elizabeth Leane, Yvette Watt and Carol Freeman (Eds.). (Burlington: Ashgate, 2011), 37.

57. Bryman, 6.

III.
Gender

Perfect Brides or Beautified Baddies: Characters' Use of Cosmetics in Disney's Feature Animation

Lauren L. Smith

Throughout recent history, cosmetics have been inexorably linked with women's identities. As Kathy Piess says in *Making Up, Making Over: Cosmetics, Consumer Culture, and Women's Identity*, "the early-twentieth-century discourse on cosmetics, as articulated by producers and consumers of these commodities, shifted the burden of female identity from an essential, interior self to one formed in the marking and coloring of the face".[1] As early as the 1920s, cosmetics were already being packaged and marketed "on the basis of personality types".[2] In this way, not only did cosmetics become an integral part of the way women's identities are constructed (both as a group and as individuals), but likewise this connection between cosmetics and identity became central to – and further promoted by – the marketing strategies of the cosmetic companies. That cosmetics should be used in the films made by the Walt Disney Animation Studio (from here on referred to as Disney) in order to construct meaning for its characters is not, therefore, particularly surprising. This chapter looks specifically at the ways in which the use of cosmetics is depicted in particular scenes within Disney's animated features in order to create meaning for its characters and the situations surrounding them.

Of the five scenes within Disney's feature films in which obvious attention is drawn to makeup and cosmetics, three revolve around villains: Ursula in *The Little Mermaid* (1989), Madame Medusa in *The Rescuers* (1977), and Yzma in *The Emperor's New Groove* (2000). The two relevant films showcasing "good" characters who use cosmetics are *Mulan* (1998), in which there is a key scene involving Mulan's face being made up, and *The Princess and the Frog* (2009), where we see Tiana's best friend, Charlotte La Bouff, use make-up. In all of these cases, the use of cosmetics as a means of artificial enhancement or even as a means for obtaining beauty, is used to highlight the artifices present in either the characters or the situations being depicted.

In the cases of both Ursula and Madame Medusa, the emphasis on their use of makeup occurs during scenes in which they are being the most manipulative and artificial in their use of language. In both cases, the characters are hiding their true natures and feelings towards other characters; in other words, they are creating artificial identities in order to manipulate other characters into doing their bidding, following their advice – to trick good characters into giving the villains what they want. Deceit plays an important part in Ursula's evil plans throughout the film, from her initial encounter with Ariel, in which she convinces the desperate girl that she really does want to help her, to her transformation into Vanessa, a beautiful girl with Ariel's voice. It is in this initial encounter with Ariel that Ursula's use of cosmetics is highlighted. When Ursula is shown applying her lipstick and using product to style her hair, it is just as Ariel has entered her under water cave, thereby allowing Ursula to begin implementing her plan to overthrow King Triton (Ariel's father). In this scene, Ursula attempts to portray herself as a "saint" who lives "to help unfortunate merfolk", posing as someone who only wishes to help others (for the appropriate fee, of course). As has already been shown in previous scenes in which she is shown plotting her revenge on King Triton, the audience is well aware that she certainly does not intend to help Ariel in her quest to become human and be with Eric (indeed, Ursula wishes to add Ariel to her garden of trapped souls). We see that Ursula is playing a part – putting on the mask of a kind, helpful person who just happens to "fortunately know a little magic".

Wearing red nail varnish, and with her lips already painted a matching crimson red, the first thing Ursula does when Ariel arrives is begin applying her makeup and fixing her hair; effectively, she is applying her mask. The use of a clam-like shell brings connotations of violence to her makeup; she not only traps sea creatures (specifically "merfolk") with her artificial niceties, but also uses them to create her artificial looks as well. As she squeezes out her "lipstick" from the shell, it is shown in close up, and having applied it to her lips, the exaggerated pout she does to ensure it is properly applied draws even further attention to her ritual and its artifice. Throughout this, she lays the foundation for her entrapment of Ariel, painting her face as she paints a metaphorical picture of herself as the kindly stranger who just wants to help, calling Ariel endearing (or possibly, in her case, saccharine) terms such as "my child" and "angelfish" whilst pretending to empathise with Ariel's situation and love for Eric.

Similarly, in *The Rescuers*, when Medusa is shown taking off her makeup (a comic affair, especially when one of her fake eyelashes proves particularly difficult to remove), she is speaking to Penny in a falsely sweet voice, trying to convince the child to try harder in her search for The Devil's Eye, a large diamond that is hidden somewhere at the bottom of a small cave prone to flooding, which she has been using the girl to try and find since only a small, thin child would be able to fit down the hole where the diamond has ended up.

Medusa's deceit in this scene is apparent right from the start, before the audience even sees her. As Penny is getting dressed for bed, Medusa shouts out in a sweet, motherly voice, "Penny dear, aunty Medusa wants to talk to you". Medusa's use of "dear" and "aunty", and the sickly-sweet voice are as artificial as the false eyelashes Medusa will later remove – by this stage in the film, we have already met Medusa, and we are well aware of her negative attitude towards Penny, so we are equally aware of the falseness of her behaviour in this scene. If one needed further clarification of the hollowness of these words, that Medusa is playing a role and masking her true feelings as she masks her face with makeup, then the dialogue provides it. When the scene cuts to Medusa's bedroom from Penny's, where Penny cannot hear, she says to herself, "High tide or not, that little brat's going to find me that diamond tomorrow or else!" As Medusa pulls off her eyelashes, removing her "mask" of makeup, continuing to talk to Penny in her sickly sweet voice, her face is pulled into comedic, elastic positions, almost as though she really is wearing a plastic mask, completely separate from her real face. Her "mask" is not as good as Ursula's, however, and Penny leaves the room in tears after Medusa asks "who would want [to adopt] a homely little girl like you?" Medusa is not as practised as Ursula in the art of the artificial caretaker. Indeed, it is interesting to note that while Medusa is shown taking off her makeup, and indeed is struggling with this task as though she is battling with her makeup mask, Ursula, by contrast, is seen applying her makeup flawlessly, and does so effortlessly as she speaks.

Both of these scenes explicitly draw attention to the way these women use cosmetics to change the way they look; both are shown to use artificial means (makeup) in an attempt to enhance their appearance, whilst simultaneously showing the artificial nature of their performances of friendliness to the other characters. As the artificial nature of both Medusa's and Ursula's appearances are emphasised, they are echoed in the artificial nature of their words.

Just like Ursula and Medusa, their fellow villain, Yzma, wears heavy makeup (including oversized false eyelashes) throughout *The Emperor's New Groove*, as well as an array of extravagant outfits, all with equally-extravagant matching hats or headdresses which serve to hide her baldness. In fact, Yzma is perhaps the most "made up" of all the female Disney villains, wearing eye shadow, extremely long false eyelashes, lipstick, and nail varnish, and always in dramatic colours, usually purple. Purple has come to be a colour that is often associated with female villains (think of Ursula and Maleficent, for example), but likewise has had a long association with royalty; Yzma has strong designs on seizing Emperor Kuzco's throne, and her use of purple is no doubt a nod to her royal aspirations.

Yzma is not the only character to wear makeup in the film; in one scene, Kuzco (by this point having been transformed into a llama by one of Yzma's potions) disguises himself with cosmetics in order to get something to eat in a restaurant in which llamas are banned. Here, the power of cosmetics and costuming is used so successfully in creating a new artificial outward identity that it successfully creates the image of a human woman on the body of a male llama (at least for the characters in the scene; to the audience, he is still unmistakably a llama disguised – rather comically – as a woman). Indeed, after Kuzco removes his makeup, although he wears the rest of his costume still, he feels he cannot go back into the restaurant because he is no longer disguised; his costume relies almost entirely upon his makeup, thereby emphasizing its heightened importance for shaping a character.

Throughout the film, emphasis is put on Yzma's age; indeed, when she is first introduced, she is described as "living proof that dinosaurs once roamed the earth". In a later scene in which Yzma is presented with a cake for her "birthday", there are so many candles that some are even stuck into the sides of the cake. There is one scene in particular in which Yzma's age is highlighted, and indeed this is used to illustrate further Kuzco's distaste for her: as close ups of Yzma's face are shown, effectively dissecting her into pieces to be analysed (and found wanting), her voice fades out in favour of Kuzco's criticism of her (which comes in the form of internal thoughts/voice-over narration) of the way she looks. Despite her obvious attempts at mimicking youth and beauty, Kuzco says to himself (and by extension the audience), "Woah, look at those wrinkles! What is holding this woman together?" Her age, and the fact that she is "past it", are highlighted once more when Kuzco says, "Everybody hits their stride; you just hit yours fifty years ago". There is a suggestion in all of these scenes that it is through Yzma's use of extravagant outfits and heavy makeup that she tries – albeit unsuccessfully – to emulate or create the allusion of youth.

Yzma is a highly exaggerated character, most definitely functioning as a "caricature", a word previously used by Ollie Johnston and Frank Thomas to describe two of their other female villains, Cruella DeVil of *101 Dalmatians*, 1961, and Medusa from *The Rescuers*.[3] Although even as a caricature she is clearly supposed to be wearing cosmetics, the fact that her appearance is created artificially is shown starkly in one particular scene. The illusion is perhaps not a brilliant one, and she might not be fooling anyone, but the artificial nature of this illusion is still shown starkly through the use of cosmetics in a particular scene. In this key scene, Yzma is not shown removing or applying her makeup, but rather is shown without her makeup or extravagant clothes on; awakened by her henchman, Kronk, in the middle of the night, her face is covered in some form of beauty cream, her bald head clearly showing, and her eyes covered in slices of cucumber which fall off to reveal that she is completely lacking in eyelashes (just like Medusa after she has removed her false eyelashes in *The Rescuers*). That Kronk recoils in shock and horror emphasises that the image of this woman, without her makeup on yet still trying desperately to improve her looks through the use of a cream while she sleeps, is a terrifying thing to behold. Likewise, throughout the film, there is a running gag that has various characters describing Yzma as "scary beyond all reason", thereby emphasising Yzma's failure to achieve an attractive physical appearance despite the time and effort she invests in her looks. The scene in which we see Yzma's face slathered with her night-time "beauty" cream, unlike those scenes in which we see Ursula's and Medusa's "beauty" rituals, does not reflect any particular or immediate artifice in Yzma's words or actions (though she does attempt to deceive Kuzco earlier in the film when she tells him she has no hard feelings after he fires her, and then invites him to dinner, officially as a peace offering, in order to poison him). Rather, in showing her without her costume and her makeup, and in the middle of a beauty regime that must be completed while she sleeps, the shot emphasises the overall artifice of her appearance – and by extension her general motivations and behaviour – to include the lengths she is willing to go to in order to achieve some form of youth and beauty, however imperfectly. This artifice in her "beauty" is reflective of her deceptions throughout the film; when she is first introduced, Kuzco says she has recently "gotten into this bad habit of trying to run the country behind my back"; when she decides to poison Kuzco, she invites him to dinner, hiding her murderous intentions behind a fake voice and honeyed words. She later pretends to be a relative of Pacha's in order to get into his house in an attempt to find Kuzco.

It is not just the aforementioned villains in specific scenes who make use of cosmetics; almost all of Disney's female villains are depicted wearing makeup. Indeed, of the nine human (or humanoid) female villains in its feature films, only the Queen of Hearts (*Alice in Wonderland*, 1951), is not shown wearing makeup. The same cannot be said of Disney's female protagonists, who are rarely depicted wearing (obvious) cosmetics. This is particularly true of Disney's "official" princesses, who, although they represent an idealised image of feminine beauty complete with long eyelashes, clear complexions, rosy cheeks and pink lips (and who, in the real world, are even used to market cosmetics ranges, for example M.A.C.'s Cinderella range), tend in themselves to represent a "natural" (and therefore genuine) beauty. Indeed, only two of Disney's princesses – Mulan (from *Mulan*, 1998) and Tiana (from *The Princess and the Frog*, 2009) are ever explicitly shown wearing or applying makeup; in both of these cases, however, there are cultural reasons for why they do so.

In Mulan's case, she only wears makeup when she has need to, and even then only against her will, in order to please her family and fulfil her prescribed role in society. In the scene in which she is going for an interview with the Matchmaker, Mulan must wear makeup as part of her transformation into a "bride" for the Matchmaker to evaluate and (it is hoped) find Mulan a husband so that she might fulfil her duty and "uphold the family honour". The scene revolves around Mulan's transformation into a "perfect" woman, and as Amy M. Davis says in *Good Girls & Wicked Witches: Women in Disney's Feature Animation*, "much emphasis is placed on just how much artifice is involved in being the 'perfect bride'".[4]

Consistently throughout the scene, the fact that being the "perfect bride" relies on how Mulan looks and conforms to a set of very rigid ideals (both physical and behavioural) of traditional femininity is emphasised. This is done both through the lyrics sung by the characters around Mulan, who tell her she must be "primped and polished" and given "a great hairdo" in order to be the "perfect match" and bring her family honour. These lyrics are paired (and contrasted) with the action of the scene, perhaps most obviously when they sing that "a girl can bring her family great honour in one way" whilst Mulan stops to study a game that two men are seen playing, helping the loser (who appears to be deep in thought, struggling with the next move) with one quick move. Mulan's mother quickly pulls her along. The message is clear: according to the dictates of her society, Mulan's intelligence is *not* the "one way" she will bring honour to her family.

Throughout the scene, Mulan is shown as being uncomfortable, and is never quite able to fulfil this role she must play; she has to pretend to be something she is not, and indeed has no wish to be: the embodiment of the "perfect bride". The application of a dramatic red colour to Mulan's lips, as well as eyeliner to her eyes, are each shown in extreme close up. This is clearly an important part of Mulan's transformation – no other part of it is shown in such detail. When Mulan is shown her new face in the mirror, the look of shock and disapproval in her face is obvious; in fact, she almost seems to not recognise herself in that first glimpse. She reaches up and teases a small piece of hair down in front of her face, and smiles; through everything else, all of the makeup and other aspects that fashion the perfect bride, she recognises herself in this small act of rebellion. That she attempts to fulfil this role and allows herself to be transformed for honourable reasons, for her family, is highlighted towards the end of the scene, as her mother puts a floral decoration in her hair and says with pride "There – you are ready now". Mulan's face loses all look of disapproval and discomfort it has harboured throughout; she is doing this for her mother (and father). That the application of makeup plays such a part in the creation of this role again shows how cosmetics are used in order to create meaning in a particular scene; here, it is used along with the rest of the processes in Mulan's transformation to show the artificial nature of the role; one which she never quite fits. This becomes an important part of Mulan's development as a character in the eyes of the audience, and explains why it is so important for her to bring honour to her family in her own way later in the film by going to war in the place of her father.

The highly superficial – and slightly ridiculous – nature of this image of the "perfect bride" which Mulan tries to emulate is highlighted in the next scene with the character of the Matchmaker. The Matchmaker is presented as impatient, demanding, judgemental, and unsympathetic (in heavy contrast to the behaviours and values she demands from the young women she is judging), and physically is depicted as an unattractive woman wearing heavy makeup. Indeed, before we meet her, the girls (including Mulan) who are going to meet with the Matchmaker declare her to be "scarier than the undertaker". The Matchmaker wears similar makeup to that which Mulan has had applied for the occasion, and which has previously been highlighted as an important part of her transformation into the perfect bride. The contrived nature of this beauty is highlighted when the Matchmaker, having smudged the ink used by Mulan to make notes on her arm, accidentally draws a moustache and goatee beard on herself. When Mulan then throws tea over her in order to put out a fire (which Mulan has started), the makeup runs down the Matchmakers face. Her hair now unruly and wet, her makeup and drawn-on beard now running down her face, the illusion of outer beauty is shattered, and as has already been made clear, the Matchmaker is a character who appears to have little inner beauty. The artificial nature of makeup is again highlighted, along with the artificial nature of Mulan's transformation, and indeed of this ideal of feminine beauty for which she must strive.

That this is not who Mulan really is (in case the audience had not quite realised yet) is highlighted in a later scene and the song *Reflection*, in which Mulan laments that she does not recognise the girl she sees on the outside, that her outward, constructed appearance does not fit with who she feels she is. Again, the makeup she is wearing is important here; much emphasis is placed on her face, as it is this that she concentrates on in her reflection. As she sings "When will my reflection show who I am inside", she is shown wiping the makeup off of one side of her face, leaving her with one side natural, her true self, and one side with the "perfect bride" makeup. She is torn between her wish to be herself and her need to fulfil the traditional feminine roles laid out for her by her society in order to bring her family honour, and makeup plays an important part in showing this. Her half made-up and half natural face is a visual symbol for the split within Mulan; it is a split that will be much echoed later in the film when, once more dressed as a woman, she pulls back her hair into a more "masculine" style (thereby, in that moment, showing herself as both female and male) to show the evil Hun leader, Shan-Yu that she was the "boy" who defeated his army in the mountains.

In fact, it is in this moment in the film that the two separate identities Mulan has adopted in the film are reconciled. Mulan comes up with a plan to sneak herself and some other soldiers into the palace by disguising the men as women (and by wearing female clothing herself), and while the men must wear the heavy makeup worn by Mulan in the Matchmaker scene, Mulan herself has a natural face (all wear traditional, feminine clothes, though the men "fill out" their garments by inserting fruit into their bodices in lieu of "cleavage"). The men may need makeup and other artifices to disguise themselves as women, but Mulan does not. It is in these feminine clothes – and now clearly as a woman, though not the primped and polished bride – that Mulan defeats Shan-Yu once and for all and rescues the Emperor. It is interesting to note that, while playing the role of a man earlier in the film, when it was thought she had initially defeated Shan-Yu, he actually survived (buried in the snow of an avalanche that Mulan triggered, but able, along with his army, to dig himself out and resume his conquest, unbeknownst to all apart from Mulan, who witnesses the scene). It is only in being her true self that Mulan defeats him completely and finally. Ultimately, she does not need the heavy application of makeup that made her unrecognisable to herself in order to be feminine and recognisable as a woman, and she can still behave in the more active, independent manner that characterised her time in the army when she lived as a man.

Like Mulan, Tiana's (and other characters') use of cosmetics in *The Princess and the Frog* can also be attributed to the cultural setting in which she appears, in this case, 1920s New Orleans. Historically, the twentieth century marked a change in the acceptance of cosmetics and makeup on a wider scale, at least for young women, when "a key sign of modernity ... was the wearing of cosmetics".[5] Indeed, for the first time, wearing cosmetics had become not just acceptable, but even "fashionable".[6] All of the female characters in *The Princess and the Frog* appear to be wearing cosmetics, and Tiana's friend Charlotte La Bouff is the only "good" character in Disney's animated features to be shown applying makeup purely to improve her appearance (unlike Mulan, who is only shown applying makeup because it serves as a part of the formal, ceremonial costume she must wear to visit the Matchmaker). The characters in *The Princess and the Frog* wear cosmetics *not* because it fulfils some ritualistic or symbolic function within their society, but rather because they believe it enhances their appearance, showing them to be well-groomed and respectable.

In the primary scene in which we see her applying makeup, Charlotte is hosting a costume ball for the visiting royal, Prince Naveen, hoping to impress him so that she might marry him and become a princess, as has always been her dream. Dressed up as a fairy tale version of the princess she so longs to be, the audience first sees Charlotte in this setting calmly spurning the advances of a young man dressed as a jester. As soon as he has gone, however, this calm image quickly evaporates, and Charlotte grabs handfuls of napkins. As she unceremoniously dabs herself all over with them, she proclaims, "I'm sweating! I'm sweating like a sinner in church!" While Charlotte is most probably sweating from how nervous she is, her choice of words, "sweating like a sinner in church" (an old saying from the often hot and humid South) helps to reflect the artifice of her costume in the same way that Charlotte's mostly un-princess-like behaviour is usually hidden beneath her costume and makeup. Just as Mulan does not fit the "perfect bride" she wishes to be for her parents, Charlotte does not quite fit the Princess image she wishes to emulate.

As Charlotte begins to panic that Naveen will not show up and that she will never get her wish to become a princess, she begins crying and complaining, much like a spoiled child. Charlotte has already been shown as spoiled at earlier points in the film, and as she storms up the stairs of her father's mansion, she shouts, "I never get anything I wish for!" This is particularly ironic as, throughout the film, Charlotte's lavish lifestyle is shown in stark contrast to Tiana's far more modest one. As Charlotte continues to cry about Naveen not arriving, her makeup begins to run down her face. Much like with the Matchmaker in Mulan, the illusion is now completely shattered – Charlotte now not only is not acting like a princess, but does not look like one. Clearly, she is not a Disney princess at all, and as she wails that it is "unfair" that she may never get the opportunity to become one, she seems about as far from the depiction of the typical Disney princess as one could appear to be.

Once Prince Naveen (or at least an individual whom the characters believe to be Prince Naveen) finally appears, Charlotte instantly stops crying and begins reapplying her makeup, grabbing from Tiana's hands the tiara she had tossed aside earlier. Within seconds, she is back to looking the part of the princess, but the speed with which she returns to her role only serves to highlight the artificial nature of it. All she need do is wipe away her running eye makeup, draw on a beauty spot, and dab on some powder, and she is magically transformed, but only in appearance. At this point in the film at least, the princess image is purely on the surface, an artificial creation, one which she is shown to need keep maintaining and enhancing in the following scene, in which she tops up her powder and mascara while looking in a mirror. It is interesting to note that there is another element of artifice here, as the visitor everyone at the party believes to be Prince Naveen is, in fact, the Prince's butler, Lawrence, who has been transformed by the voodoo magic of the villain of the film, Dr. Facilier. Charlotte's prince in this scene, ironically, is not a prince but rather his conniving, rather awkward manservant in a magical disguise.

In a similar way to the scene in *The Rescuers* in which Medusa removes her false eyelashes, Charlotte's application of mascara is shown to comedic effect. As she pulls her eye open in an extremely dramatic way, she says that she thought wishing on stars was just for babies and "crazy people". As she says the words "crazy people", her eye is pulled open to its fullest extent, and the connection is made that she perhaps is a little crazy. The application of makeup here is used to assist in the creation of further layers of meaning within the scene, in accentuating the possible irony of Charlotte's words, as she is always wishing on stars.

All of the scenes discussed here have some element of artifice and/or duality within them, and makeup is used in order to highlight this. The use of makeup is not necessarily the only signifier of artifice or duality within these scenes, and it is no coincidence that mirrors and reflections feature heavily in most of these scenes as they, too, can be used to highlight a duality of identity: Ursula and Charlotte apply their makeup in a mirror, Medusa removes hers whilst looking at her reflection, and Mulan's painted face is revealed to her in a hand mirror at the end of her transformation, as well as the subject of her gaze when it is "mirrored" back to her on the surface of a pond. Not only are mirrors central (both practically and symbolically) to the ritual of makeup application, they also further the ideas of duality – of the different "selves" created through the use of makeup.

Yzma's scene is the only one in which there are no mirrors. Despite there being no mirrors or other true reflections of Yzma, there are, however, mannequins with Yzma's costumes on. These mannequins in effect represent the different versions of her that she displays to the world, and in this way they are reflections of her. Indeed, one even has a pair of her signature fake eyelashes stuck on, thereby showing the importance of makeup in her "costumes" as a whole. The fact that these eyelashes even match the rest of the outfit demonstrates the importance of cosmetics in creating not only a single, fixed physical identity, but also in highlighting their ability to create multiple forms of the self.

Just as cosmetics can create meaning in the real world in the way they are used to construct women's identities, so too can they be employed to create meaning in the worlds of Disney's animated films. In the case of Disney's female villains, scenes which explicitly emphasise the use of cosmetics can be seen as enforcing the artificial nature of the identities they create for themselves in order to manipulate others, while for characters such as Mulan and Charlotte, the application of makeup can be seen as showing the artifice involved in the roles they are expected to (or, in Charlotte's case, wish to) play. Throughout these films, emphasis on the artificial nature of cosmetics and the false beauty they are used to create – perhaps more accurately in the cases of the villains, the ugliness that they wish to disguise – can be seen as a means of highlighting and reflecting the artificial aspects of the particular scenes in which they are used or in the people which they are used by.

Bibliography

Davis, Amy M. *Good Girls & Wicked Witches: Women in Disney's Feature Animation* (Hertfordshire: John Libbey Publishing, 2006).

Dyhouse, Carol. *Glamour: Women, History, Feminism.* Kindle Edition (London: Zed Books, 2013).

Johnston, Oliver, and Frank Thomas, *The Disney Villain* (New York: Hyperion, 1993).

Peiss, Kathy. "Making Up, Making Over: Cosmetics, Consumer Culture, and Women's Identity", in de Grazia, V., and Furlough, E. (Eds), *The Sex of Things: Gender and Consumption in Historical Perspective* (Los Angeles: University of California Press, 1996), 311–336.

Filmography

The Emperor's New Groove (2000). Directed by Mark Dindal.

The Little Mermaid (1989). Directed by Ron Clements and John Musker.

Mulan (1998). Directed by Tony Bancroft and Barry Cook.

The Princess and the Frog (2009). Directed by Ron Clements and John Musker.

The Rescuers (1977). Directed by John Lounsbery, Wolfgang Reitherman, and Art Stevens.

Endnotes

1. Kathy Peiss, "Making Up, Making Over: Cosmetics, Consumer Culture, and Women's Identity", in de Grazia, V., and Furlough, E. (Eds), *The Sex of Things: Gender and Consumption in Historical Perspective* (Los Angeles: University of California Press, 1996), 324.

2. Peiss, 324.

3. Oliver Johnston and Frank Thomas, *The Disney Villain* (New York: Hyperion, 1993), 159.

4. Amy M. Davis, *Good Girls & Wicked Witches: Women in Disney's Feature Animation* (Hertfordshire: John Libbey Publishing, 2006), 196.

5. Carol Dyhouse, *Glamour: Women, History, Feminism.* Kindle Edition (London: Zed Books, 2013), 16.

6. Dyhouse, 18.

Chapter 8

From Operatic Uniformity to Upbeat Eclecticism: The Musical Evolution of the Princess in Disney's Animated Features

Oliver Lindman

Among factors that shape and complicate analyses of Disney princesses, the music that accompanies their presence cannot be ignored. The way in which children internalise roles involves processes of identification, and arguably, one of film music's central functions is to condition such processes. Anahid Kassabian asserts that a musical score evokes connotations, which are largely determined by the spectator's previous relation to the music in question. Thereby, the music significantly helps to govern the engagement between the film and its audience.[1] She concedes, however, that other factors also condition this engagement, and that the musical score cannot guarantee any specific kind of identification.[2] This uncertainty relates to *polysemiosis*, Philip Tagg's term used to describe what evokes different responses depending on the individual. He also argues, however, that music cannot be considered polysemic, since different individuals within a culture tend to respond to the same music in similar ways. As he further remarks, if it were not for this "connotative intersubjectivity", music for film, TV, and other kinds of media would be "pointless".[3]

In acknowledging the existence of connotative intersubjectivity, scholars have sought to connect certain musical elements to certain concepts. Of particular interest to this investigation is the correlation between music and gender. Heather Laing points out that "semiotic codes which adhere to contemporaneous cultural constructions of gender have been traced in music as early as the sixteenth century".[4] Leo Treitler suggests that femininity is coded by softness, roundedness, elegance and grace, which in music take the form of ornamentation, elaboration, improvisation, and variation.[5] Tagg connects femininity to legato, regularity of rhythm, up-down-up melodic contours, and lack of strong motion.[6] Undoubtedly, such features are ideologically constructed rather than inherent to the music itself, and early Hollywood music was vital in establishing these conventions. Kassabian discusses the "possibilities" for female characters offered by scoring, implying that music can both restrict characterisation (small range of connotations) or make it more elaborate (large range of connotations).[7] The slow, lush and melodic themes so often accompanying the appearance or presence of the hero's love interest in early Hollywood films are poor in connotation. Languishing string instruments performing such themes signify little more than beauty, virtue and the promise of love – rendering classical Hollywood females, as Kassabian puts it, "severely limited". Assigning such weight to an element rarely consciously perceived by the audience may seem bold, but as Laing stresses, music reveals the emotional or moral truth about characters.[8] Most certainly in films, music has become an established tool for speaking the emotions of characters, or as Claudia Gorbman puts it, a "signifier" of emotion itself.[9]

Similar claims about music's ability to reveal and signify emotion have been made in the context of the film musical, and with specific reference to the integrated song number.[10] Importantly, as Disney composer Alan Menken points out, music in many Disney animated features is closer to musical theatre than to standard film music.[11] Laing suggests that the integrated number comes "when the need for emotional expression has reached a particularly high point". The character can no longer contain his or her feelings, thus the emotions must be acknowledged and shared. Moreover, this is where film musicals "go to the greatest lengths to collapse the sense of distance between the performer and the film audience", and where energy levels are "at their most extreme".[12] Combined with Kassabian's theories, these claims suggest that spectators are most prone to identification processes and emotional connection within the space of songs. Indeed, although one might be tempted to regard integrated numbers in Disney's musicals as so integrated with the narrative and visuals that they need no specific consideration, the spellbinding effect of songs speaks the opposite. Whereas this might seem a clichéd way of putting it (magic as a concept may seem overly commercialised – Disney being the greatest villain), Richard Dyer argues that songs have a "magical" power which lingers at the core of two words associated with magic: "enchantment" and "incantation".[13] Pointing at such linguistic relations, Dyer implies that the built-in capability of songs to forge emotional expressions and bonds lies at the core of how we understand and experience them. Dyer also proposes that songs empower the singer with authority, emphasising and validating the lyrical content.[14] He further argues that voices carry markers of gender, class, and other rudiments of identity.[15]

Regarding the voice, Susan Smith illustrates how performance affects musical characterisation. Singing marked by constantly changing timbres (a "multiplicity of voices") creates fluid, complex identities. More consistent, less vocally-adventurous performances may instead be restricting similarly to classical Hollywood scoring of female characters.[16] As Steven Cohan argues, music, when linked to a female character, may contribute to both the resistance to and compliance with male objectification.[17] This highlights the need to examine the Disney's choice of voice actors, and the effects of vocal performances.

Academic literature specifically concerned with music in Disney films is scarce. The few film and gender studies approaches to Disney that take music into account, such as Laura Sells' article "Where do the Mermaids Stand", have been of interest to this investigation.[18] Raymond Knapp's writings on music in *Snow White and the Seven Dwarfs* (1937) have also proven useful.[19] The other few texts on Disney music available, such as "Make Walt's Music" by Ross Care, tend to be more biographical than analytical.[20] Moreover, given this paper's focus on gender issues and musical characterisation, broader publications on cartoon music practice and aesthetics have been of limited value. Naturally, there are other unique aspects of Disney music worth considering. In the production of animated musicals, composing needs to start before the animation, allowing music to inform and sometimes dictate both plot development and characterisation at an early stage. For instance, it was only decided that the princess character Elsa in *Frozen* (2013) would be a protagonist, rather than an antagonist, once her show tune "Let It Go" had been composed.[21] This makes Disney musicals particularly well suited for discussions on musical characterisation. Further underpinning the relevance of a musical perspective is the great popularity of Disney songs, and their tendency to have a life outside the space of the film in everything from Billboard top lists to school talent shows. Some methods common to film music studies in general have, on the contrary, scarcely been applied. The well-established diegetic/non-diegetic discourse, for instance, is often too ambiguous an analytical entry for Disney films. Especially in the earliest films, the music constantly occupies the borderline between diegesis and non-diegesis, with characters humming along with the orchestral underscoring, or diegetic objects making noises in perfect synchronisation with the non-diegetic music.

In recognizing the impact of Disney, the enormous appeal of the Disney "princess" character, it becomes obvious why this character type is worthy of attention. In further accepting that film music conditions paths of identification, and that musical numbers break down emotional barriers between performers and audience, one must likewise accept not only the existence, but also the great significance of musical characterisation in Disney films. Thus, whilst this chapter discusses the *musical* evolution of Disney princess characters, it also, by arguing for the strength of the musical perspective, adds to the debate around the *general* evolution of the princess character as she manifests within Disney animation. To examine this idea in depth, this chapter examines – historically, analytically, and musically – a selection of films as representatives of their various eras. They are: *Snow White and the Seven Dwarfs* (the earliest or "Classical" era); *The Little Mermaid* (1989, as an example of what in this chapter is considered the "Menken Era"); and *Frozen* (2013).

The Classical Era: *Snow White and the Seven Dwarfs* (1937)

As defined here, the "Classical Era" encompasses most films produced during Walt Disney's lifetime. This period (1937–1959) comprises sixteen films, three of which feature princess characters: *Snow White and the Seven Dwarfs* (1937), *Cinderella* (1950), and *Sleeping Beauty* (1959). *Snow White*, the first animated Disney feature, was extraordinarily successful, and ended up grossing more than any other previous sound film.[22] Released during the Hollywood Golden Age, it is an adaptation of the Grimms' version of the classic fairy tale about the beautiful princess Snow White, who flees from her evil stepmother and finds shelter in the cottage of the seven dwarfs.

Snow White exemplifies Kassabian's statement that female characters in classical Hollywood tend to be defined as either the "fallen woman" or the "virtuous wife".[23] Counterbalanced by her evil stepmother, princess Snow White falls into the latter category. Congruently, character traits are as scarce as character types. From the very beginning, Snow White sings of her wish that her true love will find her. Her brief, musically guided encounter with the prince in this early scene establishes the supremacy of her desire for true love over the other desires that emerge, such as her wishes for the love and welfare of the dwarfs. Displaying almost nothing – apart from a little bit of naivety and a touch of disobedience when she allows the "old beggar woman" into the dwarfs' house – but virtues (during this era synonymous with "passivity and pre-marital chastity"), Snow White has been described as amongst the least dynamic characters of the Classical Era.[24] Her faultless looks, helplessness in dangerous situations, domestic skills, and ultimate union with the man make her a shining example of stereotypical womanhood in early Hollywood.[25] On a more positive note, Disney's Snow White is more intelligent and makes more of her own decisions than Grimm's Snow White does.[26]

Snow White's own decisions, however, are made within a very limited space, and Paul J. Smith's and Leigh Harline's music helps to confine her to that space. In a score often foregrounded by spontaneously breaking the diegesis and mimicking the animated drama (a technique known as "mickey mousing"), one might distinguish between two styles: the late romantic, serious style, and the more entertaining, vaudevillian style. Snow White is only allowed the former of these, the latter being reserved for dwarfs and animals. As was common during 1930s films, there is an "overwhelming association of women and love", conveyed through the "euphony of a string orchestra".[27] The opening and end credits are accompanied by a grand orchestral rendition of the Prince's serenade number "One Song". When the actual story begins, a quick and playful Viennese Waltz-like version of Snow White's own love number "Some Day My Prince Will Come" is heard. The same theme concludes the story in the form of a climactic choral finale, with the final chord initiating "One Song" for the end credits. Thus, the love themes of the romantic couple make both the opening and the closing musical statement, significantly diminishing the potential for other morals or messages to be conveyed.

The first images of the actual story epitomise the fallen woman/virtuous wife dichotomy. The evil queen's iconic "magic mirror on the wall" scene features sinister ascending and descending scales, with ethereal orchestral effects. As Snow White is subsequently introduced, the music immediately shifts from mysterious minor to unequivocal major, woodwinds and high tremolo violins leave room for a warm string orchestra, and there is a distinct increase in "hummability". Snow White even cheerfully hums along with the orchestra, adding a vocal dimension that the queen is denied. Indeed, the practice of actually "making music", as Douglas Brode implies, is a conventional tell for what is morally right and worthy of celebration.[28] As the prince fills in the last phrase of Snow White's song "I'm Wishing" in the subsequent scene, thereby "making music" with her, there is little ambiguity regarding their connection.

Snow White's songs – all very positive and celebratory – do little other than create a musical spectacle out of the heroine. Due to the difficulties and challenges of animating convincing human characters at the time, music and performance were needed to enable us to see Snow White as a "human presence".[29] During her songs, Snow White is rarely seen. Instead, we see charming sub-stories of animals doing dishes or dwarfs falling asleep. It is Snow White's musical presence and traditional vocal virtuosity, instead of her looks and stance, which create the potential for male objectification. The songs, written by Frank Churchill, all use recitative-like spoken introductions and various vocal elaborations, evoking conventions of the operetta genre. Indeed, the Jeanette MacDonald operetta movies of the 1930s inspired the score.[30] Unsurprisingly, orchestral accompaniments are lush and string-based, with little or no brass or percussion. The first song, Snow White's "I Want" song – the term informally applied to the song in which the protagonist expresses his or her innermost desires – is lyrically strikingly minimal; performed next to a wishing well, "I'm Wishing" sets up a call-and-response texture between Snow White and her own echo. The expressive large leaps between the notes evoke conventions of the Romantic period of classical music, and the slow tempo, along with Caselotti's graceful delivery, echoes Golden Age musical femininity. The aforementioned one-dimensionality of Snow White's desires is reflected by the mere twenty-two words comprising the lyrics. Looking at other songs, "Some Day My Prince Will Come", with its lingering on repeated notes, rubatos (speeding up and slowing down of the tempo), and dream-like chromaticism (elaborative deviations from the main scale), offers little that could be considered thematically or stylistically different from "I'm Wishing". Another popular tune from *Snow White*, "With a Smile and a Song", is what Jane Feuer terms a "reflexive song".[31] A song about singing, its self-referential nature allows it to take up space without adding either narrative motion or substantial characterisation. Lastly, "Whistle While You Work" is a happy work song in which Snow White lyrically links contentment with domestic duties. The phrase "and as you sweep the room, imagine that the broom, is someone that you love and soon you'll find you're dancing to the tune" effectively sums up contemporary views of the ideal housewife in one short passage. Given the lack of lyrical depth and variation in these songs, one might even, if somewhat crudely, use a table to show why Snow White's singing does little to augment her characterisation.

Table 1 – Snow White's four songs and what they celebrate.

The song ...	functions as a musical celebration of ...
"I'm Wishing"	love
"Some Day My Prince Will Come"	love
"Whistle While You Work"	domestic work (and love)
"With a Smile and a Song"	itself

Of equal importance is what kind of musical representation Snow White is denied. In the comedic, vaudevillian "Silly Song", performed in the dwarfs' cottage, Snow White is present. However, whereas the dwarfs try to musically "outdo each other's silliness", Snow White mostly sits and claps her hands.[32] 112 seconds into the song, she joins in with a sustained and virtuosic soprano high D, which, if anything, only testifies to her complete inability of being "musically silly" (or perhaps, from Dundes' analytical approach in his study of *Pocahontas*, to Disney's unwillingness to *allow* her to be silly). With musical traits reflecting absolute flawlessness,

Snow White never becomes a fun character. Being silly or awkward, both in music and outside of it, has only very recently begun to manifest itself as a trait among Disney's princesses.

Snow White's voice only further contributes to her lack of agency and independence. Walt himself states in an interview that he wanted Snow White to sound very young, yet be capable of the virtuosic soprano passages that the part requires.[33] Adriana Caselotti, who provided Snow White's voice, recalls that Walt was looking for someone who even sounded like a child.[34] Susan Smith argues that the classically trained soprano voice carries little subversive potential against the patriarchal value system.[35] Indeed, the countless righteous and innocent female opera heroines, such as Gilda in *Rigoletto* (1851) and Cio-Cio San in *Madama Butterfly* (1904), are typically sopranos. Lower voices – more specifically the mezzo-sopranos or the contraltos – are associated with a broader and less definite range of character types, such as villains, seductresses, mentors and nurses. Moreover, in the 1930s, Snow White could have theoretically been a jazz singer with a smoky alto voice. Nonetheless, Disney played it safe and made Snow White a classical soprano. With the addition of 18-year-old Caselotti's strikingly child-like timbre, Snow White is musically infantilised; she is diminished to a fundamental state of spotlessness and innocence – a 'beau ideal'. As such, she is immobilised, and well within male control.

Despite the twenty-two year span between *Snow White* and *Sleeping Beauty*, Snow White is a strong representative of the princesses of the Classical Era. Vanessa Matyas points out how startlingly similar Snow White and Aurora (*Sleeping Beauty*) are, and many commonalities stem from musical factors.[36] The first we hear of Aurora is her youthful, classically-trained soprano voice, provided by 19-year-old Mary Costa. Her song "I Wonder" is as if modelled on "I'm Wishing" when it comes to style and phrasing. She then performs the waltz "Once Upon a Dream", at the end of which a prince turns up and finishes the song. This love song thereby simultaneously performs the work of "One Song" and "Some Day My Prince Will Come", adding nothing of note. Cinderella (*Cinderella*, 1950) manages to be slightly different by not explicitly addressing the theme of love in every song. However, numbers like "A Dream is a Wish Your Heart Makes" and "Sing Sweet Nightingale" carry the same inherent reflexivity as "With a Smile and a Song" – they contribute, arguably, neither agency nor substantial characterisation. They are also stylistically coherent with virtually all previously mentioned princess songs. Overall, what dominates this era is a musical representation characterised by melodic richness, but stylistic and lyrical poverty, rendering the classical princesses infinitely pure and virtuous, but little more than that.

The Menken Era: *The Little Mermaid* (1989)

During a period often referred to as the "Disney Renaissance", renowned composer Alan Menken scored the majority of the films. The success of the instrumental and song scores from this period is remarkable. Altogether, the ten Menken Era films garnered eleven Academy Awards out of twenty nominations in music categories alone (Best Original Score or Best Original Song). *The Little Mermaid* (1989), which marked the rebirth of the animated fairy-tale musical, won Menken (songs and score) and Howard Ashman (lyrics) two Oscars. The fact that Ashman was also hired as a co-producer attests to the studio's willingness to let music and songs perform important narrative functions in the film.[37]

Between *Sleeping Beauty* (1959) and the Menken Era, only one Disney film features a princess character – the commercial failure *The Black Cauldron* (1985).[38] Although Princess Eilonwy is arguably the least known Disney princess – partly attributable to the fact that *Cauldron* has no songs – it has been observed that her feisty and adventurous spirit "set a new benchmark" for Disney female characters.[39] Weighing various feminist responses to *The Little Mermaid*, the most sensible conclusion regarding gender messages would be that they are mixed. Ariel, much to the despair of her father, King Triton, dreams of a life out of the sea. She eventually makes a Faustian bargain with the sea witch, Ursula, trading her voice for a pair of legs. Ariel's rebellious spirit and unwillingness to be the nurturing kind have been applauded.[40] Regrettably for her feminist status, her dream of a life on land is quickly transformed to a dream of a life with Prince Eric, whom she also marries in the end, arguably by traditionally being "handed over" from father to future husband.[41] It is typical, argues Cohan, that classical Hollywood film and musical comedy operate to "proclaim, then contain" female sexuality.[42] This holds true for Ariel and other Menken Era heroines such as Pocahontas and Mulan. Indeed, Disney has been accused of containing the "truly progressive significance" of their heroines' actions.[43]

It is with regard to such sanitisations that the score to *The Little Mermaid* becomes particularly interesting. The narrative may ultimately nullify Ariel's agency and independence, but it is unlikely that the lasting impression of her character is simply dictated by this final image of her. Therefore, the previously discussed tendency of musical numbers to speed up identification processes and collapse emotional barriers shows the importance of examining which elements of Ariel's personality are musically emphasised – at *any* point in the narrative. For example, the story sets up the expectation that we will first see Ariel as a performer in a diegetic concert held in the sea kingdom. In the song performed – "Daughters of Triton" – Ariel's six sisters sing virtuosic scales reminiscent of Snow White's operetta figurations. Towards the intended climax, they gather around a giant shell to introduce Ariel and her beautiful voice. Thus, we are led to expect the princess in the midst of a visual and musical spectacle, subjected to all diegetic and non-diegetic gazes. However, we are robbed of this conventional display of beauty, faultlessness, and virtuosity. To everybody's shock, Ariel is not there. Instead, Ariel is first seen alone, and slightly from the side, as she eagerly beholds the remains of an old shipwreck.

Here, the score presents a melodic fragment of Ariel's "I Want" number, "Part of Your World", which lends itself incessantly to the score, saturating the film with its message. Much of Ariel's own thematic treatment stems from the song's opening musical phrases, which have a strong sense of curiosity and restlessness to them. In musicological terms, this can be explained by the fact that Menken withholds from properly establishing the musical key. It is common for any Western music to both start and end with the tonic chord – the fundamental chord that defines the key of the music. Here, it takes time for the music to resolve to its tonic chord, rendering the tonal centre uncertain to the ear. Such ambiguity of key is completely absent from the music accompanying Snow White's first appearance. Snow White's initial musical treatment is direct and celebratory; Ariel's is in the process of searching. The much-applied melodic phrase mentioned above might even be called Ariel's "Curiosity" theme. Indeed, in a background score otherwise often recalling the traditional Hollywood late romantic style, Ariel's musical treatment tends to escape the usual clichés by having strong harmonic motion – a feature Tagg identifies as conventionally unfeminine.[44]

"Part of Your World" itself is a Broadway-style ballad evoking the idea of a "silent dreamer" while simultaneously giving its performer mobility. Echoing its first appearance in the instrumental score, it takes the song an entire minute to resolve to its tonic chord for the first time, further perpetuating the sense of restlessness. "Part of Your World" is also filled with short, ascending figures and repeated notes delivered almost like whispers, further contributing to that sense of yearning and desire. There is a soft quality to the song, with regular rallentandos (momentarily slowing the tempo down for expressive effect) weakening the real motion, disseminating the idea of the girl who tenderly expresses her innermost wishes. Similar features are found in Snow White's "I'm Wishing". However, many factors bring the numbers apart, the most obvious being the lyrics. A basic but important observation is that "Part of Your World" has 245 words, whereas "I'm Wishing", not counting echoing or repeated verses, has only 22. This has the implication that many more aspects of Ariel's personality are allowed musical enhancement. Moreover, the sheer amount of dynamic verbs in "Part of Your World", and the manner in which they are accented, fuels Ariel's wishes.

Table 2 – Dynamic verbs in "Part of Your World" and what they describe.

What Ariel *does*.	Flippin' (her fins), swimming
What Ariel *would do if she could*	Walkin', jumpin', dancin', strollin', run, stay, wandering, give, live (out of the waters), pay, spend (a day warm on the sand), stand, ask, get

Out of sixteen dynamic verbs, fourteen occur on strong beats, and are thus given extra emphasis. A telling example comes a minute and a half into the song; "Up where they walk, up where they run, up where they stay all day in the sun." The phrases are constructed in a way that firmly accentuates words of motion. Admittedly, "I'm Wishing" puts a similar emphasis on the verbs. However, there are only five of them, the three self-referential ones being unquestionably stative rather than dynamic:

Table 3 – Verbs in "I'm Wishing" and what they describe.

What Snow White *does*	Wishing, hoping, dreaming
What Snow White *wants the prince to do*	Find, say

Therefore, "I'm Wishing" swiftly establishes the princess as the passive dreamer and the prince as the one with agency and voice. "Part of Your World", by contrast, brings to the forefront all the things that Ariel would do had she not been a mermaid. She is physically immobile, but her spirit is not passive.

Nonetheless, it is worth discussing what musical treatment Ariel does not get. Notably, all Menken-scored heroines express their "I Want" wishes in ballads rather than more upbeat numbers. Some heroes get ballads too; however, the differences in sheer energy are noteworthy. Fans of *The Hunchback of Notre Dame* (1996) may recall the forceful number "Out There", sung by Quasimodo, the protagonist of the film. Quasimodo is in a very similar position to Ariel. He longs for another world, but is trapped where he is because of the prohibitions set by authoritative figures and his own shortcomings. However, a forceful ballad throughout, "Out There" ends in fortissimo ecstasy with trumpet fanfares and thunderous timpani lines. "Part of Your World", on the other hand, ends with a very soft extended note.

Although more aspects than gender dictate the style and structure of Disney songs, it is noteworthy that all "I Want" numbers belonging to Menken-scored Disney heroines retract to a similar "soft prayer" mode. Even Pocahontas, in the otherwise lively "Just Around the Riverbend", ends her wishes with a whisper. Hercules (*Hercules*, 1997) on the other hand, a male character, ends his "I Want" ballad "Go the Distance" in unrestrained elation with three climactic tenor notes. The Menken-Era heroines are rarely allowed that level of motion and exuberance in their musical treatment. One might draw attention to the short reprise of "Part of Your World" ten minutes after the main song, where the final phrase features a climactic forte Major chord enhanced by a cymbal hit. Arguably, the real climax of the song is delayed until this point. Unfortunately, the reprise also comes with a change in connotation. At this point, Ariel has discovered Prince Eric, and what was previously a celebration of her dreams of space and mobility is now an ode to her love for him. This change is epitomised in the lyrical shift from "part of *that* world" to "part of *your* world", and diminishes the multi-dimensionality of Ariel's mind-set, arguably bringing it closer to that of Snow White. Jubilant as this shift is, though, only a fraction of the song is reprised. The aforementioned "Curiosity" phrases of the song, which are quite distinct in character from the chorus, are not sung again; thus they do not acquire a "love" connotation. Correspondingly, unlike the unequivocally joyful "One Song" theme in *Snow White*, the "Curiosity" theme is too harmonically ambiguous to function well as a Disney love theme.

Jodi Benson's clear and tender Broadway voice chosen for Ariel has a sense of maturity to it, which Adriana Caselotti's Snow White lacks. With an emphasis on lyrics rather than virtuosic elaborations, Ariel's performances stand out as more nuanced than Snow White's from the perspective of characterisation. Hence, Ariel's voice is arguably not as overtly submissive to the patriarchal value system as is Snow White's. Nevertheless, it is interesting to examine how it is used as a narrative tool. When Eric meets Ariel after the transformation, he does not fall in love with her because, during their first encounter, he only heard her singing voice (now in Ursula's possession). Infatuated with the woman behind the voice, he is shown standing by the sea playing a theme from "Part of Your World" on a flute – even after he has met the real, albeit voiceless, Ariel. The fact that Ariel is forced to try, and almost succeeds at, seducing Eric with only her appearance and body language, conveys a problematic message. However, Ariel is never shown to truly win Eric's heart before she regains her musical identity, which is symbolised by her often-heard, non-verbal rendition of the "Curiosity" theme. Indeed, Ursula continuously uses her control over this "extract" of Ariel's voice to spellbind Eric, making him forget about the real Ariel. From a visual perspective, Laura Sells may be correct – arguably – in stating that Ariel's curiosity significantly fades once she meets Eric, but the musical signifier of that very trait remains the most fore-grounded in the score. [45]

Concerning identity, the Menken-Era princesses are not as easily linked as those of the Classical Era. However, Menken also composed the music in the era's two other films with major princess characters – *Aladdin* (1992) and *Pocahontas* (1995) – making some of the stylistic connections strong. Menken sees the adaptation of performed numbers into the instrumental score as a main unifying element, and tends to use songs thematically before they have been performed. [46] The love ballad "A Whole New World" in *Aladdin*, for instance, is sung by Aladdin and Princess Jasmine almost an hour into the film, but excerpts from it are used suggestively already when they first meet. Nonetheless, Jasmine is not confined to the partaking of Aladdin's romantic musical representation. She also has her own distinct theme, which primarily signifies her wish to be free. Pocahontas, a title character like Ariel, is represented by a multiplicity of themes, the most prevalent being those originating in songs like the aforementioned "Just Around the Riverbend" and the Oscar-winning "Colors of the Wind", which treat subjects like destiny and nearness to nature. Ariel, conversely, is primarily represented by thematic material stemming from a single song, which connotes several aspects of her personality. Love is strongly celebrated musically in both *Mermaid* and *Aladdin*. In *Pocahontas*, however, the song containing the film's six-note love theme was cut from the final version, weakening the union between Pocahontas and John Smith (indeed, they do not end up together). [47] As shown, all Menken-Era heroines do receive a somewhat more soft and contained musical identity than the heroes. Nonetheless, Menken's music tends to possess a harmonic motion and melodic restlessness, which help making his princesses considerably different – both from the Classical princesses, and from one another.

The Eclectic Era: *Frozen* (2013)

Following a ten-year period where Disney mainly produced non-musical films, the premiere of *The Princess and the Frog* in 2009 marked another return to the successful formula involving fairy-tale adaptations and singing characters. *Frozen* (2013) is the third and latest princess film following this revival, and the first Disney film to feature two princesses who are both protagonists. As the first Disney film of the new millennium to win an Oscar for best song, its musical content has garnered praise like no other animated film of the 21st century. [48] *Frozen* is inspired by Hans Christian Andersen's *The Snow Queen* (1844), but hardly based on it. [49] The film follows princess Anna and Kristoff, searching for Anna's sister, Queen Elsa, who, using her ability to create and master snow and ice, has accidentally set off an eternal winter in her kingdom, Arendelle.

As of the time of writing, feminist responses to *Frozen* have been numerous, but still mostly limited to journalists' reviews and blog posts. Heralded as one of the first proper "feminist" films due to its focus on sisterhood and lack of clichéd plot points (such as a centralised romantic love story), it has also met with criticism.[50] Danielle Colman, in an extensive response, slams the characterisation of both princesses, describing them as stupid, irresponsible, and lacking in agency and strength. Focussed on the intricacies of the plot, Colman fails to properly acknowledge musical factors, dismissing them as an "identity-claiming power anthem" or a "jazzy little song and dance number".[51] Elsa and Anna's rich musical treatment – including memorable songs by Kristen Anderson-Lopez and Robert Lopez, and a score by Christophe Beck – cannot be overlooked when evaluating their portrayal.

Unlike *Snow White* and *Mermaid*, the musical celebration of romantic love is marginalised in *Frozen*. Instead, the relationship between the two sisters receives most of the musical emphasis. In his study of *Gentlemen Prefer Blondes* (1953), Steven Cohan argues that the main characters, both female, "emanate strength and power" through their deep connection to one another.[52] Importantly, they are also musically unified through common songs and dances, whilst the men in the film are not given musical roles. Comparably, in *Frozen*, the main human male characters get only one song each. Also, both of these songs lack narrative significance, partly because the instrumental score never appropriates them. The two early songs that feature Elsa and Anna are more prominent. "For the First Time in Forever" is reprised halfway through the film, and "Do You Wanna Build a Snowman", which is all about the breakdown of the relationship between the sisters, is revised as a celebratory theme in the final instrumental cue. Furthermore, the developing romantic relationship between Anna and Kristoff is unconventionally accompanied by three contrasting themes, none of which originate in songs. The melodically sparse third theme – first hinted at fourteen minutes before the end of the film, when the reindeer Sven tries to persuade a downhearted Kristoff to return to Anna – is the only solid indicator of their emotional connection. They do somewhat unceremoniously get each other in the end, but their union is never at the forefront musically, which renders it relatively insignificant. If music, as Laing argues, reveals the emotional "truth" of characters, the music in *Frozen* neither foreshadows a romantic union, nor invites us to view Kristoff as Anna's primary concern.[53] Recalling the memorability of the love themes in *Snow White*, and how quickly "Part of Your World" acquires the "love" connotation, this suggests a change towards a less romantically inclined princess.

Anna's spirit is better communicated in her "I Want" number "For the First Time in Forever". The song directly follows our first view of adult Anna, which is unlike any other first views of Disney princesses: she is sound asleep, drooling slightly, and with a lock of her (*very* bedhead) hair stuck to her mouth. This image screams of a humanity unseen in princesses of the previous eras, and the subsequent song reflects similar characteristics. At first glance, "Forever" is a typical Broadway ballad, but in scope and energy it is more similar to Quasimodo's "Out There" than to Ariel's

"Part of Your World". With its brisk, climactic orchestral crescendo building up to Anna's final high note, it is only the second princess "I Want" number throughout Disney history not to retract to "soft prayer" mode towards the end. Furthermore, "Forever" stands apart from all of Snow White's songs in that it is difficult to boil down its lyrical content to a single wish. Colman dismisses the song as yet another primarily focussed on love, but that is a gross oversimplification. With its 367 words (around 50 percent more than "Part of Your World"), it provides a multidimensional representation of Anna's character. Whereas Anna lyrically does address the potentiality of finding a love interest, she mainly cherishes the idea of meeting people, and having nothing in her way. The song also emphasises Anna's slightly irrational nature. While fantasising about "a beautiful stranger, tall and fair", she suddenly, out of nowhere, realises that she wants to "stuff some chocolate" in her face; recalling Snow White's out-of-place soprano D in "The Silly Song", such silliness and unpredictability is new among Disney princesses. Anna also expresses uncertainty over whether she is "elated or gassy", thereby, for the first time in forever, allowing basic and unpolished human needs to become associated with a Disney princess.

Elsa's show tune "Let It Go" carries even more progressive significance. Otherwise much associated with a theme signifying her icy powers and fear of revealing them, Elsa sings "Let It Go" when the damage is done, and she has nothing to hide anymore. "Let It Go" is a power ballad with distinct rock percussion echoing contemporary popular music – an element rarely heard in Menken-Era songs to such an extent. Recalling Kassabian's theories on how audiences' previous experiences of certain musical genres inform extra-musical associations, "Let It Go" likely has connotative functions quite different from those of the Broadway ballad. For one thing, pop/rock songs and Broadway songs are generally experienced completely differently in a live setting, the former involving bodily movement, the latter sitting still. Moreover, "Let It Go", with its instantly recognisable refrain and rebellious lyrics, forms such a strong characterising statement that it arguably singlehandedly emboldens Elsa. Colman is right in asserting that Elsa for most of the film shows more vulnerability than agency and strength.[54] However, treating the "power anthem" as a negligible, three-minute exception is to undervalue its impact. "Let It Go", to borrow Dyer's terminology, names and grounds Elsa's true emotions with its subversive lyrics, while deploying the vast range of affects offered by the power ballad.[55] During this song, audiences will be the most inclined to form a lasting perception of Elsa. It is, nonetheless, noteworthy that Elsa's character as communicated in the song stands in contrast to most other scenes featuring her. In *Snow White*, storyline and musical representation blend effortlessly. In *Frozen*, that this is not the case enriches Elsa with a complexity that Snow White lacks.

Much of Elsa's perceived subversive strength resides in the fact that popular music historically has been regarded as a challenge to established value systems, as has the voice performing it.[56] Naturally, the popular music that became a reflection of youth and norm-critical perspectives in the 1950s and 60s has little symbolic weight today. What is considered different and challenging to established conventions always changes. Standing on its own, "Let It Go" is stylistically far from provocative. However, in the context of the animated Disney musical, including a song which, in its film version, has such instantaneous Billboard potential is a novel endeavour. It screams for commercial attention outside of the film itself. Moreover, the casting of Idina Menzel as Elsa's voice ("Let It Go" was written specifically for her) is significant. Best known for playing the lead role of Elphaba in the acclaimed Broadway musical *Wicked* (2003–), she had already voiced a powerful female character who breaks free from her chains through a massively energetic show tune (the signature song "Defying Gravity"). A voice that has become associated with rebellion for Broadway fans, it also has an authoritative, husky rawness to it. The maturity of then 41-year-old Menzel's timbre stands in stark contrast to the princesses of the Classical Era, whose voice actors were all teenagers when cast. Indeed, whereas the voice does not have the same narrative function in *Frozen* as in *Mermaid*, its function as a symbol for identity is important.[57] Recalling Susan Smith on how voices can convey complex identities, it is noteworthy how Kristen Bell's Anna often uses her timbre in adventurous ways, appropriating classical vibrato to mock highbrow culture, or singing with chocolate in her mouth.[58] Her singing is marked by a diversity of voices; thus her identity is marked by a variety of traits. Not counting the virtuosic figurations of Snow White and Aurora, timbral excursions among Disney princesses have been quite contained, historically. Arguably, this is another consequence of Disney's sanitisations. Female voices that wield authority or are marked by multiplicity carry subversive potential to patriarchal value systems – the former because it competes for control, the latter because it escapes it.

In the Eclectic Era, the three film musicals featuring princesses have all challenged established conventions, both generally and musically. Turning the fairy tale *The Frog Prince* into *The Princess and the Frog* (2009) involved multiple stages of reworking source material, eventually ending up with a black princess in 1920s New Orleans and the Louisiana Bayou and featuring a jazz-based score by *Toy Story* composer Randy Newman. For *Tangled* (2010), the source tale of "Rapunzel" underwent less of a geographical and temporal displacement from the popular Grimm version, but most of the songs sung by princess Rapunzel contain elements of folky rock, as do several cues from the score. Arguably, abandoning the symphonic orchestra as the main accompaniment of songs increases popular appeal. Kassabian highlights the significance of film music's potential for "extrafilmic" life. Menzel's version of "Let It Go", notably, reached the top 10 of the Billboard

Hot 100 in March 2014.[59] The image of Elsa as powerful and rebellious has thus, through the song, been revitalised millions of times outside of the film. It should be noted that the princess film scores of the Eclectic Era still subscribe to strong conventions of musical representation, but in various original ways, they all suggest a move away from the Menken formula of the 1990s. The more upbeat and stylistically-diverse musical representation of the Disney princess is new to the twenty-first century.

Conclusion

The musical development of the animated Disney princess is a slow but reasonably steady process of gradual liberation from the early Hollywood conventions of scoring stereotypical womanhood. Starting at the beginning, the coherence and symmetry of the instrumental score of *Snow White* reflect the unquestionable clarity of the morals communicated. Basic dichotomies in style and mood render the princess indisputably good, virtuous, and spotlessly feminine. The songs associated with the princesses of the Classical Era are characterised by a consistently major mode and string orchestra accompaniment. Consequently, they evoke quite a narrow range of connotations, as do their lyrics, which tend to either address the theme of love, or general topics with little narrative significance. Furthermore, all the Classical princesses are voiced by very young, classically trained singers with a sweetness and purity of tone that, symbolically, offer a portrait of young womanhood that is unchallenging to patriarchal value structures.

Princess Ariel of the Menken Era receives a more ambiguous musical treatment, though still confined to symphonic and thematic conventions. Whereas *The Little Mermaid* illustrates how melodic excerpts from one song can have multiple characterising functions, composer Alan Menken would enrich his palette for later princess films of the era. In *Pocahontas*, for instance, different themes underscore different aspects of the title character's personality. Menken's compositional style is marked by vivid melodies and a constant directionality, which provide the Menken-Era princesses with a sense of motion and agency unknown to the Classical princesses. Nonetheless, the iconic Menken "I Want" ballad tends to avoid the most ecstatic emotional highs when written for female characters. Moreover, whereas the music in *The Little Mermaid* and later princess films of the period show a wide array of stylistic influences, Menken's recognisable Broadway style is always prominent. Notably, all actors voicing the Menken-Era princesses are classically trained Broadway sopranos, and thus united similarly to the Classical princesses.

Hints at further progress are seen in the most recent Disney princess films. *Frozen*, notably, avoids the celebration of romantic love partly by rarely supporting it musically. Also, the new era brings about the first signs of a stylistic revolution. In the post-2009 musicals featuring princesses, instrumentation typical of genres such as jazz and folk-rock has become a more prominent element of the instrumental scores. Stylistic changes also carry over to the songs. The rock-inspired show tune "Let It Go" in *Frozen* is the current peak in a period that has offered "I Want" numbers in three distinctly different styles, performed by artists such as blues singer Anika Noni Rose (*The Princess and the Frog*) and singer-songwriter Mandy Moore (*Tangled*). Through widening of range of genres and varying of voice types, the image of the Disney princess has begun its transformation into one less bound to stereotypical traits. "Let It Go", which came 76 years after "I'm Wishing", stands as an example of these musical (and cultural) changes.

While this chapter offers an analytical entry and a detailed historical overview of a relatively unaddressed topic, it also shows that there is room for more exploration. Expanding on the topic of audiences and the sociocultural meanings of music is necessary for more in-depth studies of the films. Furthermore, whilst some attempts have been made at combining musical and visual analyses, a more consistently integrated approach had to be excluded for reasons of space. The lack of consideration of authorial intention is partly motivated by Philip Tagg's extensive argument concerning the value of prioritising the responses of the "final arbiters" of the music – the listeners.[60] Nonetheless, longer studies should recognise the potentials of engaging with both creators and audiences. Another area worth investigation is the level of extrafilmic engagement with the music – especially among children. Whereas this paper seeks to stress music's potentials in enriching post-filmic identification processes, the focus of princess merchandising on dolls and glittering dresses likely works against it.

Despite the inevitable limitations, this study illustrates that it cannot be assumed that what Disney songs and themes contribute to characterisation is directly proportional to their duration relative to an entire film. Music evokes connotations, which create characterisation and condition identification processes. Moreover, when music is foregrounded, emotional borders between characters and audience are often the thinnest. Thus, motion pictures, when aided by music, are powerful influences on anyone exposed to them. When such a marketable product as the Disney princess is given a strong musical identity, music-based analyses are key to evaluating her progress. As the worldwide "princessification" of children will likely prevail, one can only hope that the term acquires a new meaning. In the wake of Disney's latest success",'princessified" girls around the world get to build ice palaces and sing "Let It Go". This may indicate a step in the right direction.

Bibliography

Primary sources

Anderson, Hans Christian. *The Complete Fairy Tales of Hans Christian Andersen* (Hertfordshire: Wordsworth Editions Limited, 2009).

Grimm, Jacob and Grimm, Wilhelm. *The Complete Fairy Tales of the Brothers Grimm* (Hertfordshire: Wordsworth Editions Limited, 2009).

Secondary sources – published

Ambjörnsson, Fanny. *Rosa – den farliga färgen* [Pink: The Dangerous Colour] (Stockholm: Ordfront, 2011).

Brode, Douglas. *Multiculturalism and the Mouse* (Austin: University of Texas Press, 2005).

Byrne, Eleanor and McQuillan, Martin. *Deconstructing Disney* (London: Pluto Press, 1999).

Care, Ross. "Make Walt's Music: Music For Disney Animation, 1928–1967". In *The Cartoon Music Book*, edited by Daniel Goldmark (Chicago: Chicago Review Press, 2002), 21–36.

Cohan, Steven. *Hollywood Musicals, the Film Reader* (London: Routledge, 2002).

Davis, Amy M. *Good Girls and Wicked Witches: Women in Disney's Feature Animation* (Bloomington: Indiana University Press, 2006).

Davis, Amy M. *Handsome Heroes & Vile Villains: Men in Disney's Feature Animation* (Bloomington: Indiana University Press, 2013).

Dyer, Richard. *In the Space of a Song: The Uses of Song in Film* (London: Routledge, 2012).

Dundes, Lauren. "Disney's Modern Heroine Pocahontas: Revealing Age-Old Gender Stereotypes and Role Discontinuity Under a Façade of Liberation". In *The Social Science Journal* 38, no. 3 (2001): 353–365.

England, Dawn Elisabeth, Lara Descartes, and Melissa Collier-Meek. "Gender Role Portrayal and the Disney Princesses". *Sex Roles* 64, no. 7–8 (2011): 555–567.

Feuer, Jane. *The Hollywood Musical* (Houndmills: The MacMillan Press Ltd., 1993).

Gabler, Neil. *Walt Disney: The Triumph of the American Imagination* (New York: Random House, 2007).

Garcia Zarranz, Libe. "Diswomen Strike Back: The Evolution of Disney's Femmes in the 1990s". *Atenea* 27, no. 2 (2007): 55–66.

Gorbman, Claudia. *Unheard Melodies: Narrative Film Music* (Bloomington: Indiana University Press, 1987).

Griffin, Sean. *Tinker Belles and Evil Queens: The Disney Company From the Inside Out* (New York: New York University Press, 2000).

Kassabian, Anahid. *Hearing Film: Tracking Identifications in Contemporary Hollywood Film Music* (New York: Routledge, 2001).

Knapp, Raymond. *The American Musical and the Performance of Personal Identity* (Princeton: Princeton University Press, 2006).

Laing, Heather. "Emotion by Numbers: Music, Song and the Musical". In *Musicals: Hollywood and Beyond*, edited by Bill Marshall and Robynn Stilwell (Wiltshire: Cromwell Press, 2000), 5–13.

Laing, Heather. *The Gendered Score: Music in 1940s Melodrama and the Woman's Film* (Aldershot: Ashgate Publishing Limited, 2007).

Limbach, Gwendolyn. "'You the Man: Well, Sorta': Gender Binaries and Liminality in Mulan". In *Diversity in Disney Films: Critical Essays on Race, Ethnicity, Gender, Sexuality and Disability*, edited by Johnson Cheu (Jefferson: McFarland, 2013), 115–128.

Matthew, Patricia A. and Jonathan Greenberg. "The Ideology of the Mermaid: Children's Literature in the Intro to Theory Course". In *Pedagogy* 9, no. 2 (2009): 217–233.

Michel, Claudine. "Re-Reading Disney: Not Quite Snow White". *Discourse: Studies in the Cultural Politics of Education* 17, no. 1 (1996): 5–14.

Morgan, David. *Knowing the Score: Film Composers Talk About the Art, Craft, Blood, Sweat, and Tears of Writing for Cinema* (New York: HarperCollins Publishers, 2000).

Ross, Deborah. "Escape from Wonderland: Disney and the Female Imagination". In *Marvels & Tales* 18, no. 1 (2004): 53–66.

Sells, Laura. "Where Do the Mermaids Stand: Voice and Body in The Little Mermaid". In *From Mouse to Mermaid: The Politics of Film, Gender and Culture*, edited by Elizabeth Bell, Lynda Hass and Laura Sells (Bloomington: Indiana University Press, 1995), 175–192.

Shepherd, John. "Difference and Power in Music". In *Musicology and Difference: Gender and Sexuality in Music Scholarship*, edited by Ruth A. Solie (Berkley: University of California Press, 1995), 46–65.

Smith, Susan. *The Musical: Race, Gender and Performance* (London: Wallflower Press, 2005).

Spaeth, Jeanne. "Alan Menken on Music's Many Forms". In *Music Educators Journal* 84, no. 3 (1997): 39–48.

Tagg, Philip. *Music's Meanings: A Modern Musicology for Non-Musos* (New York: The Mass Media Music Scholars' Press, 2013).

Thompson, Teresa. L. and Eugenia Zerbinos. "Gender Roles in Animated Cartoons: Has the Picture changed in 20 Years?" *Sex Roles* 32, no. 9–10 (1995): 651–673.

Towbin, Mia Adessa, Shelley A. Haddock, Toni Schindler Zimerman, Lori K. Lund, and Litsa Renee Tanner. "Images of Gender, Race, Age, and Sexual Orientation in Disney Feature-Length Animated Films". *Journal of Feminist Family Therapy* 15, no. 4 (2008): 19–44.

Zipes, Jack. "Breaking the Disney Spell". In *From Mouse to Mermaid: The Politics of Film, Gender and Culture*, edited by Elizabeth Bell, Lynda Haas and Laura Sells (Bloomington: Indiana University Press, 1995), 21–42.

Secondary sources – unpublished

Matyas, Vanessa. "Tale as Old as Time: A Textual Analysis of Race and Gender in Disney Princess Films". In *Graduate Major Research Papers and Multimedia Projects*. Paper 6. Accessed April 6, 2014. http://digitalcommons.mcmaster.ca/cmst_grad_research/6.

Web sources

Caulfield, Keith. "'Frozen' Rules With Most Weeks at No. 1 Since Adele's '21'". *Billboard*, April 2, 2014. Accessed April 5, 2014. http://www.billboard.com/articles/news/6032586/frozen-rules-billboard-200-most-weeks-at-no-1-since-adele-21.

Chance, Molly. "Kristen Bell: 'Frozen' character is 'awkward', 'Veronica Mars' footage 'looks radical'". Zap2it, August 14, 2013. Accessed April 5, 2014. http://zap2it.com/blogs/kristen_bell_frozen_character_is_awkward_veronica_mars_footage_looks_radical-2013-08.

Colman, Danielle. "The Problem with False Feminism (Or Why "Frozen" Left Me Cold)". Medium, February 7, 2014. Accessed April 3, 2014. https://medium.com/disney-and-animation/7c0bbc7252ef.

"Frozen: Songwriters Kristen Anderson-Lopez & Robert Lopez Official Movie Interview". YouTube, LLC, October 31, 2013. Accessed March 26, 2014. https://www.youtube.com/watch?v=mzZ77n4Ab5E.

"Huell Howser Interviews Adriana Caselotti-The Voice of Snow White". Youtube, LLC, March 9, 2009. Accessed March 22, 2014. https://www.youtube.com/watch?v=PFfgRmZXJT0.

Trust, Gary. "Pharrell Williams Leads Hot 100; John Legend, Idina Menzel On the Move". *Billboard*, March 26, 2014. Accessed April 7, 2014. http://www.billboard.com/arti-

cles/news/602 1173/pharrell-williams-leads-hot-100-john-legend-idina-menzel-on-th
e-move.

Filmography

Aladdin. Directed by Ron Clements and John Musker. 1992. Stockholm: Walt Disney Studios Home Entertainment AB, 2010. DVD.

Askungen [Cinderella]. Directed by Clyde Geronimi, Wilfred Jackson and Hamilton Luske. 1950. Stockholm: Walt Disney Studios Home Entertainment AB, 2012. DVD.

Den lilla sjöjungfrun [The Little Mermaid]. Directed by Ron Clements and John Musker. 1989. Stockholm: Walt Disney Studios Home Entertainment AB, 2006. DVD.

Frozen. Directed by Chris Buck and Jennifer Lee. 2013. Burbank, CA: Walt Disney Studios Home Entertainment, 2014. DVD.

Herkules [Hercules]. Directed by Ron Clements and John Musker. 1997. Stockholm: Walt Disney Studios Home Entertainment AB, 2003. DVD.

Mulan. Directed by Tony Bancroft and Barry Cook. 1998. Stockholm: Walt Disney Studios Home Entertainment AB, 2004. DVD.

Pocahontas. Directed by Mike Gabriel and Eric Goldberg. 1995. Stockholm: Walt Disney Studios Home Entertainment AB, 2002. DVD.

Prinsessan och grodan [The Princess and the Frog]. Directed by Ron Clements and John Musker. 2009. Stockholm: Walt Disney Studios Home Entertainment AB, 2010. DVD.

Ringaren i Notre Dame [The Hunchback of Notre Dame]. Directed by Gary Trousdale and Kirk Wise. 1996. Stockholm: Walt Disney Studios Home Entertainment AB, 2002. DVD.

Snövit och de sju dvärgarna [Snow White and the Seven Dwarfs]. Directed by Larry Morey, Wilfred Jackson, Ben Sharpsteen, Perce Pearce, David Hand and William Cottrell. 1937. Stockholm: Walt Disney Studios Home Entertainment AB, 2009. DVD.

Trassel [Tangled]. Directed by Nathan Greno and Byron Howard. 2010. Stockholm: Walt Disney Studios Home Entertainment AB, 2011. DVD.

Törnrosa [Sleeping Beauty]. Directed by Clyde Geronimi. 1959. Stockholm: Walt Disney Studios Home Entertainment AB, 2008. DVD.

Endnotes

1. Anahid Kassabian, *Hearing Film: Tracking Identifications in Contemporary Hollywood Film Music* (New York: Routledge, 2001), 60, 141.

2. Kassabian, 142.

3. Philip Tagg, *Music's Meanings: A Modern Musicology for Non-Musos* (New York: The Mass Media Music Scholars' Press, 2013), 170, 200.

4. Heather Laing, *The Gendered Score: Music in 1940s Melodrama and the Woman's Film* (Aldershot: Ashgate Publishing Limited, 2007), 13.

5. Leo Treitler, in *Ibid*., 13–14.

6. Tagg, in Kassabian, 125.

7. Kassabian, 70.

8. Kassabian, and Laing, 14.

9. Laing, 14, and Claudia Gorbman, *Unheard Melodies: Narrative Film Music* (Bloomington: Indiana University Press, 1987), 79.

10. Heather Laing, "Emotion by Numbers: Music, Song and the Musical", in *Musicals: Hollywood and Beyond*, edited by Bill Marshall and Robynn Stilwell (Wiltshire: Cromwell Press, 2000), 6.

11. Alan Menken, in Jeanne Speath, "Alan Menken on Music's Many Forms", in *Music Educators Journal* 84, no. 3 (1997): 40.

12. Laing, "Emotion by Numbers", 7.

13. Richard Dyer, *In the Space of a Song: The Uses of Song in Film* (London: Routledge, 2012), 2.

14. Dyer, 30, 56.

15. Dyer, 5.

16. Susan Smith, *The Musical: Race, Gender and Performance* (London: Wallflower Press, 2005), 58.

17. Steven Cohan, *Hollywood Musicals, the Film Reader* (London: Routledge, 2002), 78.

18. Laura Sells, "Where Do the Mermaids Stand: Voice and Body in *The Little Mermaid*", in *From Mouse to Mermaid*, 175–192.

19. Raymond Knapp, *The American Musical and the Performance of Personal Identity* (Princeton: Princeton University Press, 2006), 125–131.

20. Ross Care, "Make Walt's Music: Music For Disney Animation, 1928–1967", in *The Cartoon Music Book*, edited by Daniel Goldmark (Chicago: Chicago Review Press, 2002), 21–36.

21. "Frozen: Songwriters Kristen Anderson-Lopez & Robert Lopez Official Movie Interview", YouTube, LLC, October 31, 2013, accessed March 26, 2014, https://www.youtube.com/watch?v=mzZ77n4Ab5E.

22. Neil Gabler, *Walt Disney: The Triumph of the American Imagination* (New York: Random House, 2007), 276–277.

23. Kassabian, 69.

24. Davis, Amy M. *Good Girls and Wicked Witches: Women in Disney's Feature Animation* (Bloomington: John Libbey Publishing, 2006): 102, 135.

25. Mia Adessa Towbin, Shelley A. Haddock, Toni Schindler Zimmerman, Lori K. Lund and Litsa Renee Tanner, "Images of Gender, Race, Age, and Sexual Orientation in Disney Feature-Length Animated Films", *Journal of Feminist Family Therapy* 15, no. 4 (2008): 28–30.

26. Jacob Grimm and Wilhelm Grimm, "Snow-White and the Seven Dwarfs", in *The Complete Fairy Tales of the Brothers Grimm* (Hertfordshire: Wordsworth Editions Limited, 2009), 261–271.

27. Kassabian, 35.

28. Douglas Brode, *Multiculturalism and the Mouse* (Austin: University of Texas Press, 2005), 174.

29. Knapp, 131.

30. *Snövit* [Snow White], DVD with audio commentary, 57:04.

31. Jane Feuer, *The Hollywood Musical* (Houndmills: The MacMillan Press Ltd., 1993), 50.

32. Knapp, 130.

33. *Snövit* [Snow White], DVD audio commentary, 15:00.

34. "Huell Howser Interviews Adriana Caselotti-The Voice of Snow White", YouTube, LLC, March 9, 2009, accessed March 22, 2014, https://www.youtube.com/watch?v=PFfgRmZXJT0.

35. Smith, 77.

36. Vanessa Matyas, "Tale as Old as Time: A Textual Analysis of Race and Gender in Disney Princess Films", in *Graduate Major Research Papers and Multimedia Projects*, paper 6, accessed April 6, 2014, http://digitalcommons.mcmaster.ca/cmst_grad_research/6, 22.

37. Sean Griffin, *Tinker Belles and Evil Queens: The Disney Company From the Inside Out* (New York: New York University Press, 2000), 143.

38. Davis, *Good Girls*, 155.

39. Davis, 177.

40. Davis, 181; Lauren Dundes, "Disney's Modern Heroine Pocahontas: Revealing Age-Old Gender Stereotypes and Role Discontinuity Under a Façade of Liberation", *The Social Science Journal* 38, no. 3 (2001): 358; and Deborah Ross, "Escape from Wonderland: Disney and the Female Imagination", in *Marvels & Tales* 18, no. 1 (2004): 59.

41. Sells, 179–180.

42. Cohan, 67.

43. Gwendolyn Limbach, "'You the Man: Well, Sorta': Gender Binaries and Liminality in Mulan", in *Diversity in Disney Films: Critical Essays on Race, Ethnicity, Gender, Sexuality and Disability*, edited by Johnson Cheu (Jefferson: McFarland, 2013), 126.

44. Tagg, in Kassabian, 125.

45. Sells, 180.

46. David Morgan, *Knowing the Score: Film Composers Talk About the Art, Craft, Blood, Sweat, and Tears of Writing for Cinema* (New York: HarperCollins Publishers, 2000), 118.

47. Mike Gabriel, quoted in "Deleted Sequence: 'If I Never Knew You'", *Pocahontas*, DVD bonus clip.

48. Keith Caulfield, "'Frozen' Rules With Most Weeks at No. 1 Since Adele's 0145 21'", *Billboard*, April 2, 2014, accessed April 5, 2014, http://www.billboard.com/articles/news/6032586/frozen-rules-billboard-200-most-weeks-at-no-1-since-adele-21.

49. Hans Christian Andersen, "The Snow Queen", in *The Complete Fairy Tales of Hans Christian Andersen* (Hertfordshire: Wordsworth Editions Limited, 2009), 270–302.

50. Molly Chance, "Kristen Bell: 'Frozen' character is 'awkward', 'Veronica mars' footage 'looks radical'", Zap2it, August 14, 2013, accessed April 5, 2014. http://zap2it.com/blogs/kristen_bell_frozen_character_is_awkward_veronica_mars_footage_looks_radical-2013-08.

51. Danielle Colman, "The Problem with False Feminism (Or Why "Frozen" Left Me Cold)", Medium, February 7, 2014, accessed April 3, 2014, https://medium.com/disney-and-animation/7c0bbc7252ef.

52. Cohan, 81–82.

53. Laing, 14.

54. Colman, "The Problem with False Feminism".

55. Dyer, 5.

56. John Shepherd, "Difference and Power in Music", in *Musicology and Difference: Gender and Sexuality in Music Scholarship*, edited by Ruth A. Solie (Berkley: University of California Press, 1995), 59.

57. Sells, 181.

58. Smith, 58.

59. Gary Trust, "Pharrell Williams Leads Hot 100; John Legend, Idina Menzel On the Move", *Billboard*, March 26, 2014, accessed April 7, 2014, http://www.billboard.com/articles/news/6021173/pharrell-williams-leads-hot-100-john-legend-idina-menzel-on-the-move.

60. Tagg, 198.

Chapter 9

Princess Brides and Dream Weddings: Investigating the Gendered Narrative of Disney's Fairy Tale Weddings

Kodi Maier

It is no wonder that the song "When You Wish Upon a Star" has evolved into the very theme that defines Disney's mission. The message presented is clear: in everything the entertainment company does, from movies to books to CDs, from theme parks to food to resorts, from beautiful princesses to magical beasts, Disney strives to fulfil every fantasy. Therefore, it is hardly surprising that a company whose legacy centres on fairy tales and dreams would come to flourish in one of the largest fantasy-based industries of the 21st century: the wedding industry. Since 1991, when Disney established its Fairy Tale Weddings platform, thousands of couples have chosen Walt Disney World Resort, Disneyland, the Disney Cruise Line, and other company settings as the backdrop for their perfect fantasy wedding. While Disney did not manufacture the market for its Fairy Tale Weddings from thin air, it is nonetheless situated in a unique position within the wedding industry and that industry's narratives – one which allows the company to reap enormous profits. It is only by exploring these crosscurrents, namely the construction of the wedding industry, the narrative construction of the "princess bride", and Disney's role in translating fairy tales to the silver screen that the cultural impact of Disney's Fairy Tale Weddings can be discerned.

Once Upon a Time ...

Before embarking upon an exploration of Disney's in-house wedding platform, it is first necessary to deconstruct the wedding industry as a whole. First and foremost, the industry as it exists today posits itself as a bastion of tradition. The white wedding gown, the diamond engagement ring, the multi-layered cake, and the elegant venue are all elements that many Western brides deem necessary to launch a successful marriage. If the ceremony lacks any of these elements, those particularly devoted to the "traditional" wedding may reject the rite for being incomplete and deeply flawed, dooming the young couple to an equally flawed marriage. However, this has not always been the case. According to Vicki Howard of Hartwick College, wedding rituals from the colonial period up to the nineteenth century were established by the community to mark the creation of a new household. Indeed, Howard states that any celebration "was prepared at home".[1] Nor was there a set formula for the nuptial proceedings, as "[w]edding traditions followed the dictates of custom, religion, and culture and varied widely across the country and between different groups".[2] It was not until the 1920s that the wedding industry began to emerge, driven by "jewelry retailers and manufacturers, department store bridal salons, bridal consultants, fashion designers, caterers, etiquette writers, and a host of other experts and entrepreneurs" looking to capitalise "on older wedding rituals, making them more lucrative in the process, [and] sometimes even introducing new practices as if they were timeless traditions".[3] Department stores specifically introduced "the gift registry, bridal salon, and wedding fashion show – all of which were widespread by the World War II era", while publications such as *Bride's Magazine* (launched in 1934) and *Modern Bride* (launched in 1949) introduced the perfect platform for advertising that helped expand the bridal market.[4]

The unified efforts of such commercial interests successfully laid the foundation for the so-called "traditions" that many swear by today. The jewellery industry, for example, played an active role in the establishment of engagement ring and wedding ring traditions, allowing numerous jewellers and jewellery retailers to capitalise on such traditions for decades to come. In her book *White Weddings*, Chrys Ingraham explains how, in the early twentieth century, Sir Ernest Oppenheimer of the De Beers Corporation hired New York advertising agency N.W. Ayer & Son to generate a desire for diamond engagement rings. Before De Beers became invested in selling nuptial jewellery, only the bride wore a wedding band to symbolise the pledge of the marriage contract, guaranteeing that she, as the property of her father, would be accordingly transferred to her spouse, her new "owner".[5] In an effort to increase De Beers's diamond sales, N.W. Ayer & Son launched a variety of campaigns aimed at inspiring men, the assumed breadwinners, to equate diamonds with love and eternity through the now-famous slogan, "a diamond is forever".[6] Thus, a diamond ring became more than a lovely bauble for the bride: "it was a sign of the man's ability to pay [or provide], as well as a symbol of his love".[7] These and subsequent campaigns were so successful that many Americans (and others) now believe a diamond engagement ring is a necessity, rather than the luxury it actually is.[8] The jewellery industry's innovations were not limited to bridal accoutrements. Profits were further increased by promoting the groom's wedding band and the double ring ceremony, "traditions" that were not prevalent prior to World War II.[9] Although attempts to create a market for male engagement rings in the 1920s were unsuccessful, jewellery retailers were able to naturalise the growing practice of the groom's wedding band largely, because during the 1940s, "the double ring ceremony … highlighted the bonds of marriage and family, bonds that could extend to include nation and the capitalist 'free world.' During wartime, a man could wear a groom's band as a symbol of what he was fighting to preserve."[10]

Jewellers were not the only ones invested in transforming the traditions of the wedding ceremony: the bridal gown underwent significant changes as well. As previously discussed, a couple's wedding was formerly considered a family affair, with emphasis on the formation of a new family, rather than the ceremony itself. Thus, instead of purchasing a special gown she would wear only once, the bride donned her best dress or a suit that could be worn many times after the ceremony. Such dresses were customarily black or grey, but if the bride's family could afford to spend a bit more, brocades of gold and silver or yellow and blue were used.[11] While brides did wear white on occasion, the concept of a "white wedding" did not begin to gain popularity until 1840, when Queen Victoria married Prince Albert. According to Ingraham, "When Queen Victoria was wed in a white gown, she captured the imaginations of many".[12] The young queen was wed in "an opulent ceremony where she wore a luxurious and beautiful … *white* wedding gown. Following this grand event, many white Western middle-class brides … imitated Victoria and adopted the white wedding gown."[13] At the time, white was particularly significant in that it was a sign of privilege: as a fabric, it was hard to come by and difficult to keep clean. For these reasons, white also symbolised female sexual purity. Thus, the white wedding gown became a marker of virginal purity, which in turn denoted the bride's suitability as a mother and wife.[14]

Widespread cultural changes take time, and the lavish, formal white wedding ideal so familiar today did not solidify until the 1950s. The end of World War II saw the rise of an expanding middle class economy, which included a rise in greater levels of consumer demand. According to Howard, the white wedding extravaganza gained traction during this period "because it embodied Cold War liberal values – the postwar belief that democracy and capitalism were intertwined", a statement Howard attributes, in part, to historian Lizabeth Cohen, who calls this blend of government and consumerism "a 'consumer's republic', a strategy for 'reconstructing the nation's economy and reaffirming its democratic values through promoting the expansion of mass consumption".[15] This move toward blatant consumerism is on full display in Vincente Minnelli's 1950 film, *Father of the Bride*. The film follows Stanley Banks (played by Spencer Tracey), a middle class lawyer who struggles to navigate the details, costs, and emotional weight of his only daughter's upcoming marriage. Although the family collectively agrees that Kay (Elizabeth Taylor), the Banks' daughter, will have a small wedding at home, the ceremony quickly balloons into what Stanley calls "a big, flashy show that [they] can't afford".[16] To Stanley, details that are now considered essential elements of the ceremony – the white wedding gown, bridesmaids, flowers, a church – are all superfluous expenses. It is not until his wife, Ellie (Joan Bennett), expresses a touch of regret that her own wedding did not have "all the trimmings"[17] that Stanley relents. Moreover, even Ellie's vision of a manageable reception is snubbed by the caterer, who immediately begins weaving visions of trays of salmon and cold sturgeon. When Ellie interrupts, declaring they had planned on a less extravagant reception with sandwiches, small cakes, and ice cream, the caterer replies, "Of course you can have what you wish, Madam, but that's what we usually serve for children's parties".[18] Although Ellie stands firm, the caterer's message is clear: the "simple" reception (and the "simple" wedding) is no longer the norm.

Chrys Ingraham notes that the economic policies of President Ronald Reagan, who held office from 1981 to 1989, further spurred the exponential growth of the wedding industry with its promises of "a return to American prosperity, traditional values, and happy endings. His message to Americans was to celebrate and display consumption, luxury, pleasure, and excess."[19] This, in turn, "created a seedbed for white wedding extravaganzas". Over time, the "number of weddings increased as did the amount of money people were willing to pay (or go into debt)".[20] At the same time, Lady Diana Spencer's 1981 wedding to Charles, Prince of Wales, embodied the fairy tale luxury that many Americans had begun to envision as the perfect start to a happy and prosperous marriage. According to *Bride's* magazine, the ceremony "transformed the way we think about weddings. The images of that event are so thoroughly implanted in our memories, it's hard to separate the idea of the bride from the picture of Diana emerging, Cinderella-like, from her glass coach. That early morning ... we started dreaming about the day we, too, would promise to love, honor, and cherish."[21] Ingraham elaborates, "Princess Diana's ceremony helps the new bride imagine her own, inviting her to emulate and legitimize upper-class practices, as though the average middle-class bride could ever achieve anything remotely similar to this pageant".[22] As a result of Reagan's policies and Princess Diana's fairy tale wedding, the notion that a luxurious, and costly, wedding leads to a successful marriage became firmly entrenched in a large portion of the American psyche.

In 1991, Touchstone Pictures, a subsidiary of The Walt Disney Company, released their version of Minnelli's *Father of the Bride*. Premiering ten years after Reagan took office and Princess Diana wed Prince Charles, the remake represents the full culmination of both events' impact on current conceptions of the perfect wedding. While the film closely follows the original, there is one key difference: the lavishness of each nuptial detail. Much like Stanley Banks, George Banks (Steve Martin) overtly cringes at every new cost, going so far as to propose that his daughter get married at a steakhouse. Eventually, however, George agrees to accompany his wife, Nina (Diane Keaton), and daughter, Annie (Kimberly Williams), to see Franck, a flamboyant, upscale, vaguely European wedding coordinator, who shows the family a cake priced at $1,200. George is shocked. When he protests that his first car didn't cost that much, Franck laughs, "Well, welcome to the 90s, Mr. Banks!"[23] Much like the caterer who snubbed Ellie's idea of a simple reception, Franck makes it clear that such expense is normal – even reasonable. Once the cake is decided, a host of additional decorations and details are brought in that were not in the original version, including a freshly planted tulip border, a trio of live swans, and parking attendants. George's visible stress continues to mount, until he finally has a public nervous breakdown that lands him in the city jail. Nina refuses to bail him out until he swears to "stop telling everyone [he meets] how much this wedding is costing" and "how, with every roll of [his] eyes, [he is] taking away a piece of her happiness".[24] Again, the film posits that such opulence is necessary for the ceremony to be successful and for Annie to truly be happy on her big day.

As societal expectations grew, so too did the machine behind the white wedding phenomenon. Since the 1980s, the influence and scope of the bridal industry have grown exponentially. In 1999, the average annual profit for the industry was around $32 billion dollars, which grew to $80 billion in 2006.[25] Ingraham notes that today's industry involves a long list of primary, secondary, and tertiary markets, including but not limited to wedding gowns and apparel, diamonds, venues and destinations, household goods, invitations and paper goods, flowers, photos, gifts, catering and cakes, accessories (for example, ring pillows), and limousines.[26] An estimate from 2008 notes that a couple will spend an average of $27,852 on the wedding itself, with the dress costing an average of $1,553 to $1,811, including alterations, and $258 on a headpiece and veil.[27] Moreover, the industry is not limited to the accoutrements for the wedding itself. In her article "Superbrides", British author Sharon Boden uses the term "wedding industry" "… to denote the opportunities on offer to consumers to achieve the weddings they desire as well as the methods used to generate these desires in the first place: for example, bridal magazines, the media, Internet wedding sites, wedding professionals and service providers, business promotions, wedding exhibitions and 'fayres', regional wedding directories and CD-Rom wedding planners".[28] The wedding industry has become a multimedia market where the "marriage of conspicuous consumption with the promise of love and romance combines to create a highly lucrative but virtually invisible transnational ... industry that is interdependent with the historical needs of capitalism".[29] In other words, the wedding industry has embedded itself so deeply in the economic and social needs of American (and Western) heteronormative, capitalist society that it has created a "recession-proof" market where touches such as limousines or a horse-drawn carriage are deemed to be "necessary" for a successful wedding.[30]

Here Comes the Bride

As the wedding industry increasingly manufactures and invests in strengthening the accoutrements of the white wedding, it is worth elaborating on how the bride, the central cog in the industry's machinery, is constructed. To be clear, although television shows, magazines, websites, and other media all discuss the wedding as the "bride's" special day, they are not speaking of the woman beneath the wedding gown. Rather, they are speaking of the *idea* of the bride: a composite of images and associations that the woman is expected to strive for and fulfil in order to have a "successful" wedding and, eventually, a "successful" marriage. Despite the implicit assumption within the wedding industry that a woman's primary goal in life is to get married and live happily ever after, it must be remembered that "no one is born a bride" (or a groom!).[31] This is especially evident in the language bridal magazines and other outlets use to advertise to their audiences. A quote from *Bride*'s magazine wonders "What makes a woman obsess about her wedding gown? Is it because she's been thinking about it since she was four, because it's the one item of clothing that can instantly turn her into a princess, or because 167 pairs of eyes will be staring at her as she marches down the aisle?"[32] In a segment featuring Disney's Fairy Tale Weddings platform on Walt Disney World Radio's YouTube channel, host Lou Mongello opens by asking, "What little girl doesn't dream about being a princess or having a fairy tale wedding?"[33] These examples demonstrate that the bride's desires for a lavish "fairy tale" wedding are more than merely constructed; they are *naturalised* by language that implicitly reinforces the idea that fantasising about the "perfect" "fairy tale" wedding is an inherent component of a woman's femininity. The target of this construct is by no means limited to women of marrying age, but begins with toy creators, such as Disney, and manufacturers, such as Hasbro and Mattel, who produce numerous lines of wedding products largely aimed at or featuring little girls. *New York Times* writer Peggy Orenstein states that, according to Barbie manufacturer, Mattel, one of the most popular games young girls play is "bride".[34] Ingraham elaborates: "Mattel, Disney, Hasbro, and other toy companies market a variety of children's products that feature the same dominant images of the pretty white bride whose greatest achievement is in wedding her handsome prince. The wedding becomes both the object of a young girl's dreams and the site of closure, rendering the marital relationship inevitable."[35] In the early 1990s, Mattel manufactured a line of "My Size Barbie" dolls, among them "My Size Princess Barbie" and "My Size Bride Barbie". The three-foot-tall dolls were constructed in such a way that their female owners could share Barbie's dress, allowing her to enact her assumed fantasies of being a princess or a blushing bride. Furthermore, "Disney films, television cartoons and sitcoms, soap operas, messages from family members, roles as flower girls and junior bridesmaids, and wedding toys that invite little girls to plan a pretend wedding" all further serve to solidify Western wedding norms in the imaginations of young girls.[36]

Now understood by a sizeable proportion of the Western population as unquestionable and innate, such fantasies naturalise the links between Womanhood, the romantic fairy tale, and the opulence of the modern-day wedding, all of which work – overtly or subliminally – to pressure women into manifesting the image of the perfect bride in their own weddings. As Erika Engstrom notes, there is a "pressure [for the bride] to conform to the bridal costume, rather than the costume conforming to the body".[37] Marisa Corrado unveils exactly how the wedding gown industry "teaches" brides to embody this ideal in her article "Teaching Wedding Rules: How Bridal Workers Negotiate Control Over Their Customers". Corrado states that "Bridal workers strive to gain control over their brides' behaviour by presenting a professional self. By establishing familiarity with their clients and demonstrating their expertise, bridal workers can give orders to their customers and chastise them when they deviate from appropriate behaviour without fear that the customer will not return."[38] In the course of Corrado's field research, she observed two wedding consultants, Helen and Joan, who would emphasise that "the bride's main priority is to present a flawless, beautiful image of 'the bride' on the wedding day" whenever a bride complained that her dress was uncomfortable.[39] Weight gain, a natural bodily occurrence, is frequently presented as a problem because wedding dresses are ordered months in advance and only so many alterations can be made. If the bride does not maintain a certain weight, she distorts the "perfection" of the dress. Corrado confirms that most bridal shops have their customers sign a contract promising that their measurements will not change significantly, with the understanding that if their measurements do change, the salon will not be held responsible for providing a new dress.[40]

Princess for a Day

Queen Victoria also serves as one of the major exemplars for the princess bride narrative, an important keystone within Disney's wedding industry and the wedding industry as a whole. Ingraham likens the queen to Cinderella, both being "plain" women who marry their handsome prince in an elegant, lavish ceremony. Indeed, such public, royal weddings as Queen Victoria's did much to strengthen the link between heterosexual romance and unbridled consumerism. The weddings of Princess Grace of Monaco and Princess Diana, two supposedly "common" women who married handsome princes, followed this "grand tradition" and further ignited American imaginations. This is particularly true of Grace Kelly, an internationally acclaimed film star who married Prince Rainier in a highly publicised wedding extravaganza filmed by MGM in April 1956. According to Ingraham, "For many Americans, Grace Kelly, born in Philadelphia to Irish immigrant parents, represented the merging of the Hollywood fairy-tale happy ending and the American dream of possibility and wealth. The headlines proclaimed that even a little girl from Philadelphia could become a princess."[41] Princess Diana, a school teacher, married Charles, Prince of Wales in an equally opulent ceremony. For the thousands of women who tuned in to watch these weddings on television, the lives of their idols "symbolized possibility: 'Fairy tales can come true, it can happen to you'. Neither woman came from royalty [...] yet both found 'a handsome prince', leading many to believe that fairy tales could come true."[42]

Again, this theme of the princess bride, especially the bride as a rags-to-riches Cinderella, appears over and over in the wedding industry at large. Combined with the gendered nature of the wedding narrative – all labour and focus of the wedding falls on the bride, as it is "her" special day – the ideal of the princess bride further serves to drive the ever-increasing opulence and extravagance of even the average wedding, leading one to wonder exactly where this narrative originated. As demonstrated above, real-life princess brides have certainly played a part in igniting the public's imagination. However, a bride's desire to be a princess on her wedding day stems from something more than the wish to emulate real-life royalty. In order to understand this phenomenon, one must first dissect the construction of the princess in American society, specifically that of Cinderella.

While dozens of versions of the Cinderella tale appear in fairy tale traditions from around the world, it is the Anglo-European versions, especially Disney's 1950 animated feature film, which dominate the American imagination. Traditionally, the story depicts a young, beautiful, and gentle girl whose wicked step-mother forces her to do all household labour in the family home, reducing the girl to rags while her step-mother and two step-sisters live in luxury. One day the prince of the land announces he will hold a royal ball, open to every woman in the kingdom, to help him select his new bride. Although the girl's step-mother forbids her to attend, her fairy godmother comes to her rescue and magically transforms her rags into a beautiful ball gown. Providing her with an enchanted coach and driver, Cinderella's fairy godmother then sends her off to the ball. There the prince falls madly in love with the mysterious beauty and, after she flees the ball at the stroke of midnight, vows to stop at nothing in order to find her. Thus, the young maid is elevated to royalty and, as a result, realises the fullness of her potential.

According to fairy tale scholar Maria Tatar, such stories were used to fulfil a pedagogical function and teach young children, in this instance young girls, the proper way to behave in civilised society. In discussing "The Kind and Unkind Girls" fairy tale story type,[43] Tatar notes that "Whether a tale exalts the value of hard work or praises any of a host of virtues ranging from kindness to *politesse*, it imparts specific lessons by instituting a system of rewards for one type of behavior and punishment for another".[44] In other words, Cinderella's behaviour in her various Anglo-European incarnations serves to teach young girls that their highest calling is to be gentle, kind, generous, and industrious. If girls and women manifest Cinderella's qualities in their own lives, they will surely be rewarded. Sheldon Cashdan, author of *The Witch Must Die: The Hidden Meaning of Fairy Tales*, sheds further light on this narrative in his discussion of the Russian Cinderella tale, *The Frog Princess*. In the fairy tale, the handsome prince, Ivan, is forced to take a frog as his royal wife. Cashdan notes that in this instance the princess is the lowest of the low, a slimy, ugly creature who is transformed into a beautiful princess by the prince's love. When the princess appears at court, she arrives in a gilded carriage, dressed in a stunning gown, and immediately captures the attention of those around her. Here, it seems, Cashdan is describing more than a mere transformation – he is describing an apotheosis.[45] Again, Cashdan highlights the idea that the fairy tale princess functions as a metaphor, which provides a guide for actualising the highest form of the female self.

Within the wedding industry today, that narrative has shifted slightly. Of course, given that fairy tales have retained their pedagogical function, women are still taught to be kind, obedient, hard-working, and generous. Over the years, however, the wedding industry has used the Cinderella narrative in particular to teach women how to become a bride. The notion that planning a wedding is a difficult, laborious task that spans a year (or more) certainly remains, but, as previously discussed, the wedding industry primarily depends upon the Cinderella narrative to teach the bride to emphasise luxury and beauty above all else on "her" special day. Writer Rebecca Mead illuminates the machinery behind the Cinderella bride in her *Guardian* article, "Princess for a Day". She writes:

> Throughout, the bride is encouraged from all sides – by wedding magazines, by the coverage of celebrity weddings, and by the vendors she encounters – to think of herself as a 'princess for a day', [...] Being a princess is an enduring girlhood fantasy, and when translated to the context of a wedding it is

particularly apt, given that *a princess is one who enjoys limitless wealth and childish irresponsibility*. Tellingly, a wedding is not characterised as an opportunity to be a queen, and to enjoy the perhaps more distinguished, and potent, form of regality that implies.[46]

As Mead points out, this narrative infantilises the bride, urging her to indulge in her deepest childhood fantasies.

But Where Is the Groom?

The narrative of the bride as Cinderella is further reinforced by the groom/prince's conspicuous absence from the construction of this matrimonial paradigm. In lamenting the self-centred point of view the wedding industry encourages brides to take, writers such as Shelia Gibbons frequently remark that the groom has become little more than an afterthought for the festivities. In an article for *WeNews*, Gibbons quotes scholar Erika Engstrom's analysis of The Learning Channel's series *A Wedding Story* (1997–2005) in which she states that the wedding day "revolves around (the bride) and her feminine appearance ... In contrast, although it may be an important day for the groom, his wedding day is not his most important day. Indeed [...] the expectation for him is that he simply show up."[47] Just as industry narratives assume the bride has wanted an opulent, regal wedding since girlhood, it is equally assumed that young men want nothing to do with such "romantic stuff". According to Peggy Orenstein, Disney concluded early on that "a groom or prince is incidental to [the] fantasy, a regrettable necessity at best. Although they keep him around for the climactic kiss, he is otherwise relegated to the bottom of the toy box, which is why you don't see him prominently displayed in stores."[48] Sheldon Cashdan demonstrates that this idea is not by any means a Disney creation, but instead a recurrent factor in older fairy tale traditions, noting that "[t]he prince tends to be a cardboard character, almost an afterthought, who materializes at the end of the story to ensure a happy ending. In many instances, the intervention of the prince is incidental to the heroine's survival."[49] If the bride is to be a fairy tale princess, specifically Cinderella, she needs a Prince Charming to complete the scene. Neither the fairy tale traditions nor the wedding industry, or even the bride herself, require him to do anything more than stand at the altar and bask in the beauty of his princess.

Following suit, advertisers rarely address the groom when selling wedding accoutrements. Instead, they turn their full attention to the bride, appealing to her "innate" fantasies of being a princess. In the aforementioned WDW Radio YouTube clip, Lou Mongello discusses the myriad benefits of getting married at Disney specifically as they would appeal to the bride's childhood fantasies. If wedding industry narratives address the groom at all, it is simply in his role as part of the couple, not as a person with an invested interest in the proceedings. This highly gendered rhetoric, in turn, trickles down to the public and further ingrains the already sexist division of labour of planning a wedding. Tina Lowrey and Cele Otnes interviewed a number of couples for their article, "Construction of a Meaningful Wedding: Differences in the Priorities of Brides and Grooms", including one groom who said, "I have taken a very active interest in agreeing with everything she does [...] *Once you realize you're basically organizing a coronation, then it's okay*".[50] Other grooms echo Lowrey's and Otnes's interviewee elsewhere. In Dawn H. Currie's study on the construction of the "modern traditional" wedding in Western culture, one groom, Larry, contends that the entire process of planning a wedding is somehow beyond the groom's interest or even mental capacity, saying, "I think she spends more hours a day thinking about the conscious little details which I would miss, than I do". Another groom, Brian, said, "For some reason my mind goes blank. She asks how things should happen on the day of the wedding – [...] I couldn't figure it out to save my life. And I don't know why. I have a feeling that it's not in men's genes."[51] The cardboard cut-out nature of the princely groom, then, is circular: industry giants invest in appealing to the wedding fantasies of the princess bride, upholding the erasure of the prince/groom already prevalent in fairy tales. Grooms hear these messages and bow out of the process, assuming that planning a wedding is not in their genes or is simply "girls' stuff". This then influences how the industry invests their advertising dollars, diminishing the groom's role in order to further solidify the gendered division of labour already prevalent in wedding practices.

Behind the Magic

Having established and examined the major cogs in the wedding industry's machine, it must be asked: where does a corporation like Disney, one with a vested interest in perceived traditions, fit? First and foremost, Disney is the primary curator of America's fairy tales and folk lore. Despite the fact that Disney's animated fairy tale feature films are only a fraction of the studio's total output, they are the bedrock upon which Disney's legacy rests in modern perceptions of the company. When Disney translates a fairy tale from more "traditional" or "original" versions, such as those edited by the Brothers Grimm or written by Charles Perrault, Disney's version of that fairy tale is then canonised within the American psyche.[52] In other words, "Such is the power of visual representation that children tend to believe that Disney's version of the fairy tale is the real story rather than the 'classic' version to which they may or may not have been exposed through school or home".[53] Although Disney has certainly translated more parochial fairy tale-like stories such as *Pinocchio* (1940) and *Alice in Wonderland* (1951), their princess fairy tale adaptations such as *Cinderella* (1950), *The Little Mermaid* (1989), and *Beauty and the Beast* (1991) carry the most weight. Since the establishment of the Disney Princess franchise in 2000, countless journal articles, books, and blog posts have been written that dissect, discuss, and deliberate the impact these stories have had on American people, specifically American girls, in relation to the "princess culture" explosion of the last decade.[54]

Regardless of impact, the point remains: Disney's influence over the American fairy tale narrative is so strong that they can decide with impunity who gets to be the next (American) princess and how her story will unfold. Indeed, numerous calls for greater racial diversity have been made as women search for a Disney princess in whom they can see themselves, as if a Disney princess made in their image might finally "legitimise" their place in American society. In an article for *The Christian Science Monitor*, Rebecca Hains highlights the frustrations of young girls of colour such as "[t]he little black girl who came home from first grade in tears because her classmates said she couldn't be a princess" because there were no black Disney princesses before Tiana appeared in *Princess and the Frog* (2009).[55] When fans cannot find the diversity they seek in the Disney canon, they create "racebent" versions of their favourite Disney princesses in order to fill in the gaps Disney's lack of representation leaves.[56] Such representation among Disney's official princesses plays a key role in the wedding industry and Disney's wedding industry in particular because, more often than not, when a bride talks about her visions for a fairy tale wedding or likens herself to a princess, it is the Disney imagining of the fairy tale, particularly Disney's version of Cinderella, that she is referring to. Indeed, the company has been weaving their own "happily-ever-after" fairy tales since *Snow White and the Seven Dwarfs* debuted in 1937, inspiring fans to celebrate their own happily-ever-afters either in the parks or the hotels, with or without Disney's permission. In 1991, the same year that Touchstone released its remake of the classic 1950 film *Father of the Bride*, Disney launched their Fairy Tale Wedding platform as a response to their fans' dreams, thus creating a division of the wedding industry that is uniquely their own. Today, newly-engaged couples need only visit Franck's Bridal Studio, the one-stop wedding planning shop at Walt Disney World Resort, to procure everything they could desire, including venues for the wedding and the reception, either within the parks or on their cruise ships, invitations, cakes, and royal transportation.

Just as the wedding industry uses toys to teach young girls to internalise the fantasy of the princess wedding, Disney uses their highly lucrative Disney Princess franchise to foster an interest in the Disney wedding fantasy with a young female audience. Established in 2000 by former Nike executive Andy Mooney, the Disney Princess franchise brings (at the time of writing) eleven of Disney's most popular princesses and heroines – Snow White, Cinderella, Aurora/Briar Rose, Ariel, Belle, Jasmine, Pocahontas, Mulan, Tiana, Rapunzel, and Pixar's Merida – "out of the vault", granting them merchandising immortality and expanding their worlds beyond the limits of the movies. Young girls can purchase and play with a host of toys, including dresses, tiaras, shoes, magic wands, and make-up, allowing them to "become" whichever princess they choose. If a girl wishes to dress up as Ariel and act out the entire movie, from the moment Ariel first sees the handsome Prince Eric through to their wedding at the film's conclusion, Disney provides everything she will need to fill her toy box, including numerous Ariel dolls. In addition, Disney frequently produces material solely dedicated to the princesses' weddings, regardless of whether or not the princess's nuptials are included in her movie. For instance, the Disney Princess *Wedding Wishes* colouring book, published in 2009, features the weddings of Aurora, Belle, Cinderella, Jasmine, Ariel, and Snow White, even though *Cinderella* and *The Little Mermaid* only allude to Cinderella's and Ariel's weddings, and Jasmine marries her commoner groom, Aladdin, in a direct-to-video sequel, *Aladdin and the King of Thieves*. The colouring book comes with a page of glittering stickers (bouquets, wedding cakes, wedding bells, birds, inter-locking wedding rings, and pictures of the brides) and features images of the brides preparing for and celebrating their weddings. With the help of her pet tiger, Rajah, Jasmine examines her wedding dress, sends out invitations, decorates the palace, gathers flowers for her bouquet, and dons her wedding dress before meeting Aladdin at the altar and dancing with him at the reception. Princess Aurora prepares for her wedding in a similar fashion but, instead of a pet tiger, she has the help of her fairy godmothers – Flora, Fauna, and Merryweather – and a host of woodland animal friends.[57] It is important to note that, just as the prince/groom is conspicuously absent in wedding-themed toys and the overall narratives of the wedding industry, the grooms in Disney's colouring book do not appear until the day of the ceremony, leaving the work of the wedding firmly within their princesses' purview.

This example may seem insignificant, but it nonetheless makes a significant point: if Disney has the power to shape the fairy tale canon of the collective American psyche, the narratives of that canon frequently extend beyond their movies and into their merchandise. It is here that Disney straddles a unique position within the narratives of the wedding industry: the power the company wields as the curator of America's fairy tales means that the odds are good that the average young girl is more likely to fantasise about becoming a Disney princess bride. This in turn means that Disney is able to create and retain a high demand for the products within its Fairy Tale Weddings platform. Potential brides are invited to go to their website, where they can plan out the entire wedding in any one of Disney's American venues (the Walt Disney World Resort in Florida, Disneyland in California, Disney's Aulani Resort in Hawaii, or on one of the Disney cruise ships) and, however briefly, become the Disney princess she has always dreamed of being. In 2011, Disney teamed up with wedding dress manufacturer and retailer Alfred Angelo to produce the Disney's Fairy Tale Weddings Dress Collection, allowing brides-to-be to choose from gowns inspired by Ariel, Belle, Jasmine, Rapunzel, and, of course, Cinderella. Prior to Alfred Angelo's closing in July 2017, the collection was introduced with the following: "In tribute to princesses who dare to dream, Alfred Angelo unveils a stunning collection of signature gowns that capture the essence of each Disney Princess: her grace, her spark and her legendary beauty. Your once upon a time is now in an ethereal bridal creation fuelled by fantasy, romance and adventure, from the depths of the sea to far above the clouds."[58] A free planning guide offered through the Fairy Tale Weddings website describes the Alfred Angelo line as "the quintessential fairy tale bridal collection, fit for royalty. The Collection captures the essence and style of Disney Princesses – from the independent spirit of Tiana and the pretty romance of Sleeping Beauty to the classic glamour of Cinderella." Here Disney employs a number of wedding industry motifs to sell their gowns, emphasising the bride's assumed desire to be a beautiful princess and have her every dream come true on the day of her wedding.[59]

Of course, the offerings of Disney's Fairy Tale Weddings are not limited to fantasy venues and bridal gowns. Given the prevalence of the Cinderella narrative within the wedding industry, it only makes sense that Disney would make an extra effort to go above and beyond to accommodate any bride's particular fantasies. Should she so wish, the bride has the option of renting a horse-drawn carriage for around $2,950 to arrive at her ceremony in style.[60] A key feature in Disney's marketing for the Fairy Tale Weddings platform, the real-life version of Cinderella's Glass Coach comes complete with a pumpkin-inspired crystal carriage (so everyone can admire the bride as she arrives) pulled by six white ponies, with a driver and two footmen in all-white regalia to escort her from the coach. The couple can also request a Major Domo to act as their ring bearer for $800, who will carry the rings down the aisle in a glass slipper on a red pillow reminiscent of the climactic scene from Disney's animated *Cinderella*.[61] If that is still not enough, the couple can have a white dove flyover for $250, a private firework display for $2,500, or have "uninvited guests" who will come and entertain their party for $1,800.[62] Couples who elect to get married at one of the venues in Florida can also break away from their guests for a few moments to have their wedding photos taken in front of Cinderella's castle. At the reception, they can serve a cake decorated with the phrase "They Lived Happily Ever After" and/or topped with glass slippers, Cinderella's coach, or Cinderella's castle. Light projections of Cinderella's castle or Cinderella's coach are available to decorate the reception venue. All of these details further serve to evoke an enchanted, fairy-tale atmosphere, allowing the bride to embody the ultimate Cinderella fantasy. In this way, Disney's Fairy Tale Weddings platform is an adult extension of the Disney

Princess franchise, allowing grown women to realise their childhood fantasies (real or assumed) of being a Disney princess bride.

Much like the establishment of the Disney Princess franchise in 2000, Disney created their wedding platform to fill a need – rumours of guests sneaking into the parks for a quiet, private ceremony still circulate to this day – and the business has boomed ever since. Elana Levine confirms such a demand in her own analysis of Disney's weddings when she notes, "Since couples regularly traveled to Disney World to get married anyway, the company found a way to profit even further from those couples' patronage".[63] Since 1991, more than 40,000 couples from all over the world have been married at Disney's various venues, and wedding industry experts recognise Walt Disney World Resort as the top-ranked venue for honeymoons and destination weddings.[64]

This was, of course, no accident. Disney's Wedding Pavilion was first used on June 18, 1995, for the premiere broadcast of Lifetime Television's *Weddings of a Lifetime*, a reality-based television series that showcased real life couples fulfilling their dreams of getting married at the Walt Disney World Resort.[65] Hosted primarily by *General Hospital* celebrity couple Jack and Kristina Wagner,[66] the series "teemed with layered images of weddings and romance – the real-life couples getting married, Disney fairy tales like *Cinderella*, the celebrity couples' real-life relationships, and the fictional romantic histories of their soap opera characters".[67] In the second episode, Kristina frames the episode's bride, Anne, as a Cinderella who has found her very own Prince Charming in groom-to-be Brian. Audience members are invited to hear the story of how the lovers met by chance at Disney World. Anne talks about "a spark in the air" that gave her hope this chance meeting would turn into something special, while Brian talks about falling in love at first sight, making the first move, and kissing Anne against a backdrop of fireworks. Anne's mother cements the idea of the pair as star-crossed lovers, saying that their meeting was "pre-destined" and a "blessing from above". The actual ceremony opens to a row of trumpeters heralding Brian's princely arrival on a white horse, followed by Anne's entrance in Cinderella's Crystal Coach.[68] Again, all of these elements layer together to reify and solidify the norms of the princess bride, both in the featured bride, Anne, and for all of the potential brides watching the broadcast at home. In addition, the deeply ingrained gender bias within the wedding industry is further entrenched with Disney's *Weddings of a Lifetime*. Data reveals that when the show aired, "Lifetime held the enviable position of being the only cable network exclusively targeted to women", and was able to capture "the most sought-after demographic, women aged 18 to 49 with an average household income exceeding $40,000".[69] By primarily focusing on women in what was essentially the grand opening of Disney's Wedding Pavilion, Disney further glorified the princess bride.

Anything Your Heart Desires

What about the brides who do not dream of being a princess? What about the bride who did not grow up pretending to be Cinderella at the ball or Sleeping Beauty waiting for Prince Charming to wake her from her cursed slumber with a kiss? What about the bride who wants the complete Disney experience without the weight of a tiara? Does Disney's Fairy Tale Weddings have a place for them? In short: yes. Franck's Studio, named for Franck from the 1991 *Father of the Bride*, was established alongside the Disney Wedding Pavilion in 1995 to fulfil any potential dream a bride could imagine, princess themed or no. At Franck's, couples can examine first-hand every accessory and accoutrement needed for the wedding: invitations, dinner placements, floral bouquets, cakes, dresses, videography, photography, and entertainment. If the couple finds the demands of creating a Disney wedding on their own too stressful, there is a wedding planner on hand to help them through the process. Those who wish to eschew the Cinderella/princess theme can opt for an international theme in Epcot, a Hollywood theme in Disney's Hollywood Studios, or a luau at the Polynesian Resort. Outside the wedding and the reception, custom "magic bands" decorated for the bride and groom allow the newlyweds to move about the park with ease, storing credit card information, room keys, and fast passes. Bride and groom Mickey and Minnie Mouse ears are also available for purchase, as are champagne flutes, Mickey and Minnie wedding picture frames, salt and pepper shakers, and Mickey Mouse diamond rings. In short, Disney will happily go to any length to make the couple's dream wedding wishes come true.

Happily Ever After

While critics would like to blame Disney for filling the American public's mind with images of royal weddings and extravagant happily-ever-afters, Disney did not single-handedly create the wedding industry as it exists today. Long before Disney established Fairy Tale Weddings in 1991, the wedding industry was invested in the narrative of the princess bride, especially in its promotion of a more lavish, luxurious, and opulent wedding. Items like wedding bands and intricate white gowns became seen as a "necessity" for what was once a more homely affair. Because Disney is the main proprietor and progenitor for American fairy tales and, in turn, the idea of the Americanised princess, they are able to tap into the industry to grow their wedding franchise. Thus, the company is able to turn a young girl's dreams of a Cinderella wedding into a lavish and highly profitable reality.

Bibliography

Cashdan, Sheldon. *The Witch Must Die: The Hidden Meaning of Fairy Tales*. New York, Basicbooks, 1999.

Corrado, Marisa. "Teaching Wedding Rules". *Journal of Contemporary Ethnography*, Vol. 31, No. 1 (2002), pp. 33–67.

Couch, Robbie. "This Artist Swapped Iconic Characters' Skin Colors in 'Racebent Disney'". *HuffPost UK*, 2014, http://www.huffingtonpost.co.uk/entry/race-bent-disney-characters_n_5323545.

Curie, Dawn H. "'Here Comes The Bride': The Making Of 'Modern Traditional' Wedding In Western Culture". *Journal of Comparative Family Studies*, Vol. 24, No. 3 (1993), pp. 403–421.

Engstrom, Erika. "Unraveling The Knot". *Journal of Communication Inquiry*, Vol. 32, No. 1 (2008), pp. 60–82.

"Fast Facts: Disney's Fairy Tale Weddings and Honeymoons". *Walt Disney World News*, 2017, http://wdwnews.com/fact-sheets/2016/05/04/fast-facts-disneys-fairy-tale-weddings-and-honeymoons/.

Gibbons, Sheila. "Bridal Media Promote Merchandise, Not Marriage". *Women's Enews*, 2003, http://womensenews.org/2003/06/bridal-media-promote-merchandise-not-marriage/.

Hains, Rebecca. "Disney Princess Diversity: Characters Changed Via Tumblr, D-Tech". *The Christian Science Monitor*, 2012, https://www.csmonitor.com/The-Culture/Family/Modern-Parenthood/2012/0816/Disney-Princess-diversity-Characters-changed-via-Tumblr-D-Tech.

Howard, Vicki. "'A Real Man's Ring': Gender and The Invention of Tradition". *Journal of Social History*, Vol. 36, No. 4 (2003), pp. 837–856.

Howard, Vicki. "The Bridal Business". *OAH Magazine of History*, Vol. 24, No. 1 (2010), pp. 52–56.

Hurley, Dorothy L. "Seeing White: Children of Color and the Disney Fairy Tale Princess". *Journal of Negro Education*, Vol. 74, No. 3 (2005), pp. 221–232.

Ingraham, Chrys. *White Weddings: Romancing Heterosexuality in Popular Culture*. 2nd ed., New York, NY, Routledge, 2008.

Levine, Elana. "Fractured Fairy Tales and Fragmented Markets: Disney's Weddings Of A Lifetime And The Cultural Politics Of Media Conglomeration". *Television & New Media*, Vol. 6, No. 1 (2005), pp. 71–88.

Lowrey, Tina M., and Cele Otnes. "Construction of a Meaningful Wedding: Differences in the Priorities of Brides and Grooms". *Gender and Consumer Behavior*, Sage Publications, Thousand Oaks, CA, 1994, pp. 164–183.

McDonough, Megan. "What's It Like Getting Married at Disney? It's Not Always a Fairy Tale ..". *The Washington Post*, 2017, https://www.washingtonpost.com/entertainment/whats-it-like-getting-married-at-disney-its-not-always-a-fairy-tale/2017/05/04/59390a66-2c24-11e7-be51-b3fc6ff7faee_story.html?utm_term=.4d847a81f0ca.

Mead, Rebecca. "Princess for a Day". *The Guardian*, 2010, https://www.theguardian.com/lifeandstyle/2010/aug/07/weddings-industry-commercial-giles-fraser.

Orenstein, Peggy. "What's Wrong With Cinderella?" *The New York Times Magazine*, 2006, http://www.nytimes.com/2006/12/24/magazine/24princess.t.html.

Tatar, Maria. *Off With Their Heads!: Fairy Tales And The Culture Of Childhood*. Princeton, NJ, Princeton University Press, 1992.

Wedding Wishes. New York, NY, Golden Books, 2009.

YouTube. "Disney Weddings at Walt Disney World". 2017, https://youtu.be/47G3O2I92JA.

YouTube. "Weddings of a Lifetime". 2009, https://youtu.be/Vj5XvF5i140.

YouTube. "Weddings of a Lifetime". 2009, https://youtu.be/xt78YlmfmBg.

Filmography

Father of the Bride (Vincente Minnelli, director); Warner Brothers, 1950.

Father of the Bride (Charles Shyer, director); Touchstone Pictures, 1991.

Endnotes

1. Vicki Howard, "The Bridal Business" in *OAH Magazine of History* (January 2010), 52.
2. Howard, 52.
3. Howard, 52.
4. Howard, 52.
5. Ingraham, 82.
6. Ingraham, 79.
7. Vicki Howard, "'A Real Man's Ring': Gender and the Invention of Tradition", in *Journal of Social History* (Summer 2003), 843.
8. Ingraham, 79.
9. Howard, *The Bridal Business*, 52.
10. Howard, Vicki. "'A Real Man's Ring'", 847. This article also provides an excellent in-depth exploration of men's nuptial traditions in a more general sense.
11. Ingraham, 59.
12. Ingraham, 59.
13. Ingraham, 60. Italics in original.
14. Ingraham, 60.
15. Howard, *The Bridal Business*, 53.
16. *Father of the Bride*, 1950. Dir. Vincente Minelle. Warner Brothers.
17. *Father of the Bride*, 1950.
18. *Father of the Bride*, 1950.
19. Ingraham, 65.
20. Ingraham, 65.
21. Quoted in Ingraham, 64.
22. Ingraham, 148
23. *Father of the Bride*, 1991.
24. *Father of the Bride*, 1991.
25. Ingraham, 42. Adjusted for inflation in 2017, these figures would be approximately 47 billion and 98 billion dollars respectively.
26. Ingraham, 42.
27. Ingraham, 9.
28. Boden, section 2.6.
29. Ingraham, 66.
30. Ingraham, 66.
31. Ingraham, 26.
32. Ingraham, 64.
33. https://youtu.be/47G3O2I92JA
34. Peggy Orenstein, "What's Wrong With Cinderella?" *New York Times*, 24 December 2006. Url: http://www.nytimes.com/2006/12/24/magazine/24princess.t.html
35. Ingraham, 140.

36. Ingraham, 147.

37. Erika Engstrom, "Unravelling the Knot: Political Economy and Cultural Hegemony in Wedding Media" in *Journal of Communication Inquiry* (1 January 2008), 77.

38. Marisa Corrado, "Teaching Wedding Rules" in *Journal of Contemporary Ethnography* (1 February 2002), 34.

39. Corrado, 51.

40. Corrado, 61.

41. Ingraham, 61.

42. Ingraham, 62.

43. Tatar describes "The Kind and Unkind Girls" story type (as classified by folklorist Antti Aarne in his book *The Types of the Folktale: A Classification and Bibliography*, which was translated and expanded by Stith Thompson) as a reward-and-punishment tale where a woman has two daughters, a biological daughter and a step-daughter. Frequently the step-daughter is kind and industrious while the woman's own daughter is rude and lazy. The step-daughter enters an other-worldly realm and is assigned a number of tasks by an enchanted entity; when she completes them she is rewarded with riches. When the step-daughter embarks on the same journey, she refuses to complete the tasks and is sent away with all manner of nasty things: dirt, toads, worms, etc. Although "Cinderella" does not explicitly fit this type, there is enough of an overlap that the following discussion still applies. Maria Tatar, *Off with Their Heads: Fairy Tales and the Culture of Childhood* (1992), Princeton University Press. Princeton, NJ. pp. 51–69.

44. Tatar, 56.

45. Sheldon Cashdan, *The Witch Must Die: The Hidden Meaning of Fairy Tales* (1999), Basic Books. New York, NY. 104.

46. Rebecca Mead, *Guardian* article, "Princess for a Day", emphasis added

47. Shelia Gibbons, *WeNews* article, "Bridal Media Promote Merchandise Not Marriage"

48. Peggy Orenstein, "What's Wrong With Cinderella?" New York Times, 24 December 2006. Url: http://www.nytimes.com/2006/12/24/magazine/24princess.t.html

49. Cashdan, 28.

50. Tina M. Lowrey and Cele Otnes, "Construction of a Meaningful Wedding: Differences in the Priorities of Brides and Grooms" in *Gender Issues and Consumer Behavior*, ed. Janeen Arnold Costa (1994), Sage Publications. Thousand Oaks, CA. 174. Emphasis added.

51. "Here Comes the Bride" p. 414

52. "Traditional" and "original" are used loosely here, due to the fact that fairy tales began as a primarily oral tradition of storytelling subject to numerous retellings and interpretations, making their origins almost impossible to trace to their source.

53. Dorothy L. Hurley, "Seeing White: Children of Color and the Disney Fairy Tale Princess" in *The Journal of Negro Education* (Summer 2005), 222.

54. See *Cinderella Ate My Daughter: Dispatches from the Front Lines of the New Girlie-Girl Culture* © 2011 by Peggy Orenstein and *The Princess Problem: Guiding Our Girls Through the Princess-Obsessed Years* © 2014 by Rebecca C. Hains for more information.

55. http://www.csmonitor.com/The-Culture/Family/Modern-Parenthood/2012/0816/Disney-Princess-diversity-Characters-changed-via-Tumblr-D-Tech, accessed August 24, 2015.

56. See artist TT Bret's "Racebent Disney" project: http://www.huffington-post.com/2014/05/14/race-bent-disney-characters_n_5323545.html, accessed August 24, 2015.

57. *Wedding Wishes*, illustrated by Elisa Marruchi (2009), Golden Book. New York, NY.

58. https://www.disneyweddings.com/, accessed August 24, 2015.

59. While Disney Fairy Tale Weddings does cater to brides who do not wish to be a princess and those who are not even brides – i.e. homosexual male couples – the Fairy Tale Weddings website and brochures overwhelmingly focus on the straight female bride.

60. Megan McDonough, "What's It Like Getting Married at Disney? It's Not Always a Fairy Tale" for *The Washington Post*. Published May 5, 2017. Accessed December 11, 2017. Url: https://www.washingtonpost.com/entertainment/whats-it-like-getting-married-at-disney-its-not-always-a-fairy-tale/2017/05/04/59390a66-2c24-11e7-be51-b3fc6ff7faee_story.html?utm_term=.4d847a81f0ca

61. McDonough, "What's It Like Getting Married at Disney?"

62. McDonough, "What's It Like Getting Married at Disney?"

63. Elana Levine, "Fractured Fairy Tales and Fragmented Markets: Disney's Weddings of a Lifetime and the Cultural Politics of Media Conglomeration" in *Television New Media* (2005),75.

64. Disney's Fairy Tale Weddings Fast Facts

65. Lifetime is a subsidiary of the American Broadcasting Company television network, which is in turn owned by the Walt Disney Company.

66. The couple initially met on the set of ABC's *General Hospital*, where they portrayed the popular couple Frisco and Felicia.

67. Levine, 72

68. Clips of the episode found at https://youtu.be/xt78YlmfmBg and https://youtu.be/Vj5XvF5i140

69. Levine, 76.

Chapter 10

Frozen Hearts and Fixer Uppers: Villainy, Gender, and Female Companionship in Disney's *Frozen*

Catherine Lester

Since its release in late 2013, *Frozen* has become nothing short of a cultural phenomenon, with the world's largest box office gross for an animated film (which, thanks to sing-a-long re-releases in subsequent years, only keeps climbing),[1] a triple-Platinum soundtrack, two Academy Awards, and merchandise which sold so well that Disney struggled to meet demand in the wake of the film's release.[2] The *Frozen* hype shows no signs of diminishing, as it is also now a Broadway musical, has spawned two theatrically released short films (*Frozen Fever* in 2015 and *Olaf's Frozen Adventure* in 2017), theme park attractions, and has a feature-length sequel due in 2019. In addition to this resounding commercial success it has attracted a wealth of academic debate, including a "Symfrozium", and a number of academic publications discussing the film's aesthetics, industrial significance and gender politics.[3] A large part of the film's success can be attributed to its representation of gender, which film critics celebrated as highly progressive.[4] Indeed, it marks several "firsts" in terms of gender for Disney and for Hollywood filmmaking at large: it is the first Disney animated feature[5] to be directed by a woman (Jennifer Lee, who co-directed with Chris Buck), and it is the first film, of any type, with a female director to earn over $1 billion worldwide. Narratively, it is the first Disney animated fairy tale to feature two women in central roles who, for at least a portion of the film, are both princesses. Crucially, in a departure from Disney's prior animated fairy tales, these women are not straight-forwardly pitted against each other as villain and victim; instead, the film presents Elsa, the reclusive princess with an icy magical power who later becomes

Queen of Arendelle, as someone who holds the *potential* for villainy. This is then averted thanks to the healing power of the sibling bond that she shares with her younger sister, the outgoing Princesses Anna. By focusing on the representation of villainy and the ability for it to be overcome through female companionship, this chapter argues that *Frozen* marks a significant change in the representation of women – namely, princesses and authoritative women with magical powers – and the relationships between them in Disney's animated fairy tales.

This adds to a growing body of scholarly work that examines *Frozen*'s gender politics. In contrast to the overwhelmingly positive critical and public response to the film's progressive qualities, many academic responses adopt a post-feminist approach to argue that, although film *does* mark a step forward in the representation of women in Disney's animated films, there are also a number of problematic aspects that undermine its feminist potential. For example, the film's adherence to restrictive norms of feminine beauty has been read by Madeline Streiff and Lauren Dundes as "conflating feminism with femininity and sex appeal".[6] In addition, Maja Rudloff points out that although *Frozen*'s female protagonists are indeed active and driven by their own agency, they remain surrounded by male characters.[7] This chapter does not seek to dispute these arguably valid criticisms, but to add to this debate by calling attention to two other aspects of the film's gender politics which have received less attention in academic discourse: the role of solidarity between its female protagonists and how this relates to representations of villainy, particularly in light of *Frozen*'s status as a fairy tale. As such, the chapter follows in the steps of the works of Owen Weetch and Sarah Whitfield, who discuss the film's theme of female bonding. Weetch analyses how *Frozen*'s use of stereoscopic 3D illustrates Elsa's personal journey from rejecting to embracing her community and Anna's companionship.[8] Whitfield locates the film within the Broadway musical tradition which, she argues, has a better historical record than Disney's animated films for showing female characters communicating with one another, thus allowing them "to enact the resolution to their own dramatic conflict".[9] This chapter builds on these by considering how *Frozen*'s resolution that foregrounds female solidarity, and its complex presentation of Elsa and other "villainous" characters, offers a new, progressive model for the representation of women, and their interactions with each other, in Disney's animated fairy tales.

Before Frozen: the "Disney Princess" and the Wicked Witch

That *Frozen* has two princesses as leading characters may not at first seem particularly significant. Despite only eight of Disney's animated films being based on fairy tales, when we think of the studio what often comes to mind is, if not Mickey Mouse, the iconic fairy tale castle logo and the "Disney

Princess" – both the actual princess characters in their respective films, and the Disney Princess media franchise of dolls, costumes, magazines, and a variety of other paratexts.[10] Both Disney's princess *characters* and the Disney Princess *franchise* have been widely criticised for seeming to promote to young, predominantly female viewers unhealthy ideals of body image, femininity, and romance. Indeed, the princess characters are impossibly beautiful, have dainty, slim-waisted figures, and are commonly perceived as being "helpless ornaments in need of protection, and when it comes to the action of the film, they are omitted".[11] Amy M. Davis, however, argues that in the context of the films the princesses have more agency than their detractors give them credit for, and that their representation improves over the course of the twentieth century.[12] Yet any positive representations that can be gleaned from the films are largely erased by the Disney Princess franchise, which comes under even greater fire than the films for homogenising the princesses, taking them out of their narrative contexts, and focusing on elements concerning beauty and romance.[13] For example, in 2013, controversy surrounded Pixar's *Brave* when the "tom-boy princess" Merida was due to become a "Disney Princess".[14] Merida's make-over for the franchise removed the bow and arrow with which she is extremely adept in the film and gave her a more sexualised appearance by narrowing her waist, giving her a fuller breast and wider hips, and adorning her once-bare face with make-up. The resulting image removed, or at least severely toned down, any references to her feisty, rebellious nature, which was seen by many as a refreshing departure from Disney's previous representations of fairy tale princesses. The "Disney Princess" is therefore a figure of great tension, and one that is vital to contextualising the representation of gender in *Frozen*.

Gender dynamics in Disney's princess films are further problematised due to the identities of the villains who are placed in opposition to these princesses. In the princess films up to the late 1980s, the villains are older, malevolent, single women, some of whom possess witch-like magical powers: the wicked step-mother and Queen of *Snow White and the Seven Dwarfs*; *Cinderella*'s Lady Tremaine and her obnoxious daughters, the ugly step-sisters; *Sleeping Beauty*'s Maleficent; and *The Little Mermaid*'s Ursula. The extreme contrast between the beautiful young princess and the evil older woman continues the classic black-and-white dichotomy of good versus evil established in the roots of fairy tales, allowing for streamlined story-telling. Many critics have argued that these female villains are far more compelling than their comparatively passive opponents: they are the "diva of the piece",[15] "erotic and subversive forces",[16] and *femmes fatales* who incite a love-to-hate sensation in the audience. Still, the depictions of these wicked women can be considered troubling due to the implication that their transgressive female sexuality is associated with evil, and must therefore be rejected and destroyed in the service of the heteronormative romantic narrative and re-establishment of the patriarchal status quo.[17] Furthermore, despite the fact that it might be seen positively that women feature so heavily in these films, the relationships between these women are only ever ones of antagonism and competition – competition to be the most beautiful, to marry a prince, to rule a kingdom – rather than of support between women. As suggested by Jill Birnie Henke, Diane Zimmerman Umble and Nancy J. Smith, rather than being progressive relationships of "power-with" each other, they are ones that depict the struggle for "power-over" one another.[18]

Positive change can be seen in the depiction of women, particularly the princesses, from the start of Disney's Renaissance era.[19] *The Little Mermaid*'s Ariel and *Beauty and the Beast*'s Belle – and the "non-fairy tale" princesses: Jasmine, Pocahontas and Mulan – are headstrong, pro-active young women with greater senses of selfhood and agency than their predecessors. For example, all of them take action to rescue their male love-interest (and others), as opposed to or in addition to the reverse. However, in terms of their interactions with other women, these films do little to improve upon the earlier princess films. With the exception of *The Little Mermaid*, all of these films pit their female protagonists against not wicked witches, but male villains such as *Beauty and the Beast*'s Gaston. This move from female to male villains is one which Davis suggests may have been "an attempt to steer away from sexist portrayals of evil, sexually frustrated women" in the 1990s' increasingly politically-correct cultural climate.[20] While this means that female characters are not in competition with each other in these narratives, it also means that there are very few significant female relationships in these films. Furthermore, although the princesses are often united on official Disney Princess merchandise, it is a "rule" of the franchise that wherever two or more princesses appear on a product they should never make eye contact or otherwise acknowledge one another's existence.[21] The paratexts thus focus on extending the heteronormative romantic narratives of the films and prevent opportunities to encourage female interaction where it is already absent within the films.[22]

An eleven year-long gap follows this group of films in which most of Disney's animated features focus on narratives featuring male leads, before returning to the fairy tale princess with *The Princess and the Frog*, *Tangled*, and the aforementioned *Brave*. Each can be considered progressive in its own way,[23] but it is Pixar's *Brave* – not a "Disney film" *per se*, nor based on an existing fairy tale, yet which is included in the Disney Princess franchise – that is particularly noteworthy. *Brave* is a milestone in that it is the first (and currently only) of Pixar's films with a female director (Brenda Chapman, who co-directed with Mark Andrews and Steve Purcell). It is also the only one of Disney/Pixar's fairy tale princess films to put the relationship between a princess and her *biological* mother at the forefront of the narrative – even if the latter spends most of it in the form of a bear – a relationship which, crucially, concerns their learning to support and understand each other.[24] That both *Frozen* and *Brave* are the first instances of Disney's and Pixar's fairy tale output focusing on supportive female relationships, and are also each studio's first film to have significant female creative forces behind the scenes, does not seem to be a coincidence.[25] In line with these more progressive depictions of female relationships in Disney's films in the 2010s, the "Bechdel Test" has become an increasingly popular measure of the representation of women in film; specifically, the extent to which two or more female characters communicate with each other about something other than a man.[26] The lack of female bonding in Disney's fairy tales (and the Disney Princess paratexts) is therefore a very pertinent contemporary concern.

Frozen follows in the footsteps of *Brave*, becoming the first animated Disney fairy tale (as opposed to a Disney/Pixar co-production) to place the importance of female companionship at the centre of its narrative. It does so with an intense awareness of Disney's back catalogue of fairy tales, presenting one character, Anna, who on a surface level fits the "Disney Princess" mould, and another, Elsa, who possesses characteristics synonymous with the "wicked witch". In making their relationship central to the film's narrative resolution, the film offers female bonding as a "cure" for potential villainy, thus subverting typical expectations concerning the depiction of women with magical powers in Disney fairy tales.[27] In doing so, it also prompts us to think back upon Disney's earlier female fairy tale villains and question whether or not they, too, could have been "saved" from their villainous ways with the support of their princess victims.

"Beware the Frozen Heart": Setting Up Frosty Expectations

It goes without saying that villains are a crucial element of fairy tales. Indeed, without them there would be no story; or, at least, a very uninteresting one with little at stake, as the protagonists would have "no real incentive to move forward in their lives, to undertake their adventures, and to grow as individuals".[28] Bruno Bettelheim's psychoanalytic reading of fairy tale villains proposes that they are a projection of the sinful aspects of the protagonist's personality: "victory is not over others but only over oneself and over villainy (mainly one's own, which is projected as the hero's antagonist)".[29] Similarly, Sheldon Cashdan argues in *The Witch Must Die* that the antagonists in fairy tales must always die, symbolically representing "a victory of virtue over vice, a sign that the positive forces in the self have prevailed".[30] Villains in fairy tales can thus be argued to be as important psychologically as they are narratively. It is therefore interesting that for the majority of *Frozen* it is unclear precisely who this figure is, a detail that has been the target of some criticism.[31] It is on repeat viewing and close analysis, however, that it becomes clear that this ambiguity is one of the film's most effective aspects, and crucial to the way the film subverts expectations and offers new directions for Disney's fairy tales going forward.

As stated above, *Frozen* is a film highly aware of its predecessors, and it ostensibly deals in slightly modernised versions of well-worn stereotypes.[32] Anna is the younger and more optimistic, yet naïve, of the two Arendelle princesses. She and Elsa play happily as children, before an accident (in which Elsa strikes Anna with her powers) means that Anna's memories of Elsa's powers are removed; they must spend the rest of their childhoods locked inside the castle until Elsa has learned to control her powers. Elsa and Anna grow apart, worsened by the untimely deaths of their parents, the King and Queen. Like many other fairy tale princesses who have been trapped within oppressive environments, whether their step-mother's home, under the sea, or in a tower, Anna has an idealistic and unrealistic view of the world – specifically, of love. In the musical number, "For The First Time In Forever", Anna sings of her desire to see the world outside of the castle walls and finally meet "The One" at Elsa's coronation. In a slight twist on the "perfect princess" stereotype, however, she also sings of how in her excitement she is unsure of whether she is "elated or gassy", and that her nervousness makes her "wanna stuff some chocolate in [her] face". Further displaying the film's self-awareness, on the morning of Elsa's coronation two guests are heard saying that they bet the sisters are "absolutely lovely". The film then cuts abruptly to Anna asleep in bed: snoring, drooling, and her hair a tangled mess. Nonetheless, Anna has the figure of a "Disney Princess" and shares the desires of her predecessors to see the world outside her confines and, if the opportunity arises, to fall in love. Her dreams appear to come true when she literally bumps into a suitor, Prince Hans of the Southern Isles, the epitome of the "Prince Charming" archetype. Thus, *Frozen* presents the building blocks of what seems to be a standard fairy tale princess narrative.

The speed with which Anna and Hans get engaged may be somewhat suspect and disorienting; in fact, having known each other for less than a day, their engagement comes faster than any other Disney prince and princess couple. The audience's reservations are voiced in the diegesis by both Elsa and Kristoff, Anna's eventual true love: Elsa declares "You can't marry a man you just met", and Kristoff challenges how much she really knows about Hans, concluding that her judgement is not trustworthy. However, as an audience subject to the Disney fairy tale princess narrative again and again, it is easy to accept this swift proceeding of events. It helps that Anna and Hans' "falling-in-love" duet (a Disney fairy tale staple), "Love Is An Open Door", is so sincere, persuasive and euphoric that we are swept along with Anna. Further aiding this acceptance is that their duet is filled with visual references to the love songs of earlier Disney fairy tales, most notably, *Cinderella*'s "So This Is Love". The most telling evidence that *Frozen* is deliberately dealing in archetypes in order to later subvert them is a projection of Anna and Hans' dancing silhouettes onto the sail of a nearby ship. This closely mirrors a shot in which Cinderella and Prince Charming's dancing silhouettes are cast onto a palace wall. Without context, these shadows could be depicting exactly the same couple, and indeed, Anna and Hans appear to be playing out the roles of the archetypal princess and prince that are expected from Disney's fairy tales. Disney's archetypes (and fairy tale archetypes prior to Disney's adaptations), like shadows, are not necessarily true representations of reality; they are simplified facsimiles – "typical rather than unique", as Bettelheim puts it – that function to tell a story swiftly and effectively.[33] Thus, we can read the use of shadows to convey archetype in *Frozen* as a signal of the film's intent to "fool" the audience into believing that these figures are simply stock characters (albeit slightly modernised) in a predictable narrative that will end with, or pre-empt, their marriage.[34]

Anna and Hans slotting so easily into these roles of the princess and her prince leaves open the final key role of the fairy tale villain. This is where expectations set up by Disney's established "princess versus wicked witch" dichotomy come into play, as well as our knowledge going into the film provided by its marketing and production background. Jonathan Gray argues that, through paratexts like trailers and posters, "films and television programs often begin long before we actively seek them out", and that the information we receive about a text *before* seeing it is as crucial to the construction of a text's meaning as the text itself.[35] In the case of *Frozen*, this construction of meaning begins with the common knowledge that the film is a very loose adaptation of Hans Christian Andersen's "The Snow Queen" (1844). Disney had been attempting to adapt the tale since the late-1930s,[36] and it was only in 2011 – two years before the film's release – that it was retitled *Frozen*.[37] Even to someone unfamiliar with the tale, it is arguably clear that the title role is a villainous one. Queens in fairy tales, especially magical queens, are rarely on the side of good, and "snow" brings to mind coldness, literally and figuratively. Though before *Frozen* a feature-length Hollywood adaptation of "The Snow Queen" had never been made, other wicked queens or witches associated with ice and snow have featured in well-known texts, such as the White Witch of *The Chronicles of Narnia* novels (C. S. Lewis, 1950–56) and their many film, television, radio and stage adaptations. The most basic knowledge of the source material alone therefore forces an expectation that Elsa, shown in the film's promotional materials with her white-blonde hair, ice-blue dress and magical powers, is the villain of the piece. Indeed, this was the case for much of the film's pre-production; concept art indicates that the Snow Queen character was conceived to follow in the vein of Disney's earlier female villains as a *femme fatale* or diva.[38] In these designs she has blue skin, a spiky haircut in either blue, black or white, heavy-lidded eyes, and strikes a variety of haughty, seductive poses, much unlike the character in the final film.[39] Early story concepts also reveal that the Snow Queen was to have an army of evil snowmen and a coat of live weasels.[40] The casting of the popular Broadway star Idina Menzel as Elsa's voice further associates the character with villainy. Menzel, before the release of *Frozen*, was best known for originating the role of Elphaba, the Wicked Witch of the West, in the musical *Wicked: The Untold Story of the Witches of Oz* (2003–). Despite the fact that *Wicked* is a revisionist text that shows the iconic villain to be a sympathetic, misunderstood and maligned woman with good intentions (much like Elsa in *Frozen*), this simple association of Elsa with the Wicked Witch of the West may have further led audiences to assume that Elsa's role in the film would be that of an antagonist.[41]

The film's marketing materials are also highly interesting due to the way they construct Elsa. By the time the film's marketing campaign had begun, Elsa had been re-conceptualised as a good, sympathetic character who is misunderstood and ostracised due to her powers. Yet, the trailers depict her as an antagonist – that is, when she features at all. The teaser trailer[42] features only a comical skit involving Olaf the snowman and Sven the reindeer, a scene that does not appear in the film. A theatrical trailer,[43] released later, hardly features Elsa at all, but establishes the basic premise that Arendelle is endangered by a perpetual winter caused by her magical powers. The only shots in this trailer of Elsa are an ominous shot of her from behind as she opens a window, followed by a shot of her atop a snowy hill casting her powers, which in turn is followed immediately by disaster film-esque shots of the frozen kingdom. There are a further five shots in the trailer of her using her powers, one of which is followed by a character's accusation of "sorcery". The second of these shots does not actually feature in the final film; the rest are taken out of their narrative context, and all of them last less than one second each (in a trailer of over two and a half minutes). Gray claims that trailers are almost always "carefully manicured" and obsessed-over by marketers,[44] while John Ellis describes them as a "calculated" part of the "process of meaning".[45] Thus, this *Frozen* trailer is arguably very precisely crafted in order to imply that Elsa is the film's antagonist. Although it should be pointed out that with her blonde hair, soft features and slim figure, Elsa is physically more similar to the "Disney Princess" archetype, the marketing carefully builds upon knowledge of the original fairy tale and assumptions that women with magical powers in Disney fairy tales have wicked intentions.[46]

With these expectations set up, the film's opening continues to misdirect the audience, ensuring that even viewers who had not been exposed to any of the marketing, nor bore any knowledge of the film or its source material, would expect a villainous female presence. After the title sequence, the film opens proper with the musical number "Frozen Heart". Sung by male ice harvesters as they saw chunks of ice from a frozen lake, it acts in the vein of a Greek chorus to introduce the film's themes. Its final line is an ominous warning: "Beware the frozen heart". This can be taken to mean the figuratively frozen heart of a "cold" person, but also foreshadows Anna's literally frozen heart when she is accidentally struck by Elsa's powers towards the end of the film. The song implies that the one with the "frozen heart" is a female being through the gendered lyrics such as "Beautiful! Powerful! Dangerous! Cold!", "Icy force both foul and fair", and "There's beauty and there's danger here".[47] Equally, the strong, rhythmic beat, imagery of saws and pickaxes, and verbs such as "cut", "strike" and "break" ominously imply violence and danger. With or without any other knowledge of the film, these opening moments clearly associate the ice itself, and the implied icy figure, with danger, emotional coldness, and power, which is admired but also feared and must be "broken". The song could, in fact, be describing any of the Disney witches who have come before. What is interesting, therefore, is that what follows makes it clear that this figure, assumed to be the "Snow Queen", is anything but a cruel villain.

Immediately after "Frozen Heart" we are introduced to Elsa and Anna as children, establishing their close sisterly bond. That Elsa is introduced as a child is highly significant as none of Disney's other female fairy tale villains have been shown as children, the reason for which may be that showing them as (presumably innocent) children will risk evoking sympathy from the audience. Following *Frozen*, it is interesting that *Maleficent* (2014) – Disney's live-action revisionist take on the iconic *Sleeping Beauty* villain – also shows its protagonist's formative years, serving to prove that her subsequent "evil" actions were actually justified due to her violent assault by a male, Stefan, who would go on to become the King and father of the sleeping beauty herself, Princess Aurora. Returning to *Frozen*, Elsa, during and beyond childhood, displays characteristics that could otherwise have coded her as a villain; for example, it is due to Elsa's powers that both she and Anna become locked in their own castle, in a variation of the fairy tale trope. However, rather than Elsa doing this out of any nefarious intentions, she has been *taught* that her power is dangerous by the authoritative patriarchal figures around her: her father the King, and Grand Pabbie, the leader of the magical trolls. Elsa can therefore be considered both her own captor and prisoner, who traps her sister and rejects her affections out of care rather than out of cruelty or selfishness. In this way, she is also shown to be far more (emotionally) complex than her wicked predecessors: more victim than villain, as much a fairy tale princess as a "wicked witch". It is precisely this duality to her character that subverts the typical presentation of Disney's witches and magical queens as evil. Displaying this duality more so than at any other point in the film is the song "Let It Go".

"Letting Go" and Transforming Archetypes

Lee has revealed that the key development that led to the film being re-conceived with Elsa as a victim rather than a villain was in the writing of the song "Let It Go".[48] Taking place after Elsa's powers are revealed at her coronation and she flees Arendelle, it was originally intended to show her transformation into a generic villain who swears vengeance on those who have shunned her. However, songwriters Robert Lopez and Kristen Anderson-Lopez decided to focus instead on what fearing one's own power and feeling ostracised from one's community would actually *feel* like.[49] This can be considered both a departure from, and a similarity to, previous Disney witches. They seem to lack the ability to feel sympathy and compassion, but have no trouble expressing negative emotions like anger, jealousy, and frustration. "Let It Go" retains an air of this anger and vengefulness that Elsa could have embraced had she been characterised as a traditional villain: this is illustrated by lyrics such as "Let the storm rage on", the defiant slamming of the doors of her ice palace, and looking straight into the camera – an action which Elizabeth Bell notes is usually only done by Disney's evil women[50] – and stating, "The cold never bothered me anyway". Elsa is also startlingly honest about the pressure to conform: she cynically rejects her late father's (well-intentioned, but harmful) advice to "Be the good girl you always have to be / Conceal, Don't feel", decides "I don't care what they're going to say", and that there's "No right, no wrong / No rules for me / I'm free!" For Elsa, who *looks* like a "perfect princess", to be expressing these intense, raw, and very *human* feelings of isolation and frustration feels liberating, particularly when contrasted with the serenely-smiling princesses as they appear elsewhere within the Disney Princess franchise. Out of context, these moments of Elsa's self-expression might sound like the words of someone headed on the path of evil. Yet, they are combined with gentler moments of simple pleasure as she explores the capabilities of her powers to create beauty, and without the fear of hurting anyone else – aspects that are absent from any of Disney's earlier "wicked diva" songs. (Crucially, at this point, Elsa is not aware of the severe damage her powers have had on Arendelle.) As such, in this transformation from frustration to pleasure, the song builds to an almost orgasmic experience of pure catharsis. Significantly, the songwriters have Broadway roots (and Lopez-Anderson is the first female songwriter to work on a Disney princess film), and like the Broadway diva (such as *Wicked*'s Elphaba), Elsa is the "singer of big, belting songs of self-determination and self-celebration",[51] arguably a key reason for the immense popularity of "Let It Go".[52]

As a song about a magical woman relishing in her own power, the closest comparison to "Let It Go" from another Disney animated film is, in fact, not from one of the previously mentioned princess fairy tales, but *The Sword in the Stone* (1963). The film's wicked witch, Madam Mim, has a small, but highly memorable part in which she proves herself a worthy match for her nemesis, Merlin the wizard. In her song, "Mad Madam Mim", she boasts to the young Arthur that she has "more magic in one little finger" than Merlin, and sings with egotistical glee about how she chooses to "delight in the gruesome and grim" rather than use her gift for good. She is squat, plump and ugly with purple hair and green eyes, and enjoys making herself even uglier despite being able to make herself "beautiful, lovely and fair", something she only does to deceive others. Like a *femme fatale*, she flirts, bats her eyelashes and wiggles her hips, deliberately seducing the audience (within the film and in reality) before aggressively popping back to her true, ugly form, cackling with delight at Arthur's shocked reaction. "I'm an ugly old creep!" she yells, while jumping up and down and tugging at her hair: perhaps simultaneously expressing her frustration at being penned into this category by society, yet also embracing and relishing in this identity that is so feared (as, after all, fearing something gives it a certain degree of power). *The Little Mermaid*'s Ursula, similarly, uses her grotesque, part-human, part-octopus body to strut around and preach to the naïve Ariel about what a man wants in a woman. Later in the film, she transforms her tentacular body of "gynophobic imagery"[53] into a beautiful young woman in order to seduce Prince Eric, with the intended result of capturing the soul of Ariel's father, King Triton. Mim and Ursula, in their performative displays of "transgressive excess",[54] are thus shown using their sexuality as a weapon, just another part of their inherent wickedness and difference from the beautiful, modest, and virginal princesses. Elsa, who physically resembles the princesses more than she does Mim or Ursula, uses her magic to transform herself, but only for her own enjoyment, rather than to harm or seduce another. While it might be read as troubling that her self-empowerment, freedom, and rejection of her father's "conceal, don't feel" mantra is closely tied to her gaining a more sexualised appearance – as she replaces her modest and constrictive coronation dress with a revealing gown and high heels – within the scene's diegesis she is not doing this for an audience, but only for herself.[55]

Elsa's self-transformation also sets her apart from her princess predecessors to whom she is physically similar, but whose coming-of-age moments are marked by transformations that are done *to* them by a more powerful person, and in the service of the heteronormative romantic narrative. The most iconic of these is Cinderella's tattered dress being turned into a sparkling ball gown by her fairy godmother, while another, highly problematic, example is Ariel's transformation into a human by her father so that she can marry Prince Eric. The ones performing the magic in these instances are a woman who possesses magical power but is made (sexually) unthreatening through her age and benevolent, bumbling demeanour, and a hyper-masculine king who wields a phallically-shaped trident. Elsa's transformation is thus highly progressive in this context, in that she possesses the power and agency to do it *to* herself and for no one *but* herself. Significantly, Elsa's moment of transformation is visually reminiscent of Cinderella's and Ariel's: the swirl of sparkles around the body, signalling the transformation as it progresses upward from the feet to the head. In her article on glamour in teen witch texts, in which the protagonists frequently use magic to make themselves over, Rachel Moseley discusses the sparkle as a "signifier of glamour, of superficial beauty".[56] "While the sparkle is powerfully spectacular . . . it is also highly ephemeral", emphasising surface over depth.[57] Indeed, as Moseley points out, the very word "glamour" began its existence meaning a kind of spell or enchantment, typically implying the assuming of a false appearance that is more pleasing and appealing than that of the true self.[58] Elsa's changing of her hair and clothes – from buttoned up to liberated – is, in this older meaning of the word, her casting a glamour upon herself. Although Elsa's transformation might represent her greater (magical) power than Cinderella and Ariel, it is arguably only a superficial change that lacks true transformation of the *self*. Elsa is only temporarily happy and free of her personal demons; she has escaped one castle in which she was trapped only to lock herself in another of her own making. When Anna catches up with her and Elsa realises the damage she has done to Arendelle, she loses control of her powers and emotions once again, accidentally striking Anna in the heart – an almost fatal action than can only be undone by an "act of true love".

As we find out, the act that will cure Anna's frozen heart is her own act of protecting Elsa from being killed – not, as is expected, a true love's kiss from a male suitor. In this way, Anna, in turn, steps outside of the archetypal role upon which she is based – that of the princess – by becoming the "knight in shining armour" to her own sister. Elsa is undoubtedly a popular character because of her self-expression and magical ability, but Anna has a less literal "superpower" of her own in the form of love. This is hinted toward in Elsa's dialogue after Anna has broken the news that Arendelle is in danger: "What *power* do you have to stop this winter? To stop me?" she asks, rhetorically (emphasis added). Anna is absolutely overflowing with love, and just as Elsa struggles to control her own icy power, *Frozen* is arguably just as much about Anna learning to direct her love, her power, toward the right people – an isolated sister (or the equally-isolated ice harvester, Kristoff) rather than an unfamiliar prince.[59] It is on this subject of the power of familial love between women that we must now turn to two crucial characters who stand in opposition to this, and further reveal the ways in which the film uses appearances in order to subvert expectations of villainy.

"Everyone's a Bit of a Fixer Upper": Overcoming Misogyny Through Female Solidarity

If it becomes evident quite early that Elsa is not the villainous Snow Queen that was expected of her, the film attempts to fill this lack by offering a substitute in the form of the Duke of Weselton. The Duke is deliberately offered as a red herring in order to further distract from the film's true villain, Prince Hans. With his oversized moustache, Napoleonic short stature, British accent, and his first lines stating his desire to exploit the riches of Arendelle, he is immediately coded as a nefarious person. Appropriately, the citizens of Arendelle mispronounce his homeland as "Weasel Town". His dastardly status is further cemented when, at Elsa's coronation ball, he accuses her of "sorcery", of being a "monster", and of deliberately attempting to harm him – all things that, by this point in the film, we know to be untrue. Later, he sends his henchmen after her and strongly implies that they are to kill her. However, the Duke is also strongly coded as a fool, an attention seeker, and thoroughly unthreatening: he performs a bizarre jig at the coronation and at the end of the film claims that his neck hurts (parodying the idea of the spurious "personal injury" lawsuit), as he has run out of other reasons that he shouldn't be thrown out of Arendelle. Yet despite his comic harmlessness, the Duke serves a much darker purpose in the film.

The Duke throws accusations at Elsa because he has no context nor prior knowledge of her situation, unlike Anna and the film's audience, who affectively have known her since her childhood. As far as he knows, she *is* a monster or a sorceress, one who has just been crowned Queen. In this respect, the Duke can be read as reflective of the way audiences are intended to react to prior female fairy tale villains.[60] These classic villains are introduced with no context for their "evilness" and are simply expected to be villains due to their physical appearances and that they are positioned as binary oppositions to the fair princesses. The Duke's accusations are also reflective of the many examples of highly-insidious, real-life treatment of women in the media – specifically women in powerful and authoritative positions. As documented in Laura Bates' *Everyday Sexism*, "female politicians are subjected to ridicule, criticism and dismissal on the basis of their sex".[61] This was effectively displayed by the widespread misogynistic treatment of Democratic candidate Hillary Clinton in the 2016 US presidential election. To cite just one of many examples, Clinton was labelled a "nasty woman" during a televised debate by Republican candidate Donald Trump, who would go on to win the presidency.[62] Bates suggests that such displays of misogyny toward female politicians may discourage younger women and girls from pursuing careers in politics or other male-dominated professions.[63] They may also not be a far cry from what we might imagine the Disney witches being subjected to if targeted by real-world media. We are given no, or very little, context for their being power-hungry "castrating bitch[es]"[64] – they "just are" that way. Yet, as revisionist texts like *Maleficent* and *Wicked* show, it is possible to provide justifiable reasons for their behaviour and actions, which in these re-workings are caused by their misunderstanding and mistreatment by the patriarchal societies in which they exist.

James B. Stewart's *Disney War* reveals insight into *Frozen*'s development in the early 2000s, which suggests that Elsa was close to suffering a similar, potentially sexist, treatment as the witches before her. Stewart recounts a *Taming of the Shrew*-inspired pitch to then-CEO Michael Eisner: the Snow Queen would have been a "terrible bitch" who freezes her undesirable suitors, until a "regular guy" comes along and succeeds in melting her heart, thus suggesting that the cure for bitchiness is the love of a good man.[65] Although in the final film Elsa is not a "cold-hearted bitch" to be "tamed" by a male suitor, the song "Frozen Heart" contains some of this misogynistic fear of a powerful female force, later vocalised by the Duke: the harvesters, armed with their tools, sing that "Ice has a magic can't be controlled / Stronger than one! Stronger than ten! / Stronger than a hundred men!" followed by a yell punctuated by the violent swinging of pickaxes into blocks of ice. Yet this scene also contains hints towards the film's progressive resolution that hinges on female solidarity. The sky, pink from the setting sun, tinges the snowy landscape in a warm glow, potentially suggesting the thawing power of Anna's love, as she is associated with warm colours throughout the film due to her red hair and pink cape. (The same colour tints the sky in the aforementioned scene in which Anna catches up with Elsa at her ice palace.) The lyrics further hint toward the film's resolution by speaking of the ice having a frozen heart that is "worth mining". This is more explicitly suggested in the film's final song, "Fixer Upper", in which the trolls tell us that "People make bad choices / If they're mad or scared or stressed / But throw a little love their way ... And you'll bring out their best!" They refer specifically to familial love from a father, sister or brother.[66] Can we envision this applying to Disney's earlier female fairy tale villains? Were these "witches" – potentially victimised due to their statuses as (magically) powerful women in authoritative positions, like Elsa – merely "fixer uppers" lacking the solidarity of other women? Too intent on gaining, to borrow the terminology of Henke et al again, "power-over" rather than "power-with" their princess victims?[67] *Frozen*, by "tricking" the audience into expecting Elsa to be the generic villain and antagonist to Anna's "typical" fairy tale princess, only to completely subvert this by demonstrating the power of female companionship, arguably suggests such a possibility. *Maleficent*, too, twists the original film's narrative into one in which the titular evil fairy actually comes to love Aurora. The sleeping princess is thus not awoken by the kiss of a prince, but by the kiss of Maleficent. The film then ends with Maleficent alive (rather than killed, as she is by Prince Phillip in the 1959 film) and living peacefully with Aurora in the fairy kingdom. Contra to Cashdan's argument, perhaps the witch does not *always* have to die after all.

This leaves only the film's true villain, the true possessor of a "frozen heart", Prince Hans, who is vital to the film's subversion of expectations of the typical Disney fairy tale narrative. When Anna needs an "act of true love" to cure her frozen heart, she immediately is rushed to Hans. However, although he seems like an archetypal Prince Charming, Hans reveals his truly evil nature and intentions: he does not love Anna at all, but only intended to marry her, kill her and Elsa, and take the throne of Arendelle for himself. This is a twist that, on paper, might sound clichéd and narratively unimaginative, but it works in context precisely because the film has succeeded in portraying Hans as so unequivocally *nice*. The marketing is also complicit in this, thus ensuring that audiences warm to him before even seeing the film: the aforementioned theatrical trailer specifically refers to him as "The Nice Guy", while posters position him next to Anna, implying that they are a couple. Ed Hooks criticises the film's portrayal of Hans for not providing any foreshadowing of his villainy: "Hans is a blank slate, a mental rag doll. There were opportunities galore for the animator to 'animate the thought', to capture at least a reflective shadow of Hans's plan".[68] This overlooks the subtle, doubly-coded indications of Hans' true intentions in his dialogue and body language. At Elsa's coronation, Anna slips on the dancefloor and is caught by Hans. "Glad I caught you", he says. What seems at first to be a chivalrous gesture and an indication of his attraction to Anna becomes, with the knowledge of his true nature, a sinister, predatory line – a fisherman reeling in a prize-winning catch. Owen Weetch observes further signposts in the love duet, "Love Is An Open Door": Hans tells Anna how after having met her he's "found [his] place". Although it could easily be assumed that he means this figuratively, as he says this he gestures with his hand toward the kingdom, hinting toward his plan to seize the crown for himself. He also fondly reassures Anna, "I love crazy", before they burst into song. As Weetch points out, "Of course he does", as Anna being "crazily" in love is something he can take advantage of for his own gain.[69] To turn to the marketing materials once more, one poster – which shows Hans, Anna, Olaf, Elsa, and Kristoff submerged in snow with only their heads visible – hints towards Hans' nefarious nature: he is shown gazing intently at Anna who, with Kristoff and Elsa, looks straight ahead, unaware that she is being watched. Hans' doubly-coded gaze can be read as either loving and caring or disconcerting and predatory, depending on whether one has seen the end of the film. Hans is therefore far from "under-developed", as argued by Hooks,[70] but the most dangerous type of villain: one who is not seen coming. On designing the classic Disney villains, veteran animators Ollie Johnston and Frank Thomas state that they "preferred to depict our examples of vileness through a strong design which eliminated realism and kept the audience from getting too close to the character".[71] *Frozen* takes advantage of this trend by planting the Duke, who *looks* stereotypically evil, as a red herring. Concept art shows early designs of Hans which more overtly code him as evil: while still handsome, he has a long, pointed nose, sharp, black eyebrows, a shifty stare and a smirk – a world away from the wide-eyed, soft featured, and sincere-seeming Hans of the final film.[72] Doing the opposite of the technique that Johnston and Thomas describe, and casting the villain in disguise as a handsome Prince Charming, is potentially *Frozen*'s most subversive and refreshing act. It acknowledges something that many (adult) audience members may have learned the hard way: that a charming, handsome man is not necessarily as good on the inside as he *looks* on the outside. "Don't bet on the prince", advises the title of Jack Zipes' edited collection of contemporary feminist fairy tales, published twenty-six years before the release of *Frozen*.[73] With its portrayal of Hans, therefore, *Frozen* is in the intriguing position of a Disney film criticising Disney's own tropes, and using them against the audience to challenge ingrained assumptions about what villainy does or does not look like.

Re-thinking Wickedness: New Directions for Disney's Fairy Tales

There may be many reasons for the wide appeal and success of *Frozen*. Not all of these can be addressed here, but at least part of the film's appeal may be in its acknowledgement that, unlike fairy tales, reality has few straight-forward binaries, and the true natures of people are not easily determined by the way they look. Perhaps most significantly of all, it does not place women in opposition to each other, as enemies poised to destroy one another. Instead, it offers love, communication, and companionship be-tween women as both a potential resolution and a weapon to combat sexism. With that being said, it is interesting to note that Elsa and Anna spend relatively little time together in the film. Anna, in actual fact, spends more screen time with her male companions, Kristoff and Olaf the snow-man. That a feature-length sequel is on the horizon, however, may provide opportunities for Anna and Elsa's relationship to further develop in inter-esting and progressive ways. The *Frozen* paratexts are already making headway in this respect, and are continuing to encourage female compan-ionship: whether in *Frozen Fever* (2015), a short sequel to the film; in picture books like *A Sister More Like Me*,[74] which expands upon Anna and Elsa's childhood; or on a variety of merchandise where they are shown embracing, thus breaking the Princess franchise's "no eye contact" rule.[75] Elsa and Anna have, as of yet, not been "officially" initiated into the Disney Princess line-up, but if they were, they would be further breaking ground in that Elsa would be the first queen to join the princesses.[76]

In relation to this, one other possible reason for *Frozen*'s immense popularity is that it acknowledges that being a queen or witch is actually highly appealing – perhaps even more so than being a princess. Disney's evil queens and witches have power (whether magical, political, or simply the power of being feared) and do not conform to what patriarchal ideals say that a woman should or should not be, even though this, more often than not, results in severe punishment. Most of all, they are self-expressive divas who do and say what they feel and think, especially when they feel angry, frustrated, and victimised by an unjust society. With the success of *Frozen* and *Maleficent*, Disney seems to be realising the appeal of powerful and authoritative women, particularly those with magical powers, and are increasingly acknowledging this appeal, evoking sympathy for, and inviting identification with them in their feature films. Even Cinderella, in Disney's 2015 live-action film, becomes a queen through marriage without at any point having the title of "Princess". That Elsa embodies many of the villainous queen or witch characteristics while being a sympathetic and good-hearted person, like a princess, makes her a revolutionary new type of character for Disney's fairy tales. That Elsa is not paired off with a male suitor, and remains single by the film's end, can also be seen as highly refreshing (and opens the film up to queer readings). Anna, who has been somewhat neglected in this piece in favour of Elsa, must not be forgotten as the princess who goes from besotted bride-to-be to saviour (who punches her former fiancé in the face). That both sisters nonetheless conform to the highly restrictive form of feminine beauty associated with the Disney Princesses must be acknowledged, especially in relation to Elsa, who while bearing much in common with her evil predecessors is still separated from them by her "princessy" appearance. As such, in *Frozen*'s exclusion of the sexually transgressive, grotesque bodies of the witches, it is possible to read the film as continuing to code these bodies as undesirable and associated with evil. But one film alone does not bear the responsibility to completely revise a seventy-six year history. *Frozen* can thus be considered a significant step toward more progressive and inclusive depictions of women, and their relationships with one another, in Disney's fairy tales and children's media culture more broadly.

Bibliography

August, John. "Episode: 128: Frozen with Jennifer Lee". *Scriptnotes*. Podcast audio. January 28, 2014. Accessed Feb 25, 2014. http://johnaugust.com/2014/frozen-with-jennifer-lee.

Bates, Laura. *Everyday Sexism* (London: Simon & Schuster, 2014).

Bell, Elizabeth. "Somatexts at the Disney Shop: Constructing the Pentimentos of Women's Animated Bodies". In *From Mouse to Mermaid: The Politics of Film, Gender, and Culture*, edited by Elizabeth Bell, Lynda Haas and Laura Sells (Bloomington: Indiana University Press, 1995), 107–124.

Bettelheim, Bruno. *The Uses of Enchantment: The Meaning and Importance of Fairy Tales* (London: Penguin Books, 1976).

Cashdan, Sheldon. *The Witch Must Die: The Hidden Meaning of Fairy Tales* (New York: Basic Books, 1999).

Child, Ben. "Brave director criticises Disney's 'sexualised' Princess Merida redesign". *The Guardian*. May 13, 2013. Accessed May 30, 2015. http://www.theguardian.com/film/2013/may/13/brave-director-criticises-sexualised-merida-redesign.

Davis, Amy M. *Good Girls & Wicked Witches: Women in Disney's Feature Animation* (Eastleigh: John Libbey Publishing, 2006).

Davis, Amy M. *Handsome Heroes & Vile Villains: Men in Disney's Feature Animation* (New Barnet: John Libbey Publishing, 2013).

Davis, Amy M. "On 'Love Experts', Evil Princes, Gullible Princesses, and *Frozen*". Keynote Speech, given at the "SymFrozium" One-Day Symposium on *Frozen*, held at the University of East Anglea, 12 May 2015. Currently Unpublished.

Ellis, John. *Visible Fictions: Cinema, Television, Video* (New York: Routledge, 1993).

Gray, Jonathan. *Show Sold Separately: Promos, Spoilers, and Other Media Paratexts* (New York: New York University Press, 2010).

Henke, Jill Birnie, Diane Zimmerman Umble and Nancy J. Smith. "Construction of the Female Self: Feminist Readings of the Disney Heroine". *Women's Studies in Communication* 19, no. 2 (1996): 229–249.

Hicks, Barbara Jean. *A Sister More Like Me* (New York: Disney Press, 2013).

Holliday, Christopher. *The Computer Animated Film: Industry, Style and Genre* (Edinburgh: Edinburgh University Press, 2018).

Hooks, Ed. "Disney's 'Frozen': The Acting and Performance Analysis". *Cartoon Brew*. Mar 21, 2014. Accessed Jun 1, 2015. http://www.cartoonbrew.com/ideas-commentary/disneys-frozen-the-acting-and-performance-analysis-97605.html.

Johnston, Ollie and Frank Thomas. *The Disney Villain* (New York: Hyperion, 1993).

Keane, Claire. "Early exploratory drawings of Elsa inspired by Amy.".. *Claire on a Cloud*. Jan 24, 2014. Accessed Jun 1, 2015. http://claireonacloud.com/post/74407510693/early-exploratory-drawings-of-elsa-inspired-by-amy.

Keane, Claire. "More Frozen visual development! My early …" *Claire on a Cloud*. Jan 28, 2014. Accessed Jun 1, 2015. http://claireonacloud.com/post/74858176355/more-frozen-visual-development-my-early.

Kearney, Mary Celeste. "Sparkle: luminosity and post-girl power media". *Continuum* 29, no. 2 (2015): 263–273.

Leonardi, Susan J. and Rebecca A. Pope. *The Diva's Mouth: Body, Voice, Prima Donna Politics* (New Brunswick: Rutgers University Press, 1996).

Lynskey, Dorian. "Why Frozen's Let It Go is more than a Disney hit – it's an adolescent aperitif". *The Guardian*. Apr 10, 2014. Accessed Jun 2, 2015. http://www.theguardian.com/music/musicblog/2014/apr/10/frozen-let-it-go-disney-hit-adolescent-lgbt-anthem.

Macaluso, Michael. "The Postfeminist Princess Public Discourse and Disney's Curricular Guide to Feminism". In *Disney, Culture, and Curriculum*, edited by Jennifer A. Sandlin and Julie C. Garlen (London: Routledge, 2016), 73–86.

McClintock, Pamela. "Box Office Milestone: 'Frozen' Becomes No. 1 Animated Film of All Time". *The Hollywood Reporter*. Mar 30, 2014. Accessed May 30, 2015. http://www.hollywoodreporter.com/news/box-office-milestone-frozen-becomes-692156.

Moseley, Rachel. "Glamorous witchcraft: gender and magic in teen film and television". *Screen* 43, no. 4 (2002): 403–422.

Orenstein, Peggy. *Cinderella Ate My Daughter: Dispatches from the Front Lines of the New Girlie-Girl Culture* (New York: Harper Collins, 2011).

Putnam, Amanda. "Mean Ladies: Transgendered Villains in Disney Films". In *Diversity in Disney Films: Critical Essays on Race, Ethnicity, Gender, Sexuality and Disability*, edited by Johnson Cheu (Jefferson: McFarland & Company, Inc., 2013), 147–62.

Rudloff, Maja. "(Post)feminist paradoxes: the sensibilities of gender representation in Disney's *Frozen,*" *Outskirts: Feminisms Along the Edge* 35 (2016): 1–20.

Sciretta, Peter. "Walt Disney Animation Gives 'The Snow Queen' New Life, Retitled 'Frozen' – But Will It Be Hand Drawn?" *SlashFilm.* Dec 22, 2011. Accessed Jun 1, 2015. http://www.slashfilm.com/walt-disney-animation-the-snow-queen-life-retitled-froze n-hand-drawn/.

Sells, Laura. "'Where Do the Mermaids Stand?': Voice and Body in *The Little Mermaid.*" In *From Mouse to Mermaid: The Politics of Film, Gender, and Culture*, edited by Elizabeth Bell, Lynda Haas and Laura Sells (Bloomington: Indiana University Press, 1995), 175–192.

Shone, Tom. "Frozen's celebration of sisterhood guaranteed to melt the coldest heart". *The Guardian.* Nov 23, 2013. Accessed May 30, 2015. http://www.theguardian. com/film/2013/nov/29/frozen-disney-pixar-film-criticism.

Solomon, Charles. *The Art of* Frozen (San Francisco: Chronicle Books, 2013).

Stewart, James B. *Disney War: The Battle for the Magic Kingdom* (London: Simon & Schuster, 2005).

Streiff, Madeline, and Laura Dundes. "Frozen in Time: How Disney Gender-Stereotypes Its Most Powerful Princess". *Social Sciences* 6, no. 38 (2017): 1–10.

Walt Disney Animation Studios. "Disney's Frozen Teaser Trailer". Youtube video, 1:35. Jun 19, 2013. Accessed Jun 1, 2015. https://www.youtube.com/watch?v=S1x76DoACB8.

Walt Disney Animation Studios. "Disney's Frozen Official Trailer". Youtube video, 2:32. Sep 26, 2013. Accessed Jun 1, 2015. https://www.youtube.com/watch?v=TbQm5doF_Uc.

Weetch, Owen. "Frozen (Chris Buck & Jennifer Lee, Disney, U.S., 2013)". *WeetchNotes.* Dec 22, 2013. Accessed Jun 1, 2015. https://weetchnotes.wordpress.com/2013/12/22/fro zen-chris-buck-jennifer-lee-disney-u-s-2013/.

Weetch, Owen. *Expressive Spaces in Digital 3D Cinema* (Basingstoke: Palgrave Macmillan, 2016).

Whitfield, Sarah. "'For the First Time in Forever': Locating *Frozen* as a Feminist Disney Musical", in George Rodosthenous (Editor), *The Disney Musical on Stage and Screen: Critical Approaches from* Snow White *to* Frozen (London: Bloomsbury, 2017): 221–238.

Wilde, Sarah. "Advertising in Repackaging the Disney Princess: A Post-feminist Reading of Modern Day Fairy Tales". *Journal of Promotional Communications* 2, no. 1 (2014): 132–153.

Wloszczyna, Susan. "With Frozen, Director Jennifer Lee Breaks the Ice for Women Directors". *Indiewire.* Nov 26, 2013. Accessed May 30, 2015. http://blogs.indiewire.com/womenand hollywood/with-frozen-director-jennifer-lee-breaks-the-ice-for-women-directors.

Wolf, Stacy. *Changed for Good: A Feminist History of the Broadway Musical* (Oxford: Oxford University Press, 2011).

Wood, Zoe. "Frozen: parental panic as unexpected Disney hit leads to merchandise sellout". *The Guardian.* May 17, 2014. Accessed May 30, 2015. http://www.theguardian.com/ film/2014/may/17/frozen-film-disney-success-merchandise-sellout.

Woolf, Nicky. "'Nasty woman': Trump attacks Clinton during final debate". *The Guardian.* October 20, 2016. Accessed May 22, 2017. https://www.theguardian.com/us-news/ 2016/oct/20/nasty-woman-donald-trump-hillary-clinton.

Zipes, Jack, ed. *Don't Bet on the Prince: Contemporary Feminist Fairy Tales in North America and England* (New York: Routledge, 1987).

Zipes, Jack. "Breaking the Disney Spell". In *From Mouse to Mermaid: The Politics of Film, Gender, and Culture*, edited by Elizabeth Bell, Lynda Haas and Laura Sells (Bloomington: Indiana University Press, 1995), 21–42.

Endnotes

1.   Pamela McClintock, "Box Office Milestone: 'Frozen' Becomes No. 1 Animated Film of All Time", *The Hollywood Reporter*, Mar 30, 2014, accessed May 30, 2015, http://www.hollywoodreporter.com/news/box-office-milestone-frozen-becomes-692156.

2.   Zoe Wood, "Frozen: parental panic as unexpected Disney hit leads to merchandise sellout", *The Guardian*, May 17, 2014, accessed May 30, 2015,http://www.theguardian.com/film/2014/may/17/frozen-film-disney-success-merchandise-sellout.

3.   "Symfrozium: A Study Day on Disney's 'Frozen'," University of East Anglia, Norwich, May 12, 2015; Sarah Wilde, "Advertising in Repackaging the Disney Princess: A Post-feminist Reading of Modern Day Fairy Tales", *Journal of Promotional Communications* 2, no. 1 (2014): 132–153; Mary Celeste Kearney, "Sparkle: luminosity and post-girl power media", *Continuum* 29, no. 2 (2015): 263–273; Michael Macaluso, "The Postfeminist Princess Public Discourse and Disney's Curricular Guide to Feminism", in *Disney, Culture, and Curriculum*, eds. Jennifer A. Sandlin, Julie C. Garlen (London: Routledge, 2016), 73–86; Maja Rudloff, "(Post)feminist paradoxes: the sensibilities of gender representation in Disney's *Frozen,*" *Outskirts: Feminisms Along the Edge* 35 (2016): 1–20; Owen Weetch, *Expressive Spaces in Digital 3D Cinema* (Basingstoke: Palgrave Macmillan, 2016), 127–156; Madeline Streiff and Laura Dundes, "Frozen in Time: How Disney Gender-Stereotypes Its Most Powerful Princess", *Social Sciences* 6, no. 38 (2017): 1–10; Sarah Whitfield, "'For the First Time in Forever': Locating *Frozen* as a Feminist Disney Musical", in *The Disney Musical on Stage and Screen: Critical Approaches from 'Snow White' to 'Frozen'*, ed. George Rodosthenous (London: Bloomsbury, 2017), 221–238; Christopher Holliday, *The Computer Animated Film: Industry, Style and Genre* (Edinburgh: Edinburgh University Press, 2018), 76–77.

4.   Susan Wloszczyna, "With *Frozen*, Director Jennifer Lee Breaks the Ice for Women Directors", *Indiewire*, November 26, 2013, accessed May 30, 2015, http://blogs.indiewire.com/womenandhollywood/with-frozen-director-jennifer-lee-breaks-the-ice-for-women-directors;   Tom Shone, "*Frozen*'s celebration of sisterhood guaranteed to melt the coldest heart", *The Guardian*, November 23, 2013, accessed May 30, 2015, http://www.theguardian.com/film/2013/nov/29/frozen-disney-pixar-film-criticism.

5.   Any references to "Disney's animated features" or variants thereof refer only to the theatrically released animated feature films produced by Walt Disney Animation Studios, of which *Frozen* is the fifty-third. This excludes any direct-to-video sequels, live-action films that feature animation, and films made by Pixar Animation Studios, DisneyToon Studios, or any other division of The Walt Disney Company that produces animated films.

6.   Streiff and Dundes, 7.

7.   Rudloff, 16.

8.   Weetch, 152.

9.   Whitfield, 233.

10.   The official Disney Princess "line-up" currently includes Snow White (1937), Cinderella (1950), *Sleeping Beauty's* Aurora (1959), *The Little Mermaid's* Ariel (1989), *Beauty and the Beast's* Belle (1991), *Aladdin's* Jasmine (1992), Pocahontas (1995), Mulan (1998), *The Princess and the Frog's* Tiana (2009), *Tangled's* Rapunzel (2010) and Merida of Pixar's *Brave* (2012). Perceptive readers will note various idiosyncrasies which, while a subject of inquiry worth pursuing, will not be analysed here. Chiefly, not all of these characters are actually princesses, like Mulan, and several legitimate princesses from other animated Disney films, such as *The Black Cauldron's* Eilonwy (1985), are missing, while Merida, from a Pixar film, is included. This chapter is primarily concerned with the depictions of "Disney Princesses" with fairy tale origins.

11.   Jack Zipes, "Breaking the Disney Spell," in *From Mouse to Mermaid: The Politics of Film, Gender, and Culture*, ed. Elizabeth Bell, Lynda Haas and Laura Sells (Bloomington: Indiana University Press, 1995), 37.

12.   Amy M. Davis, *Good Girls & Wicked Witches: Women in Disney's Feature Animation* (New Barnet: John Libbey Publishing, 2006), 235.

13. For an in-depth critique of the Disney Princess franchise and the wider "girl culture" in which it is situated, see Peggy Orenstein, *Cinderella Ate My Daughter: Dispatches from the Front Lines of the New Girlie-Girl Culture* (New York: Harper Collins, 2011).

14. Ben Child, "*Brave* director criticises Disney's 'sexualised' Princess Merida redesign", *The Guardian*, May 13, 2013, accessed May 30, 2015,http://www.theguardian.com/film/2013/may/13/brave-director-criticises-sexualised-merida-redesign.

15. Sheldon Cashdan, *The Witch Must Die: The Hidden Meaning of Fairy Tales* (New York: Basic Books, 1999), 30.

16. Zipes, "Breaking the Disney Spell", 37.

17. Further problematising the depictions of these villainous women is that they can be read as "display[ing] transgendered attributes", in opposition to their "hyper-heterosexual" heroes and heroines, thus associating these attributes with evil; Amanda Putnam, "Mean Ladies: Transgendered Villains in Disney Films", in *Diversity in Disney Films: Critical Essays on Race, Ethnicity, Gender, Sexuality and Disability*, ed. Johnson Cheu (Jefferson: McFarland & Company, Inc., 2013), 147.

18. Jill Birnie Henke, Diane Zimmerman Umble and Nancy J. Smith, "Construction of the Female Self: Feminist Readings of the Disney Heroine", *Women's Studies in Communication* 19, no. 2 (1996): 245.

19. The Disney Renaissance, beginning in 1989 with *The Little Mermaid*, is considered a period of creative resurgence for the studio's animated output. Significantly, this is also when Disney returned to using fairy tales as source material, which the studio had not done since 1959's *Sleeping Beauty*.

20. Davis, *Good Girls & Wicked Witches*, 217.

21. Orenstein, 13–14.

22. It is, of course, entirely possible for child consumers to make up their own games in which they interact as princesses or have their princess dolls interact with each other during play. Some princess characters have also recently appeared as "Easter Eggs" in each other's films, such as Rapunzel in the background of a scene in *Frozen*. Disney Princesses have appeared in the television series *Sofia the First* (2012–), but never in the same episode, though they do appear in the same scene in *Wreck-it-Ralph 2: Ralph Breaks the Internet* (2018). Nevertheless, it is still concerning that the princesses do not interact within the diegeses of their films or on official Disney Princess merchandise.

23. *The Princess and the Frog* introduces the first African-American Disney Princess, Tiana, who is also the first princess "career woman". It is also interesting in that Tiana's rich, white, and spoiled friend, Charlotte La Bouff, seems to poke fun at the idea of the traditional princess. *Tangled*, while reintroducing the "princess versus evil step-mother" trope and ending with the coupling of Rapunzel with a handsome man, shows a more complex female relationship than we have seen before. Rather than seeming wholly evil, Mother Gothel appears to have some affection and concern for her adopted daughter. Moreover, she relies on the magical properties of Rapunzel's hair rather than possessing any magical power of her own – power which Rapunzel comes to harness for her own use.

24. Biological mothers in fairy tales, and especially Disney's adaptations, are usually either dead or, if alive, unable to assist in their daughter's plight.

25. Many of Disney's previous animated films have had significant contributions by women, however Lee, who scripted and co-directed *Frozen*, arguably had more control over the film than any woman has had before over an animated feature film made at Disney. Chapman's situation is more complex; she exited *Brave* in 2010 due to "creative differences", and was only much later credited as a co-director.

26. The "Bechdel Test" is named after Alison Bechdel, who introduced the test in 1985 in her comic strip *Dykes to Watch Out For* (1983–2008). There are valid criticisms of the test, such as that regardless of whether a film passes, it may still contain sexist or objectifying portrayals of women. Disney's *Cinderella* passes, for example, in spite of its many traditionally-patriarchal depictions of gender roles. However, the Test is commonly used as a generally useful indicator of the representation of women in fictional texts.

27.   By "women with magical powers" this chapter is referring to villainous women only; fairy godmothers, of course, though also magically powerful, arguably exist in a separate category from other magical women.

28.   Amy M. Davis, *Handsome Heroes & Vile Villains: Men in Disney's Feature Animation* (New Barnet: John Libbey Publishing, 2013), 187.

29.   Bruno Bettelheim, *The Uses of Enchantment: The Meaning and Importance of Fairy Tales* (London: Penguin Books, 1976), 127–128.

30.   Cashdan, 36.

31.   Ed Hooks, "Disney's 'Frozen': The Acting and Performance Analysis", *Cartoon Brew*, March 21, 2014, accessed June 1, 2015,http://www.cartoonbrew.com/ideas-commentary/disneys-frozen-the-acting-and-performance-analysis-97605.html.

32.   Disney has already explored self-referential territory with the live-action-animated hybrid *Enchanted* (2007), which both pokes fun at and celebrates many of the established Disney tropes, such as the "true love's kiss". However, *Frozen* is Disney's first attempt to revise such tropes actually *within* the context of a sincere fairy tale adaptation, as opposed to an overt self-parody.

33.   Bettelheim, 8.

34.   Just previously to the shadow shot, they are also shown imitating the robotic movements of clockwork figures and singing about how their "mental synchronisation / Can have but one explanation": that they are meant to be together. These references to clockwork and mechanics further suggest that they are simply playing out pre-determined and predictable roles.

35.   Jonathan Gray, *Show Sold Separately: Promos, Spoilers, and Other Media Paratexts* (New York: New York University Press, 2010), 47–48.

36.   Charles Solomon, *The Art of* Frozen (San Francisco: Chronicle Books, 2013), 9–10.

37.   Peter Sciretta, "Walt Disney Animation Gives 'The Snow Queen' New Life, Retitled 'Frozen' – But Will It Be Hand Drawn?" *SlashFilm*, December 22, 2011, accessed June 1, 2015, http://www.slashfilm.com/walt-disney-animation-the-snow-queen-life-retitled-frozen-ha nd-drawn/.

38.   Solomon, 14, 15, 63, 76.

39.   Interestingly, visual development artist Claire Keane states on her website, which contains much of her *Frozen* art, that she drew inspiration for the visual development of Elsa from musical figures such as Amy Winehouse and Bette Midler, further establishing Elsa's early conception as a "diva"; Claire Keane, "Early exploratory drawings of Elsa inspired by Amy". *Claire on a Cloud*, January 24, 2014, accessed June 1, 2015, http://claireonacloud. com/post/74407510693/early-exploratory-drawings-of-elsa-inspired-by-amy; Claire Keane, "More Frozen visual development! My early …" *Claire on a Cloud*, January 28, 2014, accessed June 1, 2015, http://claireonacloud.com/post/74858176355/more-frozen-visual-develop-ment-my-early.

40.   *The Story of Frozen: Making a Disney Animated Classic*, ABC, Sep 2, 2014, television broadcast.

41.   Menzel, apart from physically resembling some of the Snow Queen's early designs due to her striking facial features and dark hair, has a Broadway "diva" persona of her own due partly to *Wicked*, but also her first Broadway role as Maureen, a vain performance artist, in *Rent* (1996–2008).

42.   Walt Disney Animation Studios, "Disney's Frozen Teaser Trailer", Youtube video, 1:35, June 19, 2013, accessed Jun 1, 2015, https://www.youtube.com/watch?v=S1x76DoACB8.

43.   Walt Disney Animation Studios, "Disney's Frozen Official Trailer", Youtube video, 2:32, September 26, 2013, accessed June 1, 2015, https://www.youtube.com/watch?v= TbQm5doF_Uc.

44.   Gray, 48.

45.   John Ellis, *Visible Fictions: Cinema, Television, Video*. (New York: Routledge, 1993), 54.

46.   Some versions of the film's poster and DVD cover are also complicit in this. The theatrical poster shows Elsa dominating the top-half above the other characters in a spell-casting pose,

which follows a trend of Hollywood film posters in which villains are placed in the upper half, scaled bigger and looming ominously over the protagonists. This can be seen on posters for a range of vastly different films, such as *Snow White and the Seven Dwarfs* (1937), *Star Wars* (1977), and *No Country for Old Men* (2007).

47. The use of the term "fair" is of course also reminiscent of Snow White's wicked step-mother: "Magic mirror on the wall, who is the fairest one of all?"

48. John August, "Episode: 128: Frozen with Jennifer Lee", *Scriptnotes*, podcast audio, January 28, 2014, accessed February 25, 2014, http://johnaugust.com/2014/frozen-with-jennifer-lee.

49. August, "Episode: 128: Frozen with Jennifer Lee", *Scriptnotes*.

50. Elizabeth Bell, "Somatexts at the Disney Shop: Constructing the Pentimentos of Women's Animated Bodies", in *From Mouse to Mermaid: The Politics of Film, Gender, and Culture*, ed. Elizabeth Bell, Lynda Haas and Laura Sells (Bloomington: Indiana University Press, 1995), 116.

51. Stacy Wolf, *Changed for Good: A Feminist History of the Broadway Musical* (Oxford: Oxford University Press, 2011), 228.

52. "Let It Go" was the winner of the 2014 Academy Award for Best Original Song, but has also achieved better chart success than the other songs from the film and, significantly, out-performed the more subdued "pop" version sung by Disney Channel star Demi Lovato, released by Walt Disney Records as a single. Also demonstrating the wide appeal of "Let It Go" is that it has been subject to various progressive readings, such as a queer reading of it as a "coming out" anthem; Dorian Lynskey, "Why Frozen's Let It Go is more than a Disney hit – it's an adolescent aperitif", *The Guardian*, April 10, 2014, accessed June 2, 2015, http://www.theguardian.com/music/musicblog/2014/apr/10/frozen-let-it-go-disney-hit-adolescent-lgbt-anthem.

53. Laura Sells, "'Where Do the Mermaids Stand?': Voice and Body in *The Little Mermaid*," in *From Mouse to Mermaid: The Politics of Film, Gender, and Culture*, ed. Elizabeth Bell, Lynda Haas and Laura Sells (Bloomington: Indiana University Press, 1995), 181.

54. Susan J. Leonardi and Rebecca A. Pope, *The Diva's Mouth: Body, Voice, Prima Donna Politics* (New Brunswick: Rutgers University Press, 1996), 163.

55. Her aforementioned direct gaze into the camera at the end of the sequence implies acknowledgement of an extra-diegetic audience, thus complicating this claim that she is not performing for anyone but herself. With this in mind, this moment is perhaps more akin to a teenage girl dancing and singing into a hairbrush in front of her bedroom mirror. Regardless, it goes without saying that this is an incredibly complex moment in an already complex scene, one which this chapter alone cannot do justice to.

56. Rachel Moseley, "Glamorous witchcraft: gender and magic in teen film and television", *Screen* 43, no. 4 (2002): 407.

57. Moseley, 408–409.

58. Moseley, 403–404.

59. It should be noted that Elsa's power can also be read as a metaphor for love: in containing it, she isolates herself from others. But when using her power joyfully she creates Olaf the snowman, an embodiment of the love that she has for Anna. Olaf, channelling this, considers himself to be a "love expert", and is integral to helping Anna realise what true love is.

60. The Duke is the most outspoken accuser in the film, but he is not the only character to have suspicions or make accusations about Elsa with little supporting evidence. Even Kristoff – who, unlike the Duke, has not at this point witnessed Elsa's power – is extremely dubious of Anna's plan to simply talk to Elsa, or her insistence that Elsa is good. "So you're not at all afraid of her?" he asks, to which Anna happily responds, "Why would I be?", indicating her unwavering love for her sister even when no one else understands her reasoning.

61. Laura Bates, *Everyday Sexism* (London: Simon & Schuster, 2014), 53.

62. The slur "nasty woman" was very swiftly reclaimed by feminist supporters of Clinton as a badge of honour, lending credence to the argument presented in this chapter that female villainy can actually be highly appealing due to the subversive power that such vilification often implies. Nicky Woolf, "'Nasty woman': Trump attacks Clinton during final debate", *The*

Guardian, October 20, 2016, accessed May 22, 2017. https://www.theguardian.com/us-news/2016/oct/20/nasty-woman-donald-trump-hillary-clinton.

63. Bates, *Everyday Sexism*, 67.

64. Sells, 181.

65. James B. Stewart, *Disney War: The Battle for the Magic Kingdom* (London: Simon & Schuster, 2005), 437.

66. It is interesting given the film's emphasis on sisterhood and female solidarity that the song lists these family members, two of which are male, but not the mother. In addition, Elsa and Anna's mother only has one line in the film while their father, the one who predominantly encourages Elsa to hide her powers, has several. It is disappointing that, given the film's progressiveness in other aspects, *Frozen* follows in the tradition of many fairy tales in excluding biological mothers.

67. Henke, Umble and Smith, 235.

68. Hooks, "Disney's 'Frozen': The Acting and Performance Analysis".

69. Owen Weetch, "Frozen (Chris Buck & Jennifer Lee, Disney, U.S., 2013)", *WeetchNotes*, December 22, 2013, accessed June 1, 2015. https://weetchnotes.wordpress.com/2013/12/22/frozen-chris-buck-jennifer-lee-disney-u-s-2013/.

70. Hooks, "Disney's 'Frozen': The Acting and Performance Analysis".

71. Ollie Johnston and Frank Thomas, *The Disney Villain* (New York: Hyperion, 1993), 18.

72. Solomon, 67–68.

73. Jack Zipes, ed., *Don't Bet on the Prince: Contemporary Feminist Fairy Tales in North America and England* (New York: Routledge, 1987).

74. Barbara Jean Hicks, *A Sister More Like Me* (New York: Disney Press, 2013).

75. Technically, they do not break the rule; the rule is in place in order to preserve the sanctity of the princesses' individual stories and mythologies, thus Elsa and Anna existing and interacting within the same narrative does not jeopardise this. However, that *Frozen* is a Disney animated fairy tale with two princesses who have the ability to interact with each other at all is still a highly significant step. As such, they could be said to "break the rule without breaking it", allowing Disney to seem progressive without undermining or destabilising the carefully thought out structures that are already in place.

76. Kida from *Atlantis: The Lost Empire* (2001), like Elsa, is a princess who becomes a queen by the end of her narrative. However, Kida is excluded from the Disney Princess franchise, for reasons that are unclear.

IV.
Outside the Studio

The Violentest Place on Earth: Adventures in Censorship, Nostalgia, and Pastiche (or: *The Simpsons* Do Disney)

Jemma D. Gilboy

Throughout *The Simpsons'* run, which is (at the time of writing) thirty years, the series has featured countless Disney references. In the process of cataloguing all of these incidences, it became clear that three aspects of Disney's output were consistently rewarded with the most sustained and faithful treatments: the theme parks, Walt Disney's own history (or a skewed vision thereof), and the timeline of Disney's films as they relate to *The Simpsons'* show-within-the-show, "The Itchy and Scratchy Show".

The task is thus to determine what – beyond being Disney outputs – these three elements have in common that makes them particularly tempting to the producers of *The Simpsons*. The numerous treatments of the theme parks, Disney himself, and the history of the production company in the series are executed with a blend of reverence, parody, criticism, and nostalgia. The three elements strike a sonorous-enough chord among the creative producers of the series (henceforth "creatives") not only to warrant multiple acknowledgments, but also to inspire meticulous reconstructions of animated scenes, of well-known theme park attractions, and of known or rumoured aspects of Walt Disney himself.

Modern Conventions

The attributes of Walt Disney, the theme parks, and the Disney company (henceforth "Disney") are characterised as manifestations of (or were originally presented in the context of) innocence, childlike wonder, idealism, and sweetness. The *Simpsons'* treatments of these three elements almost always subvert these notions, presenting the elements instead in a context of darkness (e.g. depicting Disney the company as an unscrupulous, money-hungry corporation, or suggesting that Walt Disney was a Nazi sympathiser with an "evil gene", or forcing the audience to conflate Mickey Mouse with Itchy the Mouse, the latter of whom is characterised only by his sociopathic and sadistic murderousness). This type of subversion is a key characteristic of postmodernism, a disillusioned worldview with which *The Simpsons* has been observably aligned since its debut in December 1989.

Before tackling the trademarks and important role of postmodernism in *The Simpsons* and in its many Disney allusions, it is crucial first to look at the concept of modernism, taking into account its key characteristics along with the social contexts of its rise and fall. Art historian Christopher Witcombe considers the origins and hallmarks of modernism:

> In the history of art [...] the term "modern" is used to refer to a period dating from roughly the 1860s through the 1970s and describes the style and ideology of art produced during that era. [...] The tenets of the movement, its belief in progress, freedom, and equality, had been sustained from the outset by artists and intellectuals, and embraced by those who reaped the material benefits it brought. [...] For some, problems in the pursuit of modernism were already apparent early in the 20th century. The senseless, mechanized slaughter of the First World War showed that modernism's faith in scientific and technological progress as the path to a better world was tragically misguided.[1]

Clearly, at the outset of the modern era, the swift progress, economic expansion, and profound changes in lifestyles that resulted from the Industrial Revolution inspired a new and unprecedented outlook for those in both the new urban and the changing rural settings.[2] New phenomena like the accumulation of wealth led to unprecedented social mobility (and increasing social equality), and the benefits enjoyed by those who profited from the transformations inspired a great deal of faith in the technology that enabled and prompted those transformations.

However, as Witcombe observes, beginning after the First World War, the first cracks appeared in the façade of modern idealism. By the 1970s, the optimism of modernism gave way to the cynical disillusionment of the postmodern era; with unprecedented media coverage of yet another war whose immense violence and destruction were enabled by the era's accelerated technological advancement, and with emergent social movements exposing deeply-ingrained institutional inequality and injustice throughout the United States and the western world, what was once the modern perception of "progress" began to give way to a more postmodern sense of scepticism and despair.

Postmodernism functions in two ways: as "anti-modern", marked by an outright rejection of the ideals that drove the modern era, and as a more moderate, revisionist approach to those ideals.[3] Like its predecessor, postmodernism is itself characterised by and expressed through several key attributes and methods; those most salient to *The Simpsons* are explored here.

Literary scholar Linda Hutcheon observes that self-reflexivity distinguishes the postmodern text, noting that parody plays a significant role in that reflexivity. Hutcheon suggests a redefinition of parody that goes beyond "ridiculing imitation"; it should instead be understood "as repetition with critical distance that allows ironic signalling of difference at the very heart of similarity".[4] She goes on to indicate that, in a given text, parody functions paradoxically by both challenging and upholding cultural continuity.

Aligning with Hutcheon's perspective on self-reflexivity, literary scholar John Alberti proposes that it is in *The Simpsons'* particular brand of self-referentiality that its postmodernity is most easily detected. *The Simpsons* is unique in that its self-awareness is not limited to its ever-present assertion that it is itself a media construct; *The Simpsons* itself can be counted among the victims of its satire:

> we can locate the postmodernity of *The Simpsons* in the program's relentless self-referentiality, a consistent foregrounding of itself as a television program and media construct that functions as an operative principle and satirical strategy of the show, not just an occasional rhetorical gesture. Thus, *The Simpsons* uses satire not only to undermine the pretensions to cultural significance of various texts from both "high" and "low" culture, it includes itself as part of that mockery, potentially undercutting the cultural critique in which the program seems to be engaged.[5]

The series' self-reflexivity is thus present not just in its self-awareness as a product of its forbears, but also in its mockery of itself as a forbear. This occurs alongside its paradoxical stance as an opponent and a proponent of the cultural status quo, in which nothing (including itself) is spared the rod of *Simpsons* parody.

Eco Echoes Baudrillard

The argument at the core of this chapter – that the postmodern perspectives of those who create *The Simpsons* inspires the parodic representations of Walt Disney, of Disney company films, and of the Disney theme parks – takes for granted the premise that Walt Disney, the Disney company and the creations and products of both are firmly planted in modernity. However, one of noted postmodern theorist Jean Baudrillard's most famous examples of his concept of hyperreality (the phenomenon in which one is unable to distinguish between that which is real and that which is simulated) is Disneyland.[6] Baudrillard contends that the meticulously-conceived and constructed Disneyland – in particular, those aspects that are meant to mirror elements of real life (such as Main Street, U.S.A) – is designed to conceal the fact that what we perceive as reality is just as false as the reality presented at Disneyland. Fellow postmodernist theorist Umberto Eco explores the Disneyland example of the hyperreal even further, observing that in using authentic adornments in some circumstances and obviously false ones in others, the park acknowledges its own simulated nature, and thus drives a desire among visitors for such pretence.[7] Eco argues that Disneyland – even more than its much larger cousin, Walt Disney World – is an allegory of consumer society. The park demands that each visitor surrender his or her will (and, therefore, his or her humanity) in order to pass through the boundaries and that they follow orders as politely requested; the compliant are subsequently rewarded with the "abundance of the reconstructed truth".[8] The implications in both authors' works are that Walt Disney (and those who contributed to the creation of the parks) fully intended to create a hyperrealist environment in order to lull attendees into surrendering their will and their money for a chance to participate in the illusion. Such a proposition would suppose that Walt Disney and his cohorts were not modernists, but were in fact cynical postmodernists all along, exploiting and capitalising upon the nostalgic desires of modernists and postmodernists alike in order to reap the profits. It also suggests that aspects of the park are constructed as reflections only of the American ideal, rather than of Walt Disney's own.

While it would perhaps be naïve to assume that all intentions behind the creation of the parks were pure, the suggestion that the entirety of Walt Disney's interest was in profiteering rather than (at least in part) in amusement does a definite (and problematic) disservice to the adventurous and ambitious innovator Walt Disney. Baudrillard in particular sheds a ghoulish light on Walt Disney, referring to the widespread (but absolutely false) rumour that Walt Disney was frozen cryogenically: "By an extraordinary coincidence [...] this frozen, childlike world is found to have been conceived and realized by a man who is himself now cryogenized: Walt Disney, who awaits his resurrection through an increase of 180 degrees centigrade".[9] There is nothing in this (or its surrounding) text to suggest that Baudrillard does not himself believe the rumour; if he does, this could explain his particularly cynical view of Walt Disney. For Baudrillard, rather than being a nostalgic idealist himself, Walt Disney is instead complicit in the illusion, helping to fool the public into thinking that when they enter Disneyland, they are leaving reality and entering a fictional space, when, in fact, every space they occupy is constructed on fiction.

It seems a simpler conclusion that, rather than being complicit in (and investing vast sums of money into) a conspiracy to shield humanity from its own reality and using the resulting illusion to drain customers of their money, based on his success in creating attractions for wide consumption, instead, Walt Disney knew that his vision of an idealised America would appeal enough to others that, if he built it, they would pay to spend time in such an environment. Even in the case of the cryogenic rumour, surely Walt Disney's supposed faith in future scientists' ability to resurrect him would exemplify his actual (and well-documented) optimistic faith in technological progress for the betterment of humanity, a hallmark of modernity – and one with which he shares a particularly strong association, as will be explored further below.

The journalists reporting on Walt Disney during his lifetime (including Paul Hollister, Walter Wanger, and Robert De Roos, whose works are collected and reprinted in editor Eric Smoodin's work *Disney Discourse: Producing the Magic Kingdom*) portray him as a pioneer who championed hard work, invention, self-reliance, and investment in technological advancement for American success in the Second World War.[10] With the hindsight of an author writing in 1994, Eric Smoodin observes Walt Disney's multifaceted public and private personae, complicated by his mixed politics and (at times) rigid ideological approaches, noting that – both during his life and in retrospect – Walt Disney was often erroneously portrayed as falling to one extreme of the political spectrum or the other.[11] Sometimes, and, perhaps, worse still, Smoodin notes a tendency among his contemporary journalists "to simplify [Walt Disney] in the extreme. As a result, television specials about Euro Disney (produced by the Disney studio) construct him as a utopian visionary seeking world peace through leisure activity".[12] Smoodin goes on to discuss the aspect of the man on which the earlier journalists and current scholars have full consensus: Walt Disney's enthusiasm for and invention of new technology, in his films and especially in his parks. He observes:

> Disney has been responsible for a kind of Tennessee Valley Authority of leisure and entertainment. That is, like Thomas Edison and Henry Ford, while celebrated for individual artifacts, Disney was actually the master of vast "technological systems". [...] Like Samuel Insull, Frederick Taylor, and Ford once again, Disney imagined his systems as blueprints for a future based on efficiency, conservation, and communal living.[13]

Though the proposition that Walt Disney was a hardened postmodernist is one worth considering, it ignores aspects of the man that so clearly materialised in his work as well as in the persona he presented to the public. This chapter does not make the argument that profit was not an important one of Walt Disney's objectives in his many endeavours; rather, the argument is that the ideals he presented in his personal appearances and the work he produced were more likely to have been rooted in genuine nostalgia, innovation and enterprise rather than to have stemmed from a conscious and calculated desire to exploit the masses and manipulate their deepest desires. Even if Walt Disney's true intentions cannot be known, upon reviewing journalistic and scholarly reports on him, observing the philosophies behind his work, and watching and reading Walt Disney's own personal public addresses, it can be concluded with confidence that, at the very least, the public presentation of the man aligns with modernist ideals – and it is to this public presentation that the creative authors of *The Simpsons* respond in their many satirical takes. Therefore, on these distinctions, Walt Disney will be considered henceforth in this chapter as a modernist.

The Wonderful World(s) of Disney

Walt Disney began making films during the modern era, when experimentation in artistic endeavours was at its height. Not among the ranks of the earliest postmodernists who had been irrevocably shaken by the First World War, Disney embraced – and encouraged his studio toward – technological innovation and progress.[14] The studio produced films that both embodied and depicted improvement through advancement; even in 1928, audiences could marvel as a synchronised-sound, problem-solving Mickey finds a way to get the hapless passengers of Podunk Landing onto his steamboat, presumably making its way to more exciting surroundings.[15]

As suggested above, nowhere are Walt Disney's modernist ideals more apparent than in the theme parks. Whether in the spaces that recollect an idealised and commodified version of the past (such as Main Street, USA) or in those that look toward a utopian future (such as Tomorrowland in the Magic Kingdom or Epcot), Disney's theme parks are an effective actualisation of the ideals of the modern era: efficiency, progress, philanthropy, cleanliness, optimism, utopianism, and truth.[16] In creating Disneyland, Disney was determined, as promised in the park's motto, to make his park "The Happiest Place on Earth".

These ideals make Disney – and Disney theme parks in particular – excellent targets for the cynical authors of the postmodern text. Naturally, then, this is where creators of *The Simpsons* would inaugurate their now-longstanding practice of Disney parody. In the second season episode "Old Money", Abe "Grampa" Simpson visits "Diz-Nee Land" in an attempt to enjoy his inheritance from his late girlfriend.[17] On the DVD commentary for the episode, at the moment that the establishing shot of Diz-Nee Land's admission gates appears, writer Al Jean announces it as "a shot at Disney" – this could be interpreted as a camera shot of the amusement park, or as a swipe at the animation giant. Creator Matt Groening lands firmly in the latter camp when he asks, "Was this the first of our taking on, uh, 'Diz-nee'?"[18]

This brief exchange between Jean and Groening introduces two more layers to *The Simpsons'* parodies of Disney. The first is that, due to its immense and unparalleled commercial and artistic success, the consistent implementation of innovative practices, and tradition of quality, the Disney Studio has long been established as an animation giant and the standard against which all animated texts are measured, particularly in the Hollywood (or American) screen industry. It would seem that Groening – who holds a reputation for taunting his series' own network, the Fox Broadcasting Company (henceforth "Fox") – sees his series as a sort of David who is challenging Disney's Goliath to take a legal swing ... and this in the days before the Walt Disney Company purchased 20th Century Fox.[19] Litigiousness and the primacy of profit are two traits that the Disney company and 20th Century Fox have in common; *Simpsons* creatives have publically shared several of their own personal accounts of Fox network executives' extreme penny-pinching.[20] These specific traits inspire annoyance in *Simpsons* creatives; their response, traditionally, has been to subject the offending parties to a great deal of satire. Thus, this is the second layer of the *Simpsons*' Disney parodies, in which Disney's notorious litigiousness presents something of a challenge to the creators of the series, who tend to push the boundaries of infringement at every opportunity.

The subject of Disney's litigiousness came up in the series itself in the season-four episode "Lisa the Beauty Queen", when Disney's lawyer appears, flanked by two goons, at the Springfield Elementary School carnival to dispute the school's use of the slogan "The Happiest Place on Earth". The lawyer (a recurring character, known only as the Blue-Haired Lawyer, who represents Disney and Disney's primary parodic stand-in "I&S Productions" in several episodes) tells Principal Seymour Skinner that, if he fails to comply with the request that he cease and desist using the "registered Disneyland copyright", his "small school carnival" is "heading for a great big lawsuit".[21] Skinner responds by engaging his ex-Green-Beret combat skills to physically assault the trio – including the goon who attempts to flee. When the briefcase Skinner throws after the escapee hits its target and knocks the man to the ground, Skinner remarks, "Copyright expired".

The series creatives have depicted a fairly extreme response to the imposition – however obnoxiously it is presented – of a copyright by a large corporation. Threatening to sue an already-impoverished elementary school for the use of a copyright-protected slogan is low, and in attributing such an action to the Disney company, the series creatives make clear their perspective on the company's attitude toward money and profit. The addition of the goons to the Disney camp in the encounter further enhances the creatives' position: money-hungry corporations that pursue small enterprises over mild infringements are no different from thugs. The violence that is then exacted upon these thugs is swift, brutal, and, in all likelihood, cathartic. It is also somewhat unexpected: the creatives chose to unleash the fury through a rather unlikely character.

Though there are frequent allusions to his former military service, Principal Skinner is consistently portrayed as a disempowered, impoverished bureaucrat who lives with (and under the thumb of) his meddlesome, overbearing mother, and who is desperate but ultimately unable to meet Superintendent Chalmers's expectations of his competence as principal of Springfield Elementary. It is rare that Skinner defends himself against attacks by his mother or his boss – or, later, his girlfriend, Edna Krabappel. Therefore, to witness him so suddenly and effectively deliver the blows of justice to Disney's lawyer and goons is to read the message encoded in his actions: until this moment, and despite many frustrations and opportunities, Skinner has never lost control and behaved violently toward his tormentors.

Thus, Disney's legal persuasions have crossed a line that inspired a generally controlled but disenfranchised man to exercise military-grade violence. He has also done so effectively; though Disney approached him with the overt threat of a lawsuit and, in the presence of the goons, the covert threat of bodily harm in the event of non-compliance, the proverbial little guy stood up for himself and won. Once again, the David-and-Goliath allegory applies to the *Simpsons'* take on Disney. On the DVD commentary for this episode, Al Jean confirms the show's determination to wake the sleeping giant. He recalls, "every third show we joke about Disney. We did this and they never said anything, so we just got more bold as the series went along."

The first in-depth take on Disney theme parks appears in the fourth-season episode "Selma's Choice", when, while contemplating starting a family on her own, Marge's sister Selma takes Bart and Lisa to Duff Gardens when Homer is too sick to take the children himself.[22] Conceptually, the park is a parody of Busch Gardens, Tampa: the absurdity that a beer company would operate a theme park, particularly one targeted to young people, is herein made ever so apparent. But aesthetically – with the exception of the prominent peak roller coaster in the skyline – Duff Gardens is a Disney doppelganger. With the distinguished (but, in this case, modest) castle just beyond the turnstiles at the entrance, Duff Gardens is dominantly Disney. To greet guests just on the other side of those turnstiles are the seven Duffs: men in adult-sized beer bottle costumes who embody the trait encapsulated in their names. In this episode, we only get to see the first four: Tipsy, Queasy, Surly, and Remorseful; just as Disney named his dwarfs according to their personalities, *The Simpsons* have named their Duffs. How ludicrous that these most egregious symptoms of drunkenness have become lovable mascot heroes to the children who visit – yet another commentary on the appropriateness of a beer company as theme park proprietors. "The Beer Hall of Presidents", in which an animatronic Abraham Lincoln (based, of course, on Disneyland's "Great Moments with Mr. Lincoln" exhibit) raps lyrical on the virtues of Duff Beer. To Lisa, and to all who bear witness, it is a disgrace.

The first ride we see the trio embark upon is also its last as a unit. It is a stunning caricature of the famed Disney theme park offering, "It's a Small World", a boat ride through shallow water that takes passengers through a colourful gallery of animatronic figures (representative of a great many nations) singing and moving in time to the very repetitive eponymous song. The aesthetics of the original (the scale, the colours, the graphics, the dolls' appearance, the music, the shape of the boat, even the red-and-white striped poles) have been meticulously reproduced in painstaking detail. Only in the *Simpsons* version, the figures are clearly children, still organised according to continents and dressed in traditional cultural dress from around the world, but each holding (and alternately swigging from) a bottle of Duff beer. The repetitive song they sing and move in time to: "Duff beer for me / Duff beer for you / I'll have a Duff / You have one, too / Duff beer for me ..."

Based on a story rumoured to have happened to *Simpsons* writer Kevin Curran (in which he drank the water surrounding the Pirates of the Caribbean boats and was delirious for the following three days), Lisa is forced to drink the water on this ride as a result of Selma's exasperated and misguided attempt at parental compromise and, as a result, winds up hallucinating.[23] Selma shortly loses track of both children; in her intoxicated state, Lisa wanders right into the Duff Gardens parade, an obvious send-up of the on-again-off-again (if you will) Main Street Electrical Parade, whose music the Simpsons writer David Stern found particularly irritating and which he and director Carlos Baeza were keen on capturing. The resulting parodic tune by Alf Clausen is virtually indistinguishable from the original, and the sparkling floats whose presence it announces include a scale version of the Duff blimp, a mug of beer being filled by a Duff tap, an American flag featuring the words "DRINK DUFF BEER", and the Statue of Liberty guzzling a Duff. The day at Duff Gardens ends when Selma is reunited with the children; Lisa is the last to return to the security building, having been found swimming naked in the Fermentarium. She is subsequently provided with a handful of pills produced from the pockets of a lab coat worn by someone who confidently assures Selma that he is not a doctor. Following her experience at Duff Gardens, Selma decides to focus her maternal energy on Jub-Jub, the unwanted iguana her mother inherited from her recently-deceased Aunt.

Itchy and Scratchy: That Happy Cat Teams up with a Psychotic Young Mouse

Before we visit The Violentest Place on Earth, it would be prudent to take a moment to discuss an important distinction in *The Simpsons'* treatment of

Disney: the difference between the notions of parody and pastiche. Piecing together notions of pastiche from the works of Linda Hutcheon and Frederic Jameson, along with the use of the term in the vernacular offered by Ingeborg Hoesterey, pastiche could be defined as an imitative celebration of a given text – one devoid of the biting satire or critique that is present in parody.[24] While it can be perceived as a lovingly-crafted replica of the original text, Frederic Jameson sees it as "a neutral practice" of the mimicry of parody, "devoid of laughter".[25] (In fact, Jameson sees all postmodern parody as pastiche, an impotent and ineffective form of imitation.)

The more positive spin on the term is bolstered by Hoesterey's etymological investigation of the word's derivation. Pastiche is a notion rooted in the Italian concept of "pasticcio", a type of pâté whose name was borrowed by the art scene of the Renaissance to describe paintings of dubious value that synthesised the styles of multiple artists, created with deceptive intentions.[26] The word took on a positive (and French) spin when it was adopted by turn-of-the-18th-century music enthusiasts and the operetti they patronised, and briefly enjoyed a new branding by Proust in the early 20th century as a receptive activity rather than a productive one, similar to the intertextual work performed by Kristeva's spectator.[27] However, within the common discourse, the productive concept of pastiche prevails, along with the positive spin; pastiche in the vernacular is a device used to incorporate traits from two of its closest relatives, parody and homage, to form a light-hearted celebration of its object. Parody diverges from pastiche at the point of celebration; while parody can be inspired by an admiration and affection for its textual object, it is characterised by a definitively critical element. In place of the adoration that might be detected in pastiche of a given text, parody offers a satirical perspective of the text that might expose unfavourable traits thereof.

When considering these perceptions of pastiche with respect to its use in *The Simpsons*, it is difficult to reconcile the show's clever takes on and adaptations of Disney history, practice and cultural impact with the absence of humour Jameson observes in pastiche and postmodern parody. Granted, Jameson was writing in 1991; perhaps he had somehow missed the first season of the series. Jameson's taste (and access to the Fox terrestrial channel in its early days) aside, what is crucial for this chapter is that there is a distinction between pastiche and parody, and that this distinction can be found at the site of intent: the sniping element of parody (similar to that of satire) and the celebratory nature of pastiche (similar to that of homage) are aspects of both the method and the objective of mimicry.

In their versions of the Disney theme parks, we find *The Simpsons* at their most parodic. We can locate the crossover to pastiche – and back again –

in the show within the show: *Itchy & Scratchy*. While the theme park Itchy and Scratchy Land is almost entirely on the side of parody, in the fourth season, *Simpsons* creators began to develop the story behind *The Itchy & Scratchy Show* – and, as has been made clear with considerable effort, they borrowed heavily from the history of Disney.

This is most easily observed in a scene of the sixth episode of the fourth season, "Itchy & Scratchy: The Movie", in which Bart and Lisa watch a report by Channel Six news anchor Kent Brockman on another Channel Six series, *Eye on Springfield*. In his report, in anticipation of the Itchy and Scratchy movie's enormous premiere that evening (for which mega-fan Bart has bought tickets well in advance), and in recognition of the associated "Itchy and Scratchy mania", Brockman provides a retrospective look at Itchy and Scratchy's long history.[28] It is worth noting that the *Eye on Springfield* story's scene opens with a strong self-parody: "a first-hand look at how American cartoons are made" which depicts the slavery-like conditions of a Korean animation studio.[29] During Brockman's introduction, the camera pans across a crowded, windowless, rat-infested animation studio in which exhausted and flagging Korean animators are kept awake by uniformed overseers who prod them with bayonets. This scene provides the backdrop for Brockman throughout his report. According to those providing commentary on the DVD, the animators at the series' own animation studio, Rough Draft Korea, were so offended by the parody that overseas animation supervisor and studio creator Gregg Vanzo initially refused to do the work.[30]

Brockman's show-within-the-show history of Itchy and Scratchy begins in 1928 with the very first Scratchy cartoon, *That Happy Cat*, in which a black-and-white anthropomorphic cat, drawn in a very similar style to silent-era rubber-hose animals (e.g. large, elliptical black pupils with a lack of delineation around the whites of the eyes, ropey extremities, white-gloved hands), walks down a city street, smiling, then whistling a tune and pausing at the end to tip his fedora at the audience. "The film did very poorly", says Brockman. "But the following year [1929], Scratchy was teamed up with a psychotic young mouse named Itchy, and cartoon history was made". It is at this point that *Steamboat Itchy* appears.

This short film-within-the-series is a very meticulous, carefully-crafted recreation of the aforementioned early Disney masterpiece, *Steamboat Willie*. Animator Rich Morin confirms that the backgrounds for the sequence are hand-painted, as opposed to the usual cel backgrounds used in the series, and the animals in the foreground are a close match to the style of Disney's first rendition of Mickey Mouse (and the rest of the menagerie aboard his vessel). The fidelity of *Steamboat Itchy* to the object of its mimicry is nearly frame-for-frame in some parts, opening with a whistling Itchy, dressed just as Mickey is in the original (buttoned short pants, white shoes, a tall engineer's cap) and whistling a similar sort of tune, and cutting to a wide shot of the boat, whose two smoke stacks coil and expand in rhythm. Cutting back to the deck with Itchy at the wheel, he is approached by Scratchy (dressed identically to the large, bullying cat-like figure from *Steamboat Willie*, later named Pegleg Pete), who picks up the tune Itchy had been whistling earlier as an apparent gesture of friendship and comradery. When Scratchy tips his hat, however, Itchy brandishes a machine gun and shoots Scratchy's kneecaps out. Bleeding profusely, Scratchy crawls around the deck with his eyes wrenched shut, crying in agony. Itchy takes advantage of Scratchy's unawareness that he is headed straight for the boat's coal oven and opens its door. When, in crawling forward, Scratchy puts his head through the open oven door, Itchy slams it shut, and Scratchy's body writhes and twitches until it is stilled by death. Itchy then opens the door and props the corpse up so its smoking, charred skull is just above his own head and utters his implied tagline of the time, "Oh me, oh my!" The short closes with an iris, followed by a title card in the style of that which concludes *Steamboat Willie* (albeit with minor allusions to the *Tom and Jerry* title cards of the 1940s, another series to which Itchy and Scratchy implicitly refer) – though the *Itchy & Scratchy* one contains the vindicating reminder: "PASSED BY NATIONWIDE BOARD OF RE-VIEW. Thus, the foundation of the cycle of violence that occurs in every *Itchy & Scratchy* short is laid: the vicious Itchy and the naïve, sweet Scratchy encounter one another and Itchy – whose exact beef with the cat is yet unknown – enacts unspeakable violence upon his nemesis.

The manifold uses of the ultra-violent *Itchy & Scratchy* cartoons in *The Simpsons* are well-articulated by Robert Sloane:

> The Simpsons has often used *Itchy & Scratchy* […] as a vehicle for commenting on the production of television shows […] generally and the state of *The Simpsons* specifically. In an episode from the second season ("Itchy & Scratchy & Marge"), Marge goes on a crusade to ban violent cartoons from television. Airing in December of 1990, when Simpson-mania was either at or approaching its peak, the episode appeared to be a direct reference to criticisms of the show (and of Bart in particular) for providing bad role models. Other episodes deal with plagiarism in animation ("The Day the Violence Died"), and/or contain references to Disney iconography ("Itchy & Scratchy Land").[31]

The violence in *Itchy & Scratchy* therefore addresses several topics frequently raised in the context of *The Simpsons* and of animation as a whole. Though *Steamboat Itchy*'s subversion through its extreme brutality of our generic expectations of the early Disney shorts takes this scene close to parody, as one prolific *Simpsons* fan-blogger has pointed out, it is "not that 'Steamboat Willie' is exactly pacific. Mickey tortures the [expletive] out of a bunch of animals in his lust for the perfect rendition of 'Turkey in the Straw'".[32] The author usefully draws attention to the fact that when modern cartoons come under fire for racy or violent content, they are often unfavourably compared to their more wholesome or innocent early counterparts, but that such a comparison overlooks the provocative content present in some (indeed, one might argue *many*) early animated works. While the extreme violence in *Steamboat Itchy* clearly far outweighs that in *Steamboat Willie*, beyond being a total subversion of an innocent original text, there is perhaps some acknowledgment and reflection in *Steamboat Itchy* of the cartoon violence that is usually omitted from the nostalgic Disney narrative.

The second scene-within-the-scene is a pastiche of a number of studios, Disney included, that were producing propaganda, informational, and educational shorts during World War II as part of Hollywood's contributions to the American war effort. The short film in question depicts Itchy and Scratchy who, having agreed an unprecedented truce, are instead focusing their violent impulses upon Adolf Hitler. Their look has evolved, somewhat in accordance with Mickey's, but (especially with Scratchy's noticeably yellow eyes) bearing perhaps more similarity to Hanna and Barbera's Tom and Jerry, the cat-and-mouse duo whose own animated shorts first appeared in 1940.

In conformance with the notion of pastiche as defined above, while having fun with the styles and conventions of *The Simpsons'* early animated forbears, nothing in either scene actually ridicules or offers any perceptible criticisms of Disney or any of the other studios referenced within. Rather, in painstakingly creating or recreating golden-era cartoons, *Simpsons* creators claim for *Itchy & Scratchy* a history, longevity, and sustained cultural relevance equal in the fictional *Simpsons* world to Disney's own in our real one.

The Violentest Place on Earth

Where *Simpsons* creators truly straddle the pastiche/parody line is in the season six episode "Itchy & Scratchy Land". According to then-showrunner David Mirkin, this episode was written in reaction to Fox censors, who told him that they had received complaints that the *Itchy & Scratchy* sequences were too violent, and that *The Simpsons* would have to stop producing them.[33] Mirkin was incensed and demanded to see the complaints, which Fox could not produce – because, Mirkin concludes, there weren't any. Mirkin promised the network they would do an entire episode devoted to the combative duo, to an "Itchy & Scratchy Land", and he and staff writer John Swartzwelder then set to work on it.

According to Mirkin, the network pursued them heavily throughout the process, stating that Fox's standards with respect to content had changed and that, therefore, the network was unwilling to accommodate the levels of violence that were previously deemed acceptable. Mirkin responded that

The Simpsons' standards had not changed, and that they would be proceeding with production on the episode. When the network threatened to cut it, Mirkin responded by threatening to go to the press with his side of the story; he contends that this ultimatum forced the network to back down, and Mirkin then acceded that he would be careful about the amounts of violence and blood in the final product.

From the grand entrance of Itchy & Scratchy Land to the Itchy & Scratchy Money (like Disney Dollars, except that it is purchased on admission for the customers to discover it is not accepted anywhere in the park), to Parents' Island (an obvious take on Pleasure Island and featuring similar offerings to its inspiration), to the gift shops peddling themed souvenirs, accessories, clothing, plush versions of obscure characters (such as Disgruntled Goat, Uncle Ant, and Ku Klux Klam), to another run at the Main Street Electrical Parade (especially the music, in which Mirkin, like Reiss and Stern were before him, was aiming for "a piece of music that, in its repetition, would start to drive you insane in less than two minutes") – every element of Itchy & Scratchy Land is a parody of the Disney theme parks.

The parody reaches its peak at the park's old-time theatre, where the Roger Meyers Story plays, just as the Walt Disney Story did at the Main Street Opera House at Disneyland. Here the audience is told, in very similar language to that used to describe Walt Disney, that Meyers was the "gentle genius behind Itchy & Scratchy". Parody does not yet cross into pastiche, when we learn that Meyers "cared about almost all the peoples of the world" and, in 1938, "was criticised for his controversial cartoon *Nazi Supermen Are Our Superiors*".[34] These are clear references to Walt Disney's persistently-rumoured but unconfirmed anti-Semitism and racism, and it is not surprising that these particular authors have proliferated these particular rumours. In fact, they laid the groundwork one season earlier when, in "The Boy Who Knew Too Much", Springfield's Dr. Hibbert testified that, along with Hitler and Freddy Quimby, Walt Disney had the "evil gene".[35]

Connected to the cynicism of postmodern thought is the inclination toward conspiracy theory. Slavoj Žižek and Frederic Jameson both observe a type of cynical paranoia emergent from the general distrust in institutions and individuals.[36] *The Simpsons* authors have painstakingly recreated the idealised version of life – and of Walt Disney – that visitors encounter at the Disney parks, but in order to unmask the dark truths concealed within. Walt Disney's idealism, especially when coupled with his interest in new technology, offer tantalising prey for experts at lampooning. For example, *Simpsons* writers incorporated the pervasive rumours about Walt Disney's cryonic state into Roger Meyers Senior's story. In a particularly dark scene of the season 7 episode "The Day the Violence Died", present-day Itchy &

Scratchy Studios head Roger Meyers Jr, son of studio founder Roger Meyers Sr, is bankrupted by an $800 billion lawsuit that posthumously exposes his father as a plagiarist (and a homeless man named Chester J. Lampwick as the true creator of Itchy the mouse). When Bart and Lisa grow desperate in the absence of their favourite show, they approach Meyers Jr., who now runs the front desk of a slum hotel, to beg him to pay royalties to Lampwick so he can keep producing *Itchy & Scratchy*. To this request, an angry, embittered Meyers responds, "Royalties? Ha! I don't have the money to produce the cartoons. I lost everything. I can't even keep my dad's head in the freakin' cryogenic centre anymore." The camera zooms out to reveal a polystyrene cooler whose contents are clearly thawing. Meyers turns to address the cooler, asking, "Ya comfortable in there, Daddy?" Roger Meyers Sr. apparently shared Disney's modernist love for and faith in technology and its promise – and Walt Disney's rumoured posthumous state – only Meyers Sr. took it a step further by having only his head preserved for future resurrection.

It is worth entertaining the thought that perhaps *The Simpsons* are not only satirising Walt Disney's dichotomous images, but also the conspiratorial hunger that proliferates these perceptions.

Walt Disney's interest in efficiency and ingenuity can be observed both above and below ground at Walt Disney World; it led to the construction of Walt Disney World's Utilidors atop which sits the visible part of the park. Unfortunately, their precise purpose – to hide the aesthetically unappealing and inconvenient aspects of such an undertaking that are necessary to run a perfect park – gives them a great deal of conspiratorial appeal. Requiring a vehicle to navigate them efficiently, the Itchy & Scratchy Land version is vast, boasting four basement levels, a control centre, the robot repair centre, the park's detention centre – and, as Marge rather unpleasantly discovers, a hole to crawl into and die, to which the guards are more than happy to escort her upon her rhetorical request.

Due to a small mathematical error on the part of the chief artificial intelligence engineer on site (resident Springfield scientist-about-town Professor John Frink who, in this circumstance, forgot to carry the one in part of his calculation), the animatronic Itchy & Scratchy robots patrolling the park turn their violence on the humans just as the Simpsons emerge from the Utilidors. Helicopter evacuations are under way, but because Bart and Homer spent the day tormenting the Itchy & Scratchy mascots, one such mascot kicks the family off the ladder, sealing their doom on the island. Once the Simpsons realise that bright, flashing lights render the robots immobile, Bart smashes the windows of the gift shops and steals the disposable cameras in order to exploit their flashes, thus saving the family. Marge, who at the beginning of the episode had expressed concern that this vacation would be a disaster, wound up acknowledging that – despite the close call – this was the family's best vacation to date, completed with the taking of hundreds of photos together.

The theme parks as reconceived in *Simpsons* style offer a substantially more complex and overt glimpse at their perceptions of Walt Disney, his films, and his company. Even the "small school carnival" discussed earlier provides some of the most biting criticisms of the company's litigiousness. Duff Gardens requires that we consider the educational value, integrity and overall appeal of audio-animatronic versions both of long-dead (and some living) former presidents and of tiny people representing the world's nations through a tremendously repetitive song (no one appears to enjoy the latter ride, and Bart is downright uneasy). Through the Itchy & Scratchy money gag, Parents' Island, and the gift shops carrying special collectors' items, "Itchy & Scratchy Land" takes an unflinching look at the consumerist aspects of theme parks – although it is prudent to note that the gift shops provide a lifesaving solution to the otherwise-doomed family.

Having taken this close reading of the challenging side of *Simpson*-flavoured parody, I will conclude with three uplifting moments of *Simpsons*-affirming pastiche. While the audience learns some chilling information about Roger Meyers, Sr. in his biopic, we are also made aware that he was immensely proud of his two films *Scratchtasia*, and *Pinitchyo*. In the scenes of each included in Roger Meyers Sr.'s biopic, the *Simpsons* creatives demonstrate their deep love of Disney films. Stylistically – from the colour palettes of each to the details to the increased quality of the animation – these echo the originals perfectly. Though these films have obviously once again thwarted the generic expectations of their predecessors, we laugh only because the Itchy-and-Scratchy violence injected into each is in such stark contrast to the otherwise artful and faithful re-creations of their muses. In this circumstance, we are not asked to laugh at the original works, but rather at their modern Simpsonian cousins.

Conclusion

This chapter has touched and elaborated upon only a tiny handful of the countless references to Disney that have been made in the series since its beginning. The objective here has been to examine the motivations and methods driving the tendency, according to showrunner Al Jean, for *Simpsons*' creators to do a Disney joke "every third show". Admiration and affection are easily observed in the above examples, particularly with respect to the cinematic history of the Itchy & Scratchy studios. Critiques begin to appear with the theme parks, which include Itchy & Scratchy Studios' (fraudulent) founder's own biography. Herein lies the parody/pastiche distinction in action: the films offer pastiche while, in their propensity toward darkness and even uncertainty, the theme parks fall clearly into the parody category. The send-ups of Walt Disney himself only slightly tip the scales toward the parody side. While both pastiche and parody are exercises of a postmodern artist, the parodies of Walt Disney himself most clearly betray *Simpsons* creatives' postmodern preoccupations with modern idealism.

Importantly, while postmodern takes on modern idealism have inspired both loving pastiche and biting parody, the Disney Company is forever evolving and expanding. Now that the company has acquired Lucasfilm, Marvel, and – in March 2019 – 21st Century Fox (and, in doing so, *The Simpsons* themselves), parodies of their products are now once and future Disney parodies.[37] This, in conjunction with *The Simpsons'* own longevity, provides a vast wealth of future fodder for our postmodern satirists.

Bibliography

Alberti, John (Editor), *Leaving Springfield: The Simpsons and the Possibility of Oppositional Culture* (Detroit: Wayne State University Press, 2004).

Baudrillard, Jean (transl. Sheila Faria Glaser), *Simulacra and Simulation* (Ann Arbor: The University of Michigan Press, 1994).

Crafts, Nick. "The Industrial Revolution: Economic Growth in Britain, 1700 – 1860", *ReFRESH* (Spring, 4, 1987), 1 – 4. http://www.ehs.org.uk/dotAsset/15457c19-e7bd-4045-a056-30a3efac2d47.pdf

Eco, Umberto (transl. William Weaver), *Travels in Hyperreality* (London: Harcourt, 1986).

Hoesterey, Ingeborg. *Pastiche: Cultural Memory in Art, Film, Literature* (Indianapolis: Indiana University Press, 2001).

Hutcheon, Linda. *A Poetics of Postmodernism: History, Theory, Fiction* (New York: Routledge, Taylor and Francis e-Library, 2004. First published 1988), 26.

Hutcheon, Linda. *A Theory of Parody: The Teachings of Twentieth-Century Arts Forms* (Chicago: University of Illinois Press, 2000).

Jameson, Frederic. *Postmodernism, or, the Cultural Logic of Late Capitalism.* (Durham: Duke University Press, 1991).

Smoodin, Eric (Editor), *Disney Discourse: Producing the Magic Kingdom* (New York: Routledge, 1994).

Sweatpants, Charlie. "compare& contrast: disney, the simpsons, & zombie simpsons" (*Dead Homer Society*, 02 December 2010): https://deadhomersociety.com/tag/fantasia/.

Witcombe, Christopher L.C.E. "Modernism: An illustrated study in five chapters", 2000, first accessed 17 July 2014, http://arthistoryresources.net/modernism/modpostmod.html.

Zizek, Slavoj. "The Big Other Doesn't Exist", *Journal of European Psychoanalysis* 5 (Spring-Fall 1997): http://www.psychomedia.it/jep/number5/zizek.htm.

Audio/Video

DVD commentary for *The Simpsons*, "Old Money" (1991), Fox Broadcasting Company, DVD (2002).

DVD Commentary for *The Simpsons*, "Itchy & Scratchy: The Movie" (1992), Fox Broadcasting Company, DVD (2004).

DVD Commentary for *The Simpsons*, "Selma's Choice" (1993), Fox Broadcasting Company, DVD (2004).

DVD Commentary for *The Simpsons*, "Itchy & Scratchy Land" (1994), Fox Broadcasting Company, DVD (2005).

Filmography

The Simpsons, "Old Money", directed by David Silverman, written by Jay Kogen and Wallace Wolodarsky, 28 March 1991, Fox Broadcasting Company, DVD (2002).

The Simpsons, "Lisa the Beauty Queen", directed by Mark Kirkland, written by Al Jean and Mike Reiss, 15 October 1992, Fox Broadcasting Company, DVD (2004).

The Simpsons, "Itchy & Scratchy: The Movie", directed by Rich Moore, written by John Swartzwelder, 3 November, 1992, Fox Broadcasting Company, DVD (2004).

The Simpsons, "Selma's Choice", directed by Carlos Baeza, written by David M. Stern, 21 January 1993, Fox Broadcasting Company, DVD (2004).

The Simpsons, "The Boy Who Knew Too Much", directed by Jeffrey Lynch, Written by John Swartzwelder, 5 May 1994, Fox Broadcasting Company, DVD (2005).

Steamboat Willie, directed by Walt Disney and Ub Iwerks, 1928. Burbank, California: Disney Brothers Studio. Walt Disney Animation Studio, 27 August 2009. Accessed 6 June 2014. https://www.youtube.com/watch?v=BBgghnQF6E4

Endnotes

1. Christopher L.C.E. Witcombe, "Modernism: An illustrated study in five chapters", 2000, first accessed 17 July 2014, http://arthistoryresources.net/modernism/modpostmod.html.

2. Nick Crafts, "The Industrial Revolution: Economic Growth in Britain, 1700–1860", *ReFRESH* (Spring, 4, 1987), 1–4. http://www.ehs.org.uk/dotAsset/15457c19-e7bd-4045-a056-30a3efac2d47.pdf

3. Witcombe, "Modernism: An illustrated study in five chapters"

4. Linda Hutcheon, *A Poetics of Postmodernism: History, Theory, Fiction* (New York: Routledge, Taylor and Francis e-Library, 2004. First published 1988), 26.

5. John Alberti, "Introduction" in *Leaving Springfield: The Simpsons and the Possibility of Oppositional Culture*, ed. John Alberti (Detroit: Wayne State University Press, 2004), xx.

6. Jean Baudrillard (transl. Sheila Faria Glaser), *Simulacra and Simulation* (Ann Arbor: The University of Michigan Press, 1994), print, 12.

7. Umberto Eco (transl. William Weaver), *Travels in Hyperreality* (London: Harcourt, 1986), print, 44.

8. Ibid, 48.

9. Baudrillard, *Simulacra*, 12.

10. Paul Hollister, "Genius at Work", *Disney Discourse: Producing the Magic Kingdom* (Eric Smoodin, ed., New York: Routledge, 1994, print), 23–41. See also Walter Wanger, "Film Phenomena", *Disney Discourse*, 42–43. See also Walter Wanger, "Mickey Icarus 1943: Fusing Ideas with the Art of the Animated Cartoon", *Disney Discourse*, 44–47. See also Robert De Roos, "The Magical Worlds of Walt Disney", *Disney Discourse*, 48–68.

11. Eric Smoodin, "Introduction: How to Read Walt Disney", *Disney Discourse*, 1–5.

12. Ibid, 3.

13. Ibid.

14. Robert De Roos, "The Magic Worlds of Walt Disney" in *Disney Discourse: Producing the Magic Kingdom*, ed. Eric Smoodin (London: Routledge, 1994), 52–55, 61.

15. *Steamboat Willie*, directed by Walt Disney and Ub Iwerks, 1928. Burbank, California: Disney Brothers Studio. Walt Disney Animation Studio, 27August 2009. Accessed 6 June 2014. https://www.youtube.com/watch?v=BBgghnQF6E4

16. Witcombe, "Modernism: An illustrated study in five chapters".

17. *The Simpsons*, "Old Money", directed by David Silverman, written by Jay Kogen and Wallace Wolodarsky, 28 March 1991, Fox Broadcasting Company, DVD (2002).

18. Matt Groening, DVD commentary for *The Simpsons*, "Old Money", Fox Broadcasting Company, DVD (2002).

19. The series' creatives, and Groening in particular, have made multiple overt attempts to provoke the infamously legally aggressive Fox network into pursuing legal action against them. In several interviews Groening has ardently contended – and Fox representatives have steadfastly denied – that the network threatened legal action against the series (*ipso facto* against itself) after derisive comments about Fox news were made in an episode, including with the use of a satirical news crawl. Groening claims that, though Fox ultimately did not make good on their threats to sue, but that the series was banned from using news crawls again lest audience members believe them to be real. A full discussion of this incident can be found in Jemma Gilboy, "Craptacular Science and the Worst Audience Ever: Memetic Proliferation and Fan Participation in *The Simpsons*" (PhD Thesis, University of Hull, 2016, pp. 209–216).

20. See Jay Kogen, Mike Reiss and Conan O'Brien, "'The Simpsons' Writers Reunion" (*Serious Jibber Jabber with Conan O'Brien*, 25 April 2013), accessed 26 April 2013: http://team-coco.com/video/simpsons-serious-jibber-jabber?playlist=x;eyJ0eXBlIjoiZXRhZyIsImlkIjoz OTIwNH0.

21. *The Simpsons*, "Lisa the Beauty Queen", directed by Mark Kirkland, written by Al Jean and Mike Reiss, 15 October 1992, Fox Broadcasting Company, DVD (2004).

22. *The Simpsons*, "Selma's Choice", directed by Carlos Baeza, written by David M. Stern, 21 January 1993, Fox Broadcasting Company, DVD (2004).

23. [Speaker could not be determined from among] Matt Groening, Al Jean, Jim Reardon, Mike Reiss, and David M. Stern, DVD Commentary for *The Simpsons*, "Selma's Choice", Fox Broadcasting Company, DVD (2004).

24. Linda Hutcheon, *A Theory of Parody: The Teachings of Twentieth-Century Arts Forms* (Chicago: University of Illinois Press, 2000), 37–39. See also Linda Hutcheon, *A Poetics of Postmodernism: History, Theory, Fiction. Electronic ed.* New York: Routledge, Taylor and Francis e-Library, 2004.

25. Frederic Jameson, *Postmodernism, or, the Cultural Logic of Late Capitalism.* (Durham: Duke University Press, 1991), 17.

26. Ingeborg Hoesterey, *Pastiche: Cultural Memory in Art, Film, Literature* (Indianapolis: Indiana University Press, 2001), 1–5.

27. Hoesterey, 9.

28. *The Simpsons*, "Itchy & Scratchy: The Movie", directed by Rich Moore, written by John Swartzwelder, 3 November 1992, Fox Broadcasting Company, DVD (2004).

29. Ibid.

30. Al Jean, DVD Commentary for *The Simpsons*, "Itchy & Scratchy: The Movie", Fox Broadcasting Company, DVD (2004).

31. Robert Sloane, "Who Wants Candy? Disenchantment in *The Simpsons*" (*Leaving Springfield: The Simpsons and the Possibility of Oppositional Culture*, John Alberti (ed.), Detroit: Wayne State University Press, 2004), 143.

32. Charlie Sweatpants, "compare& contrast: disney, the simpsons, & zombie simpsons" (*Dead Homer Society*, 2 December 2010): https://deadhomersociety.com/tag/fantasia/.

33. David Merkin, DVD Commentary for *The Simpsons*, "Itchy & Scratchy Land" (episode directed by Wes Archer, written by John Swartzwelder, 2 October 1994, Fox Broadcasting Company, DVD [2005]).

34. It is worth noting that, if Roger Meyers Sr had indeed created such a film in 1938, he would, right around the same time, have contradicted that message with the *Itchy & Scratchy* propaganda short discussed earlier, which depicts both main characters beating and killing Adolf Hitler, whose corpse then receives further abuse from a fully-able President Franklin D. Roosevelt in the background while in the foreground Scratchy holds a picket urging audience members to "SAVE SCRAP IRON!"

35. *The Simpsons*, "The Boy Who Knew Too Much", directed by Jeffrey Lynch, Written by John Swartzwelder, 5 May 1994, Fox Broadcasting Company, DVD (2005).

36. Slavoj Zizek, "The Big Other Doesn't Exist", *Journal of European Psychoanalysis* 5 (Spring – Fall 1997): http://www.psychomedia.it/jep/number5/zizek.htm. See also Jamieson, *Postmodernism, or, the Cultural Logic of Late Capitalism*, 37.

37. For more on this, see Cynthia Littleton and Brian Steinberg, "Disney to Buy 21st Century Fox Assets for $52.4 Billion in Historic Hollywood Merger". *Variety.com*, 14 December 2017, http://variety.com/2017/biz/news/disney-fox-merger-deal-52-4-billion-merger-1202631 242/. Amusingly (and relevantly), the story is illustrated by a cartoony image of Mickey Mouse's hand capturing by the ankles 3 characters owned by Fox, the central character in the image being Homer Simpson.

Chapter 12

Disney Pluralism: Beyond Disney-Formalism

Chris Pallant

You couldn't make it up. Useless so called 'academics' at a useless 'university'. What a waste of money. Sack all of them and let them try and make a living in the real world not fairy tale Disneyworld [*sic*].[1]
'V' (online comment)

On May 12, 2015, the University of East Anglia staged an event called 'Symfrozium'. As you may have guessed from the title (or maybe you were also there), this event was a symposium dedicated to the interrogation of Disney's *Frozen* (2013) from a range of different perspectives. As with any other academic event, the organisers, Su Holmes and Sarah Godfrey, publicised widely across numerous academic-specific forums and mailing lists (including those managed by the British Association of Film, Television and Screen Studies; the Fan Studies Network; the Media, Communication and Cultural Studies Association; and the Society for Animation Studies), on social media (Facebook and Twitter), and via UEA's own blog. There is nothing remarkable about this approach; however, the event's playfully-constructed title captured the popular imagination in a way that most academic events do not – and responses were decidedly mixed. The quotation at the start of this chapter is emblematic of the more extreme and negative reactions to this event. While the responses in general follow a largely predictable pattern, they raise an important question: in what ways does 'Disney' mean different things to different people?

It is with this mixed response in mind that I sat down to write this chapter. While this chapter shares the same title as the Keynote paper that I presented at the Discussing Disney conference at the University of Hull in September 2014, it is fair to say that, given the activity described above, the thrust of this chapter represents a necessary evolution from the ideas presented in Hull. Pleasingly, this natural shift in focus actually serves to align my chapter more closely with the titular ambition of this collection: not only to discuss Disney, but also to consider the ways in which various, pluralist frameworks, when applied to Disney discourse, might serve to expand such discussions in a positive fashion.

My use of the term pluralism (and its variant forms) in this chapter is not an attempt to hook into the existing critical frameworks that exist in the political sciences, stemming primarily from Robert A. Dahl's work in the 1960s, which is concerned with what he perceived to be a particularly pluralistic mode of democracy that existed in the United States.[2] With the unwieldy scale of contemporary 'Disney' in mind, my use of pluralism in this chapter is intended to foreground the fact that what 'Disney' was/is/means is not defined by any one individual – whether that is The Walt Disney Company or an online commentator going by the pseudonym 'V'. As we continue through a period of scholarly upheaval, where the meaningfulness and funding of Arts and Humanities is increasingly defined via metrics conceived for – and far better suited to – STEM subject areas, scholars committed to the study of 'Disney' as an object of significant historical and cultural importance need to continually re-evaluate how they frame and communicate this work. With this in mind, this chapter does not seek to reveal a universal truth, but rather to re-articulate the richly pluralist entity that 'Disney' is, both in terms of how we view Disney, and also in the ways that Disney has adopted various pluralist production agendas. It is clear that a chapter of this length can only scratch the surface in this regard, so, as a matter of priority, we will start by reflecting on competing popular and scholarly visions of 'Disney', including an analysis of those popular responses provoked by the Symfrozium event, followed by an brief evaluation of the merits of the scholarly notion of Disney-Formalism. The remainder of the chapter seeks to reveal the importance of pluralist activity within Disney's evolving production contexts, and how it can be seen to have informed: the development of the storyboard in the 1930s, the development of the *Disneyland* television series in the 1950s, and the self-reflexively pluralist register that is evident in the recent short *Get a Horse!* (2013).

Popular Voices: Symfrozium

At the time of writing there are 73 unique tweets when searching '#Symfrozium' on Twitter. On the whole, these tweets are positive, with many users who do not identify as being academics adopting a fan-orientated rhetoric to advertise how 'cool' and 'brilliant' this event will be; there are also a number of users that do identify as academics (myself included) that adopt a similar register when commenting on the event.[3] James Welker, who writes of a specialism in cultural studies on his Twitter profile, playfully notes: 'Did my best to ignore #Frozen. Turns out worthy of serious study!', before including a link to the notice about the Symfrozium event posted to the Fan Studies Network.[4] To read Welker's tweet as being indicative of the attitudes of the Fan Studies Network more generally would be an over-determination, yet Welker's expression suggests a self-conscious re-negotiation of cultural capital, with his tweet indicating a Bourdieusian reaffirmation of group boundaries – in this instance, those of the Fan Studies Network and his own network of Twitter followers.[5] More straightforwardly, Welker's statement is characteristic of the unease that has historically greeted the 'serious' study of Disney – and, more broadly, animation.

By comparison, the responses offered in more traditional media forms, such as television, radio and news agencies, were less favourable. The Anglia branch of the British television broadcaster ITV took an interest and sent a news crew to the event. Several academics were interviewed on camera before the day commenced, and the cameraman even stayed for the first ten minutes of Amy Davis's opening Keynote paper, awkwardly interrupting her to ask for the first slide to be brought back up on screen so that he could 'get a close up', before leaving with the rest of the crew at approximately 9:30am. Having captured little more than a snapshot of the event (which ran until 5pm), it was hardly surprising to find that the eventual broadcast VT on the evening news that day presented the event as its light-hearted 'And Finally' piece.[6]

While the general tone of the piece is indeed light, the conclusion offers a rather loaded juxtaposition, with the dialogue from an interview with co-organiser Holmes becoming an audio bed as the visual cuts from Holmes to a clip of Anna and Kristoff's first sled ride. As this cut is made, Holmes offers the following assessment: 'I actually think it's harder to make a case *not* to study *Frozen* than to study it. If something is *that* popular and has had *that* much impact on culture we think it's worth thinking about critically and indeed seriously'.[7] Following this, the short item closes by cutting back to footage of Colman infants school, which had featured at the start of the VT, with the reporter, Malcolm Robertson, offering the following summation in voiceover: 'These four and five year olds don't take it too seriously, they just think *Frozen* is a bit of fun, very good fun'.[8] ITV's rhetoric of mutual exclusivity, which casts *Frozen* as either a tenuous object of study or a simple source of fun, was repeated by BBC's Radio 1 Breakfast Show. Also in Norwich at that time, having moved up from London for the week to promote Radio 1's 'Big Weekend', which was being staged in the city the following weekend, the Breakfast Show sent a reporter to record a similar puff piece. Holmes, who was interviewed by the Breakfast Show reporter, recalls how the questions encouraged the construction of a false binary: you can either be an academic, or a concerned parent.[9]

Newspaper responses also emerged, with *The Telegraph* and *The Daily Mail* offering national coverage, while the *Eastern Daily Press* provided a more regional perspective. The respective headlines provide a good approximation of the tone adopted in each article. Kat Brown's article in *The Telegraph*, entitled 'Norwich to host academic conference on *Frozen*', stands as the most balanced, situating the film in terms of its financial and cultural impact globally, before providing a brief thematic overview of the Symfrozium event.[10] Sam Russell's article in the *Eastern Daily Press* follows a similar path, but understandably amplifies the geographical location of this event, and also placing a greater emphasis on the role of UEA as the host institute.[11] Contrastingly, Hannah Parry's article on *The Daily Mail*'s online platform, which carries the mocking headline 'University dons to study "cultural impact" of Disney fairytale *Frozen* as Princess Elsa and Olaf the snowman make it onto the syllabus', is undermined by its inaccuracy.[12] Parry's opening line serves as an immediate marker regarding the author's lack of awareness about animation studies in the UK, as she states: 'Lectures on Disney's award-winning hit children's film *Frozen* are being offered at a British university for the first time'.[13] Given the wide array of film and animation courses on offer in UK Higher Education, combined with *Frozen*'s lasting impact over the years since its release, it would truly be surprising if the Symfrozium event was indeed the first occasion where lecturers had focussed on the film.

Most disconcerting, however, is the angry resistance to the Symfrozium-related activity that is voiced within the comments sections on both *The Daily Mail* and *Eastern Daily Press* webpages. *The Daily Mail*'s comments section contains seven unique responses, four of which present negative views concerning the Symfrozium event, two of which criticise *Frozen* on a qualitative level, and one that attempts to defend *Frozen*. The strength of negative feeling towards the Symfrozium event is more exaggerated on the *Eastern Daily Press* webpage, where respondents, self-identifying as residents of the Norwich area, voice displeasure that local money is being spent on such an event, the worst being the comment from an individual only identifiable as 'V' which opened this chapter. Such a perspective, as voiced by 'V', reveals a misunderstanding of the economics of both academic symposia and the management of university estates more broadly. In reality, the UEA event took place in a single UEA room that was not in use that day, and required no specialist equipment to be bought or installed, with the expenditure on the day limited to one round of teas, coffees, and biscuits. Free speech is welcome in the UK, and whether we choose to agree with 'V' or not (and three responses on the *Eastern Daily Press* webpage do adopt a more positive stance, arguing for a more liberal and progressive view of university activity and education), what we see here, in just this small sample of reactions to the Symfrozium event, is the degree to which

Disney remains a hotly debated subject, where a range of divergent voices share a common goal: to define Disney on *their* terms.

Scholarly Voices: Beyond Disney-Formalism

Disney's animation over the past eighty-plus years does not easily coalesce into a singular aesthetic tradition. In fact, any attempt to distil Disney's animation in such a manner is to ignore the variety of aesthetic ambitions expressed throughout the studio's long history. (This is to say nothing of the non animation-related ventures that Disney has mounted during this same period, including the building of theme parks and towns, the creation of a television network, the production of nature documentaries, and the provision of tailored wedding packages.) Disney scholarship has developed in an equally-diverse manner in response to this activity, and it is beyond the remit of this chapter (and collection) to review this rich literature in full.[14] The loosely-connected scholarly perspectives below are offered simply as a shorthand means by which to rapidly re-establish my motive for publishing the article 'Disney-Formalism: Rethinking "Classic" Disney' in 2010 – an article that set out to narrow the terms with which we discussed specific aspects of Disney animation.

Disney's animation history is a deeply pluralist history that requires each generation to make sense of this disparate oeuvre afresh. It is clear that features such as *Snow White and the Seven Dwarfs* (1937), *Pinocchio* (1940), *Dumbo* (1941) and *Bambi* (1942), which represent what Steven Watts describes as 'the creative high-watermark of the early Disney Studio',[15] alongside films such as *Beauty and the Beast* (1991) and *Princess and the Frog* (2009), represent an aesthetic extreme, with films such as *Toot, Whistle, Plunk and Boom* (1953) and Oskar Fischinger's 'Toccata and Fugue in D minor' sequence from *Fantasia* (1940) thereby representing the opposing extreme; establishing such a continuum makes it relatively easy to place productions such as the Oswald the Lucky Rabbit short *Sky Scrappers* (1928), *Destino* (2003), and *Get a Horse!* somewhere in-between.

While such a mapping is easy to construct in retrospect, during his stewardship, Disney held – and promoted – a fixed, teleological vision of the development of animation at his studio. Rather than embracing the 'plasmatic' achievements of his earlier short animation, which in Sergei Eisenstein's view offered a utopian vision of metamorphic potential at a time of increasing industrial automation and reduced social freedom,[16] Disney became obsessed with a 'solemn search for perfection'.[17] This version of perfection revolved around constructing the most believable animation possible, using any available technique (which included studying live action footage to bring added fidelity in character movement and developing their own version of the Multiplane camera to bring added depth to their landscapes).[18] However, while Disney may have wished to relegate his earlier plasmatic shorts to history, they remain an important part of the studio's story. The studio's animation does not follow a predictable evolutionary trajectory, developing from a *primitive* form to a *perfected* form. Instead, as might be expected, the studio's animation reflects the conditions of its production – recording changes in artistic taste, technological affordance, and socio-political pressure, for example.[19]

In 'Disney-Formalism: Rethinking "Classic" Disney', I set out to establish an alternative method by which to describe a particular subset of Disney feature animation that developed during the late 1930s and early 1940s.[20] The article proposed that the frequently-used shorthand 'Classic Disney' had become overdetermined, not least because of the fact that The Walt Disney Company itself had co-opted the term in the 1980s as part of a re-commodification strategy to maximise profitability when re-launching its older films on the newly debuted VHS format, but also because of how the phrase can serve as a shorthand means by which to refer to both a distinct (often early) period of Disney animation and Disney's feature animation tradition more loosely. While the article offered a solid account of the development of the expression 'Classic Disney', and also how the alternative expression 'Disney-Formalism' might be used to describe the particular hyperrealist aesthetic that prioritised believability above all else, which was forged at Disney in the wake of *Snow White and Seven Dwarfs*, the limitations of word count prevented much else. Given the public discourse presented above, which assumes as its starting point a rather one-dimensional viewpoint on Disney animation, it is useful to push beyond the relatively tight, aesthetic focus of my earlier article to place greater emphasis on other aspects of Disney production activity that resist – through their inherent plurality – the narrow visions of 'Disney' promoted in many of the popular assessments noted above (as well as my own article, albeit with good intention).

Production Pluralism: Storyboarding

Disney has played a key role in pluralising the pre-production animation environment, both in terms of facilitating a more pluralistic production process and also by taking steps to reveal this pluralism to popular audiences. In the first instance, Disney's conventionalisation of the storyboarding process in the late 1920s and early 1930s directly expanded the pluralist potential of animation production.

While the Disney studio is frequently cited as having created the storyboard form in many of the 'How To' books that describe the storyboarding process,[21] as I have discussed at length elsewhere,[22] this is a considerable oversimplification. Those individuals working at Disney were certainly not the first people to make use of visual pre-production materials, particularly of a type that today would easily be identified as storyboards, but rather their extensive and consistent use of storyboards played an important role in conventionalising the form. Given the types of animated film that Disney began to prioritise throughout the 1930s, the storyboard can also be read as symbol of the studio's shift from a reliance on individual creativity and skill to a reliance on collective endeavour.

It is well documented that the Disney studio's embryonic successes were driven by a very small group of individuals. Through the transition from being known as The Disney Brothers Studio to The Walt Disney Company, and during the production of the *Alice Comedies* (192 3–2 7) and *Oswald the Lucky Rabbit* (192 7–2 8), the brothers Walt and Roy, along with the influential animator Ub Iwerks, directly shaped this early development. The tightknit and relatively equal nature of this group is borne out in the competing stories that describe the conception of Disney's most important character, symbol, and intellectual property: Mickey Mouse. At a meeting in New York with Charles Mintz of Winkler Productions, the copyright holder of *Oswald the Lucky Rabbit*, Walt Disney learned that he was the victim of a coup. Mintz, believing that the Oswald character was something of a golden ticket, sought to knock the fledgling Disney studio out of business by taking control of the series and stealing Disney's few staff members in order to meet the production demands. In response to this, Disney suggests that he immediately got back on the front foot, claiming that during his train ride back to Los Angeles he had imagined a new character – a mouse – and that in his mind he had already 'dressed [his] dream mouse in a pair of red velvet pants with two huge pearl buttons, had composed the first scenario and was all set'.[23] Contrastingly, Dave Iwerks, son of Ub, suggests that 'Mickey was Ub's character' – although it is worth noting that this statement appears in Marc Eliot's book, *Walt Disney: Hollywood's Dark Prince* (2 003), which seeks to dismantle Walt Disney's reputation through a tactic of contesting his personal contribution to the studio's development and broad character assassination.[24] Whether it was Walt Disney or Iwerks who contributed most to the development of Mickey Mouse, it is also important to recognise that they were not working in a vacuum, and many of the 'mice that had appeared in earlier silent cartoons and the [. . .] popular Felix the Cat' clearly influenced Mickey's visual construction.[25] As John Canemaker notes, 'ear shapes distinguished one round character from another; remove pointed ears and add two long oblong ones and Felix became a Rabbit named Oswald; substitute two round circles, and Oswald begat a mouse named Mickey'.[26]

With the development of the *Mickey Mouse* (192 8–present) cartoons, demand quickly increased for animated work produced by the studio. This also led to the development of another short form series, the *Silly Symphonies* (1929–1939). On a practical level, this increase in production activity necessitated an expansion in studio staff numbers and, consequently, more efficient ways to manage collective activity than had been required when all of the key individuals (the Disney brothers and Iwerks) were working on a single project and could therefore resolve creative dilemmas with a quick face-to-face meeting. However, with Disney's increased production commitments, coupled with his feature film ambition (realised through *Snow White and the Seven Dwarfs*), story development and management became a crucial preproduction concern. These pressures, where contrasting versions of Disney animation – each reflecting different historical trajectories, with the aesthetic concerns of the short animation pointing towards Disney's recent past, and the aesthetic concerns of *Snow White and Seven Dwarfs* pointing towards Disney's immediate future – occupied the same production space, thereby encouraged a more pluralist agenda at Disney, to which the answer was the storyboard.

Although the storyboard's origin story at Disney feels more than a little apocryphal, it is also probably anchored in truth.[27] The tale goes that Walt Disney had fallen into the habit of holding meetings in Story Department member Webb Smith's office. During these meetings, Smith would rapidly sketch out the ideas approved by Disney. At the end of these meetings, Smith would then be asked to file these sketches into an appropriate order. Relatively early in this process, Smith had the idea of pinning his sketches to the walls of his office, thereby visually presenting the intended short's narrative in order. While Disney embraced the idea of wall mounting these pre-production sketches, having recently spent money redecorating the studio he introduced an inexpensive intermediate layer: large corkboards. In Disney's opinion, it was Smith who therefore had given birth to the storyboard.[28]

The material qualities of the storyboard responded perfectly to the production conditions that solidified at Disney during the 1930s, where multiple short films competed with the long-term evolution of *Snow White and the Seven Dwarfs* for time and resources. Given this ambition, Disney had little alternative but to adopt a much more pluralist approach to production than had been employed in the very early years of the studio. The storyboard, which occupied a central position in this expanded production environment, enabled multiple artists to contribute to the same board, and thereby contribute to the development of the same production. The storyboard's material nature at this time, being constructed in a modular fashion from multiple sheets of paper, meant that all aspects of the narrative remained simultaneously fixed, yet easily unfixable – in short, every ideas was potentially open to continual development by multiple individuals until gaining final approval by Disney. At the point of approval, the storyboard then provided a means by which to distribute visual information throughout the studio, enabling multiple departments to work towards a shared creative vision. With Disney's push towards increasingly detailed, complex and lengthy animation projects, the studio's pluralist approach described above became a source of pride – as well as productivity – for Disney.

Promoting Pluralism: Going Behind the Scenes

During the 1950s, Disney's activities expanded dramatically. While the storyboard serves as a convenient record of the pluralist activity that took place at Disney during the 1930s as the studio sought to develop the scope of its animation, Disney's various television series, appearing first under the *Disneyland* title in 1954, provide an even greater window onto the pluralist activities of Walt Disney and his staff. Today we take for granted the extensive 'behind the scenes' access that DVD, Blu-ray, and online special features grant, yet in the middle of twentieth century, consumer access to production narratives was limited. Recognising the promotional potential of such an activity, Walt Disney took the plunge, opting to host a show that included as part of its running order a wide range of 'behind the scenes' activities.[29]

The first episode of this venture, entitled *Walt Disney's Disneyland* and airing on 27 October 1954, provides a good model of how the show developed over the years to come. Within the first seven minutes we are shown a range of Disney activities from theme park building, through live action filmmaking, to feature animation production. The opening of the episode is accompanied by a male, voice of god-style narration, which informs the viewer that over the course of the television series, 'many worlds will open to you'. With this statement, the narrator starts to describe the various worlds that will be encountered, keeping time with the visual imagery that changes to reflect his description: 'Frontierland: tall tales and truth from the legendary past'; 'Tomorrowland: the promise of things to come'; 'Adventureland: the wonder world of nature's own realm'; and 'Fantasyland: the happiest kingdom of them all'. Following what is essentially an opening teaser, we are given a quick overview of Disney's pristine Burbank studio, where a tracking crane shot highlights the large numbers of staff bustling along Mickey Avenue.

As the camera comes to rest on a sign that reads '"20,000 Leagues Under the Sea" Company', the focus shifts from the commuting masses navigating Mickey Avenue to the recognisable faces of Kirk Douglas, Peter Lorre, and James Mason, who form the star-studded cast for *20,000 Leagues Under the Sea* (1954). We are also shown Mason, who plays Captain Nemo, filming the scene where he defends the stricken Nautilus from the clutches of a giant squid. Via a dissolve transition, we see a sign that reads: '"Sleeping Beauty" Models Stage'. This triggers another shift in focus, this time to a sound stage, where actress Helene Stanley, dressed as Princess Aurora, spins in time with a recording of the song 'Once Upon a Dream', while three Disney artists each sketch rapidly, attempting to capture a sense of this motion. Following this, the opening montage concludes by providing a glimpse of Disney's Foley Artists in the midst of concocting all manner of fantastical sound effects. After the playful juxtaposition of the voiceover stating that 'On the surface things here appear to be following their normal pattern', which runs parallel with the surreal Foley soundscape, we learn that: 'the truth of the matter is something unusual is going on in the studio today, something that never happened before'. With that tantalising remark we are introduced to Walt Disney. Immediately Disney adopts a practical tone, talking in terms of scale and geography, before announcing his vision for 'Disneyland the place', and his hopes that 'it will be unlike anything else on this earth: a fair, an amusement park, an exhibition, a city from Arabian Nights, a metropolis from the future, in fact, a place of hopes and dreams, facts and fancy, all in one'.

The opening six minutes of *Disneyland*, the first instalment of what would become a long running fixture of Disney television programming, effectively showcases the multiple activities in which Walt Disney and The Walt Disney Company were invested at that time. This period in the mid-1950s marked a significant step change for Disney: from this point forward, Disney's film production, whether animated or live action, ceased to be the main focus, becoming instead an important – but integrated – ingredient in a wider, pluralistic entertainment agenda. This agenda placed equal weight on reaching new audiences by: attracting them to the physical spaces of Disney's theme parks; infiltrating their domestic spaces through the reach of television programming; and continuing to seduce them via the cinematic space of fantasy, escapism and spectacle.

The success of the *Disneyland* show quickly established a convention whereby short, behind the scenes sequences would precede the screening of an animated short. Amusingly, on more than one occasion, the need to *find* such production footage resulted in Disney taking the decision to recreate a moment of production. An example of this restaging can be seen in the *Cavalcade of Songs* episode of the *Disneyland* series, which aired on February 16, 1955. As a prelude to a screening of the *Silly Symphony* instalment *Three Little Pigs* (1933), we see a pivotal moment of invention, with Walt Disney playing a leading role in the composition of the song: 'Who's Afraid of the Big Bad Wolf'. On the surface this is clearly an absurd sequence, featuring individuals, such as Marc Davis and Ward Kimball, who were not employed by Disney in 1933, but who can be seen contributing directly to the song's development, as well as featuring awkwardly choreographed moments, such as when the group of men suddenly pick up musical instruments and begin to perform the song in a precise and well-practiced fashion.[30] Artificiality aside, such sequences reveal a desire on Disney's part to showcase not only the skilled creativity that had unquestionably been the foundation of their success in the past, but also a desire to promote a more pluralistic vision of Disney in the present – where the company's parallel practical, professional, and, ultimately, human stories gained added – and arguably equal – importance.

Self-Reflexive Pluralism: *Get a Horse!*

Paul Wells observes that, following Disney's effective usurpation of North American animation with films like *Snow White and the Seven Dwarfs* and *Bambi*, 'it might properly be argued that all cartoon animation that follows the Disney output is a *reaction* to Disney, aesthetically, technically, and ideologically'.[31] This is a useful perspective, and immediately calls to mind the reactionary attitudes of United Productions of America (UPA) and, more recently, DreamWorks, whose animation, produced within a North American context, overtly rallies against the Disney-Formalist aesthetic. While Wells is most interested in establishing a broader framework of American animation production agendas and contexts, it is also possible to regard some of Disney's own animation production in the years following as adopting a reactionary stance.

The recent short *Get a Horse!*, which accompanied the theatrical release of *Frozen*, could be viewed as such a reaction, and highlights the continued importance of Disney's early period animation to those working at the studio today. The short begins as if it were an original 1920s *Mickey Mouse* cartoon, with the eponymous hero encountering a number of his regular gang riding a horse-drawn hay wagon in the manner of a charabanc. After Mickey joins the brigade, via Minnie Mouse's extending leg (which transforms into a staircase), Pete roars up behind the wagon in an automobile. Pete, one of Mickey's long-standing arch rivals, immediately grows impatient with the wagon's slow progress as it blocks the country lane, and squeezes his horn so that it proclaims: 'Make way for the future'. However, Pete's anger quickly transforms into lust once he spots Minnie Mouse. With Pete capturing and seeking to hold onto Minnie (whether she likes it or not), and with Mickey fighting to rescue Minnie from Pete's clutches, the cartoon's primary narrative drive is quickly established. What makes this cartoon so pertinent is not the rescue narrative, but rather the self-reflexive interrogation of space and form that takes place once the overarching conceit is established: that the characters are able to travel between the 2D, black-and-white, hand-drawn (*old*) world behind the cinema screen, and the 3D stereoscopic, colour, computer generated (*new*) world in front of the screen.

Get a Horse! reveals on a number of levels a commitment in terms of the short's conception and production to playfully engage with a range of subjects that foregrounds the plurality of Disney's own animation history. The short employs a range of formal devices to amplify this pan-historical subtext. For the first 96 seconds a flat, black-and-white aesthetic is adopted, with all of the action taking place within a small 1.33:1 aspect ratio frame that occupies only the central space of the surrounding, black 2.39:1 widescreen frame. Furthermore, the implied projection upon the 1.33:1 frame contains many of the characteristics of early film: a slight vignetting of the image at its periphery, inconsistent exposure (manifest in the flickering brightness of the image), and visible scratch marks on the image itself. Following Pete's hurling of Mickey and Horace Horsecollar through the cinema screen, the surrounding colour, three-dimensional, stereoscopic space becomes fully visible, filling the 2.39:1 frame; where the screen is ripped, we see within the frame hints of the still-flat but more artistically-advanced background that characterises Disney's Technicolor shorts beginning in 1932. In other words, in a single shot we are shown three important stages of Disney's animation aesthetics for its short subjects. In terms of character design, within the black and white realm of early cinema the characters are animated in a flat, two-dimensional style, whereas once they step beyond the cinema screen into the surrounding frame they appear in full colour and in three-dimensions.

While the sound design neatly captures the historic conventions of the two frames, with the early cinema realm featuring several examples of 'Mickey Mousing' (where non-diegetic music is tightly synchronised with diegetic action), and the modern realm featuring a much more balanced soundscape, as an example of pluralistic ambition and awareness, the short's visual storytelling is far more revealing. Throughout the short, the characters situated within the diegetic world frequently transgress the implied fictional frame, seemingly altering, at will, the terms on which the diegetic world is founded. For example, at one point we see Mickey pull back the theatrical curtains of the surrounding frame, so that he might better follow Pete's evasive manoeuvres, contained within the central frame, as Pete passes out of frame. Mickey's actions cause the central screen to extend along its X-axis, allowing him to follow more of Pete's movement. While such an act would be difficult to replicate in the real world (without careful choreography the image would spill onto the curtain in a distorted form), in the metamorphic realm of the animated cartoon Mickey's actions are simply the latest in a long tradition of characters who exert control over the animated landscapes in which they appear (such as Koko The Clown in the Fleischer Studio's *Out of the Inkwell* series [1918–1929] and Bugs Bunny in the famous conclusion to *Duck Amuck* [1953]). In another example, the three-dimensional Mickey removes his tail, and then straightens it into a needle so that he might pierce the cinema screen and release the water in which Pete is threatening to drown Minnie Mouse; such re-appropriations of body parts were a constant feature of Disney's early *Oswald the Lucky Rabbit* and *Mickey Mouse* cartoons. This ability on the part of the characters to transform their animated world foreshadows the short's conclusion.

While the control exerted by Mickey over the animated world described above pays homage to similar conceits found in early Disney animation, at the short's conclusion Mickey realises that the surrounding frame – the digital world – affords new methods of manipulation. Technologically, whereas the celluloid filmstrip, by virtue of its material affordances, encouraged linear modes of production and consumption, digital filmmaking supports alternative forms of moving image creation. Living, as we do, in a digital age, it is easy to take for granted our ability to pause the viewing experience, skip forwards and backwards and varying speeds, and randomly access scenes at a speed limited only by competence with the device on which we access the chosen film.[32] These new affordances form the basis of Mickey's climatic torture of Pete, carefully flipping the cinema screen to freeze his enemy in time, before exacting his revenge in a selective and technologically-empowered way.

In *Get A Horse!*, it seems that Disney is facing a profound moment of technological plurality: one where traditional technology meets transitional technology. With this short, accompanying as it did the theatrical release of *Frozen*, in which the present/future shape of Disney animation could be seen 'spiralling in frozen fractals all around' thanks to the computer-managed processes of diffusion-limited aggregation (snow generation), Disney has explicitly acknowledged an awareness of its own aesthetic plurality. Given the singular focus on stylised CGI in their recent feature films (*Zootopia*, 2016; *Moana*, 2016; *Ralph Breaks the Internet*, 2018; *Frozen 2*, 2019), *Get a Horse!* hints at an approach that the studio might seek to revisit in order to keep this aesthetic plurality alive in the years to come.[33]

Conclusions

Why is this notion of plurality important? Throughout his life, when asked to reflect on the success of his studio, Walt Disney was fond of rehearsing the line: 'I only hope that we never lose sight of one thing – that it was all started by a mouse'.[34] Even during his lifetime, Disney would have been acutely aware that while this line might have carried a certain amount of truth, 'Disney' had certainly come to represent far more than just Mickey Mouse. In the decades since Walt Disney's death, the company that carries his name has woven itself deeply into our cultural DNA. For example, at the time of writing, Disney offers a product range called 'Disney Baby', which bids to guide you and your new-born 'along the way with little smiles, trusty tips and of course a sprinkle of Disney magic'.[35] At a time when large corporations like Disney are seeking to manage our journey through life, it is critically important that we continue to interrogate the terms on which we interact with them. By adopting a pluralist framework, we might find a more nuanced and flexible means with which to negotiate the 'Disney' world in which many of us now live. This pluralist approach is intended to encourage competing perspectives. Whether you are an anonymous artist working under the pseudonym 'Banksy' and promoting a satirical theme park,[36] or an anonymous online commentator, known only as 'V', these divergent perspectives concerning what 'Disney' means to the individual are crucially important to our wider, collective understanding of what 'Disney' means with each passing generation.

Bibliography

Barrier, Michael. *Hollywood Cartoons: American Animation in its Golden Age* (Oxford: Oxford University Press, 1999).

Bell, Elizabeth, Lynda Haas, and Laura Sells, *From Mouse to Mermaid: The Politics of Film, Gender and Culture* (Bloomington, IN: Indiana University Press, 1996).

Bolter, Jay David, and Richard Grusin. *Remediation: Understanding New Media* (Cambridge, MA: MIT Press, 1998).

Bourdieu, Pierre. "The Forms of Capital (1986)". In *Cultural Theory: An Anthology*. Edited by Imre Szeman and Timothy Kaposy (Malden, MA: Wiley-Blackwell, 2011), 81–93.

Brown, Kat. 'Norwich to host academic conference on Frozen', *The Telegraph*, May 11, 2015. Accessed August 20, 2015, http://www.telegraph.co.uk/film/frozen/UEA-symfrozium-academic-conference-Norwich/.

Canemaker, John. *Before the Animation Begins: The Art and Lives of Disney Inspirational Sketch Artists* (New York: Hyperion, 1996).

Cristiano, Giuseppe. *Storyboard Design Course: Principles, Practice, and Techniques* (Hauppauage, NY: Barron, 2007).

Cristiano, Giuseppe. *The Storyboard Artist: A Guide to Freelancing in Film, TV, and Advertising* (Studio City, CA: Michael Wiese, 2011).

Dahl, Robert A. *Pluralist Democracy in the United States: Conflict and Consent* (Chicago, IL: Rand McNally, 1967).

Dahl, Robert A. *Who Governs?: Democracy and Power in an American City* (New Haven, CT: Yale University Press, 1961).

Davis, Amy M. *Good Girls & Wicked Witches: Women in Disney's Feature Animation* (New Barnet: John Libbey, 2007).

Davis, Amy M. *Handsome Heroes & Vile Villains: Masculinity in Disney's Feature Films* (New Barnet: John Libbey, 2014).

Disney Miller, Diane, *The Story of Walt Disney* (New York: Henry Holt, 1958).

Eisenstein, Sergei. *Eisenstein on Disney*. Edited by Jay Leyda; Translated by Alan Upchurch (London: Methuen, 1986).

Eliot, Marc. *Walt Disney: Hollywood's Dark Prince* (London: André Deutsch, 2003).

Finch, Christopher. *The Art of Walt Disney: From Mickey Mouse to the Magic Kingdom* (New York: Harry N. Abrams, 1973).

Hart, John. *The Art of the Storyboard: A Filmmaker's Introduction* (Burlington, MA: Focal Press, 2008).

ITV. "Disney's hit film Frozen – why academics just can't let it go". *ITV Online*, May 12, 2015. Accessed September 12, 2015, http://www.itv.com/news/anglia/2015-05-12/disneys-hit-film-frozen-why-academics-just-cant-let-it-go/.

Mulvey, Laura. *Death 24x a Second: Stillness and the Moving Image* (London: Reaktion Books, 2006).

Pallant, Chris and Steven Price. *Storyboarding: A Critical History* (London: Palgrave, 2015).

Pallant, Chris. "Disney-Formalism: Rethinking 'Classic Disney'". *Animation: An Interdisciplinary Journal* 5 (2010): 341–352.

Pallant, Chris. *Demystifying Disney: A History of Disney Feature Animation* (New York: Continuum, 2011).

Parry, Hannah. "University dons to study 'cultural impact' of Disney fairytale *Frozen* as Princess Elsa and Olaf the snowman make it onto the syllabus". *Mail Online*, May 8, 2015. Accessed September 11, 2015, http://www.dailymail.co.uk/news/article-3073218/University-dons-study-cultural-impact-Disney-fairytale-Frozen-Princess-Elsa-Olaf-snowman-make-syllabus.html.

Russell, Sam. "UEA academics to spend one-day conference talking about Disney movie Frozen". *Eastern Daily Post*, May 6, 2015. Accessed August 25, 2015, http://www.edp24.co.uk/news/uea_academics_to_spend_one_day_conference_talking_about_disney_movie_frozen_1_4062289.

Schickel, Richard. *The Disney Version: The Life, Times, Art and Commerce of Walt Disney* (Chicago, IL: Elephant, 1997).

Smith, Dave, and Steven Clark. *Disney: The First 100 Years* (New York: Disney Editions, 2002).

Smoodin, Eric. *Disney Discourse: Producing the Magic Kingdom* (New York: Routledge, 1994).83

Solomon, Charles. *The Disney that Never Was: The Stories and Art from Five Decades of Unproduced Animation* (New York: Hyperion, 1995).

Telotte, J. P. *The Mouse Machine: Disney and Technology* (University of Illinois Press, 2008).

Telotte, J.P. "Ub Iwerks' (Multi)Plain Cinema". *Animation: An Interdisciplinary Journal* 1 (2006): 9–24.

Wasko, Janet. *Understanding Disney: The Manufacture of Fantasy* (Cambridge: Polity Press, 2001).

Watts, Steven. *The Magic Kingdom: Walt Disney and the American Way of Life* (Columbia, MO: University of Missouri Press, 1997).

Wells, Paul. *Animation and America* (Edinburgh: Edinburgh University Press, 2002).

Endnotes

1. Sam Russell, 'UEA academics to spend one-day conference talking about Disney movie Frozen', *Eastern Daily Post*, May 6, 2015, accessed August 25, 2015, http://www.edp24.co.uk/news/uea_academics_to_spend_one_day_conference_talking_about_disney_movie_frozen_1_4062289.

2. See, in particular, Robert A. Dahl's books *Who Governs?: Democracy and Power in an American City* (New Haven, CT: Yale University Press, 1961) and *Pluralist Democracy in the United States: Conflict and Consent* (Chicago, IL: Rand McNally, 1967).

3. Twitter search: 'Symfrozium', *Twitter*, accessed August 26, 2015, https://twitter.com/search?q=symfrozium&src=typd.

4. James Welker, Twitter post, *Twitter*, February 9, 2015, accessed September 10, 2015, https://twitter.com/james_welker/status/564946358444892160.

5. See Pierre Bourdieu's 'The Forms of Capital (1986)', in *Cultural Theory: An Anthology*, eds. Imre Szeman and Timothy Kaposy (Malden, MA: Wiley-Blackwell, 2011), 87–88.

6. ITV, 'Disney's hit film Frozen – why academics just can't let it go', *ITV Online*, May 12, 2015, accessed September 12, 2015, http://www.itv.com/news/anglia/2015-05-12/disneys-hit-film-frozen-why-academics-just-cant-let-it-go/.

7. Su Holmes interview, 'Disney's hit film Frozen …'.

8. Su Holmes interview, 'Disney's hit film Frozen …'.

9. Chris Pallant email correspondence with Su Holmes, June 4, 2015.

10. Kat Brown, 'Norwich to host academic conference on Frozen', *The Telegraph*, May 11, 2015, accessed August 20, 2015, http://www.telegraph.co.uk/film/frozen/UEA-symfrozium-academic-conference-Norwich/.

11. Russell, 'UEA academics'.

12. Hannah Parry, 'University dons to study "cultural impact" of Disney fairytale *Frozen* as Princess Elsa and Olaf the snowman make it onto the syllabus', *Mail Online*, May 8, 2015, accessed September 11, 2015, http://www.dailymail.co.uk/news/article-3073218/University-dons-study-cultural-impact-Disney-fairytale-Frozen-Princess-Elsa-Olaf-snowman-make-syllabus.html.

13. Parry, 'University dons …'.

14. Again, this is by no means an attempt to provide an exhaustive list of resources, but for readers interested in gaining a fuller picture of Disney scholarship I would recommend the following texts: Eric Smoodin's collection, *Disney Discourse: Producing the Magic Kingdom* (1994), which despite being over twenty years old, remains a good resource; Elizabeth Bell, Lynda Haas, and Laura Sells's collection, *From Mouse to Mermaid: The Politics of Film, Gender and Culture* (1996); from an economic perspective, Janet Wasko's *Understanding Disney: The Manufacture of Fantasy* (2001) and Richard Schickel's *The Disney Version: The Life, Times, Art and Commerce of Walt Disney* (Chicago, IL: Elephant, 1997); from a technological perspective J. P. Telotte's *The Mouse Machine: Disney and Technology* (2008); and for consideration of identity politics through close textual analysis, Amy M. Davis's two companion studies *Good Girls and Wicked Witches: Women in Disney's Feature Animation* (2007) and *Handsome Heroes and Vile Villains: Masculinity in Disney's Feature Films* (2014).

15. Steven Watts, *The Magic Kingdom: Walt Disney and the American Way of Life* (Columbia, MO: University of Missouri Press, 1997), 83.

16. See Sergei Eisenstein, *Eisenstein on Disney*, ed. Jay Leyda, trans. Alan Upchurch (London: Methuen, 1986).

17. Michael Barrier, *Hollywood Cartoons: American Animation in its Golden Age* (Oxford: Oxford University Press, 1999), 245.

18. For a more detailed discussion of Multiplane camera technologies and Disney's contribution to the development of them, see Chris Pallant, *Demystifying Disney: A History of Disney Feature Animation* (New York: Continuum, 2011), 27–30, and J.P. Telotte, 'Ub Iwerks' (Multi)Plain Cinema', *Animation: An Interdisciplinary Journal* 1 (2006): *passim*.

19. For an extended discussion of the significance of material affordance to the development of technology, see Jay David Bolter and Richard Grusin's still influential *Remediation: Understanding New Media* (Cambridge, MA: MIT Press, 1998).

20. Chris Pallant, 'Disney-Formalism: Rethinking "Classic Disney"', *Animation: An Interdisciplinary Journal* 5 (2010): *passim*.

21. See, for example, John Hart's *The Art of the Storyboard: A Filmmaker's Introduction* (Burlington, MA: Focal Press, 2008), Giuseppe Cristiano's *Storyboard Design Course: Principles, Practice, and Techniques* (Hauppauage, NY: Barron, 2007) and *The Storyboard Artist: A Guide to Freelancing in Film, TV, and Advertising* (Studio City, CA: Michael Wiese, 2011).

22. Chris Pallant and Steven Price, *Storyboarding: A Critical History* (London: Palgrave, 2015), 26–44.

23. Schickel, *The Disney Version*, 116.

24. Marc Eliot, *Walt Disney: Hollywood's Dark Prince* (London: André Deutsch, 2003), 36.

25. Charles Solomon, *The Disney that Never Was: The Stories and Art from Five Decades of Unproduced Animation* (New York: Hyperion, 1995), 6.

26. John Canemaker, *Before the Animation Begins: The Art and Lives of Disney Inspirational Sketch Artists* (New York: Hyperion, 1996) 4.

27. Although the specifics of this story differ slightly, the general impression is consistent in both the accounts presented by Diane Disney Miller in *The Story of Walt Disney* (New York: Henry Holt, 1958), 123, and by Schickel in *The Disney Version*, 148.

28. Christopher Finch, *The Art of Walt Disney: From Mickey Mouse to the Magic Kingdom* (New York: Harry N. Abrams, 1973), 82.

29. It is worth noting that the short film, "How Walt Disney Cartoons are Made", was made for RKO execs in 1937 when they became Disney's distributor, which was converted shortly afterward into a rudimentary 'behind the scenes/Snow White trailer' and put into distribution in RKO theatres. This short ancillary project may well have planted the seed in Walt Disney's mind that would later blossom into the 'behind the scenes' element of *Disneyland*.

30. Employment commencement dates for Davis and Kimball are verified on Disney's official *D23* 'Disney Legends' webpages: https://d23.com/disney-legends/

31. Paul Wells, *Animation and America* (Edinburgh: Edinburgh University Press, 2002), 45.

32. For an excellent discussion of how digital technologies have refashioned the cinematic form see Laura Mulvey's *Death 24x a Second: Stillness and the Moving Image* (London: Reaktion Books, 2006).

33. Upcoming film information accurate at time of writing, based on the information provided on the Walt Disney Animation Studios' *IMDB.com* webpage: http://www.imdb.com/company/co0074039/?ref_=tt_dt_co

34. Dave Smith and Steven Clark, *Disney: The First 100 Years* (New York: Disney Editions, 2002), 1.

35. 'Disney Baby', *Disney.com*, accessed September 10, 2015, http://family.disney.co.uk/disney-baby.

36. In the summer of 2015, the artist Banksy opened a 'Bemusment Park' called 'Dismaland', which sought to critique the carefully-regulated, censorial marketplaces of fun that are Disney's theme parks. On the Dismaland website, Banksy offers the following warning with characteristic wit: 'Contains uneven floor surfaces, extensive use of strobe lighting, imagery unsuitable for small children and swearing. The following are strictly prohibited in the Park – spray paint, marker pens, knives and legal representatives of the Walt Disney Corporation'. 'About', *Dismaland*, accessed September 17, 2015, http://dismaland.co.uk.

Index

Lightning Source UK Ltd.
Milton Keynes UK
UKHW012302241119
354104UK00013B/37/P